Christian Generosity according to 2 Corinthians 8–9

Its Exegesis, Reception, and Interpretation Today in Dialogue with the Prosperity Gospel in Sub-Saharan Africa

Viateur Habarurema

© 2017 by Viateur Habarurema

Published 2017 by Langham Monographs
An imprint of Langham Creative Projects

Langham Partnership
PO Box 296, Carlisle, Cumbria CA3 9WZ, UK
www.langham.org

ISBNs:
978-1-78368-260-7 Print
978-1-78368-262-1 Mobi
978-1-78368-261-4 ePub
978-1-78368-263-8 PDF

Viateur Habarurema has asserted his right under the Copyright, Designs and Patents Act, 1988 to be identified as the Author of this work.

All rights reserved. No part of this publication may be reproduced, stored in a retrieval system or transmitted, in any form or by any means, electronic, mechanical, photocopying, recording or otherwise, without the prior written permission of the publisher or the Copyright Licensing Agency.

Unless otherwise stated, Scripture quotations are from the New Revised Standard Version Bible, copyright © 1989 National Council of the Churches of Christ in the United States of America. Used by permission. All rights reserved.

British Library Cataloguing in Publication Data
A catalogue record for this book is available from the British Library

ISBN: 978-1-78368-260-7

Cover & Book Design: projectluz.com

Langham Partnership actively supports theological dialogue and a scholar's right to publish but does not necessarily endorse the views and opinions set forth, and works referenced within this publication or guarantee its technical and grammatical correctness. Langham Partnership does not accept any responsibility or liability to persons or property as a consequence of the reading, use or interpretation of its published content.

Pentecostal/charismatic Christianity constitutes the growing edge of Christianity in Africa today. Viateur Habarurema's book is an excellent addition to the growing number of critical biblical studies that looks at important theological themes associated with Pentecostalism. This is an important exegetical work that deepens our understanding of the practical outworking of the prosperity gospel that has become a hallmark of contemporary Pentecostalism.

J. Kwabena Asamoah-Gyadu, PhD
Baëta-Grau Professor of Contemporary African Christianity and Pentecostalism,
Trinity Theological Seminary, Ghana

This is a fine study which combines precise exegesis of the biblical texts with most relevant reflections on its corollaries for present-day theology and the church, based on first-hand knowledge and sound academic analysis.

Riemer Roukema, PhD
Professor in Early Christianity,
Protestant Theological University, Amsterdam and Groningen, Netherlands

What are crucial elements of a Christian theology of generosity? In his enlightening study, Viateur Habarurema carefully analyzes Paul's text on the collection for Jerusalem in 2 Corinthians 8–9, with an astute eye to the wider Pauline corpus and the Christian tradition, and engages Paul in a fascinating dialogue with various shapes of African prosperity gospel. A model of scholarly clarity and contextual sensitivity!

Benjamin Schliesser, PhD
Professor of New Testament Studies, Faculty of Theology,
University of Bern, Switzerland

Contents

Abstract ix

Acknowledgments xi

Abbreviations xvii

Introduction 1
    1. Motivation for the Study 1
    2. Major Scholarly Studies on Paul's Collection 7
    3. New Areas to Be Explored 23
    4. The Aim and Nature of This Research 27
    5. Presuppositions and Approach 29
    6. Structure of the Study 31

Chapter 1 33
The Background of Christian Generosity
    1.1 Charity in the Old Testament and Early Judaism 34
        1.1.1 The Hebrew Bible and Social Justice 34
        1.1.2 The Septuagint 37
        1.1.3 Early Judaism 39
    1.2 Charity in the Greco-Roman Context 41
    Conclusion 45

Chapter 2 47
Paul's Corinthian Correspondence
    2.1 1 Corinthians 5:9–11 47
    2.2 2 Corinthians 2:1, 5; 7:12 ("The Letter of Tears") 49
    2.3 Partition Theories 51
    2.4 Marks of Discontinuity in 2 Corinthians 1–7 55
    2.5 The Unity of 2 Corinthians 8–9 in Recent Scholarship ... 56
    2.6 2 Corinthians 10–13 61
    2.7 The Text of 2 Corinthians 8–9 64
    Conclusion 69

Chapter 3 71
Paul's Collection in 2 Corinthians 8–9
    3.1 The Macedonians as a Good Example of Generosity
        (2 Cor 8:1–6) 72

    3.2 The Corinthians Exhorted to Complete the Collection
        (2 Cor 8:7–12) 95
    3.3 The Purpose of the Collection (2 Cor 8:13–15) 109
    3.4 The Delegates, Their Commendations and Mission
        (2 Cor 8:16–9:5) 117
    3.5 God Reciprocates the Generosity of a Cheerful Giver
        (2 Cor 9:6–10) 140
    3.6 The Outcomes of the Collection and Doxology
        (2 Cor 9:11–15) 156
    Conclusion 168

Chapter 4 171
2 Corinthians 8–9 from Late Antiquity to the Reformation Period
    4.1 John Chrysostom 172
        4.1.1 The Benefits of God's Grace, Mutuality and the
            Dangers of Wealth 174
        4.1.2 The Justification for Christian Generosity 176
        4.1.3 The Special Place of the Poor in Chrysostom's Thought 180
        4.1.4 The Ways of Giving 181
    4.2 Theodoret of Cyrus 184
        4.2.1 God's Grace and Its Effects 185
        4.2.2 Motivations, Ways of Giving and the Danger of
            Possessions 186
    4.3 Ambrosiaster 188
        4.3.1 Different Meanings of Gratia 189
        4.3.2 The Use of Possessions and Care for the Needy 189
        4.3.3 The Language of Retribution 192
    4.4 Thomas Aquinas 193
        4.4.1 Gratia, Genuine Generosity and Its Benefits 194
        4.4.2 Poverty Praised and Concern for the Poor 200
    4.5 John Calvin 202
        4.5.1 Gratia in Relation to Christian Generosity in
            2 Corinthians 8–9 204
        4.5.2 Christian Generosity and Reward 206
        4.5.3 Alms as a Due to the Poor 208
        4.5.4 The Ways of Giving 209
    4.6 Summary 211
    Conclusion 215

Chapter 5 217
Pentecostalism in Sub-Saharan Africa: An Overview

    5.1 Pentecostalism as a Global Movement............................217
    5.2 The Use of the Bible in African Pentecostalism........................227
        5.2.1 The Bible as a Devotional Book 227
        5.2.2 The Talismanic and Symbolic Use of the Bible...............236
    Conclusion 241

Chapter 6 243
The Prosperity Gospel in Sub-Saharan Africa
    6.1 Background 243
    6.2 The Major Teachings of the Prosperity Gospel 245
        6.2.1 Atoning Death of Christ, Abrahamic Covenant and
             Prosperity...246
        6.2.2 Faith and Prayer as Ways to Material Prosperity.............247
        6.2.3 Christian Giving and Financial Prosperity 255
        6.2.4 Anointing as a Route to Prosperity................................259
    6.3 A Positive Import of the Prosperity Gospel? 260
        6.3.1 A Genuine Quest for the Fullness of Life
             Promised by the Scriptures.....................................260
        6.3.2 Audacity to Address Real-Life Problems........................263
        6.3.3 A Reverential Attitude to the Bible as God's Word..........266
    6.4 Concerns about the Prosperity Gospel 269
        6.4.1 Moral and Social Weaknesses: Greed, Inequalities and
             Unaccountability..269
        6.4.2 Theological Shortcomings..273
    Conclusion 280

Chapter 7 283
The Reading of 2 Corinthians 8–9 in Africa Today in Dialogue with the Prosperity Gospel
    7.1 Matthew Ashimolowo: 2 Corinthians 9:5–13 285
        7.1.1 The Motivations for Giving 285
        7.1.2 The Kinds of Offerings and Ways of Giving...................287
    7.2 Mensa Otabil: The Principles of Productivity and
        Multiplication 290
    7.3 Dag Heward-Mills: The Law of Sowing and Reaping...............291
        7.3.1 Tithing: 2 Corinthians 8:7 291
        7.3.2 How to Activate the Principle of Sowing and Reaping:
             2 Corinthians 9:6–10..293
    7.4 David O. Oyedepo 295
    7.5 Enoch Adejare Adeboye 298
    7.6 Benson Andrew Idahosa...300

    7.7 Discussion and Evaluation 303
        7.7.1 The Concept of Grace in the Hermeneutics of
        2 Corinthians 8–9...304
        7.7.2 The Farming Metaphor of Sowing and Reaping...............305
        7.7.3 The Ways of Giving and Care for the Poor.......................307
        7.7.4 Christian κοινωνία 308
        7.7.5 The Lord's Voluntary Poverty and Attitude to
        Material Possessions 310
        7.7.6 A Theology of Stewardship and Giving............................313
    Conclusion 317
Conclusion.. 319
Bibliography... 333

Abstract

This work seeks to engage a constructive discussion with current interpretations of 2 Corinthians 8–9 by some Pentecostal teachers of prosperity in sub-Saharan Africa who argue that Christian giving secures financial wealth to faithful givers. A solid exegesis through the grammatico-historical approach which at times borrows insights from rhetorical analysis serves as a basis to interact with several readings of this passage. Moreover, the study presents an overview of Pentecostalism as a charismatic movement significantly attested among mainline Protestantism and the Roman Catholic Church in sub-Saharan Africa. It also sketches the major traits of the prosperity gospel which is one of the main features of this movement on the continent. These two points frame the general context in which today's interpretations of Paul's text by most African Pentecostals are appraised.

In this study, a case is made that while organizing his collection, Paul was driven not by the motives of Greco-Roman patronage/benefaction, but by the conviction that the God of Israel commands his people to care for the poor. Although his undertaking has no clear antecedent in Jewish history, the apostle must have merged several Jewish conceptions and applied them in a creative organizational manner. Furthermore, Paul believed that Christ, who himself had demonstrated much concern for the needy, gave the same instructions to his followers. By the concept of divine χάρις, capable of different meanings and central to 2 Corinthians 8–9, Paul redefines Greco-Roman social exchange practices. In the same vein, the notion of αὐτάρκεια, sufficiency does not aim neither at self-enjoyment nor at one's total independence from others concerning financial and spiritual needs. Rather, its purpose consists in constantly serving those in need.

The exploration of sermons by John Chrysostom and commentaries from Theodoret of Cyrus, Ambrosiaster, Thomas Aquinas and Calvin, reveals that the notion of χάρις, which is badly missing in the prosperity discourses, has caught their attention to varying degrees. Their main contention is that participation in or the collection itself are termed χάρις to teach that all that we have or accomplish originates in God. The text of 2 Corinthians 8–9 is strictly and uniquely correlated with almsgiving. For their part, the preachers of prosperity employ it almost uniquely to promote the belief that giving is a route to financial prosperity. The belief in reward, mostly drawn from Paul's reference to the metaphor of sowing and reaping in 2 Corinthians 9:6-11, is investigated to point out similarities and discrepancies among the authors considered in this dissertation. As a way of conclusion, a point is made that the centrality of the concept of grace in 2 Corinthians 8–9 directs that we must conceptualize Christian giving in terms of responsibility, gratefulness and trust that God is faithful to his promise to take care of his children however the circumstances might be, rather than as a way to attract God's favors and material prosperity. Besides, a series of hermeneutical and theological recommendations are spelled out to promote a reading which is faithful to Paul's thoughts in 2 Corinthians 8–9, fully integrated in his overall theology, and remains open to some insights provided by Pentecostal hermeneutics.

Acknowledgments

Surely goodness and mercy shall follow me all the days of my life, and I shall dwell in the house of the LORD my whole life long. (Ps 23:6)

Now to him who by the power at work within us is able to accomplish abundantly far more than all we can ask or imagine, to him be glory in the church and in Christ Jesus to all generations, forever and ever. Amen. (Eph 3:20–21)

Writing a doctoral dissertation is a long journey of commitment and sacrifices. It also offers moments of joy through the opening of new horizons not only in the realm of knowledge but also in that of human relations. When in August 2010 I started the one-year master's program at the Protestant Theological University (PThU), Kampen, I also had the dream of doing doctoral research thereafter. It was therefore a great joy for me to be given a chance to undertake this project in 2012. The relocation of the PThU to Groningen the same year was another new turn in my life experience in the Netherlands. It meant making new friends and adjusting to a broader university community which is much more conducive to academic work. However, to carry out this work, sometimes far away from my family left behind in Rwanda, has not been an easy task. At the end of this journey, I want to thank first of all our heavenly Father who, in Jesus Christ and through the vivifying Holy Spirit, has stretched his caring hand upon me and my family. Hope and healing have been graciously extended to us in various ways and circumstances, and through different institutions and individuals.

The Protestant Institute of Arts and Social Sciences (PIASS) deserves special recognition because it provided me with the necessary time to write the present study. Moreover, it recommended me to its partners for sponsorship. This was possible thanks to its leaders' invaluable support. These are Professor Benoit Girardin, former Vice Chancellor; Rev Professor Elisée Musemakweli, Vice Chancellor; and Rev Professor Viateur Ndikumana, Deputy Vice Chancellor for academic affairs. Similarly, I express my gratitude to the PThU for granting me a scholarship for the master's program and admitting me in the doctoral program, as well as for the wonderful facilities and an appropriate atmosphere for academic work. I thank all my professors at the PThU and the remaining staff for their friendly cooperation for the success of this study project.

I also acknowledge here the priceless support which I received from my home denomination, The Pentecostal Church in Rwanda (ADEPR). In this respect, the names of its former legal representative, Rev Pastor Samuel Usabwimana, and its current legal representative, Rev Pastor Jean Sibomana, are worth mentioning here. Other institutions and foundations have contributed to raise the funds needed for my studies. In the Netherlands, I have benefitted from the generosity of *Icco* and *Kerk in Actie*, Utrecht; *Protestantse Gemeente De Rank, Staphorst* and French-speaking churches in different locations. The latter are *Église wallonne, Amsterdam; Église wallonne, Arnhem; Église wallonne, Delft; Église wallonne, Groningen; Église wallonne, Utrecht; Église wallonne, Zwolle* and *Commission pour la mission des Églises wallonnes. Je vous exprime ma profonde gratitude pour votre contribution à la réussite de mon projet d'études aux Pays-Bas. Je garde toujours le bon souvenir des moments de joie que j'ai partagés avec certains d'entre vous notamment dans les cultes dominicaux à Zwolle et à Groningue.*[1] I cannot omit to mention other Dutch foundations that donated joyfully their financial support to make this research possible: *Sint Geertruidsleen te Abbega, Stichting Zonneweelde, Ms. C. Helder-Corporaal, Zwolle* and *Christina Maria Stichting, Haarlem.* Outside the Netherlands, sponsorship came from *PMU Interlife, Sweden; WCC* and *FAP, Switzerland* and *Communauté Evangélique Philadelphie, Belgium.*

---

1. Translation: I express to you my deepest gratitude for your contribution to the success of my studies in the Netherlands. I have great memories of the precious moments I have shared with some of you, in particular during the Sunday services at Zwolle and Groningen.

Acknowledgments

A study like this one cannot be completed without assistance and inspiration from many individuals as well. For the sake of space, I can just name those who were the most influential. I am particularly grateful for the multifaceted support of Professor Dr Riemer Roukema, my doctoral supervisor, who patiently listened to me when I mentioned the idea of writing a doctoral thesis while I was still in the master's program. I still remember the times I spent in his former office in Kampen discussing the early stages of my research and other theological concerns. His encouraging advice and appreciation of my abilities have always provided me with the help I needed to carry out my academic work. This was supplemented by the words of encouragement which I received from his wife, Rev Lily Burggraaff, several times in their house. Professor Dr Mechteld Jansen, the current PThU rector and co-supervisor of the present research, has granted me the insightful guidance to complete the thesis. Her comments and questions on both the content and structure have enabled me to further develop my writing style and argumentation.

Rev Dr Gerard van't Spijker and his wife Rev Auli van't Spijker have been instrumental not only in opening doors for me to study at the PThU, but also in enabling me to find useful networks and tools for the research. I have enjoyed their company during my stays in the Netherlands. I am indebted to Dr van't Spijker who graciously accepted to read a part of the thesis, and who offered some invaluable observations. In addition, he has agreed to translate into Dutch parts of this study. Similarly, Herma and Gerard Lof deserve my appreciation here. Their hospitality has made me feel at home in the Netherlands. I treasure the precious moments we spent together sharing meals; visiting places, churches and people; discussing my research; in a nutshell sharing our joys and sorrows. Mr Lof volunteered to make some useful translations both into English and Dutch which I needed for this work. I also thank both of them for their ability to discern and anticipate my financial needs. They allowed the Lord to use them to be a blessing to my studies and life in general.

I am grateful to the Burgwalkerk in Kampen for its initiative to introduce international students to the Dutch context. My special thanks go especially to Arjen and Annemarie Salverda as well as to Henny and Henny Boxman. From their being my church contact persons, Arjen and

Annemarie have become close friends whose company has enabled me to learn much about the Netherlands and at times cope with difficult situations. I also treasure the hospitality of Masego and Jeroen Kanis from the SOZO International Fellowship in Kampen in which I was involved during my one-year stay there. My fellow students, especially Sung-Eun Yoo, a close friend and fellow postgraduate, has helped me in several ways. Besides his intellectually stimulating conversations, his presence and encouraging words when I was confronted with health problems remain engraved in my heart. My visits to him have allowed me to get to know his wife Han-Saem Song whose kindness and humility have comforted me whenever I entered their house.

I also want to thank Rev Pieter Dirk Wolthaus and his wife Anneke Wolthaus for their love and friendship during my stay in Groningen. Towards the end of my research, I came to know *emeritus* Professor Dr Johannes Roldanus and his wife Nely Roldanus and was offered a warm welcome in their house. I enjoyed a long discussion with Professor Dr Roldanus about my thesis and received some insights which enriched the final version of the thesis. Likewise, Professor Benno van den Toren and his wife Berdine van den Toren have enriched me with their experience of many years outside their home land. I thank them for the many opportunities afforded to international students to help them reflect on and engage positively with the inevitable culture shock while in the Netherlands, and on the reverse culture shock once back in each one's home country.

I owe a debt of gratitude to my colleagues within the academic staff and other workers at PIASS for their company in this learning process. Especially, I appreciate the contribution from Rev Dr Faith Lugazia who spent many days reading and commenting on parts of the thesis. Similarly, Rev Mary Catherine Day joyfully offered her expertise as a native English speaker to improve my writing style in some parts of the present work. My thanks are also extended to my colleagues in ministry as well as to several church members at ADEPR-Butare Parish for having always stood by me and my family throughout this academic journey.

To my parents Matthieu Sebisogo and Marthe Nyirakanazi, my brothers, sisters and my in-laws: Thanks for your love, support and encouragement. Finally and most importantly, my wife, Enatha Nyirahabimana, and our three daughters and our son, respectively Délices Ingabire, Emérance Munezero, Elpis Gwiza Mbabazi, and Blessing Hirwa have made enormous sacrifices because of my pastoral and academic obligations. I want to express my appreciation to you for your continued and renewed patience, understanding and support by dedicating this thesis to you. I am confident that the achievement of this study project will fill you with joy having realized that your sacrifices were not in vain.

Finally, I address a word of recognition to the board of examiners who assessed my dissertation. Their critical questions prior to and during its oral defense have enabled me to further clarify some elements of the present study.

To all these persons and institutions, as well as those that are not mentioned here, I wish God's grace.

Abbreviations

AIC: African Independent Church
BCE: Before the Christian Era
BFC: Bible en français courant
CCSL: Corpus Christianorum Series Latina
CE: Christian Era
CJB: The Complete Jewish Bible
CSEL: Corpus Scriptorum Ecclesiasticorum Latinorum
FBJ: French Bible de Jerusalem
LCL: Loeb Classical Library
LSG: French Bible translation by Louis Segond (1910)
LXX: The Septuagint
NAS: New American Standard Bible
NICNT: New International Commentary on the New Testament
NIV: New International Version
NKJV: New King James Version
NPFP: Nicene and Post-Nicene Fathers
NRSV: New Revised Standard Version
NTS: New Testament Studies
PG: Patrologia Graeca
SC: Sources Chrétiennes
TDNT: Theological Dictionary of the New Testament
TOB (NT): Traduction œcuménique de la Bible (Nouveau Testament)
WUNT: Wissenschaftliche Untersuchungen zum Neuen Testament

Introduction

1. Motivation for the Study

The relationship between the exegesis, reception history and the actualization of biblical texts in different social and ecclesial contexts is a fascinating subject. The present research investigates these three areas with regard to Paul's treatment of the collection for poor Christians in Jerusalem in 2 Corinthians 8–9. Besides a sound exegesis of this text, this work explores its interpretation from late Antiquity to the Reformation and its contemporary usage by some Pentecostal preachers from sub-Saharan Africa in relation to the motivations of Christian giving.[1] My interest in the interpretation of New Testament texts has developed over the years of my theological education. The investigation into the social implications of the Christian gospel pursues the same aim of searching for the meaning of biblical texts. In this respect, while completing the four-year bachelor's program, I studied and wrote a thesis on the gospel of Luke with much emphasis on the parable of the good Samaritan. In my master's research, the same motivation led me to reflect on Paul's collection. Paul's collection remains a

---

1. I do not pretend to carry out a thorough research in all sub-Saharan countries. The point is that experiences and resources which underpin this study are taken from this broader context. However, sub-Saharan Africa cannot be perceived as one homogeneous entity. There has always been a great diversity in terms of tribal groups, religions, cultures, and socio-political realities. But studies have also pointed out many commonalities among the populations of this part of the continent: Mutombo-Mukendi, "Le nouveau culte de la prospérité," 80, 85–86. This diversity is also reflected in the many expressions of Christianity in sub-Saharan Africa. This is why in his article Mutombo-Mukendi rightly speaks of African Christianity in plural ("les christianismes africains"). For the sake of brevity, I will often use the term Africa to designate sub-Saharan Africa. In some other instances the context will indicate clearly that the appellation refers specifically to the whole continent of Africa.

remarkable example of how the Christian faith can be lived out as a proactive presence in the midst of concrete social realities. The apostle Paul exhorts his converts to exercise generosity to relieve the needs of their poor fellow believers in Jerusalem.

Since the gospel was spread in sub-Saharan Africa by Euro-American missionaries,[2] Paul's epistles, like the rest of the Scriptures, are read and studied as a source of inspiration. Within the broader sphere of the social aspect of the Christian message as witnessed by some texts of the New Testament, the question of the use of biblical texts by today's preachers gradually took shape in my mind. As I studied Paul's conceptualization of the collection in 2 Corinthians 8–9, especially 9:6–11 and its promise of God's intervention in favor of cheerful givers, a new perspective of research was opened to my theological reflections. The question of the way this text is quoted and alluded to by African Pentecostal preachers today in particular became vital to my engagement with Paul's text on the collection in 2 Corinthians 8–9.

From the start, it is important to note that my interest in the exegesis, reception history and the actualization of the Pauline texts was the result of the interaction of at least three main factors: my Christian background in Pentecostalism,[3] an observation of different religious phenomena within African Christianity and a personal reading of Paul. To start with, I was born and raised in a Pentecostal church; and today I carry out pastoral ministry in the same denomination.[4] This experience in the church, coupled with personal observations of other Pentecostal churches, and the readings of the

---

2. Ethiopia is a special case since Christianity emerged there most probably much earlier than the middle of the fourth century as an entirely indigenous undertaking. Its encounter with Western Christianity began in the sixteenth century through Portuguese Catholicism. Protestant missionaries came later on in the nineteenth century, while Evangelicals and Pentecostals followed in the twentieth century (Abbink, "Bibliography on Christianity," 1–2.)

3. As it will be explained in the fifth chapter of the present research, "Pentecostalism" indicates the diverse movements and denominations which insist on the experience of the activity of the Holy Spirit and the practice of the charismata in the Christian life and church liturgy (Anderson, *Introduction to Pentecostalism*, 6; Asamoah-Gyadu, *Contemporary Pentecostal Christianity*, 1, 6).

4. The Pentecostal Church in Rwanda (ADEPR) is the first Pentecostal denomination that started in Rwanda in 1940. It is by far the largest church of Pentecostal persuasion. Its history is directly related to the efforts of evangelization deployed by the Swedish Free Mission (MLS) in Tanzania and the Democratic Republic of the Congo (DRC, former

literature on Pentecostalism have exposed me to its main teachings. I have been struck by the strong emphasis laid on Christian giving in the form of tithes and a certain number of regular offerings. Biblical resources for this teaching are mostly drawn from the Old Testament. Johnson Kwabena Asamoah-Gyadu explains that Christian offerings are the reinvention of the Old Testament practice of sacrificing to God. In this context, worship includes bringing some offering to God.[5] Granted, outside the context of the cult, the Old Testament also contains repeated instructions to give to the needy; these include the poor, the orphan, widow and the immigrant, as we will see in the first chapter of this study. Therefore, concerns about the motivations, forms and benefits of Christian giving have always been present in my mind.

Pentecostalism greatly insists on tithes and other offerings in the perspective of worship rather than on giving for caritative purposes. In the Mosaic law the instructions on tithing are clear and describe the overall conditions of their collection (Lev 27:30–33). Prior to this law we learn that Abraham gave to Melchizedek the tithe of his spoil of war (Gen 14:18–20) and that Jacob vowed to offer ten percent of his increase as a response to God's providential protection in his journey back home to meet his brother Esau whom he had defrauded of his birthright (Gen 28:20–22).[6] The most important Old Testament text invoked to teach tithing as a doctrine in Pentecostalism is Malachi 3:8–12.[7] The New Testament alludes to the practice of tithing in four passages (Matt 23:23; Luke 11:42; 18:12; Heb 7:1–10).[8] Tithing Christians believe that it is the latter passage that establishes a bridge between the Old Testament and the New Testament on the value of this practice. The text tells how Abraham met with Melchizedek and paid his tithe to him. Verse 8 is seen as revalorizing the practice of tithing since it reads: "In the one case, tithes are received by those who are mortal; in the other, by one of whom it is testified that he lives." The writer

---

Zaïre) in the 1920s (Spijker, *Les usages funéraires*, 37; Nsanzurwimo, *Histoire de l'Église*, 48; Habarurema, "Histoire de l'Église de Pentecôte," 177.

5. Asamoah-Gyadu, *Contemporary Pentecostal Christianity*, 83.
6. Ibid., 84.
7. Ibid., 85.
8. Ibid.

of Hebrews believes that Jesus Christ, the Son of God and priest for ever like Melchizedek (v. 3), collects tithes.

Second, my interest in Christian giving has also been instigated by the astounding spread of the overwhelming preaching on giving as a way to secure every sort of wellbeing. This trend of teaching commonly known as the prosperity gospel is gaining ground as Pentecostalism is growing rapidly in sub-Saharan Africa.[9] It covers different aspects of Christian faith and life; that of economic prosperity remaining predominant. It is strongly affirmed that through the suffering and death of Christ, God has provided for all the needs of human life. As a consequence, every Christian believer has been entitled to "the victory over sin, sickness, and poverty."[10] It is said that this share in economic prosperity and good health through Christ can be attained "merely by a positive confession of faith."[11] Concerning economic prosperity, it is generally affirmed that God blesses free givers in proportion to the amount of offering one gives, which is literally called "banking in faith."[12] Some preachers speak of the so-called "seed-faith" concept according to which the "Old Testament tithing to God out of obligation was replaced by a New Testament version – giving in order to expect a blessing."[13] In any case, Pentecostalism speaks of any type of offering in terms of a sown seed that will produce harvest. For faithful givers this harvest includes money, success and any other happy event in one's life.[14] In this line of thought, poverty or any kind of misfortune is often viewed as the normal result of a lack of uprightness in giving to God. Thus, African Pentecostalism has made tithes and offerings not only an element of Christian responsibilities as is the case in African Christian religious services, but also a "sort of sacramental duty" since they are believed to mediate divine graces in one's struggles of life.[15] The importance of tithing in Pentecostalism is evident. Tithes are the main source of income

---

9. Mbe, "Asceticism," 48; Gifford, "Ritual Use of the Bible," 179.
10. Mbe, "Asceticism," 47–48.
11. Ibid.
12. Ibid., 57.
13. Coleman, *Globalization*, 42.
14. Asamoah-Gyadu, *Contemporary Pentecostal Christianity*, 83.
15. Ibid., 84.

for Pentecostal congregations to run their different, often grandiose projects.[16] Furthermore, planting a "seed" often amounts to giving funds to the preacher. This principle also known as "sowing and reaping" has become popular in sub-Saharan African Christianity through the media programs led by North American televangelist Oral Roberts.[17]

The third reason for my investigation into Christian giving is the corollary of the second. The earliest text of the New Testament about Christian giving is from Paul whose authentic letters are generally recognized as the earliest Christian writings we possess. So 2 Corinthians 8–9 deals extensively, not with tithing, but with Paul's collection for the poor Christians in Jerusalem.[18] Indeed, it can be argued that care for the needy was not peripheral to Paul's preaching; it was rather part and parcel of the latter.[19] Concerning the collection for the poor in Jerusalem, Paul's care for the poor was not underprivileged in comparison with his ministry of preaching the gospel. In fact, when Paul returned to Jerusalem to deliver his collection, this action took priority over his planned visit to Rome which he expected to be an important launching point for his impending preaching ministry to Spain (Rom 15:23–33).[20] It is arguable that the collection was so vital to the apostle that its conveyance was at that moment a more pressing duty than his desire to proclaim the gospel and plant Christian congregations in that new mission field. Christopher J. H. Wright indicates that this cannot be seen as "an interruption or neglect" of the ministry of the Word; Paul rather regarded it "as a crucial demonstration of the gospel at work."[21]

---

16. Ibid., 87.

17. Ibid., 79.

18. I agree with D. J. Downs that the use of the term "Christians" to refer to Jesus' followers in Paul's time is historically anachronistic but that for the sake of convenience we need to acknowledge the usefulness of this designation (Downs, *Offering of the Gentiles*, 1, n. 2).

19. Longenecker, *Remember the Poor*, 309.

20. Hood, "Theology in Action," 134, quoted by C. J. H. Wright, *Mission*, 215.

21. Wright, *Mission*, 215. The author is struck by the fact that little attention is paid to Paul's collection in standard studies on his theology or his mission, despite the fact that the project occupied years of Paul's life, and the fact that he mentions it in his largest letters, devoting two whole chapters to it in 2 Corinthians. For their part, Safrai and Tomson maintain that Paul's collection project was central to his apostolate and "has correctly been understood as a key to his intentions and theology" (Safrai and Tomson, "Paul's 'Collection'," 158).

Therefore, Paul's collection requires deeper investigation.[22] Interestingly enough, Paul's vocabulary in 2 Corinthians 9:6–11 anticipates the language of the prosperity gospel preachers referred to above. This makes the study of this text all the more fascinating. It runs as follows:

> And what I say is this: the one who sows sparingly will also reap sparingly, and the one who sows bountifully will also reap bountifully. May each person give as he has decided in his heart, not reluctantly or under compulsion, for God loves a cheerful giver. And God is able to provide you with every blessing in abundance, so that by always having enough of everything, you may abound in every good work. As it is written, "He has dispersed abroad, he has given to the poor; his righteousness endures forever." He who supplies seed to the sower and bread for food will supply and multiply your seed and increase the harvest of your righteousness. You will be enriched in every way in order to show every kind of generosity, which will produce thanksgiving to God through us.[23]

The alleged "language of prosperity" used by Paul in 2 Corinthians 9:6–11 needs extensive consideration. By the analogy of "sowing" and "harvesting" Paul seems to maintain that one's efforts will be proportionally rewarded. The apostle brings in the principle of reciprocity to say that God will provide for free givers.

Actually, the scriptural proofs for the blessing of the righteous and the misfortune of the sinner are mostly found in the Old Testament, but the New Testament also holds some.[24] Since 2 Corinthians 9:6–11 is one of those texts invoked by the preachers of the prosperity gospel, a thorough investigation of this passage is needed. Such a careful study becomes all the more necessary if we bear in mind that most African Christians read the Scriptures with the conviction that God certainly speaks through them.[25]

---

22. Punt, "Some Perspectives," 333.

23. This is the NRSV with some adaptations.

24. Roukema, "Les Églises," 69: Lev 25:3–5; Deut 8:18; 28:3–14; Prov 11:24; Mal 3:10; Luke 6:38; John 10:10; 2 Cor 9:6–11; 3 John 2.

25. The reality of poverty prevailing in the churches in Macedonia and Corinth involved in Paul's collection has drawn my attention to the similar current situation of

The reading of 2 Corinthians 8–9 raises the question of the motivations of Christian giving.[26] I wonder whether Paul's discourse in 2 Corinthians 9:6–11 is to be understood in line with the prosperity gospel. To put it differently, it is crucial to ask whether Paul tells the Corinthians to give their generous contributions to the collection in the hope of experiencing economic boost as a reward. And if so, how can we make sense of the situation of these Macedonians and most of the Corinthians who were poor? Does Paul imply that this was caused by their lack of faithfulness in giving? Moreover, it is crucial to consider Paul's purpose of his fundraising and ask whether it features in the prosperity gospel proponents. These questions will be addressed in the present work. But before I proceed, an overview of the main studies on Paul's collection is necessary to frame the general context of my investigation.

2. Major Scholarly Studies on Paul's Collection[27]

Many studies have been conducted on Paul's collection from various perspectives. However, it is beyond the scope of this research to present a

---

financial difficulties of many churches, if not all, in Africa in general and in Rwanda in particular. Concerning the Macedonians, we learn that "Out of the most severe trial, their overflowing joy and their extreme poverty welled up in rich generosity" (2 Cor 8:2). As for the Corinthians, "not many were influential; not many were of noble birth" (1 Cor 1:26). On a large scale, it is most probable that most of the Christian congregations founded by Paul belonged to the lower economic categories (Longenecker, *Remember the Poor*, 279). Furthermore, as notes Ogereau, the majority of the Palestinian population lived in poverty (Ogereau, "Jerusalem Collection," 360, n. 1; Jeremias, *Jerusalem*, 87–144; Meggit, *Paul, Poverty and Survival*).

26. I agree with Safrai and Tomson ("Paul's 'Collection'," 139) that in 2 Cor 8–9 Paul seeks to convince the Corinthians to renew their commitment to the collection, and that we need to consider other sources namely 1 Cor 16, Rom 15, and other passages in Acts to construe Paul's motivations for it. However, against their view that 2 Cor 8–9 as such cannot be trusted as to the real reasons behind the apostle's fundraising project for Jerusalem, I suggest that his statements should be taken on trust. In my opinion, Paul, who was not writing a systematic treatise on Christian almsgiving, laid emphasis differently on various motivations of his collection depending on the situation he had to handle. As this project extended over most of the duration of Paul's apostolate, it is reasonable to say that Paul developed subsidiary motifs in the course of time. What started as a relief project was enriched with deeper theological insights.

27. An extensive survey of studies on 2 Cor as a whole will be presented in chapter 2 which is concerned with Paul's Corinthian correspondence. However, such a survey is not possible in the case of the reception history of 2 Cor 8–9. To my knowledge, no studies have been conducted on the interpretation history of this passage. We find lists of existing

detailed review of the history of scholarship on the matter. Some selected works will be sufficient to give the complexity of scholarly views on the motivations and the meaning of Paul's collection. But it must be noted that these views "are not necessarily mutually exclusive."[28] The first influential study to be mentioned is that of Johannes Munck, *Paulus und die Heilsgeschichte* from 1954. Munck interpreted Paul's collection "in light of Old Testament and early Jewish traditions" regarding an eschatological pilgrimage of the Gentiles with their offerings to Jerusalem as expressed, for instance, in Isaiah 2:3; 60:5–15; 66:18–20; Jeremiah 3:17; Micah 7:12, 17; Haggai 2:7; Zechariah 8:21–23; 14:16.[29] Munck was the first scholar to stress the eschatological aspect of the collection by drawing a link between Paul's collection and these Old Testament and early Jewish traditions.

Munck's thesis was followed by Dieter Georgi's and Keith F. Nickle's studies. Georgi argues that participants at the apostolic council mentioned in Galatians 2:10[30] "must have reflected back on the old motif of the nations' pilgrimage" and on the related vision of the offering the Gentiles would bring to the holy city of Jerusalem.[31] He notes that the same views influenced Paul's theology in general and his conceptualization of the collection in particular.[32] In Georgi's view, the collection and its delivery to Jerusalem by an important delegation from the Gentiles, "simply had to revive in Jewish eyes the old concept of the eschatological pilgrimage of the peoples."[33] He maintains that Paul's intention in securing the collection

---

commentaries and sermons from different periods. I will present these resources in chapter 4. As for the prosperity gospel, I will engage with the abundant literature on the subject in chapter 6.

28. Ogereau, "Jerusalem Collection," 362.

29. Downs, *Offering of the Gentiles*, 3.

30. Georgi argues that "the poor" was a self-designation of the Jewish Christians in Jerusalem which demonstrates their self-understanding as the eschatological people of God. Further, he notes that in the context of Gal 2:10 "remembering the poor" was primarily to recognize that eschatological self-designation of the Christians at Jerusalem; the bestowal of financial assistance was only conditioned by that. Georgi also contends that the use of a present subjunctive (μνημονεύωμεν), and not an aorist tense, indicates that Paul has in mind a continued action (Georgi, *Remembering the Poor*, 34–35, 40, 41–42).

31. Ibid., 42.

32. Ibid., 39.

33. Ibid., 119.

and its conveyance to Jerusalem was to provoke the Jews to the faith in Christ upon seeing this symbolic action from the Gentiles.

For Nickle, Paul's collection aimed at expressing Christian charity, achieving Christian unity, and at the anticipation of Christian eschatology.[34] Nickle points out that this unity was exclusively built upon the person of Christ who realizes and maintains it.[35] Concerning the eschatological meaning of Paul's collection, Nickle sees it as the fulfillment of Old Testament prophecies regarding the end-time pilgrimage of the nations to Jerusalem.[36] He also argues that Paul expected that his collection would provoke the conversion of Israel (Rom 11:11–26); it is part and parcel of Paul's priestly mission for "the fullness of nations" (Rom 11:25; 15:16, 28). Nickle attempts to demonstrate that in 2 Corinthians 9:10 Paul quotes Isaiah 55:10 and Hosea 10:12 to express his "conviction that the effectiveness of the Word of God among the Gentiles was of instrumental significance for the conversion of Israel."[37] Nickle is obliged to force the meaning of the text to fit in his overall interpretation. He asserts that the supply and multiplication of the Corinthians' seed for sowing and the increase of the harvest of their righteousness mentioned by Paul do not refer to funds. Rather, he explains, Paul was telling the Corinthians that their involvement in the collection "would be used by God to produce an abundant harvest in connection with the proclamation of the gospel of redemption

---

34. Nickle, *Collection*, 100.

35. Ibid., 118.

36. D. Bolton recently made the same claim with slight variations (Bolton, "Paul's Collection," 347–359). He argues that Paul makes an eschatological twist in which he blends the classical motif of the pilgrimage of the Gentiles with their offering to serve Israel (Isaiah), and that of the return of Israel from exile (Isaiah and Hosea). In Bolton's understanding, Paul's view that the Christian Gentiles are God's people and thus part of Israel explains why he deliberately refrains from equating them with "the nations as second class citizens in the kingdom of God who will be bringing gifts to Zion," but at least symbolically as the exiled returning home. In the same vein, according to Bolton, it is precisely "this very happy twist" which may account for the lack of "any explicit reference to a classical Zion-pilgrimage text of servitude within the collection verses themselves" (ibid., 358). Bolton concludes that the debt theology that transpires in Isa 60:1–14 or Zech 14:16–21, for instance, is reversed in the sense that instead of "the nations being subservient to Israel," through Paul's collection, the Gentiles "are proclaiming aloud their salvation, in Jerusalem, that they, too, are an expression of Israel" (ibid., 359).

37. Nickle, *Collection*, 137.

among Israel."[38] Nickle understands that the many thanksgivings to God (2 Cor 9:12) expected by Paul as a result of his collection will mainly be motivated by the conversion of Israel. He concludes that both the Gentiles and the converted Israel will join their voices to address their thanks to God. Moreover, Nickle entertains that the delegation that traveled with Paul to Jerusalem for the delivery of the collection was in effect "the firstfruits" of the fulfillment of the old Jewish traditions regarding the Gentiles flooding into Jerusalem.[39] But he notes that instead of coming to receive salvation as it was expected in Jewish traditions, the Gentiles, "represented by the delegates from the churches," were to stream to Jerusalem "as the true Israel of God."[40] By doing so these delegates were to realize the mission entrusted to Israel by the prophets, which consisted in proclaiming God's salvation. Nickle makes it clear that the collection, rather than being seen as "a shameful imposition which revealed his [Paul's] subservience to Jerusalem," must be regarded as "a valid endeavour" which was for Paul a genuine way of expressing the Christian faith.[41] Nickle points out that for the Gentiles the collection would display "the legitimate Christian character" they had acquired by their faith in Christ and their full participation in the Christian fellowship.[42] One of the main merits of Nickle's study is that it underlines the centrality of the notion of χάρις in 2 Corinthians 8–9 as Paul conceptualizes his collection. Nickle notes that this term chosen by Paul to talk about his collection "was endowed with rich significance from within the context of Judaism."[43]

However, the alleged eschatological dimension of Paul's collection defended by Munck, Georgi and Nickle as presented above has been challenged. David J. Downs observes that none of these scholars has demonstrated "how and where" Paul makes a connection between his collection and the Jewish pilgrimage texts.[44] Moreover, as James R. Harrison aptly

---

38. Ibid.
39. Ibid., 138.
40. Ibid., 139.
41. Ibid., 101.
42. Ibid., 125.
43. Ibid., 109.
44. Downs, *Offering of the Gentiles*, 3, 9. It is important to note that the Old Testament texts on the Gentiles' pilgrimage to Jerusalem indicate that their offerings will be intended

demonstrates, in his treatment of the collection, Paul never hints at pilgrimage texts, nor does he explicitly assign to its delivery a provocative function for the conversion of Israel.[45] He observes that there is no trace of the intertestamental messianic expectations related to Isaiah 66:20. In his view, even 2 Corinthians 9:10, which quotes Isaiah 55 and Hosea 10:12 and to which Georgi attributes an eschatological significance, does not have this meaning since it conspicuously expresses human dependence on and trust in God as the motivation for generous giving.

Another study worthy of mention is that of Verlyn D. Verbrugge. Although he recognizes that Georgi's and Nickle's studies on the collection are useful for his research, he argues that they did not investigate how "Paul's authority intersected with the Corinthians' participation in the collection."[46] Verbrugge also notes that the above-mentioned works did not examine the noticeable change in Paul's strategies to raise funds, from 1 Corinthians 16 to 2 Corinthians 8–9. He points out that in 1 Corinthians 16 Paul commands, whereas in 2 Corinthians 8–9 he formulates requests. It is remarkable that Verbrugge's interest in Paul's collection as evidenced in the Corinthian correspondence lies ultimately in the investigation of Paul's church leadership. Verbrugge analyzes three types of fundraising practices in Greco-Roman society which may have influenced Paul's conceptualization of the project in 2 Corinthians 8–9. These means were used to collect funds in order to give help to the poor and the hungry.[47] The imperial government would use a λειτουργία to raise public funds. Wealthier citizens would give their contributions in money or services for a specific activity in a city-state, such as public festivals and other forms of public entertainment and the covering of military expenses in times of war. These λειτουργίαι were originally bestowed voluntarily, but this changed gradually.[48] Indeed, with time they became an obligation, partly because of the

---

for the Temple of the Lord and not for assistance to the needy (Isa 56:6–8; 60:1–14; cf. Isa 2:1–4; 66:18–20).

45. Harrison, *Paul's Language of Grace*, 304–307.

46. Verbrugge, *Paul's Style*, 2.

47. Ibid., 146. Apart from these public funds which were used to meet the needs of the destitute, the wealth captured in wars was another source of securing the necessary funds needed for this purpose (ibid., 147).

48. Ibid., 147–148.

spirit of competition among the rich people who strived for public praise. In Ptolemaic times, λειτουργίαι were made mandatory by the government in order to perform public functions.[49]

Another institutionalized practice analyzed by Verbrugge is the Greco-Roman clubs and associations whose membership was volitional. Their activities were mostly concerned with the cult.[50] Most of these guilds got their financial support thanks to donations from wealthy members who would act as their benefactors.[51] These associations provided a social environment in which the poor could come together and see "their expenses paid," whereas the rich "received honor" in recognition for their deeds.[52] However, these associations were not charitable. For instance, Verbrugge notes that the association would cover the expenses for the burial of their poor members, but if any money was left, "it would go for a monument, not to the bereaved family."[53] Similarly, at the monthly club banquets, "the more prominent members received a greater share than the ordinary members."[54]

The Greek institution of ἐπίδοσις is the third form of fundraising studied by Verbrugge in his quest for parallels to Paul's collection. Two important features of this system are spelled out by Verbrugge. It consisted in an occasional fundraising when there was a specific need to meet in the public life of a Greek city-state such as food shortage or war. Furthermore, the appeal for donations was addressed to the masses. Verbrugge concludes that among the three systems he has analyzed, "the notion of ἐπίδοσις does serve as a true parallel to Paul's notion of raising money for the poor in Jerusalem."[55] He also recognizes significant differences.[56] While Paul writes a letter to collect the money for distant beneficiaries, in the ἐπίδοσις a decision is made by the people to make a contribution for the common good of their own community. Moreover, at a formal level, Paul uses a letter

---

49. Ibid.
50. Ibid., 150.
51. Ibid., 151.
52. Ibid.
53. Ibid., 152.
54. Ibid.
55. Ibid., 157.
56. Ibid., 175–176.

as a medium of communication, whereas for the ἐπίδοσις, the message was recorded on inscriptions in an appropriate style of language specifically different from the epistolary style. On the basis of these observations, Verbrugge rightly states that it would be inappropriate to push further the comparison between the ἐπίδοσις inscriptions and Paul's letters on the collection because "each is a different type of document."[57]

New inscriptional discoveries, which were not available when Verbrugge published his study, opened room for the reexamination of the practices of social exchange and benefaction within Judaism and in Greco-Roman culture.[58] Some contributions will be indicated here to illustrate current scholarly interest in ancient social exchange practices as the interpretive framework of Paul's collection. Hellen-Ann Hartley argues that Paul's manual work and collection project for the poor Christians in Jerusalem are an expression of "*euergetism.*"[59] The latter is explained as "the socio-political phenomenon of voluntary gift-giving to ancient communities."[60] However, Hartley reaffirms the theological meaning of Paul's project that she summarizes in its four common purposes: help for the poor, promotion of unity in the church, almsgiving from the Gentile Christians as a substitute for sacrifices and circumcision, and the provocation of Israel to believe in the Messiah thanks to the eschatological gifts from the Gentiles to Zion. Furthermore, she admits that Paul's understanding of his collection must have evolved with time to include many goals: "What began as an act of kindness may well have, as a result, become an act of unity and eschatological provocation."[61]

There is no need to repeat here criticisms formulated by Downs against the interpretation of Paul's collection as an eschatological offering to

---

57. Ibid., 176. He makes an important observation on the fact that the ἐπίδοσις inscriptions use third person imperatives frequently but never employ them for "the actual appeal to make a pledge" for donations. Verbrugge concludes that this avoidance of imperatives in such a context indicates that "asking directly for money is not an appropriate thing to do" (ibid., 209).
58. Downs, *Offering of the Gentiles*, 26.
59. Hartley, "Financing Paul," 69.
60. Ibid., 71.
61. Ibid., 74.

Jerusalem.[62] The attempt to understand Paul's fundraising project as an expression of *euergetism* is equally questionable. The civic elite alone could engage in public benefactions, and this could take different forms such as the building of gymnasia, roads, theatres, aqueducts, and temples as well as food provision and protection against enemies.[63] However, it must be noted that the practice of *euergetism* did not emerge "from altruism or municipal spirit, but from the interests of the wealthy."[64] The main reason to deny the altruist character of *euergetism* is the fact that the benefactors were legally entitled to receive honor and material rewards; which brought the recipients to view benefaction as a loan.[65]

For Hans-Dieter Betz, Paul's collection which involved the Greek Christians offering their benefaction to Jewish Christians in Jerusalem was "a matter of ecclesiastical politics."[66] He explains that this is evidenced by the fact that in 2 Corinthians 9:6–15 the apostle expects his collection to promote unity within the Church between the Jewish and Greek Christians. Another argument for Betz' interpretation of the collection is Paul's statement that he intends it to bring about equality consisting in reciprocity (2 Cor 8:14). Julien M. Ogereau expands Betz' view and contends that Paul's undertaking was an instance of "socio-economic politics" motivated by "the conviction that the advent of the eschatological kingdom of God had inaugurated a new socio-economic order, which was to become distinctive of the emergent Christ-believing communities on a global scale."[67] But it seems exaggerated to ascribe to Paul the ambition to reform the structural imbalances of Greco-Roman society as Ogereau claims.[68] Perhaps Paul's view that his collection aims to create ἰσότης, "fair balance" among believers (2 Cor 8:14) can be understood as an indirect

---

62. Downs, *Offering of the Gentiles*, 3, 9.
63. Marshall, *Jesus, Patrons, and Benefactors*, 24–173.
64. Kim, *Stewardship and Almsgiving*, 269.
65. Ibid., 270–271.
66. Betz, *2 Corinthians 8 and 9*, 68.
67. Ogereau, "Jerusalem Collection," 362.
68. Ibid., 377.

criticism against social inequalities in Greco-Roman society.⁶⁹ Paul might imply that there is a pressing need for the restoration of "a certain balance between need and surplus," as remarks Ogereau.⁷⁰ Evidently, when Paul associates ἰσότης with κοινωνία, fellowship in the treatment of the collection, he gives to his relief project a "socio-economic dimension."⁷¹

The view that the collection represents a matter in which socio-economic Church politics come into play within nascent Christianity is much elaborated by Stephan Joubert.⁷² He esteems that the Greco-Roman practice of patronage/benefaction which was known in Judaism of the first century must be viewed as "the interpretative framework" of Paul's collection.⁷³ Joubert criticizes earlier studies by observing that Paul's collection has so far been interpreted in a theological perspective as though Paul and other parties involved in this project were systematic theologians.⁷⁴ Yet he agrees that the very fact that this project is mentioned in four of his letters explains that "this was no 'ordinary' fund raising project."⁷⁵ Moreover, Joubert notes that the collection had important implications for the participating parties. By recapitulating earlier studies on the matter, he wonders what function it did actually fulfill within the early Christian movement.⁷⁶ He insists that the socio-historical context of the collection cannot merely be viewed as "background information" from which one will understand its "actual theological" meaning. He explains that patronage was a voluntary benefit relationship "between socially disproportionate individuals, as well as between socially disproportionate individuals and groups."⁷⁷ This system found expression in relations between "landlords and tenants," "patricians

---

69. J. P. Becker is right to suggest that ἰσότης should be translated as "*equity*, which connotes *proportional correspondence*, rather than the word *equality*, which connotes *identical correspondence*" (Becker, *Paul's Usage of* χάρις, 111).

70. Ogereau, "Jerusalem Collection," 366.

71. Ibid., 373.

72. Joubert, *Paul as Benefactor*.

73. Ibid., 5.

74. Ibid., 4. Ogereau ("Jerusalem Collection," 362) formulates the same complaint to the effect that much attention is paid to "the theological rationale of the collection, ignoring its more practical economic implications, or even its political dimension."

75. Joubert, *Paul as Benefactor*, 2.

76. Ibid., 2–3.

77. Ibid., 23.

and their freedman," "members of *collegia*," "Rome and occupied territories," and "officially appointed patrons and Roman communities."[78] As for benefaction, he says that it was not voluntary and consisted in "exchange of services."[79] Joubert notes that at least three areas were shaped by reciprocal obligations: "Children to parents; beneficiaries to private benefactors, and cities to their public benefactors."[80] He concludes that the meeting between Paul and the leaders of the Jerusalem church at which the apostle pledged to take care of the poor of the Jerusalem community (Gal 2:10) can be interpreted in the perspective of the theory of agonistic benefit exchange. Consequently, the collection has to be viewed as an obligation laid upon Paul by the Jerusalem leaders in exchange for their recognition of his ministry to the Gentiles.[81] Joubert notes that the leaders of the Jerusalem church perceived the collection as a charitable project aimed to place Paul and Barnabas in a long-term debt.[82] He indicates that Paul and his Gentile churches were obligated to Jerusalem (Rom 15:25–27). Correspondingly, through the collection, Paul reciprocated the benefit received from the Jerusalem church; which would bring about solidarity (Gal 2:9) and balanced reciprocity among the early Christians (2 Cor 8:13–15).[83] Joubert insists that Paul's successful completion of the collection would place the initial benefactors in the Jerusalem church under the obligation to give thanks and honor to God (2 Cor 9:11–15).[84] For him, Paul passes from the view of the collection as a "benefit exchange" to its theological understanding as a χάρις.[85] Joubert remarks that the term χάρις commands the structure of 2 Corinthians 8–9. He writes that this text illustrates the concrete functioning of God's χάρις in the lives of all those who were involved in the collection.

However, Harrison shows that Joubert fails to realize that Paul implicitly criticizes "the Greco-Roman benefaction system and shapes

---

78. Ibid., 36.
79. Ibid., 37.
80. Ibid.
81. Ibid., 107, 114–115.
82. Ibid., 106.
83. Ibid., 102–103, 114–115, 121–124, 128–134, 140–144.
84. Ibid., 144–152.
85. Ibid., 152–153, 202–203, 135–152.

an alternative vision of social relations" through his theology of χάρις.[86] According to Harrison, Paul's association of χάρις, κοινωνία, and διακονία in 2 Corinthians 8:4 attests to his effort to socially and theologically redefine the Greco-Roman conventions of benefaction.[87] He contends that to this end Paul introduces Jesus' example to avoid that the Corinthians might finally meet his request "and fulfill their promised contribution, not because of any sense of gratitude for the divine grace as revealed in the impoverished Christ (2 Cor 8:9), but more due to the silent demands of Graeco-Roman reciprocity system."[88] Harrison adds that, through Paul's theology of grace, all the parties involved in the collection are invited to regard themselves as beneficiaries of God's grace, tied together by the reciprocal obligation of love and by the recognition of the Jews' priority in salvation history.

Steven J. Friesen takes the debate further and points out that Joubert's treatment of the collection in terms of patronage/benefaction is encumbered by three problems.[89] In the first place, the description of benefaction as an arrangement in which "the parties were benefactors to each other" overlooks the asymmetric character of this social exchange. Second, it turns out that Joubert's description of the collection does not take into consideration areas in which Paul's project does not fit the system of patronage or benefaction. Third, Joubert based his description of this type of social exchange on elite texts. Consequently, his oversight of the widespread economic poverty in the Greco-Roman society of Paul's times led him to wrongly assume that the same "elite practices" would be present in the Pauline congregations.[90] Friesen points out two main features of Paul's collection which demonstrate again the unlikelihood of the influence of *euergetism* or benefit exchange on the apostle's project. First, the communal character of the collection: the fund was raised from different churches whereas patronage practices "operated primarily on the principle of one wealthy benefactor or one wealthy family (or several families) giving

---

86. Harrison, *Paul's Language of Grace*, 311.
87. Ibid., 343.
88. Ibid., 313.
89. Friesen, "Paul and Economics," 48.
90. Ibid.

a large sum that would allegedly benefit many less fortunate people."[91] Next, Paul's collection involved "people with modest living resources living mostly around subsistence" committed to helping the Jerusalem Christians in a strained financial situation and not from wealthy individuals or families that could invest the surplus of their resources in patronage.[92]

From a different standpoint, the social and theological meanings of Paul's collection have been assessed by Ze'ev Safrai and Peter J. Tomson.[93] They feel that the fact that Paul designates his fundraising campaign, "the service to the saints" (2 Cor 8:4), the expression which is found only in Paul's writings, has an important significance. They are of the opinion that it was of quite a different nature in comparison to the common practice of charity or almsgiving known in ancient Judaism and early Christianity, and to other particular fundraising activities attested in the New Testament. They argue that like others, Paul viewed the church at Jerusalem as "the mother of all churches' and, in spite of later tensions, her leaders as 'pillars' (cf. Gal 4:26; 2:9)."[94] Safrai and Tomson contend that Paul's fundraising project would enable him to acquire a social and religious status and help him to silence criticism of him in Jerusalem.[95] They state that examples of

---

91. Ibid., 49.
92. Ibid., 50.
93. Safrai and Tomson, "Paul's 'Collection'," 132–220.
94. Ibid., 132.
95. Ibid., 132–133. Like many scholars, Safrai and Tomson believe that the Jerusalem apostles' request to remember the poor and Paul's wholehearted agreement refer to the collection. They esteem that it was the outcome of this mutual agreement and was meant "to be a tribute from the gentile diaspora churches to the Jewish church of Jerusalem" (ibid., 160). However, I agree with Longenecker (*Remember the Poor*, 198) who shows that there is every reason to think that the recommendation to remember the poor as recorded in Gal 2:10 (μόνον τῶν πτωχῶν ἵνα μνημονεύωμεν) has no geographical limitations. Furthermore, this request entails that concern for the poor should be a continuous action, as suggested by the use of the present subjunctive. Therefore, the injunction to remember the poor cannot be limited to the collection, which was a project restricted in time. Rather, the Jerusalem church leaders, for whom care for the poor was a highly distinctive feature of the faith in the God of Israel that Paul had also been preaching, insisted that the apostle should continue to emphasize it in his law-free gospel to the Gentiles. Dunn holds a similar point of view about the interpretation of Gal 2:10. He concludes that it is most likely that "Paul was simply affirming his long-standing and sustained eagerness as a Jesus-believer to maintain the traditional Jewish concerns for the 'poor', a concern he continued to enact during his days as a church founder without reference to and prior to the idea of the collection as such" (Dunn, *Beginning from Jerusalem*, 933–934, 935). To me, this reading does not affect the view that Paul acknowledged the special place of the Jerusalem church. In a broader perspective, Paul

money functioning in this way are attested by rabbinic sources. They conclude that the collection is a remarkable acknowledgement of the central place of Jerusalem and of its Christian community in early Christianity.[96] Safrai and Tomson argue that Paul's collection served to provide "financial support for the foremost church and its leaders."[97] They esteem that this interpretation can be supported by the fact that in the late Second Temple period, the priests in Jerusalem were provided with money to compensate their work in the Temple.[98] Moreover, it is argued that the fact that in 1 Corinthians 16:1–5 Paul does not state that his collection is destined for the poor believers entails that the apostle thought that the church would "know what to use it for" (i.e. to support the poor and provide financial support for leaders).[99]

One of the main merits of the interpretation proposed by Safrai and Tomson is that Paul's collection was an expression of his recognition of Jerusalem's hegemony and loyalty to the mother church.[100] In fact, despite Paul's denial of the Jerusalem church leaders' influence on him in Galatians 2:6, it is clear that he was aware that he needed their approval of his ministry among the Gentiles, or better, it was essential for him to be in agreement with the Jerusalem church about his law-free gospel to the Gentiles (Gal 2:2). In other words, the reciprocal recognition of the two missions of equal status to the Jews and to the Gentiles spearheaded by Peter and Paul respectively is crucial in this context. The agreement sealed in Galatians 2:7–10 implies the recognition by Paul of the primacy of the Jerusalem apostles, insofar they had approved of his gospel to the

---

did not doubt the Jews's priority in God's revelation of his salvation plan (Rom 1:16; 3:1–4; 9–11). Furthermore, the view that the actual reason behind the collection was the payment of a tribute by the Gentiles to the Jerusalem church is hard to maintain. While Rom 15:25–27 clearly underpins this motivation, I suggested earlier that one should consider that Paul laid emphasis differently on various motivations of his collection depending on the situation he had to deal with. There is a perceptible development in Paul's thought concerning the conceptualization of his fundraising campaign. At any rate, the motif of compassion for the poor of the mother church in Jerusalem remains essential.

96. Safrai and Tomson, "Paul's 'Collection'," 191.
97. Ibid., 132.
98. Ibid., 177.
99. Ibid., 140.
100. Ibid., 132.

non-Jews.[101] Against the view that Paul's fundraising was meant to respond to a pressing situation of financial poverty among the members of the church at Jerusalem (2 Cor 8:13–15; 9:12),[102] the idea that it was intended to give financial support to Christian leaders in the Jerusalem church is the most difficult to grasp.

The last work to be considered in this research is from Joseph P. Becker, to which I referred to previously. It focuses on the unifying character of the concept of χάρις in 2 Corinthians 8–9. Becker argues that Paul's usage of this concept is quite occasional and tied to nascent Christianity as a subculture in which it is employed and becomes normative.[103] In this context of the collection, Becker explains that χάρις displays two main features. As a "doxological agent," he notes, χάρις is received from God, and when it is translated into acts of faith, it is given back to God in the form of δόξα, glory. In this sense Becker can speak of the trajectory of χάρις, whose starting and end points are located in God. The second aspect of χάρις mentioned by Becker is that Paul presents it as something which engages with both the spirits and bodies of believers and interacts with the latter. He calls this the *pneumasomatic* property of χάρις. He concludes that these two aspects appear frequently across the New Testament corpus. He strives to prove especially the materiality of χάρις, an aspect which he thinks is less noticeable and contested.[104]

---

101. Ibid., 143, 158.

102. Dunn, *Beginning from Jerusalem*, 939. The cause of this situation of poverty is not easy to decipher. In Dunn's view, it is possible that it was the result of periodic famines which would have affected poorer people in Judea. Equally possible, this was an endemic situation in the Jerusalem church which resulted from the massive conversion of poorer Jews to the Christian movement, "putting a strain on the common fund in Jerusalem," if it was still functioning as Luke depicts it in Acts 2:44–45; 4:32–37. In either case, Paul was well informed about the developments in Jerusalem. However, Safrai's and Tomson's explanation cannot be ruled out. They think that Acts 4:32–35 implies that "those who did not work because they continuously attended the Temple, were in need of donations for living" distributed from the common treasure of the community (Safrai and Tomson, "Paul's 'Collection'," 157).

103. Becker, *Paul's Usage of* χάρις, i–ii.

104. As far as 2 Cor 8–9 is concerned, Becker (*Paul's Usage of* χάρις, 197–243, 255–277) notes different instances which reflect the materiality of χάρις: it is bestowed as an observable reality (8:1), it overflows (8:2); it is received in hands (8:4), brought to completion (8:5); it is a concrete action or benefaction (8:7), administered to produce fair balance or "proportional equality" as he says (8:9, 11–15); transported and managed with care (8:19) and seen as a vital force (8:20). Moreover, he notes that χάρις is presented as a

According to Becker, this doxological feature of χάρις is implicitly present in 2 Corinthians 8–9; it remains its main function and appears in all of the ten occurrences of the word in this passage.[105] But to his disappointment, Becker observes that this dimension has perhaps been taken for granted so that little has been written about it. He strongly maintains that in this text Paul conceives χάρις as "an objective reality – as some *thing* with ontological status" for which Paul plots a clear trajectory in his treatment of the collection in 2 Corinthians 8–9.[106] Moreover, he indicates that his insistence on its somatic function is due to the fact that it has been generally neglected in modern academic studies. He remarks that, from its start, Orthodox Christianity has perceived "grace as an uncreated energy of God" by which Christians are enabled to participate in the divine nature.[107] Becker notes that this points to the fact that χάρις is physical. He continues to show that, on the contrary, in the Roman Catholic tradition, "grace has long been considered a spiritual substance of sorts which is poured into the heart of the believer."[108] But he indicates that in both traditions these conclusions have been reached not through grammatico-historical exegesis but through a dependence on patristic works, church doctrines, and arguments from pure reason. He sees that universalizing and theologizing tendencies have too often overloaded the word χάρις with abstract and post-biblical notions. Such approaches seek to separate the theological from the practical.[109] Becker indicates that none of the extant scholarly literature speaks

---

substance in 9:4 (that is how he translates ὑπόστασις); it can be sowed and reaped sparingly or bountifully (9:6), overflow (9:8), multiply (9:10). Becker also observes that Paul depicts χάρις as something you can locate in the heart or upon believers (9:7; 9:14). He adds that it can not only be seen but also recognized as a proof of something; it can be poured out in an exceeding measure (9:13–15). These considerations lead Becker to conclude that Paul presents χάρις as "something tangible and concrete." In my view, these observations point to the fact that the term χάρις has different meanings in the passage under consideration here. In addition, Paul sometimes refers to χάρις in a quasi-empirical sense just as in 1 Cor 13:4–7 he speaks of love as a personified agent: "Love is patient; love is kind; love is not envious or boastful or arrogant or rude. It does not insist on its own way; it is not irritable or resentful; it does not rejoice in wrongdoing, but rejoices in the truth."

105. Becker, *Paul's Usage of* χάρις, 1, 58–144, 330.
106. Ibid., 1, 2, 196–277.
107. Ibid., 3.
108. Ibid.
109. Ibid., 56–57.

expressly about the doxological trajectory or pneumasomatic ontology of χάρις in Paul. He thus justifies his preference for the grammatico-historical approach with some modifications as he exegetes the texts at stake.[110] However, Becker cites with satisfaction some scholars who, without intending to investigate pneumasomatic elements in Paul's employment of χάρις, identify them to some degree.[111] As far as our text on the collection is concerned, Becker's conclusion is that "χάρις is presented as something which not only freely traverses both the pneumatic and somatic planes, but does so purposively; for as it flows its trajectory from God to man, from believer to believer, and back to God, it fulfills its reason-for-being, to produce glory (δόξα) for God."[112]

The main merit of Becker's characterization of χάρις lies in its general affirmation that this term has both spiritual and material connotations. However, one may question Becker's view that in its ten occurrences in 2 Corinthians 8–9 χάρις is "consistently pneumasomatic" and that other allusions and representations of this kind involve almost every verse in this passage.[113] In other words, one wonders whether Becker is not tempted to force the text into an internal agreement as far as the different occurrences of χάρις are concerned. His conclusion gives the impression that in 2 Corinthians 8–9 Paul sets out to write a treatise on χάρις. In Becker's words, χάρις "is more than simply a frequent-occurring word in 2 Corinthians 8–9; rather, it is actually the subject of the entire pericope. For the trajectory of χάρις is either directly in view, or operating as a subtext, in every verse of 2 Cor 8–9."[114]

To conclude this survey of studies on Paul's collection, it turns out that the diversity of approaches to it reveals not only the importance that scholars have attached to it, but also its great significance in the apostle's career and theology. In this research, Nickle's and Harrison's interpretations will serve as the general framework of my reading of 2 Corinthians 8–9. Paul's words that his collection was to meet the needs of poor Christian believers

---

110. Ibid., 3, 58.
111. Ibid., 47–48.
112. Ibid., 332.
113. Ibid., 277.
114. Ibid., 144.

in Jerusalem and establish a fair balance between them and the Corinthians will be taken on trust. In other words, Paul's collection in 2 Corinthians 8–9 will be treated as a charitable work with theological significance. The centrality of the term χάρις will receive due attention not only as a strong motivation for Christian giving, but also as Paul's means to redefine human reciprocity and sufficiency. However, Nickle's eschatological aspect of the collection and Harrison's view about the supremacy of the Jews in salvation history will not be integral to this interpretive framework of 2 Corinthians 8–9. Moreover, some exegetical insights into this text from those other perspectives will be picked up to enrich this study.

3. New Areas to Be Explored

In addition to the literary analysis of 2 Corinthians 8–9 to identify the motivations set by Paul for his collection and thus for Christian giving, this study explores first the interpretation of this text by selected authors from late Antiquity to the Reformation period. To my knowledge, no previous research has been conducted in this perspective. Generally speaking, the period running from patristic times down to the Reformation has provided Christianity with an enormous literary production which exceeds by far the works of the nineteenth century which was mostly engaged with mission overseas. It is therefore interesting to investigate the content of sermons and commentaries on 2 Corinthians 8–9 stemming from these historical and ecclesial contexts. The intent of this investigation will be to assess to what extent the function of the term χάρις and the motivations of Christian giving as established by the literary analysis of this passage come up in these interpretations handed down to us. In fact, besides my scientific curiosity about the reception history of biblical texts, research in this area expresses a strong awareness that we are not the first readers of the Bible. Within the Pentecostal tradition in which I grew up and am currently carrying out pastoral ministry, there is a tendency to neglect this historical reality of biblical hermeneutics. For instance, in an article on recent debates on early Christianity, François Bovon notes that there is a remarkable historiographical lacuna on the side of evangelical scholars with regard to patristic writings.[115] It is true that Bovon's observation does not refer specifically to patristic interpretation of the New Testament. However, it points out this general attitude towards patristic literature. His remark applies to the attitude of Pentecostal interpreters of the Bible towards the reception history of the Scriptures. It is my conviction that research in this area reveals that we can always learn from those who preceded us in the interpretation of the Bible. The errors and insights (as far as we can judge them with our standards) of our predecessors can stimulate our continuous quest for the meaning of biblical texts.

The second new area to be explored concerns the use of 2 Corinthians 8–9 by some prosperity gospel preachers in sub-Saharan Africa. There is no need to explain that a solid and sound exegesis is needed before one engages a constructive dialogue with the prosperity gospel teachers. It is crucial to constantly check if all teachings on a given text, in this case 2 Corinthians 8–9, are reliable. This is all the more crucial if we bear in mind that religious teachings and beliefs exert a great influence on people, and specifically sub-Saharan Africans. The justification of an investigation into the reception history is probably the most difficult to grasp for many readers. My contention is that even Pentecostals have greatly inherited from previous ancient readers of the Scriptures. Indeed, the absence of any explicit reference to previous traditions among Pentecostals does not necessarily mean that they do not make use of them at all. A certain interpretation which has been in circulation and thus believed to emanate from a spiritual leader will *ipso facto* receive credentials and will be seen as the only one inspired by God's Spirit. A close investigation will reveal that on a given subject matter, Pentecostals expound perhaps unconsciously the views of Tertullian, Origen, Augustine, Thomas Aquinas, Calvin and others. This unconscious influence can be partly explained by the fact that Pentecostalism is essentially an oral tradition. In addition, it is important to bear in mind that, as in Latin America for instance, most of African Pentecostals used to belong to the Roman Catholic Church and mainline Protestant churches started mostly by European missionaries. That the Roman Catholic Church has engaged more with church fathers than

---

115. Bovon, "Beyond the Canonical," 126.

Protestants have remains unquestioned. Also, its old and overwhelming presence on sub-Saharan African soil explains why its influence in terms of beliefs and practices is perceptible even among people's ordinary lives though they have never officially adhered to its confessions. Similarly, the legacy of the Reformation is confessed at various levels among historical Protestantism in sub-Saharan Africa as well. It is equally true that like other Evangelicals,[116] Pentecostals hold on to some themes (with certain variations of emphasis) such as the authority of the Bible, and the central role of the cross in salvation and regeneration.[117] These themes can certainly be traced back to the Reformation. It goes without saying that some beliefs, thoughts and practices from the former traditions are still alive and operational among Pentecostals. Therefore, it seems to me that it is crucial to check whether there is a relation of continuity or discontinuity between the interpretation of our passage by the prosperity gospel preachers (Pentecostals) and selected readings handed down to us from late antique Christianity to the Reformation. The unifying element of the three steps of this study remains the function of the term χάρις and the motivations of Christian generosity in 2 Corinthians 8–9. They are established through the literary analysis of the text before their occurrence, interpretation and implications are checked in different contexts covered by the present research.

Further insights can be gained through the awareness that although people's contexts may be different, they share many preoccupations, as explains Elisée Musemakweli. On the basis of Paul Tillich's sermons, he undertook to reflect on the art of preaching in Africa though Tillich had

---

116. In the sixteenth century, the term "evangelical" was applied to the churches stemming from the Reformation in Germany and Switzerland because of their emphasis on the "gospel," the good news of justification of sinners by grace through faith, and their claim to base their teaching not on the church's tradition but on the supreme authority of Scripture (Johnston, "Evangelicalism," 219). It was thus roughly synonymous with "Protestant" in that context (Noll, "Future of Protestantism," 421). From the eighteenth century onwards it has been applied to various Christian movements and denominations which share "a dedication to the gospel that is expressed in a personal faith in Christ as Lord, and understanding of the gospel as defined authoritatively by scripture, and a desire to communicate" it passionately for conversion (Johnston, "Evangelicalism," 218). To various degrees depending on contexts these groups have insisted on the communication of the gospel in evangelism and social reform.

117. Asamoah-Gyadu, *Contemporary Pentecostal Christianity*, 2.

never engaged with this continent and its diversity of religions, cultures and socio-political challenges.[118] Indeed, the context of the church fathers and the Reformers studied in this research is quite distant in time and space from sub-Saharan Africa. This implies that every theological discourse is contextual. The ancient authors analyzed here did not talk about the African context. However, I have demonstrated that their views have penetrated the sub-Saharan African world especially through the spread of Christianity on its soil. Moreover, it is notable that these ancient authors addressed religious and social concerns which preoccupy believers in sub-Saharan Africa today. These include poverty and selfishness in society in general and among church members in particular. Furthermore, like other people on earth, Africans ask the question of the significance of human existence and the value of individual and collective actions in the present life and in the hereafter. Today, sub-Saharan African people read the Scriptures and ask how to correlate their content with the Christian life and the above-mentioned challenges. These questions moved the hearts of the ancient readers considered in the present study. Therefore, seeking to understand their reflections and solutions as readers of the same Scriptures is an intellectually and pastorally worthwhile activity.

However, I do not pretend that the earlier interpretations of biblical texts are always correct or normative. Concerning patristic interpretation, for instance, Riemer Roukema is right in conceding that very often the fathers provide us with "different interpretations that deviate considerably from each other, so that it is unwarranted to say that patristic interpretation is always valuable for historical-critical exegetes."[119] But this holds true of any hermeneutical approach to the Bible, however fascinating it may be. Correspondingly, the study of different interpretations of 2 Corinthians 8–9 is undergirded by the commonly accepted truth that we are always consciously or unconsciously influenced by our own complex contexts and presuppositions when we read the Bible, and that we constantly need to listen to others in this act of reading.[120] Ultimately, the combination of

---

118. Musemakweli, *La dynamique*, 29–31.
119. Roukema, "Value of Patristic Interpretation," 5.
120. Conradie, *Angling for Interpretation*, 109–119. In other words, there is no neutrality or objectivity in text-reading processes. People apply their limited perspectives to

the exegesis, reception history and current readings of 2 Corinthians 8–9 agrees with the conviction that God continues to speak to people through the Bible as he did in the past.

For the purpose of this study, the investigation into the reception history of 2 Corinthians 8–9 will focus solely on Paul's main thoughts in this passage. To this end and for practical reasons, I will select five authors of whom we have full commentaries on 2 Corinthians and translations in English or French. The influence that these Christian figures have exercised on Christian thought also explains why they will be studied. It is with such running commentaries that one gets the whole view of an author on the motivations of Christian generosity in the above-mentioned Pauline passage. With regard to the interpretation of our biblical passage in current African Pentecostalism, this will unfortunately not be possible. I will have to rely only on quotations from 2 Corinthians 8–9 used in the context of Christian giving. These are the only written materials available to us since the prosperity gospel – and Pentecostalism in general as we will see – operate in an oral tradition. I will therefore discuss six famous African prosperity gospel teachers whose voices are undoubtedly representative of the movement on the African continent.

4. The Aim and Nature of This Research

The ultimate aim of this study is not to analyze the organization and the implementation of Paul's collection. Rather, its focus will be upon the interpretation of 2 Corinthians 8–9 from late Antiquity down to the Reformation and its use in African Pentecostalism today in relation to the motivations of Christian giving. However, it remains a modest contribution to this vast area of research because it will solely focus on specific authors.

2 Corinthians 8–9 is about the raising of financial relief organized by Paul in favor of the poor of the Christian community in Jerusalem. This event is clearly mentioned elsewhere in Paul's writings (1 Cor 16:1–4, Rom 15:25–32). The apostle Paul devoted himself to this collection within the

---

enable the text to be alive for them (Jeanrond, *Theological Hermeneutics*, 2). In D. Jasper's words, we all approach the text with our "presuppositions," "presumptions" and "prejudices," which "may not necessarily be either good or bad" (Jasper, *Short Introduction*, 13–14).

churches he had founded in the Gentile land. The importance of this work in Paul's mission is attested to not only by the fact that it appears in his main letters, but also by the fact that even the strong opposition he faced in the Corinthian and Galatian churches against his apostleship did not deflect him from his focus. Furthermore, its value is reflected in Paul's report in Romans 15:30–31, where he testifies "his willingness to risk both his life and the possible rejection of his efforts by the Jerusalem church in order to deliver the funds personally to Jerusalem."[121] Its theological content is also of paramount importance in Paul's overall thought.[122]

It turns out that 2 Corinthians 8–9 is by far the most elaborated text on the collection and on Christian giving in general in the New Testament. Paul conceptualizes his relief project by offering a series of motives. To make sense of Paul's teaching on Christian generosity in 2 Corinthians 8–9 today, some heuristic questions need to be formulated from the outset, so that they may guide the analysis of this passage:

- What is the meaning of the frequently used term χάρις in this passage (16 times)? Does it have the same meaning in all its occurrences in our text? How does this term relate to its other usages elsewhere in Paul's writings, when we know that it remains one of the most favorite words in the apostle's vocabulary?[123]
- What are the motivations of Christian giving according to Paul in 2 Corinthians 8–9?
- Did Paul create such an undertaking, the collection, from scratch or did he draw on existing religious and social practices in the Jewish and Greco-Roman contexts?
- How can we interpret the tension between Paul's commendation of the Macedonians' contribution above their means (8:1–3) and his strong and repeated recommendation to the Corinthians that one must give according to one's possessions (8:11–12)?

---

121. Downs, *Offering of the Gentiles*, 1.

122. Nickle, *Collection*, 10: "Just as the project extended directly or indirectly over the whole temporal duration of Paul's missionary activity, so did it objectively incorporate the entirety of Paul's ministry in all of its theological depth."

123. Kohlenberger III et al., *Exhaustive Concordance*, 999–1001. The term χάρις occurs 155 times in the New Testament, 98 of which appear in Paul's writings.

- How was 2 Corinthians 8–9 interpreted over the centuries in the history of the church, precisely with regard to the concept of grace, the motivations of Christian generosity, the ways of giving, and the attitude to possessions?
- How can we make sense of 2 Corinthians 8–9 in a context, such as that of most African countries, where poverty and the prosperity gospel prevail?

5. Presuppositions and Approach

In this study, I will argue that in 2 Corinthians 8–9 Paul addressed Christian giving primarily for a charitable purpose from which he inferred theological significance.[124] The Jewish practice of charity informed Paul's collection among the Gentile Christian communities. It is possible that the apostle has merged several Jewish practices and applied them in a creative organizational manner.[125] At the same time the apostle shaped the understanding of charity in his theological framework of God's grace as a benefaction made to human beings and requiring gratitude in the form of every good deed, especially care for the needy. Moreover, Paul held the Jewish view that God reciprocates generous giving performed by believers.

In keeping with many scholars such as I. Howard Marshall, who agree that the biblical text must address our present context,[126] this research will assess how 2 Corinthians 8–9 makes sense in a particular ecclesiastical and social setting. With Ben Witherington III, I am convinced that "Paul's words are the Word of God and if properly handled and interpreted can

---

124. Nickle (*Collection*, 13) notes that the meaning of the collection "was clearly more than that of a simple act of charity" and the apostle must have devoted much of his "third missionary journey" to it according to Luke's account in Acts 18:23—21:16. But it is striking that Acts does not relate anything about the collection as such. The same account indicates that Paul was arrested in Jerusalem when he traveled there. There is no clear indication that Paul brought with him material assistance for the Jerusalem Christian community. We are only told that Paul agreed to pay for the expenses incurred for the purification of four men who had made a vow. He did so to prove his allegiance to the law of Moses as he had been advised by the Jerusalem church leaders (Acts 21:17—26). It is only in passing, when Paul presents his plea before Felix, that Acts tells about the alms that Paul would bring to his nation (24:17).

125. Safrai and Tomson, "Paul's 'Collection'," 217.

126. Marshall, *New Testament Interpretation*, 1.

still meaningfully address the *ekklèsia* today."[127] For this reason, the ultimate purpose of biblical interpretation does not consist in establishing the text of Scripture and its original meaning to its primary readers.[128] Rather, biblical interpretation goes further to examine the meaning of the text for current readers and allow the text to affect their attitudes and understanding.[129] In this way the Scriptures remain authoritative, as rightly notes Thomas A. Bennett.[130] In other words, investigation into the formation and transmission processes of biblical texts and their meaning to their original readers has to be supplemented by a serious consideration of the context of present readers. The dialogue with the prosperity gospel[131] on the interpretation of 2 Corinthians 8–9 with regard to Christian giving is crucial for this study since it responds to this need. I will discuss the points at which there is tension between my reading of the text, some elements of its interpretation encountered in the reception history, and the perspectives put forward by the prosperity gospel teachers. The purpose of this confrontation of views will be to build up a constructive and well-informed debate. Eventually, some interpretative principles will be formulated as safeguards for a reading which is consciously rooted in the literary context of 2 Corinthians and in Paul's overall theology and, at the same time, is open to the new insights generated by Pentecostal hermeneutics.

---

127. Witherington III, *Conflicts and Community*, xiv.

128. This tendency to reduce biblical scholarship to an essentially "historical science," typical of modern hermeneutics, has been challenged. In this line of thought, the search for the meaning of a text for current readers is thought to be the task of a totally different discipline (i.e. systematic theology) (Decock, "On the Value," 58, referring to Stendahl, "Biblical Theology, Contemporary," 418–432).

129. Marshall, *New Testament Interpretation*, 7.

130. Bennett, "Paul Ricoeur," 229: "Theological interpretation, by the nature of what it is trying to accomplish, expects the Bible to speak authoritatively to various ecclesial contexts is such a way that the church can return again and again to the texts, always encountering fresh meaning, always being pulled into and transformed by ever-novel scriptural worlds."

131. A genuine dialogue brings two or more interlocutors to understand one another. This research seeks to grasp the presuppositions of this teaching with regard to the motivations of Christian giving especially in relation with 2 Cor 8–9. The present study also invites these preachers to learn from other expressions of the Christian faith. Mutombo-Mukendi ("Le nouveau culte," 102) is right to write that since dialogue is becoming normative in dealing with relations among different religions, it is important to initiate such a dialogue with the prosperity gospel preachers. But he observes that dialogue can be successful if both parties involved in it have a good knowledge of each other.

The research methodology used in the present study is entirely a documentary analysis. It consists in a critical examination of information related to the issues under investigation which is accessible in printed and electronic sources. Specifically, in the exegetical analysis of 2 Corinthians 8–9 and the exploration of its reception by earlier interpreters, I will use the grammatico-historical approach. It means that words, expressions, and practices have to be set in their original socio-historical and literary contexts for a sound interpretation. However, I am aware that during the last decades many rhetorical analyses of the New Testament epistles have been made, with very different results.[132] Opposition to this method has also been expressed, since these epistles are no oral discourses and it is unlikely that the authors had been trained in Greek rhetoric. Since one cannot be sure whether Paul consciously used Greek rhetorical partitions,[133] I prefer to work with a more "traditional" analysis of the structure of the two chapters. Nonetheless, I will sometimes pick up precious insights from rhetorical approaches to this text which I find relevant to my argumentation.

For the last three chapters concerned with Pentecostalism in sub-Saharan Africa, the prosperity gospel and the contextual reading of 2 Corinthians 8–9, the documentary investigation will be supplemented by data from my personal experience of many years of observations of Pentecostal spirituality and practices.

6. Structure of the Study

This research is divided into seven chapters. In the first chapter I will explore the background of Christian generosity in Judaism and Greco-Roman culture. In the second chapter, some critical questions pertaining to the Corinthian correspondence will be addressed. Much attention will be paid to the discussion of the integrity of Paul's second letter to the Corinthians. The third chapter of this research will be concerned with the exegesis of 2 Corinthians 8–9. It will seek to identify the motivations of Christian giving in this passage according to Paul. It is in this sense that the meaning and function of the term χάρις will be investigated.

---

132. Watson, "Rhetorical Criticism," 400.
133. Ibid., 401–402.

In the fourth chapter, I will deal with some elements of the reception history of 2 Corinthians 8–9, especially with regard to the motivations of Christian giving. Chapter 5 will be concerned with a general introduction to African Pentecostalism which will be followed, in chapter 6, by the presentation of the prosperity gospel as it stands today in sub-Saharan Africa. Some think, wrongly or rightly, that the gospel of prosperity presents itself as a timely solution to the problem of economic poverty with which this continent is confronted. The seventh and last chapter will consist of investigating the use of 2 Corinthians 8–9 by the prosperity gospel teachers in sub-Saharan Africa in relation to the motivations of Christian giving.

In this study English translations are generally taken from the New Revised Standard Version (NRSV, 1989). However, in a few instances, some adjustments of its text will be called for. Very occasionally a different translation will be introduced. All the Bible versions quoted in this study for New Testament references are provided by Bible Works 7 unless otherwise indicated. As for the Septuagint quotations, I will use the New English Translation of the Septuagint (NETS).[134]

---

134. Pietersma, *New English Translation*.

CHAPTER 1

The Background of Christian Generosity

In Israel, charity was initially the expression of social justice. This justice stipulated that the destitute had the right to be cared for according to God's commandments to his people. The instruction to care for the poor was embedded in the conception of the covenant between God and Israel. In the Old Testament, it is repeatedly recommended to remember the widow, orphan, and the immigrant. It is confessed that God rewards such acts and punishes whoever offends the vulnerable. With time, the idea of righteousness acquired a new dimension and was equated with almsgiving, especially in the Apocrypha[1] included in the Septuagint (LXX). In this chapter I will explore briefly this development in the Hebrew Bible, the LXX and early Judaism. Christianity, which sprang from the diverse Judaism of the first century, took up its ethical values. Moreover, the influence of Greco-Roman culture on Judaism has been reassessed and proved to have permeated even Palestine, at least in the cities and the nobility.[2] Therefore, the second part of this chapter will deal with the practices of liberality and social exchange in the Greco-Roman society in which Christianity emerged.

---

1. Ferguson, *Backgrounds of Early Christianity,* 440: These books called "Apocrypha" in Protestant circles, and "Deuterocanonical" by the Roman Catholic Church, were produced in pre-Christian and early Christian times.

2. Ibid., 403.

1.1 Charity in the Old Testament and Early Judaism

1.1.1 The Hebrew Bible and Social Justice

In Genesis 18:19 we read that God's purpose when he chose Abraham was that the latter might perform righteousness and justice and impart them to his children.[3] This mission was so crucial that it remained the condition for the fulfillment of God's promises to Abraham.

> כִּ֣י יְדַעְתִּ֗יו לְמַ֩עַן֩ אֲשֶׁ֨ר יְצַוֶּ֜ה אֶת־בָּנָ֤יו וְאֶת־בֵּיתוֹ֙ אַחֲרָ֔יו
> וְשָֽׁמְרוּ֙ דֶּ֣רֶךְ יְהוָ֔ה לַעֲשׂ֥וֹת צְדָקָ֖ה וּמִשְׁפָּ֑ט לְמַ֗עַן הָבִ֤יא
> יְהוָה֙ עַל־אַבְרָהָ֔ם אֵ֥ת אֲשֶׁר־דִּבֶּ֖ר עָלָֽיו׃

> For I knew that he will instruct his sons and his household after him, and they will keep the ways of the LORD by **doing righteousness and justice** so that the LORD may bring upon Abraham all the things that he has talked to him about.

> ᾔδειν γὰρ ὅτι συντάξει τοῖς υἱοῖς αὐτοῦ καὶ τῷ οἴκῳ αὐτοῦ μετ᾽ αὐτόν καὶ φυλάξουσιν τὰς ὁδοὺς κυρίου ποιεῖν δικαιοσύνην καὶ κρίσιν ὅπως ἂν ἐπαγάγῃ κύριος ἐπὶ Αβρααμ πάντα ὅσα ἐλάλησεν πρὸς αὐτόν.

The root צדק conveys the idea of what is straight, in a fixed position and is what it is supposed to be. In this sense it can mean "something by which other things can be measured" (Lev 19:36; Deut 25:15).[4] In human dealings, it means what is in compliance with what is right or expected in a concrete situation. Righteousness is not an abstract concept, but consists in doing exactly what a given situation demands. As for the root משפט, its broadest sense connotes the idea of intervening in a situation which has gone wrong in the sense of oppression or being out of control, and put it right. It is in this sense that the root refers to judicial processes at various levels and rescue (hence the judges as saviors in the book of Judges). Its verbal form can thus indicate "to act as a lawgiver; to act as a judge by arbitrating between parties in a dispute; to pronounce judgment by declaring

---

3. Weinfeld, *Social Justice*, 7.
4. Wright, *Mission*, 90.

who is guilty and who is innocent respectively; and to execute judgment in carrying out the legal consequences of such a verdict."[5] The substantive form מִשְׁפָּט can depict the whole process of litigation as well as the verdict and its execution.[6] On a personal level, the noun can indicate one's legal right or the case one brings to the elders of the community against possible mistreatments by others. It is in this respect that מִשְׁפָּט is rendered by "justice" with an active connotation while צְדָקָה has a relatively more static dimension. One can rightly say that although both terms are often interchangeable, מִשְׁפָּט should be understood as what needs to be done in a given situation in order to restore people and circumstances in conformity with a right state of affairs, צְדָקָה.

God expected his people, Abraham's descendants, to commit themselves to the execution of righteousness and justice (Isa 5:7; Jer 4:2; Amos 5:24; Mic 6:8).[7] The eschatological Davidic king was expected to realize this ideal of justice (Isa 9:7; 32:1; Jer 23:5). The expression "**to do righteousness and justice**" cannot be reduced to judicial proceedings in a court. It also contains the notion of "*mercy* and *loving-kindness*," whose aim is the improvement of the living conditions of the helpless.[8] The paring of צְדָקָה and מִשְׁפָּט can be approximately rendered in English by the single complex idea of social justice. It always has an ethical dimension and is related to the ways of God (i.e. the ways he acts towards his people by saving them from all that alienates them from him and oppress them). The ways of the Lord in Genesis 18:19 mean his "character, actions and requirements."[9]

The book of Deuteronomy reflects the concern for social justice, and its traditions run through the corpus Joshua – 2 Kings, which scholars call "Deuteronomic History" for that reason.[10] This ethic is theologically rooted in the experience of Israel from bondage to freedom enacted by God's initiative.[11] Therefore, human care for the needy in Israel can only be

---

5. Ibid., 90.
6. Ibid., 91.
7. Ibid., 7.
8. Ibid.
9. Ibid., 92.
10. Hamilton, *Social Justice and Deuteronomy*, 3.
11. Kim, *Stewardship and Almsgiving*, 277–278.

seen as the imitation of God, who saved his people and provided for their needs when they were destitute (Deut 24:17–18). In the Torah five provisions at least prescribe benevolence to the economically disadvantaged: a special tithe collected every three years for the Levites, the resident aliens, the orphans, and the widows (Deut 14:28–29); the right for the poor to get food from the unplowed land in the seventh year (Exod 23:10–11); the restitution of the land to the poor who had been compelled to sell it in order to survive (Lev 25:25–28); prohibition of usury among Israelites (Lev 25:35–38); and regulations on slavery which favor the Israelites (Lev 25:39–55).[12]

In addition to the view of charity as a necessary response to God's gift of freedom to Israel, the prospect of punishment of whoever mistreats the weak is presented as another motivation for benevolence (Exod 22:21–24). By contrast, benevolence to the needy would be rewarded and this prompted the Israelites to commit themselves to assisting the needy in their midst (Deut 14:28–29). Deuteronomy 15 elaborates this promise of blessing as a reward for assistance to the poor in Israel.

Outside the Torah, the focus shifts from sacrificial rituals to the issues of ethics.[13] In some instances it is even said that sacrifices are unnecessary (1 Sam 15:22; Ps 50:12–15; Prov 21:3; Isa 1:10–17; Hos 6:6; Mic 6:6–8; Jer 7:21–23). In the Prophets we hear repeatedly the voice calling for social justice.[14] For instance, in Isaiah 1:10–17 it is declared that the abundance of sacrificial offerings was null in the eyes of God and that what counted was the pursuit of justice to be expressed through the care of orphans and widows. Isaiah 58:6–10 goes further and says that true fasting means setting free the oppressed, providing food to the hungry, shelter to the homeless, clothes to the naked, comfort to the afflicted.[15] The people of Israel are not only exhorted to assist the needy, but are also warned against God's judgement which awaits those who mistreat the weak (Isa 1:23; 3:13–15; 10:1–3; Jer 5:26–29; Ezek 22:29; Amos 2:6–7; 4:1; 5:11–15; 6:4; 8:4–6; Mic 2:1–2; 7:11). It is remarkable that prophetic condemnation of various

---

12. Ibid., 278.
13. Garrison, *Redemptive Almsgiving*, 47.
14. Ibid., 48.
15. Weinfeld, *Social Justice*, 18.

types of injustice done to the poor is an essential characteristic of Jewish communal ethic.[16] Furthermore, there is hope that in the end the rights of the poor will be restored (Isa 11:1–4; 26:1–6; 61:1).[17]

In the Writings we also encounter the same belief that almsgiving is rewarded by God and that the wicked are punished. Although the author of Job intends to challenge[18] this view, this book remains a good illustration of this theology. Job denies that his sufferings are the consequence of any hidden wrongdoing as his friends claim (22:6–13). He admits that if he had neglected the helpless, he would deserve the plight he is suffering (29:12–16, 23–25; 31:16–23; 22:6–13). It turns out that, although Eliphaz and Job "disagree as to how charitable the latter was, they are nevertheless united in the belief that the generous man ought to be protected by God and the man who abuses the poor ought to suffer."[19]

As for the Psalms, we are told that good treatment of the needy will earn protection and prosperity from God (Ps 41:1–3). It is clearly stated that righteousness is demonstrated through ethical works in favor of the needy. As in the Prophets, the warning of God's judgement against the wicked goes hand in hand with the promise of blessing to the one who cares for the poor. The book of Proverbs endorses the same trend and goes further in asserting that charity provided to the poor is in fact given at God himself and sometimes as a loan (11:25; 14:21, 31; 19:17; 22:9; 28:27). Conversely, injustice committed against the poor is directed to God and will bring divine judgement (14:31; 17:5; 28:27).[20]

1.1.2 The Septuagint

The LXX translates צְדָקָה by δικαιοσύνη to mean moral uprightness (Gen 18:19; Isa 5:7; Isa 9:4; 32:1; Jer 4:2; 23:5; 33:5; Amos 5:24; Mic 6:8; Prov 21:21). Proverb 21:3 uses δίκαια, which is synonymous with δικαιοσύνη. However, in the book of Daniel we find an important linguistic and theological development in this area. For Daniel 4:24 (MT), צִדְקָה is rendered

---

16. Dunn, *Beginning from Jerusalem*, 936.
17. Garrison, *Redemptive Almsgiving*, 48.
18. It is true that the theological viewpoint of the author of the book of Job represents a minority in Judaism.
19. Garrison, *Redemptive Almsgiving*, 49.
20. Ibid., 50.

by ἐλεημοσύνη in 4:27 LXX, and not by δικαιοσύνη as we would expect.[21] This tendency finds expression more significantly in the Greek translation of Ben Sira, where ἐλεημοσύνη means almsgiving (3:14, 30; 7:10; 12:3; 40:17 [cf. Ps 112:1–9], 24).[22] It is important to note that in Greek, this word is not restricted to almsgiving, but encompasses any good works of kindness or mercy. Ben Sira accords remarkably more value to the care of the poor than to ritual sacrifices. Whereas the offerings of those who mistreat the poor are worthless (34:18–22), almsgiving remains a sacrifice of praise (35:2). Moreover, Ben Sira expresses the view that almsgiving effects redemption from sin and provides protection from any existential harms (3:3, 4, 14, 15, 30, 31). Kyoung-Jin Kim thinks that the identification of almsgiving with righteousness itself resulted from the ardent enthusiasm of the Israelites to keep the regulations regarding care for the destitute.[23] But it is difficult to imagine that religious zeal alone can explain this change. It is more reasonable to situate this evolution in the vast context of historical, social, and political changes that occurred in Israel, especially from the Babylonian exile onward. The identification of righteousness and almsgiving was accompanied by the belief in the redemptive power of the latter. Granted, in the Second Temple period, the language to speak about sin shifted from the metaphor of a burden borne by the transgressor to the imagery of a debt which must be paid off.[24] In this setting of multifaceted evolution, charity came to be seen as an alternative to obtain salvation from sin, its consequences, and other disasters as well. This function of almsgiving presupposes the belief that giving to the poor stores up credits in one's

---

21. Ibid., 53. It is interesting to realize that in the LXX the same word ἐλεημοσύνη translates the Hebrew חֶסֶד (Prov 16:6 [15.27a in the LXX]; 20.28) in the sense of mercy or kindness. We learn that חֶסֶד preserves the king and sustains his throne. Furthermore, חֶסֶד וֶאֱמֶת (mercy and truth) effect atonement. Garrison concludes, not without reason, that this overlapping of terms "may well point to the evolution of the belief that almsgiving is both an act of kindness and mercy, and that it is a righteousness that redeems from sin and death, a righteousness more acceptable to the Lord than sacrifice. Sirach and Tobit provide considerable evidence of this stage of the doctrine" (ibid).

22. Ibid., 54–55. The references are found in Beentjes, *Book of Ben Sira in Hebrew*, 23, 24, 30, 39, 70.

23. Kim, *Stewardship and Almsgiving*, 280.

24. Anderson, *Sin*, 13, 15–39; Gregory, *Like an Everlasting Signet Ring*, 235. The same termnology is taken up in early Christianity as witnessed by Matt 6:12.

account which can be used later if one is in trouble (Sir 29:8–13).[25] I recall that atonement of sin was initially made possible on the basis of sacrificial rituals, which were construed as a divine means to restore relationships. However, even before the exile, prophets like Isaiah, Jeremiah, Amos, and Micah had claimed that sacrifice offering had to go hand in hand with "repentance, that is, 'return' to God."[26] In the absence of the temple for sacrifices, from the exilic period onward, new alternatives were provided, one of which was almsgiving.[27]

The book of Tobit is another clear example where almsgiving (ἐλεημοσύνη) has both philanthropic and theological dimensions. Charity remains the central theme of this book.[28] Its first-person narrator is introduced as a man who accomplishes different kinds of charitable deeds such as providing food for the hungry, clothing the naked, exercising hospitality, and burying the dead (1:3, 16–17; 4:16). The high value conferred to almsgiving is clearly reflected in the conviction that it is much better than any other religious practices such as prayer and fasting (12:8–9), and above all effects redemption from sin and death (4:7–11).

1.1.3 Early Judaism

At Qumran the pooling of personal property permitted the community to address the needs of its members equally.[29] The strong awareness of the

---

25. Gregory, *Like an Everlasting Signet Ring*, 234.
26. Nickelsburg, *Ancient Judaism*, 65.
27. Ibid., 69. Other means of redemption are advocated in the books dating from the exilic and post-exilic times. It was believed that God will send his Spirit to effect spiritual renewal (Ezek 36:25–27), and that the suffering of Israel and that of the Servant of the Lord would enact expiation (Second Isaiah). The motif of suffering as discipline or chastisement is developed in 2 Maccabees and the *Psalms of Solomon*. In the same context the death of martyrs was understood as a way of expiation (2 and 4 Maccabees). In other works, prayers of confession have propitiatory virtues (Ps 51; Esd 9; Neh 1; 9; Bar 1:15–3:8; Dan 9; Prayers of Azariah and Manasseh). Atonement and cleansing were also envisioned in the future as attested for instance in 1 *En.* 10:20, 22 (*1 Enoch* [The Hermeneia Translation], edited by G. W. E. Nickelsburg and J. C. VanderKam, 30), and in 1QS 4:20–22 (Charlesworth, *Dead Sea Scrolls*, 9).
28. Weinfeld, *Social Justice*, 225; Longenecker, *Remember the Poor*, 110.
29. Kim, *Stewardship and Almsgiving*, 235, n. 61. The existence of private property is suggested by the Damascus Document known also as the Zadokite Work (CD 9.10–16; 14.12–13; Charlesworth, *Dead Sea Scrolls*, 43, 57), but is absent from the Manual of Discipline also called the Community Rule (1QS). However, both documents agree on the existence of a common fund "out of which the poor, the orphans, the homeless and widows

centrality of charity in Judaism is reflected in the sect's emphasis on good works.[30] The members of the community had the obligation to exercise hospitality towards travelers, redeem captives, provide for brides, escort and bury the dead, love one's neighbor, etc.[31]

In Philo generosity is presented as the most laudable of the attractions of the Mosaic law.

> Is it not then fit to love these laws which are full of such abundant humanity? by which the rich men are taught to share the blessings which they have with and to communicate them to others: and the poor are comforted, not being for ever compelled to frequent the houses of the indigent to supply the deficiencies by which they themselves are oppressed.[32]

Philo enumerates the virtues which Jewish Scripture instills into people. The last moral attribute on the list which he considers the crown of those virtues is "the love of mankind, goodwill, equality beyond all power of description, and fellowship."[33] Philo finds that this moral principal is exemplified in a community whose description echoes that of the Qumran community.[34] Philo advises the wealthy to use their possessions to care for the destitute since the beauty of one's wealth lies in its enabling the owner to assist those who are in need: "Have you great abundance? Share it with others; for the beauty of riches is not in the purse, but in the power it gives one to succor those who are in need."[35]

The rabbinic literature provides us with an extensive development of the value and practices of almsgiving. However, it must be noted that rabbinic traditions cannot automatically be used as a background to the New Testament because they are hard to date, and in many cases reflect a later

---

were provided for." The discrepancies between both documents probably indicate that although they belong to the same circles, they may have sprung from different settlements or periods in the history of the sect (Ferguson, *Backgrounds of Early Christianity*, 467–468).

30. Nickle, *Collection*, 98–99.
31. Weinfeld, *Social Justice*, 19.
32. Philo, *Spec.* 2.107 (Colson, LCL).
33. Philo, *Prob.* 84 (Colson, LCL).
34. Philo, *Prob.* 84.85–87.
35. Philo, *Ios.* 144 (Colson, LCL).

context³⁶. Admittedly, the Mishnah contains "much material from the first century and earlier," but their assessment is not an easy task. For this reason, rightly notes Everett Ferguson, "the use of this literature for the backgrounds of early Christianity is problematic."³⁷ This explains why I have not investigated rabbinic sources.

1.2 Charity in the Greco-Roman Context

From the outset it must be noted that classical Greek has no term to indicate "'alms' or 'a gift to the poor'."³⁸ The use of the term ἐλεημοσύνη to mean almsgiving originated from the literature of Hellenistic Judaism and was later on adopted by pagan writers.³⁹ Roman Garrison thinks that this absence of terminology betrays "a certain disinterest in the plight of the impoverished."⁴⁰ Pheme Perkins writes that "poverty was despised" in Greco-Roman society as a whole and that public care for the needy was prompted only by "the peculiar political pressures of the city of Rome."⁴¹ It is commonly agreed that except for Judaism concern for the poor was of marginal interest "in the religious, moral and legal structures of ancient society"⁴² until the rise of Christianity.

Greco-Roman society had different practices which involved important expenditures for the benefit of the public but which cannot be reasonably called charity or care for the poor. In this society, liberality (ἐλευθεριότης) was one of the virtues characteristic of the good man.⁴³ Some philosophers castigated the lust for wealth, but welcomed its enjoyment with moderation.⁴⁴ The emergence of cynic philosophers brought a change in the per-

---

36. Safrai and Tomson, "Paul's 'Collection'," 132, 160–161.
37. Ferguson, *Backgrounds of Early Christianity*, 442.
38. Garrison, *Redemptive Almsgiving*, 38.
39. Ibid., 39.
40. Ibid.
41. Perkins, "Taxes," 186.
42. Longenecker, *Remember the Poor*, 60.
43. Ibid., 67.
44. Garrison, *Redemptive Almsgiving*, 39–40.

ception of and attitude towards wealth. They advocated renunciation of material wealth and rejected honor in order to lead an independent life.[45]

As noted previously, public benefaction known as "*euergetism*" was widespread in Greco-Roman society and consisted in doing good to the public.[46] By the time of the New Testament, this public generosity of wealthy people had become the main source of food supply in the Roman Empire. But as observed earlier, benefactors were much driven by the desire for public praise. Moreover, no specific acts of generosity were directed to the poor of society as a vulnerable group.[47] On the contrary, this type of benevolence benefitted the whole community. Furthermore, non-citizens were not concerned by this type of generosity.[48] It is true that in some cases benefactors would "extend some generosity to poor relations, clients, and favorite slaves."[49] It is even probable that some so-called public benefactors attempted to hoard grain and sell "it later at a higher price than usual."[50] Others exported grain abroad and blocked its importation from other areas in order to inflate its price.[51]

The public honor due to the benefactor could "take many forms, such as sacrifices, memorials, grants of land, public burials, seats, etc."[52] It could also be expressed through a crown to be displayed at a public function, a statue to be presented ostentatiously "and crowned periodically," or an inscription praising the benefactor's generosity, excellence and honors

---

45. Ferguson, *Backgrounds of Early Christianity*, 348, 349: Cynic philosophy was founded by Diogenes of Sinope (c.400–c.325 BCE) whose shamelessness even in public, as a way of getting full independence, was unusual. Cynicism failed to be a real school of thought but gained followers, and proved to be "a way of life more than a doctrine or school of thought." It is remembered for its shocking breaking of social norms such as "using violence and abusive language, wearing filthy garments, performing acts of nature (defecation, sex) in public, and feigning madness." However, there was another trend of Cynicism that was very positive to society and its norms. This contributed enormously to popular philosophy through the leading of a wandering life in public places especially under the early empire.

46. See the discussion on different interpretive frameworks of Paul's collection on previous pages of this study. See also Longenecker, *Remember the Poor*, 71.

47. Perkins, "Taxes," 186.

48. Dunn, *Beginning from Jerusalem*, 936.

49. Perkins, "Taxes," 186.

50. Ibid.

51. Kim, *Stewardship and Almsgiving*, 269–270.

52. Joubert, *Paul as Benefactor*, 38.

conferred to him/her.[53] Benefactors themselves could inscribe their achievements for public information. In both cases these inscriptions not only served to remind the society of the generosity of benefactors, but also to motivate the latter to continue their benevolence once they are assured that they would be publicly lauded for it.[54]

The crucial role of benefactors can be well grasped if one realizes that in the Greco-Roman society of the first century CE food shortage was a constant problem. Admittedly, there were not often famines, but "crop failure, war and epidemics" occurred frequently and threatened many lives.[55] On the whole, there existed from time to time distribution of food by the government and cities, but this was neither free nor at low prices.[56] Although Greco-Roman public benefaction was self-centered in nature and insufficient in scope, one should note that the material support from rich citizens "was not in the least insignificant to the poor, however small it might have been."[57] Moreover, there must have been some isolated cases in which individual rich people bestowed help out of humanitarian concern, although they must be seen as an exception. Tacitus (55–120 CE) reports that "in Fidena (near Rome) in A.D. 27, the wealthy opened their homes to help victims of the collapsed amphitheater (Annals 4.63)."[58]

Patronage was another form of generosity common in ancient societies. This system provided "people of lesser socio-economic status" with the possibility to become "clients to patrons of higher socio-economic status."[59] As noted previously, patronage found expression in relations between "landlords and tenants," "patricians and their freedman," "members of *collegia*," "Rome and occupied territories," and "officially appointed patrons and Roman communities."[60] It is the clients who would usually initiate such a relationship because they sought protection and help from the patrons.[61]

---

53. Hendrix, "Benefaction/Patron Networks," 42.
54. Marshall, *Jesus, Patrons, and Benefactors*, 4.
55. Kim, *Stewardship and Almsgiving*, 281.
56. Ibid., 257.
57. Ibid., 276.
58. Schmidt, *How Christianity Changed*, 127.
59. Longenecker, *Remember the Poor*, 73.
60. Joubert, *Paul as Benefactor*, 36.
61. Marshall, *Jesus, Patrons, and Benefactors*, 5.

Thus, it is correct to say that the voluntary character of patronage was purely theoretical. As such, patronage was not the right type of benevolence needed to relieve the poor. Worse, the clients benefitting from patronage "did not include those in lower economic levels"[62] because they had nothing to offer in return to their patrons.[63]

The imbalance in the distribution of wealth and power permitted the rich to prosper and the poor to become more and more vulnerable. Apart from the slaves, who could at least get food and shelter from their masters, and the unskilled workers, who could from time to time obtain a job to earn their living, the term πτωχός applied more specifically to the category of people who could not work at all and lived by begging (i.e. "the blind, the crippled, the lame, the lepers, the deaf, and the mentally handicapped" [Luke 4:18; 7:22; 14:13, 21]).[64] Nonetheless, it would be misleading to argue that Greco-Roman society was devoid of charitable practices. There must have been some "low-level forms of care" for the destitute in that world.[65] For instance, the existence of beggars implies that they could expect some help from passers-by.

Some Stoics advocated and practiced almsgiving. For instance, Musonius Rufus (30-101 CE),[66] Roman Cynic-Stoic, is remembered for his insistence that one should spend one's wealth on charity (*caritas*). Although he taught

---

62. Longenecker's economy scale classifies the urban population of the Roman Empire in the New Testament times into seven categories, from ES_1 (the wealthiest) through to ES_7 (the most destitute), as follows: ES_1-ES_3 (3%), ES_4 (15%), ES_5 (27%), ES_6 (30%), ES_7 (25%): Longenecker, *Remember the Poor*, 46.

63. Ibid., 73.

64. Kim, *Stewardship and Almsgiving*, 256. However, Longenecker (*Remember the Poor*, 38) remarks that the terminology used by ancient authors to depict the phenomenon of poverty is fluid: ". . . Some ancient authors show a preference for using only one term to connote a spectrum of poverties, rather than dissecting poverty into various terminological compartments. Whereas the authors collected in the New Testament make far greater use of πτωχός than πένης, Josephus and Philo much prefer πένης and its cognates to πτωχός."

65. Longenecker, *Remember the Poor*, 66, 74. It seems that some characters went to the extreme in begging: "This is evident in the Elder Seneca's *Controversiae* (10.4), which records how one loathsome man made his living by collecting exposed children who had been left for dead along the roadside and then mutilating their bodies (i.e. slicing off their tongues, chopping off their limbs, etc.) in order to augment the pity of passers-by and to increase his income through alms. Such a thing would not have happened in a world devoid of charitable initiatives and concern for the needy."

66. Ferguson, *Backgrounds of Early Christianity*, 365.

and practiced austerity, he displayed a great concern for human beings.[67] He himself would give alms because free giving is the imitation of "God's own generosity," but also "an obligation and privilege."[68]

Conclusion

I can conclude that in Judaism a lot of attention is given to care for the poor in general, and through almsgiving especially. This ethics is grounded in the fact that Israel received the same treatment from God in their exodus experience. Reward is promised to the righteous person, the one who provides for the needy; whereas God's judgement awaits whoever mistreats the poor. The idea that ethical uprightness not only meets the needs of the poor but can protect the alms giver, emerged with the Writings and found extensive expression in the Apocrypha. Greco-Roman society practiced different forms of benefaction prompted not by love for the needy, but by the search for social praise by benefactors. Nonetheless, some low-level forms of care for the poor existed in this culture.

It turns out that while organizing his collection, Paul was driven not by the motives of Greco-Roman patronage/benefaction, but by the conviction that the God of Israel commands his people to care for the poor. Although Paul's undertaking has no clear antecedent in Jewish history, the apostle must have merged several Jewish conceptions and applied them in a creative organizational manner.[69] Furthermore, Paul believed and proclaimed that Christ, who himself had demonstrated much concern for the needy, gave the same instructions to his followers. In the following chapter I will deal with the Corinthian correspondence, which is most likely the earliest literary source in which Paul conceptualized his collection for the poor Christians in Jerusalem.

---

67. Garrison, *Redemptive Almsgiving*, 45.
68. Ibid.
69. Safrai and Tomson, "Paul's 'Collection'," 217.

CHAPTER 2

Paul's Corinthian Correspondence

After he left Corinth, Paul kept in touch with the young community that he had founded there.[1] He would write to and receive letters from the people of Corinth regarding the situation on the ground (1 Cor 1:11, 5:9; 16:15–18). And if necessary, he used to send his representatives to continue the work of the Lord or settle some difficulties between him and his converts (1 Cor 4:17; 7:1; 16:10–12; 2 Cor 8:16–24; 7:13–15). The Corinthian correspondence reveals the difficulty of identifying the number and extent of the letters Paul wrote to the church in this city. We have two canonical letters and each of them alludes to a previous one that is not easy to identify, as we will see. In this chapter, I will first try to reconstruct the Corinthian correspondence as far as the two canonical letters allow us. Then, much attention will be given to 2 Corinthians from which the passage focused on in this study is taken.

2.1 1 Corinthians 5:9–11

The letter referred to in 1 Corinthians 5:9–11 is seen by many scholars as pre-canonical. They consider that it has not been preserved in the extant Pauline corpus.[2] At Ephesus, during his third missionary journey, Paul learned about the disorder which prevailed in the Corinthian church and reacted through that letter, which perhaps was concerned only with disciplinary matters in the community. The apostle urged the church to

---

1. Senft, *La première épitre*, 16. Paul's first visit to Corinth, during which he founded a church there, is to be dated from 49 to 51 or less probably from 50 to 52.
2. *La Bible T. O. B. (N.T.)*, 507–508.

take disciplinary measures against the members who were leading a dissolute life, especially in sexual immorality. Shortly after the redaction of the above-mentioned letter, and still in Ephesus, the apostle learned especially from Apollos, Chloe's people (1 Cor 1:11) and Stephanas with his companions about the alarming news (16:17–18). This news was about divisions (1:10–30; 3:1–23), scandals of sexual immorality and lawsuits among Christians (chapters 5 and 6), disorder in worship (chapters 11, 12, 14). Moreover, Paul received a letter from the Corinthians raising different issues and decided to respond to the whole situation by writing our canonical 1 Corinthians. The Corinthians wanted the apostle to clarify among other things the issues regarding marriage (chapter 7), food sacrificed to idols (chapters 8–10), the resurrection of the dead (chapter 15), and the collection for the poor in the Jerusalem church (chapter 16).[3] Our canonical 1 Corinthians was written between 52 and 57; many scholars support the summer of the year 54[4]. Maurice Carrez thinks that 1 and 2 Corinthians were written in 55 and 56 respectively.[5] There is a consensus among schol-

---

3. Safrai and Tomson ("Paul's 'Collection'," 137–138) wonder why would Paul so elaborately write to the Corinthians about the collection in 2 Cor 8–9 while he had given them a year before clear instructions in 1 Cor 16:1–4. They esteem that this was due to the fact that rival preachers had compromised his mission at Corinth. These were Judaeo-Christian missionaries whose opposition Paul came up against elsewhere, in Galatia for instance.

4. Brown, Fitzmyer and Murphy, *New Jerome Biblical Commentary*, 799.

5. Carrez, *La deuxième épitre*, 30. The question of the reliability of Acts as a historical source for the knowledge of the history of early Christianity in general and Paul's career in particular has preoccupied scholars. While some find the author of Acts was Paul's companion (Dunn, *Beginning from Jerusalem*, 66), others esteem that he was a Pauline disciple belonging to the third generation (D. Marguerat, *Les Actes des apôtres*, 19–20). It is observed that Luke presents a selective history and an idealized picture of the early church. Marguerat (*Les Actes des apôtres: 1–12*, 19) is one of those who insist on the sharp difference between the portrayal of Paul and the presentation of his theology in Acts and the information offered by his epistles. But Dunn (*Beginning from Jerusalem*, 77–81, 86–87) identifies impressive correlations between Acts and Paul's letters concerning his movements. Another striking point emphasized by Dunn is that unlike the gospels, an important number of details are correlated with non-biblical sources. He concludes that the inadequacies of Luke's narrative cannot discount the value of Acts as a historical source of information. In this respect, Paul's first visit in Corinth under Gallio (Acts 18:2) is one of those historical details corroborated by non-biblical information. An inscription discovered at Delphi referring to Gallio's term as proconsul in Corinth offers a reliable landmark in Paul's biography (D. Marguerat, *Les Actes des apôtres: 13-28*, 170–171). Concerning the relationship between Paul's letters and Acts, one of the most difficult questions to solve is the location of the Pastorals in the apostle's career. Some trace them back to Paul's lifespan. They posit Paul's relaxation after his imprisonment in Rome recounted in Acts 28, and a second

ars over the Pauline authorship of both letters. The difference in tone between the two letters can be explained by the rising of "judaizing zealotry in Judaea and in the Judaean churches" and its impact on Gentile Christian communities as attested in Galatia and Corinth.[6] But 2 Corinthians poses serious problems of literary unity and scholars are divided in this regard. I will deal with this issue in another section of this chapter.

2.2 2 Corinthians 2:1, 5; 7:12 ("The Letter of Tears")[7]

In 1830 Friedrich Bleek developed two theories about Paul's visits and letters to Corinth.[8] On the premises of Paul's announcements in 2 Corinthians 12:14 and 13:1, Bleek understood that the apostle visited the Corinthians twice before he wrote 1 and 2 Corinthians. Furthermore, he suggested the idea of an "intermediate letter" between 1 and 2 Corinthians. He also argued that this letter, thought to be a response to the incident of 2 Corinthians 2:3–4; 7:12, is lost today. Bleek esteemed that a member of the Corinthian church, different from the evildoer of 2 Corinthians 2:5; 7:12, instigated by Jewish opponents, insulted Paul in public.[9] This public confrontation damaged the apostle's authority.[10] However, the notion of an intermediate visit and a related letter (the tearful letter) is rejected by Niels

---

imprisonment inferred from 1 Clem. 5.7, but not mentioned in Acts. This hypothesis leaves some room for the writing of these letters (Dibelius and Conzelmann, *Pastoral Epistles*, 3; Towner, *Letters to Timothy and Titus*, 10–26). The majority of exegetes ascribe their writing to a later Paulinist.

6. Safrai and Tomson, "Paul's 'Collection'," 161.

7. This letter is also called the "severe letter", or "sorrowful/painful letter" (Harris, *Second Epistle*, 3).

8. Betz, *2 Corinthians 8 and 9*, 11; Bleek, "Erörterungen in Beziehung," 614–632.

9. The evildoer of 1 Cor 5:9 was involved in fornication (πορνεία) which took the form of incest. Tertullian was the first to make this distinction between the two persons: Tertullian, *La pudicité (De Pudicitia)* 13–14 (SC 394).

10. Betz (*2 Corinthians 8 and 9*, 97) affirms confidently that the frequent reference to the issue of πλεονεξία (greed, avarice) in the current 2 Cor and Paul's repeated refutations suggest that an individual in Corinth accused the apostle of this offence. In Betz's view, this person must have accused Paul of having organized the collection for Jerusalem as a disguised means of securing funds for his own interest. However, Carrez (*La deuxième épître*, 33) thinks that the offender cannot have been a member of the Corinthian church, but was somebody from outside. As for the person offended, he thinks that it was probably Paul's envoy in Corinth. But a close look at Paul's argumentation in 2 Cor leads to the conclusion

Hyldahl.[11] He identifies 1 Corinthians with the tearful letter which was written to prevent the trouble that could be caused by the fact that the visit planned by Paul did not materialize (2 Cor 1:23—2:2). In my view, the content and tone of 1 Corinthians can hardly show that this letter was written "out of much affliction and anguish of heart" (2 Cor 2:4). And if one opts for Hyldahl's theory, one has to explain what situation Paul alludes to in 2 Corinthians 2:1 when he maintains that he determined within himself that he would not come to the Corinthians in sorrow.

The idea of an intermediate visit and an intermediate letter is however plausible. It seems that despite the canonical 1 Corinthians delivered by Timothy and the latter's efforts to settle the problems which the Corinthian congregation was confronted with (1 Cor 4:17; 16:10–12), the situation did not improve much. Paul thus decided to go there personally from Ephesus. Unfortunately, his visit was aborted following the harsh opposition which he met with and in which he was publicly offended (2 Cor 2:1, 5; 7:12). After he returned to Ephesus, Paul wrote the so-called "Letter of Tears" (2 Cor 2:2–3).[12] He sent Titus to Corinth carrying the letter. Although Paul does not spell out what happened exactly, it is clear that it affected him so much that he felt compelled to change his plan to stop by there on his way back from Macedonia before he continued to Judea (2 Cor 1:15–16). He explains that he changed his previous plan for the benefit of the Corinthians (2 Cor 1:23—2:1).

All in all, we may assume that the letters alluded to in 1 and 2 Corinthians have not been preserved because they were not copied by different Christian communities as was the case for other New Testament writings. One reason may be that the churches probably found them dealing with issues bound to a specific context without any appeal for a larger audience. The case of a Corinthian who offended Paul and the fact that the apostle reacted to it by means of his "Letter of Tears" may fit in this explanation. Furthermore, this sorrowful letter evidenced an "unedifying chapter in the history of the Corinthian church that reflected poorly on that church and was an

---

that the apostle was offended by a Corinthian Christian. Otherwise, it is difficult to imagine how Paul could expect this church to discipline a person from outside.

11. Hyldahl, "Die Frage," 289–306, quoted by Betz, *2 Corinthians 8 and 9*, 32–33.
12. Betz, *2 Corinthians 8 and 9*, 12, 11.

embarrassment to its spiritual father."[13] One may presume that there was every good reason not to preserve it. However, the disappearance of the letter relating to disciplinary matters in the church (cf. 1 Cor 5:9) cannot fit in with this line of thought. I leave this question open.

Within the scope of this research, it is not possible to address all the issues raised in the previous section. In the following pages I will restrict myself to the literary unity of 2 Corinthians in general, and have a close look at chapters 8 and 9 on which this study is based. In fact, the integrity of 2 Corinthians has preoccupied scholars and has not received a satisfactory explanation. As Reimund Bieringer et al. note, the past two and a half decades have witnessed "a growing interest" in 2 Corinthians but the latter "continues to be in the shadow" of 1 Corinthians.[14]

2.3 Partition Theories

The history of partition theories in the interpretation of 2 Corinthians began with Johann S. Semler who, in 1776, suggested that the document is composed of two distinct letters.[15] According to him, the first letter, delivered by Titus, was sent to the Christians in Achaia and comprised 2 Corinthians 1–8; Romans 16; 2 Corinthians 9, and 13:11–13. The second letter was written later as a response to the distressing news Paul had heard. It included 2 Corinthians 10:1–13:10. However, Betz thinks that this was not Semler's own intuition, but that he owed his inspiration to the analysis made by his former professor, Siegmund J. Baumgarten. The history of partition theories after Semler can be divided into four stages:
- From Johann S. Semler to Adolf von Hausrath;
- From Hausrath and George A. Kennedy to Hans Windisch;
- From Windisch to Walter Schmithals;
- In Dieter Georgi's and Günther Bornkamm's works.[16]

---

13. Harris, *Second Epistle*, 8.
14. Bieringer et al., *Theologizing*, 1.
15. Betz, *2 Corinthians 8 and 9*, 3.
16. Ibid., 10.

Hausrath[17] took 2 Corinthians 10–13 as his starting point to deal with the question of the integrity of 2 Corinthians. Like his predecessors, he ascribed the differences between its sections to "the change of psychological mood."[18] Hausrath concluded that 2 Corinthians 10–13 was composed by Paul from Ephesus, shortly after 1 Corinthians, and preceded 2 Corinthians 1 to 9. At around the same time as Hausrath, Kennedy developed his own partition theory.[19] He identified 2 Corinthians 10–13 with the intermediate letter but admitted that these chapters also contain the earliest material in the canonical epistle. Kennedy argued that the intermediate letter, which he terms 2 Corinthians, was written from Ephesus whereas chapters 1–9, which are part of what he calls 3 Corinthians, were composed from Macedonia after the successful mission of Titus in Corinth. Kennedy maintained that the earlier parts of the intermediate letter have not been preserved.

Later developments of the study of 2 Corinthians raised criticisms against Hausrath's hypothesis. It was shown that he failed to realize that there are important disparities within chapters 1–9 and that he overestimated the contrast between 2 Corinthians 1–9 and 10–13 with regard to Paul's mood.[20] One of the main issues raised was the problem of chapters 8 and 9. Suffice it to note here that Johannes Weiss assigned these two chapters to two separate letters.[21] At his death, his ambition to write a commentary on 2 Corinthians was taken up by his former student Windisch.[22] The latter concluded that 2 Corinthians 10–13 belonged to an individual letter which cannot be equated with the tearful or intermediate letter. On the contrary, he argued that these chapters were a fragment of a later letter that Paul composed after Titus had left for Corinth. This letter was a response to new criticisms spread by the apostle's opponents over the integrity of his collection.[23] Moreover, Windisch doubted the literary unity

---

17. Hausrath, *Der Vier-Capitel-Brief*.
18. Betz, *2 Corinthians 8 and 9*, 12.
19. Kennedy, *Second and Third Epistles*; quoted by Betz, *2 Corinthians 8 and 9*, 13.
20. Betz, *2 Corinthians 8 and 9*, 14.
21. Weiss, *Der erste Korintherbrief*; quoted by Betz, *2 Corinthians 8 and 9*, 16.
22. Windisch, *Der zweite Korintherbrief*; quoted by Betz, *2 Corinthians 8 and 9*, 16.
23. Betz, *2 Corinthians 8 and 9*, 17–18. But Betz observes that this new crisis is hypothetical because almost nothing in the sources documents it.

of chapters 1–7 and supported the theory that takes chapters 8 and 9 as portions of separate letters which "should not be integrated into any of the other letters or fragments of letters."[24] Rather, they have to be treated as two literary units which, however, deal with the same theme of the collection: chapter 8 was sent to Corinth while chapter 9 was thought to be "a kind of accompanying letter" addressed to the Achaean congregations. For Windisch, 2 Corinthians 9:1 introduces a new independent subject, "not merely a new section of the previous letter."[25] Rudolf Bultmann's incomplete lecture notes, published in 1976 by Erich Dinkler, reflect the former's agreement with Hausrath's theory, though in revised version.[26] Bultmann suggested that 2 Corinthians 1:1–2:13; 7:5–16 and 8 belong to what he terms the last letter. While he saw 6:14–7:1 as non-Pauline, he assigned 2:14–6:13; 7:2–4; 10–13 and 9 to the intermediate letter.

Schmithals, Bultmann's student, was motivated by his master's lectures on the Corinthian correspondence. His first focus was on the question of Paul's opponents. He suggested that Paul was confronted with Gnostic opponents in both of his canonical letters.[27] As for the formal composition of 2 Corinthians, Schmithals placed 2 Corinthians 6:14–7:1 before 1 Corinthians 9:24 but agreed with Weiss, Windisch and Bultmann in general.[28] Concerning chapters 8 and 9, he argued that the latter was composed before chapter 8. Moreover, he inserted chapter 8 in the "letter of joy" (1:1–2:13+7:5–16+8) as a conclusion. Except for chapter 8 and 9 Schmithals maintained his position; he presented new arrangements of the sections of the canonical 2 Corinthians in later editions of his work.[29]

At the same time as Schmithals, Georgi proposed his own partition theory. Unlike Schmithals who thought that Paul's opponents are the same in both canonical letters, Georgi observed that they belonged to two different theological tendencies.[30] In his treatment of Paul's collection Georgi

---

24. Ibid., 18.
25. Ibid.
26. Bultmann, *Der zweite Brief*, quoted by Betz, *2 Corinthians 8 and 9*, 19.
27. Betz, *2 Corinthians 8 and 9*, 19.
28. Schmithals, *Die Gnosis in Korinth*; quoted by Betz, *2 Corinthians 8 and 9*, 19–20.
29. Becker, *Letter Hermeneutics,*" 7–9. Becker notes that Schmithals happened to divide the Corinthian correspondence into thirteen letters.
30. Georgi, *Die Gegner des Paulus*; quoted by Betz, *2 Corinthians 8 and 9*, 20.

investigated the literary question raised by 2 Corinthians 8 and 9.[31] He ascribed these chapters to two individual letters, chapter 8 being a "letter of recommendation for Titus and his companions," whereas chapter 9 was considered a "circular letter" to the Achaean churches.

The most prominent partition theory in the twentieth century was advanced by Bornkamm.[32] He took up the original version of Hausrath's theory. Bornkamm esteemed that 2 Corinthians 10–13 derived from the intermediate letter (letter of tears) which comprised 2:14–6:13+7:2–4. In his view, 6:14–7:1 has to be excluded from this letter because it is seen as Paul's earlier "first apology" written after 1 Corinthians interpolated here. Thus his partition theory identified the following fragments in 2 Corinthians: 2:14–6:13+7:2–4+6:14–7:1; 10–13+1:1–2:13+7:5–16 (the "letter of reconciliation"). As for chapters 8 and 9, Bornkamm agreed with some of his predecessors that these chapters belonged to two separate epistles. He assumed that chapter 8 is "a letter of recommendation for Titus and his companions" from which the names of the latter were omitted. Bornkamm did not take a strong stance on whether it was an individual letter or the conclusion of the letter of reconciliation. Concerning chapter 9, he asserted that it was an independent letter, "the last piece of Paul's Corinthian correspondence," composed "later than chapter 8" and delivered to the Achaean congregation.[33] Bornkamm contended that the final verses 13:11–13 cannot however be given a decisive location in one of the above-mentioned letters he had identified. In his view, they should preferably be seen as the conclusion of the letter of reconciliation, but can also be thought to be the end of the letter of tears (10–13).

It is possible that the admiration of many scholars for Bornkamm's hypothesis lies partly in the fact that he "paid special attention to the reconstruction of Paul's dealings with the Corinthians and endeavoured to trace the stages by which the original five letters were combined to form the canonical 2 Corinthians."[34] Recently, Eve-Marie Becker noted that al-

---

31. Georgi, *Die Geschichte der Kollecte*; quoted by Betz, *2 Corinthians 8 and 9*, 21.
32. Betz, *2 Corinthians 8 and 9*, 21–22; quoting Bornkamm, *Geschichte und Glaube*, 162–194.
33. Betz, *2 Corinthians 8 and 9*, 22.
34. Harris, *Second Epistle*, 9, 10.

though the interest in *Literarkritik* has declined, the question of literary unity is still raised.[35] In the case of the Pauline letters, it deals with interpolations and compilations of several letters. In Becker's view, "a deliberate editorial revision of the Pauline epistles" must have taken place by 90–100 CE.[36] However, for 2 Corinthians, Becker esteemed that the compilation of originally individual letters into one "came about less through a so-called 'editing' of the Pauline letters than by individual letters becoming attached to one another in the course of their being 'copied'."[37]

2.4 Marks of Discontinuity in 2 Corinthians 1–7

I will not spend much time on this section. It will suffice to note that both the language and the content of these chapters have given rise to the hypothesis that they are a compilation of excerpts from two originally separate letters.[38] Indeed, the passage from 2 Corinthians 2:13 to 2 Corinthians 2:14 is troubling. Paul shifts from the use of "I" to "we." The same phenomenon repeats itself between 7:4 and 7:5. It is suggested that 1:1–2:13 and 7:5–16 belonged to one letter, whereas 2:14–7:4 constituted another, which in the current 2 Corinthians establishes a link between 2:13 and 7:5. Murray J. Harris notes that there is no doubt about the literary unity of 2:14–7:4. Structural and thematic considerations are called upon to demonstrate this affirmation. He concludes that this passage should be read as "'the great digression' . . . which, as Paul's apology for the apostolic ministry, is the heart of chs. 1–7."[39] Another mark of incoherence has been

---

35. Becker, *Letter Hermeneutics*, 1. Becker indicates that as a method of biblical criticism, *Literarkritik* deals with "the delimitation, the structure, the inner unity or sources of a text and the so-called introductory questions of the author, place and date of the respective document." However, I must admit that I do not see in what way *Literarkritik* is different from literary criticism. As M. Oeming notes, literary criticism is one of the tools of the historical-critical method, which examines the text "according to its structure, its inner consistency and logical coherence in order to determine whether the text is a literary unit or a composite of different redactional layers." (Oeming, *Contemporary Biblical Hermeneutics*, 33–34).

36. Becker, *Letter Hermeneutics*, 2.

37. Ibid., 148. In her view, this process may have taken place around 70 to 90 and been completed by the end of the first century.

38. Ibid., 5.

39. Harris, *Second Epistle*, 11, 14.

found by scholars in 6:14—7:1, considered by some to be an interpolation reflecting a kind of "Christianized" Essene theology.[40] The majority of the most recent specialized studies on the passage "have defended not only its Pauline authorship, but also its integrity in the context."[41] It is possible that Paul uses and modifies existing materials in this part of his letter.[42]

2.5 The Unity of 2 Corinthians 8–9 in Recent Scholarship

Nickle agrees with the partition hypothesis that suggests that 2 Corinthians 8 and 9 were originally part of two separate letters "written within a short time of each other."[43] He notes that 9:1 seems to introduce a new subject with no logical continuation with chapter 8. He indicates that the idea of a long dictation pause between 8 and 9 may be advanced to account for these discrepancies, but it seems to him "more natural to regard them as two separate portions."[44] However, he admits that it is extremely difficult to determine in our current 2 Corinthians the other portions of letters to which these two chapters were related. Although Nickle recognizes that the identification of 2 Corinthians 10:1–13:10 "as the 'letter of tears' is not completely verifiable," he states that it "appears to be the most plausible solution."[45]

For his part, Betz also affirms that 2 Corinthians 8 and 9 belonged to two originally separate letters. He goes further and states that as they stand now, these two chapters should be interpreted in the framework of "Greco-Roman rhetoric and epistolography."[46] Betz assumes that the letter of chapter 8 was sent to the Corinthian church,[47] that of chapter 9 to the

---

40. Ibid., 15.
41. Harris, *Second Epistle*, 15.
42. Carrez, *La deuxième épitre*, 168–169: "Ce texte ne paraît pas avoir été dicté par Paul dans une première venue. Il présente par contre les caractéristiques d'un texte retravaillé, adapté, donc adopté."
43. Nickle *Collection*, 17.
44. Ibid., 17, n. 17.
45. Ibid., 17, n. 18.
46. Betz, *2 Corinthians 8 and 9*, 35, 131–140.
47. Ibid., 37.

Christians of Achaia.[48] In his view, chapter 8 displays the features of an administrative letter of the time, whereas chapter 9 reflects the characteristics of an advisory letter; and that its rhetoric is deliberative.[49] He argues that 2 Corinthians 8:23 can only make sense to the Corinthian congregation, whereas 9.2–5a is specifically related to Achaea.[50] Following Anton Halmel[51] against Karl F.A. Fritzsche[52] and Nils A. Dahl,[53] Betz argues that it is hardly possible to conceive of περὶ μὲν γὰρ (9:1)[54] as a transitional phrase between 2 Corinthians 8:16–24 (the recommendation of the delegates) and the new development on the collection in chapter 9.[55] However, not all the exponents of the partition theories agree with Betz about his view of both chapters. Joubert thinks that 2 Corinthians is a composite letter made up of two originally distinct letters (chapters 1–9 and 10–13), but agrees that there is neither manuscript nor patristic testimony to support this view. Therefore, Joubert suggests that our letter circulated only under its current form; "any redactional combination of originally separate letters must have taken place before the circulation of any one of them."[56] As noted earlier, a similar hypothesis is also defended by Becker. Her investigation into *Literarkritik* and communicative theory with regard to this letter leads her to conclude that the general practice of letter compilation was known in Antiquity. She adds that in the case of Paul's letters, this was done "when the letters were copied from wax or wooden tablets onto more extensive codices which were intended to serve the conservation of and transmission of the letters."[57] Having said that, she allows that 2 Corinthians is

---

48. Ibid., 87.
49. Ibid., 134, 139.
50. Ibid., 139.
51. Halmel, *Der zweite Korintherbrief*, 11ff. Helmel pointed out that the introductory phrase περὶ μὲν γὰρ is quite different from περὶ δὲ that Paul uses in 1 Cor 7:1; 8:1; 12:1; 16:1. He maintained that instead of connecting chapter 9 to 8, περὶ μὲν γὰρ marks the beginning of a new letter. Moreover, Helmel insisted that μέν in 9:1 points foreword to δέ in 9.3 (Betz, *2 Corinthians 8 and 9*, 26).
52. Fritzsche, *De nonnullis posterioris Pauli*, 19–20.
53. Dahl, *Studies in Paul*, 38–39.
54. Another argument invoked by partition theories exponents is the use of "we" in chapter 8 and "I" in chapter 9: Panikulam, "Koinonia in the New Testament," 45.
55. Betz, *2 Corinthians 8 and 9*, 26, 35.
56. Joubert, *Paul as Benefactor*, 134, n. 57.
57. Becker, *Letter Hermeneutics*, 70.

made up of four or five letters (1:1—7:4; 7:5—16; 8; 9; 10—13) that Paul wrote "one after the other at intervals, and very soon after their arrival in Corinth they were copied and thereby compiled, strung together."[58] As for chapters 8 and 9, Becker admits the existence of links between them at a semantic level and that there are some arguments to support their original unity. For instance, both chapters stand in inclusion by the term χάρις (8:1; 9:14—15). This view is also defended by Harris who correctly notes that this cannot be a coincidental presence of the term at the beginning and the end of this passage about the collection, the same phenomenon being observed in Paul's letters.[59] Yet Becker emphasizes that the "pragmatic function of the two chapters" remains unresolved,[60] whereas Betz observes that "thematic connections hardly demonstrate literary unity; they can just as easily be explained as links between successive letters."[61] Nonetheless, Reimund Bieringer has recently defended the literary unity of the canonical 2 Corinthians on the basis of semantic considerations. While he remains open to other views about this question, he esteems that the pervasiveness of the αγαπ-language confirms the hypothesis of the unity of this letter.[62]

The basic formal argument put forward by scholars in the nineteenth century, which Betz and others follow, is that the opening expression περὶ μὲν γὰρ has to be distinguished from περὶ δὲ often used by Paul to start new sections (1 Cor 7:1, 25; 8:1; 12:1; 16:1; 1 Thess 4:9; 5:1).[63] Besides, the presence of the particle μέν indicates decisively that γάρ (for) does not refer to anything preceding but to what follows. In the same vein, it is said that the particle δέ that would normally correlate with μέν is found in v. 3. Like Windisch, Betz concludes that in this instance περὶ μὲν γὰρ functions as the opening of a new letter.[64] However, a thorough discussion of the meaning and function of this expression in and outside the New Testament provided by Stanley K. Stowers challenges the reliability of Betz's theory.[65]

---

58. Ibid., 70.
59. Harris, *Second Epistle*, 559.
60. Becker, *Letter Hermeneutics*, 5.
61. Betz, *2 Corinthians 8 and 9*, 35.
62. Bieringer, "Love," 24.
63. Betz, *2 Corinthians 8 and 9*, 26, 90.
64. Ibid., 90; Windisch, *Der zweite Korintherbrief*, 268—269.
65. Stowers, "*Peri men gar*," 340—348.

Stowers points out that Halmel's detailed study of 2 Corinthians 9:1 "contains a flaw" because the author unfortunately did not investigate the broader use of περὶ μὲν γὰρ that includes extra-biblical sources. He adds that neither Halmel nor those following him have looked closely at Acts 28:22, the only other place in the New Testament where the expression is found.[66] Concerning this reference, Stowers notes that περὶ μὲν γὰρ "comes at the end of the episode where Paul meets with the Jewish leaders in Rome." Moreover, it occurs in the concluding statement of the Jewish leaders' response to the apostle's speech "and closely connects with what precedes."[67] Stowers' investigation on the use of περὶ μὲν γὰρ outside the New Testament drives him to conclude that very frequently it "serves to introduce a reason, warrant, or explanation for what was just said" as is the case in Acts 28:22 with regard to the Christian group.[68] In other words, after an introductory section, the author comes to his actual point. To believe Stowers, the second frequent use of περὶ μὲν γὰρ is found in instances where "the discourse which proceeds makes a general statement or claim"; the expression comes in to introduce a specific statement by mean of "an example, case, or subtopic."[69] For this use Stowers gives an example from a speech by Demosthenes and relates it to 2 Corinthians 9:1.[70] In *Against Spudias* Demosthenes makes a speech in the context of a dispute over a property. He introduces the case and explains to the jury how the matter ought to be addressed. In 41:6 he mentions the main point of the dispute (i.e. the contested house and mortgage: πρῶτον μὲν οὖν ὑμῖν μάρτυρας παρέξομαι τοὺς παραγενομένους, ὅτ᾽ ἠγγύα μοι Πολύευκτος τὴν θυγατέρ᾽ ἐπὶ τετταράκοντα μναῖς ἔπειθ᾽ ὡ῾ς ἔλαττον ταῖς χιλίαις ἐκομισάμην ἔτι δ᾽ὡς ἅπαντα τὸν χρόνον ὀφείλειν ὡμολόγει μοι Πολύευκτος, καὶ τὸν Λεωκράτην συνέστησε, καὶ τελευτῶν διέθεθ᾽ ὅρους ἐπιστῆσαι χιλίων δραχμῶν ἐμοὶ τῆς προικὸς ἐπὶ τὴν οἰκίαν [In the first place, then, I shall bring before you as witnesses those who were present when Polyeuctus betrothed his daughter

---

66. Ibid., 340–341.
67. Ibid., 341; see also Witherington III (*Conflict and Community*, 423) for the same observation on the use of this expression in Acts 28:22.
68. Stowers, "*Peri men gar*," 341.
69. Ibid., 342.
70. Ibid.

to me with a portion of forty minae; then I shall prove that what I received was less by a thousand drachmae; and further that Polyeuctus always admitted that he was in my debt, and that he introduced to me Leocrates as guarantor; and that at his death he directed by his will that pillars should be set up on the house in my favor for a thousand drachmae due on account of my wife's portion]).[71] After making other points, Demosthenes comes back to the issue of the house in 41:15–16: οὐ μὴν ἀλλ' εἰ καὶ μηδὲν τούτων ὑπῆρχεν ὑμῖν, οὐδ' ὥς χαλεπόν ἐστι γνῶναι περὶ αὐτῶν, ὁπότεροι τἀληθῆ λέγουσι. περὶ μὲν γὰρ τῆς οἰκίας, εἰ φησὶν ὑπ' ἐμοῦ πεισθέντα Πολύευκτον προστάξαι τοὺς ὅρους στῆσαι τῶν χιλίων . . . (However, though you had none of these facts to aid you, even so it is not difficult to form an opinion as to which of the two parties is speaking the truth. *For regarding the house, if he maintains that Polyeuctus was induced by me to order that mortgage-pillars be set up for the thousand drachmae . . .*).[72] In Stowers' view, one can normally render περὶ μὲν γάρ as "now back to the case of . . ."; which sense is precisely found in 2 Corinthians 9:1.[73] Besides, Stowers indicates that Paul's phraseology which coordinates μέν and δέ is common in classical Greek. This construction is found in Plato more than fourteen times. Stowers observes that this construction "occurs with all of the basic usages of περὶ μὲν γάρ and in every case the γάρ connects with what precedes."[74] From these observations Stowers concludes that the view that "the presence of μέν . . . δέ means that γάρ does not or need not connect with what precedes" is groundless.[75]

Another important insight we gain from Stowers concerns Paul's use of περὶ μὲν γάρ in connection with the phrase περισσόν μοί ἐστιν τὸ γράφειν ὑμῖν in 2 Corinthians 9:1. Stowers remarks that "Paul is employing a variation on a standard phraseology used with περὶ μὲν γάρ, which can mean 'Concerning such and such it is necessary' (or 'it is not necessary') to speak"[76] Stowers goes on to explain that in hortatory rhetoric, this expres-

---

71. Demosthenes, *Orations* 41.6 (Murray, LCL).
72. Demosthenes, *Orations*, 41.15-16.
73. Stowers, "*Peri men gar*," 342.
74. Ibid., 343.
75. Ibid.
76. Ibid., 344.

sion can express "confidence in the audience," or "the strength of the claim which is being made and the lack of need to elaborate."[77] He concludes that "The περὶ μὲν γάρ material of 9:1–4 provides a warrant and explanation for the exhortation of 8:24."[78] This formal link between chapters 8 and 9 is a good argument in favor of their literary unity. Similarly, J. P. Becker indicates that a consensus on the literary integrity of 2 Corinthians is emerging thanks to the reexamination of ancient rhetoric.[79] This point is made for instance by Frederick Long and J. David Hester Amador who place Paul's text within classical literary and rhetorical conventions found in the traditions of Andocides, Socrates, Isocrates and Demosthenes. Especially as regards chapters 8 and 9 scholars are inclined to take this text as a literary unit since there is no compelling evidence for its composite character. This also allows some to perceive in this text "a conventional tripartite rhetorical pattern" of a persuasive speech.[80]

2.6 2 Corinthians 10–13

The discrepancies between 2 Corinthians 1–9 and 10–13 are based on syntactic, semantic and pragmatic considerations. The phrase αὐτὸς δὲ ἐγὼ Παῦλος suggests that Paul begins a new development in 10:1.[81] E. M. Becker summarizes the difficulties presented by chapters 10–13.[82] In these chapters Paul frequently uses "I" language while in chapters 1–9 he also employs the first person plural. As for semantic differences, it is observed that the verb καυχάομαι appears in chapters 10–13 with a negative meaning in contrast with its positive connotation in chapters 1–9. Furthermore, important concepts in chapters 1–9 "such as δόξα, θλῖψις,

---

77. Ibid., 345.
78. Ibid., 346.
79. Becker, *Paul's Usage of* χάρις, 62–64.
80. Safrai and Tomson, "Paul's 'Collection'," 135, 145–149. After the general introduction of the theme (A: 2 Cor 8:1–15) follow illustrative or motivating digressions (B: 8:16–24; digression about the recommendations of Titus and the other two collaborators). The third part (A': 9:1–15) consists in a matter-of-fact and detailed discussion of the theme. In 2 Cor 8–9, one of the persuasive themes used by Paul is poverty. Reference is made to the Macedonians and to the Lord Jesus Christ. There is mention of the Corinthians being enriched, which entails a certain kind of poverty. Paul also speaks of the needs of the saints.
81. Becker, *Letter Hermeneutics*, 4.
82. Ibid.

χαρά, and παράκλησις are missing in chs 10–13."[83] Finally, the atmosphere of reconciliation that dominates 7:4–16 contradicts the polemical situation of chapters 10–13.

I will not deal with all of these questions. Some remarks about the use of the singular and the difference in tone will suffice here. It is true that the first person plural predominates in the first nine chapters, whereas the first person singular is the most used in chapters 10–13. However, such a shift occurs elsewhere in Paul's letters. As in Philemon where Paul also has Timothy as a co-author, the distinctly personal character of the issues treated in chapters 10–13 impelled him to prefer the first person singular to the plural.[84] The different tone reflected by 2 Corinthians 10–13 can be understood if one recalls that such a phenomenon is not infrequent in Paul (Rom 9:1–2 after 8:31–39; Rom 16:17–20 between 16:16 and 16:21; 1 Cor 1:10–13 after 1:4–9; Gal 5:2 after 5:1; Phil 3:2 after 3:1).[85] Moreover, it is important to acknowledge that even 2 Corinthians 1–7 has polemical passages (2:17; 3:1–6; 4:2; 5:12–13; 6:14–16a). Thus, one can conclude that "2 Corinthians is polemical in tone, with 10:1 marking an intensification of degree, not a variation of kind."[86] Ralph P. Martin suggests that the opposition between these two sections should not be overrated.[87] He shows that even chapters 1–7 contain signs pointing to the persisting opposition against Paul. The apostle presents his self-defense in 1:17–22. For Martin, when Paul writes that the offender was punished by the majority (2:6), the implicit suggestion is that a minority may have opposed the decision.

It is equally important to realize that even chapters 10–13 sometimes use the language of tenderness and affection (11:2–3; 12:14–15a; 13:7). Although it is impossible to verify, a "dictation pause" is to be detected after 9:15. During that pause whose length is undetermined, Paul received alarming news to the effect that the situation had deteriorated, "so that he

---

83. Ibid.
84. Harris, *Second Epistle*, 33.
85. Ibid.
86. Harris, *Second Epistle*, 30.
87. Martin, *2 Corinthians*, xlviii.

deemed it necessary to add a detailed vindication of his apostolic authority and dire warnings concerning his forthcoming visit."[88]

For those who see 2 Corinthians as a composite letter, the chronological place of these chapters depends on the defended theory of reconstruction of events. It is assumed that chapters 10–13 were composed by Paul and sent to the Corinthians either before or after chapters 1–9.[89] Both chapters are sometimes thought to belong to the intermediate letter, the so-called "Letter of Tears." This was the view of Kennedy and Bornkamm as discussed earlier.[90] One of the objections to be raised here is that these chapters are completely silent about the Corinthian offender who is at the center of the painful letter, but mention an earlier visit of Titus at Corinth (2 Cor 12:18).[91] Rather, Paul is opposed to those he calls the ψευδαπόστολοι (2 Cor 11:13).

To conclude, partition theories raise more questions than they solve as far as the literary unity of 2 Corinthians is concerned. The lack of positive evidence for any partition theory weakens the plausibility of the hypothesis.[92] For instance, one wonders how the alleged compiler of the independent letters did not realize that his work was strikingly incoherent. Moreover, no explanation is provided concerning the motivation for this compilation. If these so-called separate letters really existed, why did the early church decide to compile them when we know that even such a short and scope-restricted letter as that to Philemon was preserved as such?[93] It is even questionable whether a disciple respectful of his master would easily do such an arbitrary cut-and-paste in the letters of his apostle. Jan Lambrecht shows that no manuscript points to the lack of integrity of this letter.[94] Harris is right to conclude that "there are fewer difficulties with the hypothesis of the letter's integrity than with either the Hausrath or the Semler hypothesis."[95]

---

88. Harris, *Second Epistle*, 31.
89. Ibid., 29.
90. Betz, *2 Corinthians 8 and 9*, 13, 22.
91. Witherington III, *Conflict and Community*, 424, n. 50.
92. Safrai and Tomson, "Paul's 'Collection'," 136.
93. Carrez, *La deuxième épitre*, 24.
94. Lambrecht, *Second Corinthians*, 9.
95. Harris, *Second Epistle*, 51; Safrai and Tomson, "Paul's 'Collection'," 136–138.

2 Corinthians forms a single letter, but it was written in two stages. Paul had written 1 to 9 at the return of Titus, the main purpose being to defend his ministry and celebrate the repentance of the Corinthians, and remind them about the collection. Before he sent it, he received further news about the alarming development of the situation following the intrusion of the opponents from Jerusalem. Apparently, "Paul's authority could have been jeopardized by whatever internal development within the community."[96] Since the letter was to be delivered by Titus (8:16, 23), some time was needed to organize another trip to Corinth (8:18–22). The apostle himself added chapters 10 to 13, which explains the lack of the usual Pauline address and greetings in 9:15 and 10:1.

2.7 The Text of 2 Corinthians 8–9[97]

2 Corinthians 8–9 is relatively stable in its early witnesses. Only a few variants which are likely to affect the meaning of the text deserve our attention here.

> Ch. 8:4: μετὰ πολλῆς παρακλήσεως δεόμενοι ἡμῶν τὴν χάριν καὶ τὴν κοινωνίαν τῆς διακονίας τῆς εἰς τοὺς ἁγίους

At the end of the verse the minuscules 6 and 945 add the words δέξασθαι ἡμᾶς. The reading suggests that the phrase τὴν χάριν καὶ τὴν κοινωνίαν τῆς διακονίας τῆς εἰς τοὺς ἁγίους forms the complement of the verb δέξασθαι whose subject is ἡμᾶς. In this case, the point is that the Macedonians begged Paul and his co-workers to "receive the gift and the fellowship of the ministering to the saints" (NKJV). However, the weak attestation of this variant in the manuscripts makes it improbable. It attests to the copyists' efforts to solve the problem of translation caused by Paul's uneasy syntax.

> Verse 7: Ἀλλ' ὥσπερ ἐν παντὶ περισσεύετε, πίστει καὶ λόγῳ καὶ γνώσει καὶ πάσῃ σπουδῇ καὶ τῇ ἐξ ἡμῶν ἐν ὑμῖν ἀγάπῃ, ἵνα καὶ ἐν ταύτῃ τῇ χάριτι περισσεύητε

The words ἡμῶν ἐν ὑμῖν (our love in you) are replaced by ὑμῶν ἐν ἡμῖν (your love in us) in the following witnesses: ℵ, C, D, F, G, K, L, P,

---

96. Safrai and Tomson, "Paul's 'Collection'," 148.
97. *Novum Testamentum Graece*, 28th rev. ed.

Y, the minuscules 81, 365, 1241, 1505; the Majority text, the Vulgate and a part of the old Latin manuscripts, and the Harklean version. The reading ὑμῶν ἐν ἡμῖν fits superficially better in the context. V. 7 states that the Corinthians have other spiritual qualities: faith, eloquence, knowledge, and zeal. Therefore, it is more natural to imagine that Paul says that they also abound in or have love for him and his collaborators. For this reason, the variant ὑμῶν ἐν ἡμῖν can be regarded as a later correction of the text to fit in the flow of thought of the whole verse. However, the phenomenon of iotacism as the origin of this variant cannot be ruled out.

Another variant with weak support (the minuscules 326, 629 and 2464) reads ὑμῶν ἐν ὑμῖν (your love in you). It is an attempt to clarify Paul's statement. The text proposed by the Nestle-Aland 28th edition is transmitted by many manuscripts most of which are credible (P46, B, 0243, 6, 104, 630, 1175, 1739, 1881, the Old Latin manuscript named r, the Peshitta, Coptic versions and Ambrosiaster). The reading with ἡμῶν ἐν ὑμῖν literally "our love in you" is the most difficult, and should thus be preferred.[98] The delicateness of its translation is reflected in various Bible versions and commentators. It is rendered by "our love for you"[99] or "the love that you have received from us"[100], or "the love we inspired in you"[101].

Verse 9: γινώσκετε γὰρ τὴν χάριν τοῦ κυρίου ἡμῶν Ἰησοῦ Χριστοῦ, ὅτι δι' ὑμᾶς ἐπτώχευσεν πλούσιος ὤν, ἵνα ὑμεῖς τῇ ἐκείνου πτωχείᾳ πλουτήσητε

In some witnesses the pronoun ὑμᾶς, strongly attested in early traditions (P46, ℵ, B, D, F, G, L, P, and others) is replaced by ἡμας whose support is weak (C, K, 6, 323, 614, Eusebius and Didymus of Alexandria in part). Although the phenomenon of iotacism can explain this change, it is more probable that a later copyist altered the text to apply the statement to all Christian believers. The point is, Christ impoverished himself not for the sake of the Corinthians alone (ὑμᾶς), but also for Paul and other

---

98. Metzger, *Textual Commentary*, 512–513.
99. This is how *La Nouvelle Bible Segond: Edition d'Etude*, understands it: "... l'amour que nous vous portons ..."
100. Carrez, *La deuxième épitre*, 181: "L'amour que vous avez reçu de nous. Litéralement, 'l'amour qui vient de nous en vous'."
101. Harris, *Second Epistle*, 573.

believers who read this text (ἡμας). Therefore, the reading with ὑμᾶς is to be preferred.[102]

Verse 16: Χάρις δὲ τῷ θεῷ τῷ δόντι τὴν αὐτὴν σπουδὴν ὑπὲρ ὑμῶν ἐν τῇ καρδίᾳ Τίτου.

Some witnesses (Ὰ*, B, C, I probably, K, P, Y, 0243, 33, 81, 104, 365, 630, 1175, 1739, 1881, 2464, the Majority text, and the Sahidic version) read διδοντι instead of δοντι. The former, which was maintained until the 25th edition of the Greek New Testament, is a present participle of διδωμι whereas the latter is its aorist form. The present tense conveys the idea of continuity here. The point is that Titus still has goodwill or enthusiasm for the Corinthians. But with the aorist participle, the focus is on the fact that the goodwill was given to Titus during his recent visit to Corinth (2 Cor 7:7, 13b, 15). It is clear that the scribes' use of διδοντι was aimed at introducing a sort of clarification found in v. 17. Therefore, the aorist participle is very likely to be the original lesson. It is supported by P[46], some uncials (Ὰ[2], D, F, G, L), some minuscules (6, 323, 326, 1241, 1505), the Vulgate and a part of the Old Latin tradition, Syrian and Bohairic versions, as well as Ambrosiaster.

Verse 19: οὐ μόνον δέ, ἀλλὰ καὶ χειροτονηθεὶς ὑπὸ τῶν ἐκκλησιῶν συνέκδημος ἡμῶν σὺν τῇ χάριτι ταύτῃ τῇ διακονουμένῃ ὑφ' ἡμῶν πρὸς τὴν [αὐτοῦ] τοῦ κυρίου δόξαν καὶ προθυμίαν ἡμῶν

In this verse one variant will occupy my attention since it is likely to affect the meaning of the text: πρὸς τὴν [αὐτοῦ] τοῦ κυρίου δόξαν (for the glory of the Lord himself). Important manuscripts both in number and weight omit the genitive αὐτοῦ (B, C, D*, F, G, L, 81, 104, 326, 365, 629, 1175, 2464, the Vulgate and a part of the Old Latin tradition, Coptic versions and Ambrosiaster). The witnesses that support the reading with αὐτοῦ are Ὰ, D[1], K, Ψ, 1241, 1505, 1881*, the Majority text and all Syriac versions. Since the omission of αὐτοῦ offers the easier reading (πρὸς τὴν τοῦ κυρίου δόξαν, for the Lord's glory), it is suspected to be secondary.[103] The

---

102. Metzger, *Textual Commentary*, 513.
103. Ibid.

issue is compounded with the fact that several other witnesses have αὐτήν in place of αὐτοῦ (P, 0243, 630, 1739, 1881ᶜ and some individual Vulgate manuscripts): πρὸς τὴν αὐτὴν τοῦ κυρίου δόξαν (for the very glory of the Lord). All these observations point to the fact that αὐτοῦ was probably in the original text.[104]

Ch. 9:4: μή πως ἐὰν ἔλθωσιν σὺν ἐμοὶ Μακεδόνες καὶ εὕρωσιν ὑμᾶς ἀπαρασκευάστους καταισχυνθῶμεν ἡμεῖς, ἵνα μὴ λέγω ὑμεῖς, ἐν τῇ ὑποστάσει ταύτῃ

The last part of this verse (ἐν τῇ ὑποστάσει ταύτῃ) presents a textual problem. The word ὑπόστασις can mean substantial nature, reality, essence, actual being. It can also be rendered by undertaking or project as is the case in this verse. It seems that the latter two meanings were not current in the early church. For this reason, we find some witnesses that read ἐν τῇ ὑποστάσει ταύτῃ τῆς καυχήσεως, in the reality of this boasting: А², D², K, L, P, (Ψ), 0209, 104, 365, 630, 1175, 1241, 1505, the Majority text, all the extant Syriac versions except the Peshitta which presents some slight variations. One may suspect that the scribes derived this addition from 11:17 as an explanatory gloss.[105] In the latter reference we read: ὃ λαλῶ, οὐ κατὰ κύριον λαλῶ ἀλλ' ὡς ἐν ἀφροσύνῃ, ἐν ταύτῃ τῇ ὑποστάσει τῆς καυχήσεως (What I am saying I say not with the Lord's authority but as a fool, in this boastful confidence, NRSV). These remain the only two occurrences of the term in Paul and in the whole New Testament. In our verse, the point is that the possible unpreparedness of the Corinthians upon arrival of the Macedonians will be a cause of shame or humiliation because Paul's pride will be found void. In other words, the variant focuses on Paul's boasting whereas the reading retained by the 28ᵗʰ Nestle-Aland edition and to which I subscribe, stresses the collection itself as a project. It is transmitted by the following witnesses: P⁴⁶, А*, B, C, D*, F, G, 048, 0243, 33, 81, 629, 1739, 1881, 2464, the entire Latin tradition and the whole Coptic tradition. The point is that if the Corinthians fail to make their contributions ready before Paul and his Macedonian companions arrive, the apostle will lose his name in the undertaking of the collection.

---

104. Ibid.
105. Ibid., 514.

Verse 7: ἕκαστος καθὼς προῄρηται τῇ καρδίᾳ

Some witnesses (D, K, L, Ψ, 048, 81, 630, 1241, 1505, 2464 with slight differences, and the Majority text) read the present προαῖρεται (decides) in place of the perfect προῄρηται (has decided) supported by many manuscripts (P⁹⁹, Ἀ, B, C, F, G, P, 0243, 6, 33, 104, 365, 1175, 1739, 1881, the Vulgate and a part of the Old Latin tradition, all Coptic versions, and Cyprian). Whereas in the present verse the perfect refers to "a specific, past decision made by each Corinthian," the present expresses "a general timeless principle of giving."[106] The present tense is secondary and may have resulted from iotacism. Thus it has to be rejected.

Verse 10: ὁ δὲ ἐπιχορηγῶν σπόρον τῷ σπείροντι καὶ ἄρτον εἰς βρῶσιν χορηγήσει καὶ πληθυνεῖ τὸν σπόρον ὑμῶν καὶ αὐξήσει τὰ γενήματα τῆς δικαιοσύνης ὑμῶν

In this verse emphasis is put on the idea of God's provision for the needs of the Corinthians. The text adopted by the Nestle-Aland 28th edition, supported by many witnesses (P⁴⁶, Ἀ*, B, C, D*, P, 33, 81, 104, 326, 1175, 2464 and the entire Latin tradition) has indicative future forms χορηγήσει καὶ πληθυνεῖ . . . αὐξήσει "[God] will supply and multiply . . . enlarge" to express "calm confidence" to the Corinthians.[107] But some witnesses (Ἀ², D², F, G, K, L, Ψ, 0209, 0243, 365, 630, 1241, 1739, 1881, and the Majority text) prefer the aorist optative forms χορηγήσαι . . . πληθύναι . . . αὐξήσαι. In this case the verbs express a wish and not a statement: "May he [God] supply. . . multiply. . . enlarge."[108] It is possible that the scribes have introduced this change into the original text "to avoid having Paul suggest that God would invariably act in a particular way."[109] Some other witnesses mix the indicative future and the aorist optative. The reading with indicative future verbs is preferable.

---

106. Harris, *Second Epistle*, 632.
107. Ibid.
108. Ibid.
109. Ibid.

Conclusion

The two canonical letters of Paul to the Corinthians pose literary, historical, and theological problems that are not easy to solve. The number and diversity of partition hypotheses advanced to account for discrepancies in 2 Corinthians reveal the difficulty of the question. However, the lack of any attestations of the alleged originally individual letters makes the hypotheses suspect. Moreover, the motivation of their compilation has not received any satisfactory explanation. Therefore, while it is important to take seriously the questions raised about the literary integrity of 2 Corinthians letter, it is preferable to maintain its unity.

As far as the text of 2 Corinthians 8–9 is concerned, the manuscript tradition is more or less stable. Only a few variants have been studied in this chapter. Now that the question of the literary integrity of 2 Corinthians has been discussed and the attestation of chapters 8 and 9 in early witnesses, the following chapter of this research will be concerned with the exegetical investigation of our pericope in order to grasp its theological content.

CHAPTER 3

Paul's Collection in 2 Corinthians 8–9

Chapter 7 ends with Paul's rejoicing about the restoration of a good relationship with the Corinthians: χαίρω ὅτι ἐν παντὶ θαρρῶ ἐν ὑμῖν, "I rejoice, because I have complete confidence in you" (7:16). With this confidence that mutual understanding is restored, although it may not be as it was before, Paul considers it enough to resume the collection to which he devotes two consecutive chapters of his letter.

As stated earlier, 2 Corinthians 8–9 is treated as one unit. I propose the following division to analyze the flow of Paul's argumentation.[1]

- 8:1–6. The Macedonians as a good example of generosity: Paul praises the Macedonians for the way they engaged in the collection with great enthusiasm despite the dire poverty they were confronted with.
- 8:7–12. The Corinthians are exhorted to complete the collection. Paul challenges the Corinthians to live up to their excellence in other areas of their Christian lives by completing the work they have already started.
- 8:13–15. The purpose of the collection.
- 8:16–9:1–5. The delegates, their commendations and mission.
- 9:6–10. God reciprocates the generosity of a cheerful giver.
- 9:11–15. The outcomes of the collection and doxology.

---

1. I adopt the division suggested by Harris (*Second Epistle*, 558–660) and Carrez (*La deuxième épître*, 177–196) with some adjustments.

3.1 The Macedonians as a Good Example of Generosity (2 Cor 8:1–6)

Verse 1: Γνωρίζομεν δὲ ὑμῖν, ἀδελφοί, τὴν χάριν τοῦ θεοῦ τὴν δεδομένην ἐν ταῖς ἐκκλησίαις τῆς Μακεδονίας

Now we want you to know, brothers and sisters, about the grace of God that has been granted to the churches of Macedonia;

Paul introduces a new subject here with his normal combination of δε, (now) and ἀδελφοί.[2] The word ἀδελφός expresses both physical and spiritual brotherhood among Jews and Christians.[3] 2 Corinthians 8:1 uses it in its spiritual sense to mean fellow members of a local congregation who see themselves as God's common family.[4] Since the term claimed to designate generically male and female Christ-followers as "siblings," we can correctly translate ἀδελφοί as "brothers and sisters."[5] Besides συνεργός, διάκονος, and ἀπόστολος, the appellation ἀδελφός is the most used in the Pauline letters to refer either to a fellow worker or to one who has a certain leading position in a Christian community (1 Cor 1:1; 16:19–20; Phil 1:1, 14; 4:21–22; Gal 1:1–2; 2 Cor 1:1; 2:13; 8:18, 22–23; Col 1:1; 1 Thess 1:1).[6]

The new theme introduced by Paul deserves much attention. The apostle often uses the expression γνωρίζομεν ὑμῖν to draw the attention of his readers to an important piece of information (1 Cor 12:3; 15:1; Gal 1:11). In some cases, he wants to remind them of an important issue, as is the case here.[7] J. P. Becker draws our attention to the fact that in the Johannine literature γνωρίζω is synonymous with φανερόω, which means to reveal, to show, to disclose before the eyes.[8] From that semantic relation, he con-

---

2. Harris, *Second Epistle*, 559. The same construction can also introduce a new aspect within the discussion of the same topic. This construction is found in 1 Cor 1:10; 12:1; 15:1; 16:15. But Betz (*2 Corinthians 8 and 9*, 41, n. 3) thinks that the particle δὲ "sets the sentence off from the preceding section." In Betz's view, that section, which is not 2 Cor 7, initially formed "the epistolary prescript which the editor has omitted."
3. Soden, "ἀδελφός, ἀδελφήν, ἀδελφότης," 144.
4. Punt, "He is heavy . . . he's my brother," 153.
5. Ibid.
6. Punt (Ibid., 164) drawing on Elliot, "Paul and his coworkers," 183.
7. Carrez, *La deuxième épitre*, 179.
8. Becker, *Paul's Usage of* χάρις, 197.

cludes that Paul may be referring in 2 Corinthians 8:1 to something which, directly or indirectly can be "beholdable," "seen, perceived, or recognized." To support this view Becker resorts to Galatians 2:9 where Paul uses the related word γινώσκω which conveys the idea of empirical sense and knowledge through experience. He insists that Paul clearly says that the Jerusalem church leaders perceived or recognized the grace which had been granted to him (γνόντες τὴν χάριν τὴν δοθεῖσάν μοι) and not some of its effects. He concludes that for Paul, χάρις is something which in some sense, is subject to empirical observation, and that this is accessible to all believers.[9] But this interpretation is not convincing. The fact that Becker resorts to the Johannine literature and not to the rest of the Pauline corpus demonstrates the difficulty he has to explain the empirical meaning allegedly tied to the verb γνωρίζω. As for the leaders of the Jerusalem church, their experiential knowledge of the grace which was at work in Paul was acquired through the fascinating story that Paul recounted and brought them to understand the reality of his missionary work on the ground. The notion of experience cannot be reduced to the visual and tactile senses. Therefore, it is logical to interpret γνωρίζω in 2 Corinthians 8:1 in the sense of making something known, which meaning it carries elsewhere in the Pauline literature as mentioned earlier.[10]

Paul wants the Corinthians to know the χάρις τοῦ θεοῦ, grace of God, which has been given to the Macedonian churches. As noted previously, the word χάρις appears 155 times in the New Testament and is central to Paul's writings where it is used 98 times.[11] Paul employs it 18 times in 2 Corinthians with different meanings.[12] In the context of the collection (2 Cor 8–9), the term appears ten times (seven occurrences in ch. 8 and three in ch. 9).[13] The word is related to the verb χαίρω, to rejoice.[14] Χάρις thus means: what gives delight. Very often, poets would use χάρις and

---

9. Ibid., 198–199.
10. Danker et al., *Greek-English Lexicon*, 203.
11. Kohlenberger III et al., *Exhaustive Concordance*, 999–1001.
12. Ibid., 1000.
13. Panikulam, *Koinonia in the New Testament*, 38. This term is rare in the gospels: John (3 times), Luke (8 times).
14. Conzelmann, "χαίρω, χαράν," 373.

χαρά interchangeably.¹⁵ This basic idea remained throughout the developments of the word in later Antiquity which are vital to the understanding of its uses in the New Testament.¹⁶ χάρις appears in inscriptions to refer to a favor bestowed by a ruler. For instance, the edict promulgated by Emperor Tiberius Alexander would be called a demonstration of χάρις. People would say that they got some advantages τῇ τοῦ θεοῦ Κλαυδίου χάριτι,¹⁷ "by the favor of Claudius the god."¹⁸ χάρις can also indicate a "gracious disposition."¹⁹ Most often its plural form has the meaning of a gift in a concrete sense.²⁰ With regard to the beneficiary of a gift, χάρις is used to mean "thanks" to the giver.²¹ It is noteworthy that the inscriptions do not relate χάρις to God. But philosophers speak of God's χάρις. For instance, Epictetus wrote that Zeus deserves praises for the wonderful things which he has made in nature and the many benefits (τὰς χάριτας), that he has granted to human beings.²²

In the LXX χάρις translates the Hebrew חֵן, the infinitive substantive *qill* of the verb חנן, whose basic meaning expresses "the kind turning of one person to another as expressed in an act of assistance," and thus favor.²³

---

15. Danker et al., *Greek-English Lexicon*, 1079.

16. Conzelmann, "χαίρω, χαράν," 375–376. Ogereau ("Jerusalem Collection," 373), following Harrison, points out that in classical Greek literature, χάρις does not always have a theological meaning; rather, it is used in connection with public benefaction. He concludes that this warns us against a tendency to give it a purely theological connotation everywhere in Paul. He notes that Paul's thought "is not solely animated by lofty theological motives, but is also deeply concerned with social, political, and economic issues" (Harrison, *Paul's Language of Grace*, 294–303).

17. Conzelmann, "χαίρω, χαράν," 375, referring to Dittenberger, *Orientis Graecae Inscriptiones*, 669, 28, 29; Danker et al., *Greek-English Lexicon*, 1079.

18. My translation.

19. Conzelmann, "χαίρω, χαράν," 375, referring to Dittenberger, *Orientis Graecae Inscriptiones*, 139, 20f.

20. Conzelmann, "χαίρω, χαράν," 375, referring to Dittenberger, *Sylloge Inscriptionum Graecarum*, 814, 18f.

21. Conzelmann, "χαίρω, χαράν," 375, referring to Dittenberger, *Sylloge Inscriptionum Graecarum*, 613, 36f.

22. Epictetus, *Discourses* I.16.15 (LCL); Epictetus, *Discourses* I, 33. Another important development in the use of χάρις emerged in Antiquity. The word came to denote a supernatural power of love (Euripides, *Hippolytus*, 93) or the power of oaths (Euripides, *Medea*, 121). This power has ultimately a religious connotation because it is thought to be "from above" and manifests itself through the beauty of the θεῖος ἀνήρ (the divine man) who performs wonders by magic (Conzelmann, χαίρω, χαράν, 375, 376).

23. Zimmerli, "χαίρω, χαράν," 660.

In 3 Macc. 5:20 χάρις means gratitude. From the sphere of human relations (Gen 18:3; 32:6; 33:8; 2 Chr 7:21; 1 Esdras 8:77), the term was predominantly used to refer to God's loving attitude demonstrated in his turning to the helpless (Gen 6:8; 18:3; 30:27). But the noun חֵן gradually lost the meaning of its stem to generally mean what is good or beautiful.[24] This usage is attested in Ecclesiastes 10:12 to mean attractiveness. Similarly, χάρις occurs in Sirach 7:19 to denote the beauty of a woman.[25] This gap between the original meaning of χάρις and its new connotation was filled in by another word, חֶסֶד (mercy/compassion). In the LXX, חֶסֶד is usually translated by ἔλεος.[26] Apart from two occurrences in Esther 2:9, 17 where the phrase חֵן וָחֶסֶד is translated by χάρις, the LXX uses the latter to render חֵן.[27] It is worth noting that in many instances the word χάρις in the LXX does not have a theological meaning (Prov 1:9; 3:22; 10:32; 3:34; 11:27; 30:7; 22:1; 28:23; Wis 3:9, 14; 4:15; 8:21; 14:26; 18:2).[28] The various meanings of χάρις sketched above are confirmed by the recent scholarship of Frederick W. Danker et al. and Harrison for instance as I will demonstrate below.

From this short analysis, it is possible to conclude that Paul's use of the word χάρις is more informed by the Hellenistic context than the LXX. As observed by Harrison, the fact that Paul prefers χάρις and its cognates to the most obvious ἔλεος and its related words used by the LXX to say God's mercy is evocative.[29] But he explains that this does not imply at all that, for instance, the notion of God's saving grace is unknown in Judaism. Zechariah 12:10 refers explicitly to God's gracious and compassionate disposition towards Israel. The reference is about God's promising to pour out "a spirit of grace and supplication," πνεῦμα χάριτος καὶ οἰκτιρμοῦ, upon the house of David and the inhabitants of Jerusalem.[30] Moreover, in the Old Testament, God, who is mindful of his covenant, reveals his

---

24. Ibid., 381.
25. Lust, Eynikel and Hauspie, *Greek-English Lexicon*, 660.
26. Zimmerli, "χαίρω, χαράν," 381.
27. Harrison, *Paul's Language of Grace*, 107. Conversely, there exist only three instances where the LXX employs ἔλεος to render חֵן (Gen 19:19; Num 11:15; Judg 6:17).
28. Conzelman, "χαίρω, χαράν, 389.
29. Harrison, *Paul's Language of Grace*, 2.
30. Ibid., 108.

faithfulness by showing "mercy even in the face of sinful Israel" and this aspect dominates its use in Paul.[31] George W. E. Nickelsburg has forcefully demonstrated that the Old Testament concepts of election and covenant are rooted in the notion of God's grace.[32] Even the ideas of reward and punishment do not contradict this belief. The God who punishes the sinner is the same who also calls instantly his people to repentance. From Paul's times onwards, χάρις is used to mean divine favor "in fixed formulas at the beginning and end of letters."[33] The word can be applied to human beings and God as well as we shall see in the following instances:[34]

- It may designate a human quality (appearance or speech) that prompts a kind reaction of someone else, "attractiveness, charm": Luke 4:22; Colossians 4:6[35]. It is in this sense of beauty or charm that the word χάρις is used for instance in Josephus with reference to Moses's appearance when he was three years old.[36]

- It refers to a disposition to act beneficently towards others. It thus means favor, grace, care or goodwill. This usage reflects the context of reciprocity dominated by Hellenistic influence as well as the Semitic notion of social obligation expressed in the Hebrew word חֶסֶד.[37] To be sure, χάρις was in the first century CE the leitmotiv of the reciprocity system, and it was widely understood in this way even in Judaism at that time.[38] It refers thus to a volitional act towards the other. This includes imperial dispensations, and especially the beneficent intention of God. God's grace basically signifies the undeserved gift he makes to

---

31. Panikulam, *Koinonia in the New Testament*, 39.
32. Nickelsburg, *Ancient Judaism*, 36.
33. Danker et al., *Greek-English Lexicon*, 1079.
34. Ibid., 1079–1080.
35. We have here a genitive of quality: οἱ λόγοι τῆς χάριτος, the gracious words (Ibid., 1079).
36. Ibid., 1079 ("ἡ χαρις ἡ παιδικὴ πολλὴ καὶ ἄκρατος περὶ αὐτὸν οὖσα κατεῖχε τοὺς ὁρῶντας": Josephus, *Ant.* 2.231 [Thackeray, LCL]).
37. Danker et al., *Greek-English Lexicon*, 1079; Harrison, *Paul's Language of Grace*, 2, 26–96.
38. Harrison, *Paul's Language of Grace*, 345. He indicates that the Hebrew sources, by contrast, generally maintained the Old Testament stress on "the unilateral nature of covenantal grace, as did some preachers in the first-century Greek-speaking synagogues" as attest the homilies of Pseudo-Philo.

human beings through Jesus's sacrificial death (Rom 3:24; Gal 1:15; Eph 1:6–14; Titus 2:11; Heb 2:9). The same beneficent disposition characterizes Christ (Rom 5:15b; 2 Cor 8:9; 1 Tim 1:14).

- The word χάρις can mean the proof of goodwill, a gift, a benefaction, an act of generosity, or a concrete deed accomplished by a human being to benefit others (2 Cor 1:15; 1 Cor 16:3; 2 Cor 8:6, 7, 19; Eph 4:29). This meaning also applies to political favor as in Acts 25:3.
- χάρις also signifies a response to generosity or beneficence in terms of thanks or gratitude. This is an essential element of the Greco-Roman practice of benefit exchange. In this context χάριτες means proofs of gratitude.[39] Gratitude is expressed to human beings as in Epict. 4.7, 9; Luke 17:9 and Philemon, but it is also used in a religious context. In Judaism and early Christianity, it is directed to God and/or Christ (3 Macc. 5:20; Josephus, *Ant.* 7. 208; 2 Tim 1:3; 1 Tim 1:12; Heb 12:28; 2 Cor 9:15; Rom 6:17). Elsewhere it is rendered to the Deity for the benefits granted as attested for instance in papyri, inscriptions, Philo and pagan popular philosophers.[40]
- χάρις means a divine action in human life that enables a believer to perform a good action (2 Cor 8:1; 9:8, 14). It is thanks to God's χάρις that Paul has been called to the apostolate. The same χάρις manifests itself in various gifts of the Spirit, χαρίσματα (Rom 12:6; Eph 4:7; 1 Pet 4:10).[41] In some contexts χάρις has a concrete sense which can hardly be differentiated from δύναμις, γνῶσις, or δόξα θεοῦ (2 Cor 1:12; 1 Cor 15:10; 2 Pet 3:18; Acts 6:8).

---

39. χάριτες, which could also refer to the Greek goddesses, is totally absent from Paul (Harrison, *Paul's Language of Grace*, 285). It is possible that Paul wanted to strictly prevent any polytheistic confusion that such a term could generate in his readers. By contrast, it is employed by Philo and Josephus to designate great deeds of beneficence performed by God and humans (ibid., 120, 136–137, 139).

40. Ibid., 26–96, 114–210.

41. Danker et al., *Greek-English Lexicon*, 1080.

- χάρις is also a privilege to do something (2 Cor 8:4).[42]

The significance of this term in 2 Corinthians 8–9 cannot be sketched here before the whole passage has been analyzed. Its various meanings and function in this text will be presented in the conclusion of the present chapter. In the text under discussion (2 Cor 8:1), the expression τὴν χάριν τοῦ θεοῦ contains a subjective genitive, and not a possessive one. It points to the source of the grace received. In the case of the Macedonians, this χάρις means God giving them willingness and ability to participate in the collection.[43] The same holds true of Paul's own calling to ministry (Rom 1:5; 12:3; 15:15; 1 Cor 3:10; 15:10; 2 Cor 12:9; Gal 2:9; Eph 3:2; Phil 1:7).

Macedonia, the country of Alexander the Great and a Roman province since 146 BCE, was a senatorial province in Paul's times.[44] Its capital city was Thessalonica. Paul arrived in Macedonia for the first time during his second missionary journey, and founded the churches of Philippi, Thessalonica and Berea.[45] He visited and sent them his delegates several times (Acts 16:9–12; 18:5; 19:21–22; 20:1–3; 2 Cor 1:16; 2:13; 7:5; Phil 4:15; 1 Thess 1:7–10; 4:10). They became remarkably dynamic and supported his ministry (2 Cor 11:9; Phil 4:15–16). During his captivity in Rome or Ephesus, the Philippians assisted him. Not only did they give him material provisions, but they also sent Epaphroditus to stay with him (Phil 4:18; 2:25–30). In Romans 15:26 Paul also indicates that the Macedonians were committed to the collection. Martin rightly notes that in 2 Corinthians 8:1 Paul indirectly tells the Corinthians, among whom his authority was challenged, that his apostleship is accepted in Macedonia and that he has an excellent rapport with the believers in that province.[46]

---

42. Joubert, *Paul as Benefactor*, 136.

43. Harris, *Second Epistle*, 560. Although Paul does not use the term χάρις in Phil 2:13, he expresses there his view that God enables people to do his will. However, it is interesting to note that the concept of willingness (τὸ θέλειν), emphasized in the context of the collection (2 Cor 8:10, 11), also occurs here: θεὸς γάρ ἐστιν ὁ ἐνεργῶν ἐν ὑμῖν καὶ τὸ θέλειν καὶ τὸ ἐνεργεῖν ὑπὲρ τῆς εὐδοκίας (for it is God who works in you both to will and to do for his good pleasure).

44. Danker et al., *Greek-English Lexicon*, 611.

45. Carrez, *La deuxième épitre*, 179. Therefore, when Paul speaks of the Macedonians in relation to the collection, he is referring to the churches of Philippi, Berea and Thessalonica (Joubert, *Paul as Benefactor*, 135).

46. Martin, *2 Corinthians*, 252.

Paul indicates that this χάρις (i.e. the ability to take part in the collection) was given to the churches of Macedonia (τὴν χάριν τοῦ θεοῦ τὴν δεδομένην ἐν ταῖς ἐκκλησίαις τῆς Μακεδονίας). It is worth mentioning Paul's use of the perfect passive δεδομένην, meaning that such ability and goodwill to give to the needy have their source in God and not in human nature or zeal.[47] This divine passive in the perfect implies here that God is "the giver of a gift that has not ceased to be bestowed."[48] At the same time Paul himself admits that the Macedonians' achievements cannot be attributed to "his own successful ministry."[49] Moreover, the perfect participle indicates that God's granting of his grace to the Macedonians is not an act belonging to the past, but is still at work among the Macedonians when Paul writes to the Corinthians. The fact that Paul mentions the Macedonians is understandable. When the apostle writes 2 Corinthians, he is in Macedonia (7:5) visiting congregations (9:2).[50] The apostle can thus see God's grace at work in the life of this church. One may correctly say that for Paul God's grace always produces in the life of a Christian believer the ability to serve others. This calls for a fresh understanding of spiritual gift. It is in this light that Paul speaks not only of spectacular spiritual gifts such as prophecy, healing, and tongues (1 Cor 12:4–11) but also of the acts of giving "with liberality" and showing mercy "with cheerfulness" (Rom 12:8).[51]

> Verse 2: ὅτι ἐν πολλῇ δοκιμῇ θλίψεως ἡ περισσεία τῆς χαρᾶς αὐτῶν καὶ ἡ κατὰ βάθους πτωχεία αὐτῶν ἐπερίσσευσεν εἰς τὸ πλοῦτος[52] τῆς ἁπλότητος αὐτῶν.
>
> For during a severe ordeal of affliction, their abundant joy and their extreme poverty have overflowed in a wealth of generosity on their part.

---

47. Harris, *Second Epistle*, 560.
48. Antony, "He Who Supplies Seed," 307.
49. Furnish, *II Corinthians*, 413.
50. Harris, *Second Epistle*, 558.
51. Talbert, "Money Management," 362.
52. Harris, *Second Epistle*, 559, 563. "In Paul πλοῦτος is neuter (in the nominative and accusative) eight times and masculine (in the nominative, accusative, and genitive) five times." It is used in the Pauline corpus for moral or spiritual riches. When the term and its cognates are applied to material wealth, a qualifier is added (1 Tim 6:17).

The word θλῖψις, which is rare in non-biblical Greek, indicates distress caused either by outward circumstances or an inward experience.[53] It occurs 45 times in the New Testament, 24 of which are found in the Pauline corpus.[54] Its remarkable recurrence in 2 Corinthians (1:4, 8; 2:4; 4:17; 6:4; 7:4; 8:2, 13) sheds some light on Paul's reflection on human sufferings. In the case of the Macedonians, we are informed that their distress was caused by the situation of deep poverty they were confronted with (ἡ κατὰ βάθους πτωχεία αὐτῶν). One may wonder whether the Macedonian believers were alone in such a situation of poverty or whether their compatriots were going through the same experience. Harris remarks that although it is true that the situation of poverty was shared by all Macedonians in general, as notes Betz,[55] the dire poverty of the Christians was certainly related to their θλῖψις.[56] Their "persecution created or at least aggravated their destitution."[57] Paul adds the qualification κατὰ βάθους, "at the deepest" to express the degree of destitution they were confronted with. The genitive θλίψεως indicates that the test or trial undergone by the Macedonians was caused by affliction.[58] The situation of persecutions in Macedonia is mentioned in Paul's letters (Phil 1:29, 30; 1 Thess 1:6; 2:14; 3:3; 2 Thess 1:4–10).[59]

---

53. Danker et al., *Greek-English Lexicon*, 457. The verb θλίβω is found in 2 Cor 1:6; 4:8; 7:5.

54. Kohlenberger III et al., *Exhaustive Concordance*, 437.

55. Betz, *2 Corinthians 8 and 9*, 43.

56. But Perkins ("Taxes in the New Testament," 193) notes that some scholars suspect that Paul's mention of the dire poverty of the Macedonians "may be somewhat hyperbolic. Since the province as a whole was prosperous and the churches there were enthusiastic supporters of other aspects of Paul's mission." But nothing indicates that such a financial comfort remained unaffected by several crises which may have hit the region. Moreover, the impact of the situation of hostility faced by the Macedonians at the hands of their compatriots cannot be ignored. As for the Macedonian churches' sponsorship of Paul's ministry, this cannot be an argument against the idea that they were poor. Nothing indicates that the poor cannot participate in such an undertaking. Indeed, Paul commends the Macedonians because they have behaved in a way that one could hardly expect from people who are in a similar situation.

57. Harris, *Second Epistle*, 562.

58. In this case it is a subjective genitive (Harris, *Second Epistle*, 561). But it can also be construed as epexegetic (genitive of quality); which would mean that the test consisted of affliction. Both translations are possible and hard to differentiate.

59. Martin, *2 Corinthians*, 252.

The word δοκιμή carries the double meaning of a difficult situation, trial, test, and a proof (2 Cor 13:3). It focuses more on the positive result of this test than on the test itself.[60] The Macedonians' trial became the proof that God was at work through them.[61] This explains the paradoxical nature of their attitude. In spite of the distressing context they were in, they displayed an exemplary abundance of joy (ἡ περισσεία τῆς χαρᾶς) and rich generosity (ἁπλότητος). The Macedonians' joy is brought about by the Holy Spirit and belongs to the new creation (Rom 14:7; 1 Thess 1:6).[62] As such, it is more than a mere "happy mood" but a "saving gift from God" which characterizes the life of a Christian believer in all that he or she can share with other fellow believers as a community (2 Cor 7:13; Phil 2:2; 1 Thess 3:9).[63] In Paul's thought χάρα is related to faith (Phil 1:25), to hope (Rom 15:13) and above all it is one of the fruit of the Spirit (Gal 5:22).[64]

Paul notes that the Macedonians' poverty abounded in the riches of liberality (πτωχεία αὐτῶν ἐπερίσσευσεν εἰς τὸ πλοῦτος τῆς ἁπλότητος αὐτῶν). It is worth noting here that the same words πτωχεία and πλοῦτος used to express the outstanding example of the Macedonian generosity will also be applied to Christ in v. 9. Paul is probably saying indirectly that the Macedonians have been transformed by the salvific work of Christ. However, Gesila Nneka Uzukwu argues that the categories of riches and poverty are used by Paul as rhetorical devices in this context. In my view, no compelling evidence plays against a material interpretation of these terms.[65]

---

60. Danker et al., *Greek-English Lexicon*, 255; Betz, *2 Corinthians 8 and 9*, 43.
61. Carrez, *La deuxième épitre*, 180.
62. Georgi, *Remembering the Poor*, 71.
63. Ibid.
64. Panikulam, *Koinonia in the New Testament*, 48.
65. Uzukwu, "Poverty and Wealth," 321–323. She argues that the view that the Macedonian Christians were materially poor has to be questioned. She shows that in Paul the term πτωχός has both a material meaning (Gal 2:10; Rom 15:26–27) and a figurative one (Gal 4:9). In 2 Cor 6:10 Paul speaks of himself as someone who is poor. In addition, 2 Cor 8:9, as many scholars maintain, denotes Jesus' incarnational experience and not material poverty as such. She indicates that the difficulty is compounded by the use of πένες in 2 Cor 9:9 in Paul's quotation from the LXX which also employs it to describe someone who is materially or spiritually poor. From these observations Uzukwu notes that the term πτωχεία in 2 Cor 8:2 is ambiguous. But it is important to note that Paul's use of the phrase δοκιμῇ θλίψεως in the same context to describe the Macedonians' situation indicates that this needs to be taken at face value. Uzukwu also remarks that it is debated whether the believers mentioned in 2 Cor 8:1 were located in the kingdom of Macedonia including

In the Pauline epistles ἁπλότης occurs seven times with different meanings: sincerity or simplicity (2 Cor 11:3), simplicity of heart (Eph 6:5; Col 3:22), simple-heartedness leading to action, open hearted liberality/generosity (Rom 12:8; 2 Cor 8:2; 9:11, 13).[66] The religious component of the word in this context has to be recognized. In the Testaments of the Twelve Patriarchs, ἁπλότης is frequently used in the sense of liberality which results from piety and materializes in the community life (Reuben 4:1; Levi 13:1; Simeon 4:5; Issachar 4:1; 5:1).[67] Paul states that the Macedonians succeeded in demonstrating generosity because "they had been enabled by the gift of God's grace."[68] Whereas Paul commends the Thessalonians for their ability to rejoice in the midst of trials (1 Thess 1:6), he exhorts the Philippians to rejoice always in the Lord (Phil 4:4).[69] For Magarett Thrall, ἁπλότης could easily be translated by sincerity, single-mindedness or generosity, the three terms carrying the same meaning in a context of giving.[70]

Philippi, Thessalonica and Berea or whether they were part of the Roman province which extended to Thessalys and Epirus. More importantly, she writes that in 2 Cor 11:9 and Phil 4:15 Paul mentions financial contributions without indicating their economic status. She surmises that Paul uses an exaggerated expression which functions here as a rhetorical device to convince the Corinthians. A similar interpretation is proposed by Safrai and Tomson ("Paul's 'Collection'," 145, 146, 150) who argue that the themes of poverty and riches are tactfully employed by Paul in the context of 2 Cor 8–9 as rhetorical devices to convince the Corinthians to resume their contributions to the collection. They esteem that even the phrase ὑστερήματα τῶν ἁγίων, the needs of the saints (2 Cor 9:12) probably refers more to "economic wealth and mental reservations in Corinth" than to the real financial situation prevailing in the Jerusalem church. Their main evidence lies in the fact that 1 Cor 16:1–4 is silent about the situation of poverty in Jerusalem as a motivation for the collection. In my view, this line of thought is not convincing. There is no need to apply a hermeneutic of suspicion to Paul's depiction of the general situation of all the parties involved in his project. Furthermore, it is possible that Paul laid emphasis differently on various motivations of his project depending on the situation he had to address. This is correct inasmuch as Paul was not writing a systematic treatise on Christian almsgiving. Mutombo ("Le nouveau culte," 111) esteems that the Macedonians' poverty was not spiritual, but material.

66. Harris, *Second Epistle*, 563.

67. Carrez, *La deuxième épitre*, 180. References are found in De Jonge, *Testaments*, 7, 40, 18, 84, 85.

68. Betz, *2 Corinthians 8 and 9*, 45.

69. Ibid., 42–43. Betz notes that in early Christian theology, this paradox is seen as a model of Christian experience. Paul mentions it in 2 Cor 1:3–7, 8–11, 12, 24; 2:3, 4, 7; 7:4, 7, 9, 13–16; 4:7–18; 11:23. The apostle could even boast of his sufferings (10:8; 12:9, 10; 13:9). This theme is also present in the synoptic gospels (Luke 10:17–20; 15:5–7, 32; Matt 5:12), and originates from Judaism.

70. Thrall, *Critical and Exegetical Commentary*, 523–524.

However, J. P. Becker rejects this interpretation of ἁπλότης as meaning liberality and prefers "single-mindedness," "a deep-seated sense of one's *reason-for-being*," which meaning he also finds in 9:11, 13.[71] In my view, the notion of liberality or generosity does not necessarily refer to the size of the gift only, as contends Becker. It also indicates the willingness to share with others what one has, especially when it is not even enough for oneself. The Macedonians were able to give "not from their surplus, but out of their limited resources."[72] The difficult experience of poverty of the Macedonians "gave them a special empathy" with the poor members of the Jerusalem church (Rom 15:26).[73] In 1 Thessalonians 2:14 Paul writes that, like their fellows in Judea, the Macedonian Christians suffered at the hands of their compatriots. Given the difficult situation of the Macedonians, Nickle insists that Paul did not use ἁπλότης to speak of the amount of money given, but rather of their inner disposition in giving.[74] For this reason, he suggests that the term ἁπλότης should be translated here by "singleness, simpleness, sincerity."[75] In fact, the word ἁπλότης precisely means "generosity arising out of pure intentions," as opposed to calculations for any kind of material or moral interest.[76] It is crucial that Paul highlights "the joy and the love expressed in the gifts" by the givers "and not so much the financial aspects involved in generosity."[77]

> Verses 3–4: ὅτι κατὰ δύναμιν, μαρτυρῶ, καὶ παρὰ δύναμιν, αὐθαίρετοι ⁴ μετὰ πολλῆς παρακλήσεως δεόμενοι ἡμῶν τὴν χάριν καὶ τὴν κοινωνίαν τῆς διακονίας τῆς εἰς τοὺς ἁγίους.

---

71. Becker, *Paul's Usage of* χάρις, 73, 74.
72. Martin, *2 Corinthians*, 253.
73. Harris, *Second Epistle*, 562.
74. Nickle, *Collection*, 105. Uzukwu ("Poverty and Wealth," 324–326) holds the same view. She remarks that τὸ πλοῦτος means riches or wealth as well as abundance, fullness and plenitude whereas ἁπλότης denotes generosity, simplicity, frankness, simple-mindedness. For her, the combination of τὸ πλοῦτος and ἁπλότης needs to be understood figuratively as suggests Harris (*Second Epistle*, 563). This genitive of content, she argues, conveys an inclusive idea; Paul refers to an abundance of simple-mindedness, simplicity, and generosity on the part of the Macedonians. She concludes that given the Macedonians' willingness to engage in the collection, the question of whether they have contributed in terms of monetary value is not important.
75. Nickle, *Collection*, 105.
76. Kamalakar Jayakumar, "System of Equality," 248.
77. Punt, "Some Perspectives," 333.

> For, as I can testify, they voluntarily gave according to their means, and even beyond their means, begging us earnestly for the privilege of sharing[78] in this ministry to the saints . . .

In verse 3 a verb has to be supplied: they gave or contributed.[79] First of all, on their own initiative (αὐθαίρετοι),[80] the Macedonians decided to give their contributions for the collection. This means that neither Paul nor any of his delegates asked them to do so. It is possible to argue that Paul's initial intention was to involve in his collection those churches whose contribution would not mean "a big sacrifice."[81] Furthermore, one senses that Paul was reluctant to ask the Macedonians to give money because he knew about their deep poverty. Thus, in this verse, Paul may be saying that no one put any pressure on them to participate.[82] Paul's hesitation to ask for aid from the Macedonians may be explicable if we remember that they have been sending him material aid for his apostolic work in different congregations (Phil 4:15–16). This, coupled with their known poverty, put Paul in an uneasy situation. He resolved to tell them only about the Corinthians and other Achaeans in general without saying explicitly that he wanted them to contribute (2 Cor 9:2). In this context, Paul "could hardly have hoped for substantial financial assistance from them, but he had expected to receive

---

78. Carrez, *La deuxième épitre*, 180. The Greek text has two words at the same level, joined by a conjunction (τὴν χάριν καὶ τὴν κοινωνίαν). This construction, known as hendiadys, leads to the translation adopted in the main text. In English the same figure of speech uses two words joined by "and" to express an idea that is more naturally expressed by an adjective and a noun. Example: one can say "by length of time and siege" instead of "by a long siege" (R. Nordquist, About.com Guide: http://grammar.about.com/od/fh/g/hendiadysterm.htm, accessed on 21 May 2011). Therefore, unlike Witherington III (*Conflict and Community*, 413) and Nickle (*Collection*, 110) who translate χάρις respectively by "benevolence" or "gracious action," and "a direct expression of Christian brotherly fellowship," I align with Joubert (*Paul as Benefactor*, 136) who renders this word by "privilege." This is the translation adopted by the NKJV. Harrison (*Paul's Language of Grace*, 295–296) admits that it is possible that we have a hendiadys construction here. But in his view, it is more likely that τὴν χάριν is the direct object of δεόμενοι and that καί is epexegetic. In either case the meaning remains the same.

79. Becker (*Paul's Usage of χάρις*, 80) indicates that there exists another verb which fits the context: αἱρετίζω which means to choose or to will.

80. Harris, *Second Epistle*, 565. The adjective αὐθαίρετος is totally absent from the LXX, whereas the New Testament uses it twice: in this verse and in 8:17 in relation to Titus.

81. Panikulam, *Koinonia in the New Testament*, 35.

82. Harris, *Second Epistle*, 565.

some."[83] We may thus assume that the Macedonians were moved by the plight of the poor believers in Jerusalem, and got excited by this laudable initiative. As a result, they begged Paul to let them contribute to it (μετὰ πολλῆς παρακλήσεως δεόμενοι ἡμῶν).

Paul realizes that the Macedonians' distress spilled over into rich generosity (v. 2). They contributed beyond their means (παρὰ δύναμιν), and surpassed Paul's natural expectations given their pressing financial situation (v. 5a).[84] The apostle's point here is that "the Macedonians had given not simply what they could afford but beyond what their very slender means really allowed. He is not suggesting that their judgement was unbalanced or reckless but is affirming that their generosity surpassed any natural expectation (cf. v. 5a)."[85]

To sum up, the exemplary behavior of the Macedonians does not only lie in their ability to give generously, but also in the fact that they begged Paul to be allowed to participate in the collection. Their example does not

---

83. Betz, *2 Corinthians 8 and 9*, 47.

84. Becker presents an interesting explanation of what surprised Paul here. He draws on Schütz's view that Paul's usage of χάρις carries the notions of power. It is Paul's power (2 Cor 2:12; 12:10; 1 Cor 15:10); the domain in which Christians find their place (Gal 5:4; Rom 5:2). The same χάρις is the sphere of God's calling and thus the source of Paul's authority. He indicates that most of the transactions involving χάρις presented by Paul espouse a top-down relation. χάρις is from God to believers (Rom 1:5; 3:24; 4:4, 16; 5:2, 15); or just as often χάρις goes from God to believers and is mediated by Paul (Rom 1:7; 12:3; 15:15; 16:20; 1 Cor 1:3, 4; 3:10). Becker says that Paul was aware that the grace had been bestowed to the Macedonians through him (Acts 16:19–40). Becker concludes that Paul was surprised that the Macedonians begged him and his companions to receive their χάρις; which was in fact a redefinition of "what had always been a top-down relationship" to become "mutual reciprocity," κοινωνία. For Uzukwu ("Poverty and Wealth," 328–329), Paul's use of the antithesis in 2 Cor 8:5b entails that Paul was surprised by the Macedonians' giving themselves. In the same vein, she thinks that the expression κατὰ δύναμιν which refers to the Macedonians' contribution in terms of "abundant simple-mindedness or generosity or giving out of their limited resources" was not meant to be taken literally (ibid., 328). She sees that Paul uses again an exaggerated expression to stir the Corinthians' emotions. In my view, there is no need to doubt the condition of poverty of the Macedonians as the apostle presents it. To argue that such a situation would have meant that the Macedonians "would not be able to contribute" but would on the contrary need to be assisted, as writes Uzukwu (ibid., 322), does not do justice to Paul. Logically speaking, that is what may surprise any person as it did Paul. The Macedonians' felt financial shortage did not deflect them from giving to the collection. But Uzukwu (ibid., 329) is right to show that in the context of 2 Cor 8–9 Paul uses each of both communities' example, the Corinthians (9:1–5) and Macedonians (8:1–5), to motivate them to give generously, freely and according to one's means (8:3, 11–12; 9:5, 7).

85. Harris, *Second Epistle*, 565.

primarily consist in the fact that they gave or in the amount they contributed, but rather in their "spirit of giving that manifests itself in various ways."[86] J. P. Becker observes that even here Paul alludes to God's χάρις, as he refers to δύναμις.[87] He explains that elsewhere in the Pauline corpus, both terms are used in parallel (2 Cor 12:9; Eph 3:7). Becker concludes that in the context of the collection, Paul was telling the Corinthians that the Macedonians' free choice expressed by the adverb αὐθαίρετοι was in fact not completely their own. Rather, he explains, their impulse was instigated by the δύναμις of χάρις which God had conferred to them (8:1). However, in my view, Becker goes too far when he takes χάρις and δύναμις as synonyms in this context. He writes that the χάρις bestowed on the Macedonians (8:1) is that power beyond their own according to which they were "impelled from within to reveal a new χάρις paradigm to Paul – a paradigm in which recipients of χάρις reciprocate with those from whom they have received χάρις."[88]

The way Paul expresses the content of the Macedonians' request is instructive. They begged the apostle τὴν χάριν καὶ τὴν κοινωνίαν τῆς διακονίας τῆς εἰς τοὺς ἁγίους. The participation in the collection is depicted as a χάρις, a privilege. Victor B. Furnish translates it as "benefit" as he does in 1:15 and 9:8.[89] This implies that the Corinthians should not take it for granted. They should rather view it as a "favor" (RSV) or a "privilege" (NRSV) granted by God to them. Furthermore, the participation in the collection is regarded by Paul as a κοινωνία τῆς διακονίας τῆς εἰς τοὺς ἁγίους, a share in the fellowship of service to the saints. The word κοινωνία occurs nineteen times in the New Testament, thirteen of which are in Paul's writings.[90] In connection with the collection Paul uses it three times (Rom 15:26; 2 Cor 8:4; 9:13), and the verb κοινωνέω once (Rom

---

86. Uzukwu, "Poverty and Wealth," 330.
87. Becker, *Paul's Usage of* χάρις, 82.
88. Ibid., 89.
89. Furnish, *II Corinthians*, 401.
90. Kohlenberger III et al., *Exhaustive Concordance*, 535. Outside the Pauline writings, the word appears in Acts 2:42; Heb 13:16; 1 John 1:3, 6–7 (Ogereau, "Jerusalem Collection," 371, n. 58).

15:27).⁹¹ Κοινωνία means communion, with the idea of association, connection, combination, and relationship. It can also mean the act of sharing expressed in community life or participation in action.⁹² The same term designates a tangible symbol of fellowship such as a material gift or contribution (Rom 15:26).⁹³ However, Ogereau rejects this material interpretation. Perhaps the TOB, which translates the clause Μακεδονία καὶ Ἀχαΐα κοινωνίαν τινὰ ποιήσασθαι εἰς τοὺς πτωχοὺς τῶν ἁγίων τῶν ἐν Ἰερουσαλήμ by "la Macédoine et l'Achaïe ont décidé de manifester leur solidarité à l'égard des saints de Jérusalem," is to be preferred. In 2 Corinthians 8:4 it is the idea of participation or sharing in something that is meant.⁹⁴

---

91. In Phil 4:15 Paul commends the Philippians because when he returned from Macedonia, "not one church shared with me in the matter of giving and receiving, except you only" (οὐδεμία μοι ἐκοινώνησεν εἰς λόγον δόσεως καὶ λήμψεως εἰ μὴ ὑμεῖς μόνοι).

92. Danker et al., *Greek-English Lexicon*, 552.

93. Ibid., 553. Ogereau ("Jerusalem Collection," 368–369) contests this interpretation. He points out that the term κοινωνία never has a concrete meaning of financial contribution in ancient sources. He bases his conclusion on Peterman's study of three sets of literary and epigraphic materials (Peterman, "Romans 15:26"). This thorough investigation covers about 25 inscriptions and 120 papyri dated from IV BCE to VI CE, and some other analogous literary constructions from antique writers such as Dionysios of Halicarnassus, Isaeus, Demosthenes, and Plato. Ogereau esteems that these sources probably best reflect "the everyday language of the time." He notes that κοινωνία refers to "sharing in sacrifice," "participation in the *politeia*, festivals or public projects," "marriage relationships," "political alliance," as well as to "professional associations or business partnerships." Ogereau also observes that unlike κοινωνία the noun κοινωνός is frequently used in ancient literature to refer to "political allies, business associates, or the recipients of some benefaction" ("Jerusalem Collection," 370). He concludes that the early Christians in Rome must have understood Paul's view in the sense of "partnership or association with socio-political ramifications, which Paul envisaged between Gentile churches and their Judean counterparts, and which would ultimately manifest itself in the form of a concrete monetary gift" (ibid., 371). He contends that this interpretation could also make sense for 2 Cor 8:4 and 9:13. But Ogereau's confident assertions seem overstretched. First, if κοινωνός was frequently used in a political context, nothing indicates that it was a technical term referring to political partnerships. A fortiori, the word κοινωνία which was employed for different forms of sharing cannot be given a strictly political dimension here as Ogereau does. Ogereau himself concedes that he "cannot be as definite *vis-à-vis* the literary sources" because he has "only conducted a limited and sporadic examination of the 812 instances of the term prior to II CE" documented by the *Thesaurus Linguae Graecae*. Moreover, Ogereau, like Betz (*2 Corinthians 8 and 9*, 46, 124) to whom he refers, does not explain why such a political partnership that he reads in Paul's statement was necessary to realize the collection for Jerusalem. Finally, it is important to bear in mind that one term can be used in different contexts with different perspectives. Thus, a close look at the context is always important. It seems that it is exaggerated to lend to Paul's readers such an extended political view. And above all, we are unable to know how the Roman Christians understood Paul's statement.

94. Witherington III, *Conflict and Community*, 413, n. 9.

Elsewhere Paul talks of the sharing of Christ's sufferings (Phil 3:10), and the participation in the Holy Spirit (2 Cor 13:13).

The implications of the term διακονία in Paul's conceptualization of the collection are far-reaching. The apostle uses it five times in connection with this project (Rom 15:31; 2 Cor 8:4; 9:1, 12, 13). Whereas in Romans 15 Paul employs the term to refer to the whole collection as his undertaking (ἡ διακονία μου), we find it three times in 2 Corinthians with specific qualifications: κοινωνία τῆς διακονίας τῆς εἰς τοὺς ἁγίους (8.4), διακονία τῆς λειτουργίας (9:12), δοκίμα τῆς διακονίας (9:13), and once in the absolute (διακονίας τῆς εἰς τοὺς ἁγίους in 9:1).[95] The noun διακονία derives from the verb διακονέω which means to act as an agent or a go-between for someone, to accomplish specific obligations, to meet somebody's needs or help, to discharge official duties, and to take care of things and people.[96] Paul often uses the term διακονία as a designation of his ministry (Rom 11:13; 1 Cor 3:5; 2 Cor 3:6; 4:1; 5:18; 6:3; 11:8, 23). The same word refers to a single function or a collective term for various functions in a Christian community viewed as the body of Christ (Rom 12:7; 16:1; 1 Cor 16:15).[97] When Paul calls the collection a διακονία (2 Cor 8:4; 9:13), he points out that it should not be viewed "as an external incident but as a true act of love" (2 Cor 9:1, 12; cf. Acts 11:29–30; 12:25), "an essential act of Christian fellowship fulfilled in the service to the Lord."[98] Furthermore, the collection as a service expressed the presence of God's grace in the midst of the contributing churches, and embodied the unity between the Jerusalem Christian community and the Pauline congregations.[99] One may also argue that the efforts which Paul invested in the collection in Corinth reveal his concern for the legitimacy of his apostleship which was contested there.[100]

It is worth noting that the recipients of the collection are designated as ἅγιοι. In the LXX the word ἅγιος and its derivatives translate frequently the

---

95. Panikulam, *Koinonia in the New Testament*, 40.
96. Danker et al., *Greek-English Lexicon*, 229–230.
97. Panikulam, *Koinonia in the New Testament*, 41.
98. Nickle, *Collection*, 109.
99. Joubert, *Paul as Benefactor*, 137.
100. Martin, *2 Corinthians*, 254.

Hebrew stem קדש.[101] In Semitic languages, the root carries in the first place the meaning of consecration, and that of separation in the second place.[102] The root קדש often refers to priest, as in Exodus 30:30 where Moses is commanded to anoint Aaron and his sons, and sanctify them to serve God. The adjective קָדוֹשׁ is used 116 times to refer to God, people, and things (places, times, and objects used in cult). In a priestly perspective, this adjective specifically relates to the people of Israel. The entire community is called to be holy, which always entails "dissociation from unholy matters" (Lev 11:44, 45; 19:2; 20:7, 26; 21:6; Exod 22:30).[103] And it is even called holy (Exod 19:6; Deut 7:6; 14:21; 28:9). This holiness expresses above all an exclusive relationship between God and Israel grounded in the fact that it is God himself who saved this people from the Egyptian bondage. However, the concept of holiness in the Old Testament also contains an ethical dimension.[104] Outside the context of the sanctuary, the term is applied to Elisha, a holy man of God (2 Kgs 4:9); while in Psalms 16:3 and 34:10 it is used in the plural to refer to humans[105] These are in fact the loyal believers among the people of Israel (Isa 4:3; Tob 8:15).[106] The same meaning is found in Psalms of Solomon 17:34. The word occurs in Zechariah 14:5 with a different meaning in relation to the Day of the Lord. In the expression πάντες οἱ ἅγιοι μετ' αὐτοῦ, all the holy ones with him, the term seems to indicate angelic beings. A special meaning of this word emerges in the book of Daniel. In the Aramaic apocalypse in chapter 7, the expression קַדִּישֵׁי עֶלְיוֹנִין, ἅγιοι ὑψίστου, the holy of the Most High, was probably used to designate the loyal believers among the people of Israel as a whole or the faithful from its midst (Dan 7:18, 22, 27).[107] We learn that the evil king wages war against the saints and defeats them, but in the end they are given the kingdom (7:21f). This usage is continued in the Hebrew part of the book of Daniel. We read in 8:24 about the mighty men and

---

101. Auneau, "Sainteté-Théologie biblique," 1043.
102. Ibid.
103. Safrai and Tomson, "Paul's 'Collection'," 162.
104. Evans, *Saints in Christ Jesus*, 15.
105. Safrai and Tomson, "Paul's 'Collection'," 162.
106. Danker et al., *Greek-English Lexicon*, 11.
107. Redditt, *Daniel*, 128.

the people of the saints who are destroyed by the king of Greece. Safrai and Tomson remark that the Danielic terminology is attested in Qumran sources, although it often relates to angelic beings.[108] The same apocalyptic traditions are found in 1 Enoch, whose connections with early Christianity have been established.[109] It appears that in early Judaism the expression the "holy ones" acquired an eschatological meaning to mean the elect who were to inherit the messianic kingdom.[110]

In the New Testament the designation οἱ ἅγιοι, "the saints" is used sixty times in reference to Christians, whereas the participle which is almost its synonym (οἱ ἡγιασμένοι or οἱ ἁγιαζομένοι) appears eight times.[111] It turns out that its usage originated from biblical tradition, because at that time no social group carried this appellation in the Greek-speaking context.[112] Besides ἀδελφοί (brothers [and sisters]), οἱ ἅγιοι is another term applied frequently to the Christians.[113] While ἀδελφοί refers to their relationship to one another, ἅγιοι insists on their newly acquired status before God through Jesus Christ. All in all, the term οἱ ἅγιοι occurs forty times in the Pauline corpus to indicate the members of the early Christian communities.[114] In keeping with Paul's view that a new covenant has been established for all humanity through Jesus (2 Cor 3:7–18; 5:11–21), the church is seen as the eschatological people of God. The early Christians appropriated the Old Testament concept of election applied exclusively to Israel as a people set apart for God (1 Pet 2:9–10). To the Corinthians whose spiritual health was wanting, Paul does not hesitate to write the following in 1 Corinthians 1:2: τῇ ἐκκλησίᾳ τοῦ θεοῦ τῇ οὔσῃ ἐν Κορίνθῳ, ἡγιασμένοις ἐν Χριστῷ Ἰησοῦ, κλητοῖς ἁγίοις (To the Church of God which is at Corinth, to those who are sanctified in Christ Jesus, called to be saints). Paul also speaks of the churches of the saints, ἐκκλησίαι τῶν ἁγίων (1 Cor 14:33). In this

---

108. Safrai and Tomson, "Paul's 'Collection'," 162–163.

109. Ibid., 163. For instance, Jude 14 borrows from 1 En. 1:9 the tradition about the coming of the Lord "with ten million of the holy ones to execute judgement upon all," which echoes Zech 14:5.

110. Evans, *Saints in Christ Jesus*, 27.

111. Ibid., 29.

112. Safrai and Tomson, "Paul's 'Collection'," 161–162.

113. Gorman, "You Shall Be Cruciform," 150.

114. Ibid., 150, n. 12.

larger context of early Christianity, the appellation "the saints" indicated the Christian community in its sacred gathering.[115]

It is remarkable that in 2 Corinthians 8:4 Paul does not explain that the saints are the members of the Jerusalem church. The same occurs in 1 Corinthians 16:1 and 2 Corinthians 9:1, 12. It implies that the Corinthians have already been acquainted with the project and know about the intended receivers of the collection. Therefore, when Paul refers to the Christians in Jerusalem he uses ἅγιοι without clarification because this was not needed. But when he applies this designation to the members of other congregations, he indicates their location (2 Cor 1:1; Phil 1:1 [Col 1:1; Eph 1:1]). Peter H. R. van Houwelingen maintains that the term "the saints," applied to Christian believers in Lydda and Joppa (Acts 9:32, 41), was generally used to refer to the members of the Jerusalem church (Acts 9:13; 26:10; Rom 15:25–26, 31). He indicates that the saints are in fact "sanctified by the Spirit."[116] In other words, the term was initially used to designate the Jerusalem church and Paul deliberately extended it later to Gentile Christian congregations.[117]

> Verses 5–6: καὶ οὐ καθὼς ἠλπίσαμεν ἀλλὰ ἑαυτοὺς ἔδωκαν πρῶτον τῷ κυρίῳ καὶ ἡμῖν διὰ θελήματος θεοῦ ⁶ εἰς τὸ παρακαλέσαι ἡμᾶς Τίτον, ἵνα καθὼς προενήρξατο οὕτως καὶ ἐπιτελέσῃ εἰς ὑμᾶς καὶ τὴν χάριν ταύτην.
>
> and this, not merely as we expected; they gave themselves first to the Lord and, by the will of God, to us, ⁶ so that we might urge Titus that, as he had already made a beginning, so he should also complete this generous undertaking among you.

The Macedonians' contribution to the relief fund for Jerusalem exceeded Paul's expectations in two ways.[118] First, considering the situation of poverty the Macedonians were facing, Paul was surprised by the amount of the contribution they gave. Second, Paul had expected them to give a material gift, but he realized with amazement that they were highly committed

---

115. Safrai and Tomson, "Paul's 'Collection'," 161–165.
116. Houwelingen, "Jerusalem, the Mother Church," 20.
117. Safrai and Tomson, "Paul's 'Collection'," 141, 161, 168.
118. Harris, *Second Epistle*, 568.

to the Lord and to himself as an apostle, Christ's "official emissary."[119] Martin argues that what surpassed Paul's expectations was not the amount of the contribution they may have made. It is rather their self-giving to the Lord and to him, by the will of God.[120] Martin understands that the Macedonians have recognized the nature of Paul's apostleship, and have submitted themselves to the Lord's authority in him. Therefore, πρῶτον is not to be understood in a temporal sense, but as synonymous to ἐν πρώτοις (as of first importance) used in 1 Corinthians 15:3. Betz also thinks that this adverb has no temporal connotation, but "means first in importance," and implies that they gave themselves before Paul asked them, or before they made their contribution.[121] However, I think that it is more natural to maintain both aspects of the adverb (priority in importance and time) in relation to the recipients of the Macedonians' self-giving (i.e. the Lord and Paul). But Thrall argues that the reflexive pronoun ἑαυτούς in an emphatic position suggests that πρῶτον expresses the contrast between the Macedonians' self-dedication to the Lord and their giving contributions to the collection.[122] In any case, what matters here is that their surrender to the Lord Jesus brought them in a close relationship with Paul and his ministry. In doing so, they agreed with the early Christian conviction that God's gift of grace came about by Christ's self-sacrifice.[123] This idea of self-sacrifice is central to Romans 12:1–2 and Philippians 2:17 for instance.[124]

It is highly remarkable that Paul testifies that the Macedonians' dedication to the Lord Christ and to him was by the will of God (διὰ θελήματος θεοῦ), as he does when he talks about his calling to the apostolic ministry.[125]

---

119. Joubert, *Paul as Benefactor*, 137.
120. Martin, *2 Corinthians*, 255.
121. Betz, *2 Corinthians 8 and 9*, 48.
122. Thrall, *Critical and Exegetical Commentary*, 526.
123. Panikulam, *Koinonia in the New Testament*, 50. The wholehearted involvement of the Macedonians in Paul's collection is stressed here by Paul's employment a soteriological formulation (ἑαυτοὺς ἔδωκαν). A similar construction of the verb δίδωμι and the reflexive pronoun is used elsewhere in Paul with reference to the self-giving of Christ (Gal 2:20; Eph 5:25; 1 Tim 2:6; Titus 2:14).
124. Nickle, *Collection*, 105. Nickle esteems that Paul's thought in 2 Cor 8:5 is well understood if this verse is related to v. 2 in which the apostle uses the term ἁπλότης to describe the inner disposition that prompted the Macedonians' contribution to the collection.
125. Martin, *2 Corinthians*, 252.

This self-giving to the Lord cannot refer to the Macedonians' conversion experience because the καὶ ἡμῖν that follows excludes this possibility. Rather, it refers to a certain renewal of commitment to the Lord through a specific task that required their close collaboration with the apostle Paul, namely the facilitation of the collection project among the Macedonian congregations.[126] Martin rightly concludes that 2 Corinthians 8:5 is a central statement in Paul's effort to conceptualize the collection.[127] Paul sees it as a basically theological enterprise. This is substantiated by the striking lack of terms such as ἀργύριον (money) and χρυσίον (coined gold) to qualify it.[128] But J. P. Becker has a different view which is consistent with his refusal to admit that χάρις may have different meanings in the passage we are studying. He says that the recurring use of this term with a demonstrative, thus τὴν χάριν ταύτην (8:6), ταύτῃ τῇ χάριτι (8:7) and τῇ χάριτι ταύτῃ (8:19) indicates that Paul wanted to say that the Corinthians received the same χάρις the Macedonians had received.[129] But it is more consistent to see here Paul's way of terming the collection. Nevertheless, Becker brings some insights here. He rejects the view of some scholars who argue that Paul used the term χάρις for his collection to manipulate by spiritualizing money, a mundane thing. He explains rightly that the apostle is using the most evocative terminology to depict what Becker terms "an ontological reality," which means that when the Macedonians offered "their mundane currency" to the collection; it was turned into "holy currency."[130] This line of interpretation, as Becker notes, is consistent with Paul's depiction of the Philippians' material assistance to him as a sacrifice offered to God,

---

126. Harris, *Second Epistle*, 568.

127. Martin, *2 Corinthians*, 251–253.

128. Hartley, "Financing Paul," 69. Ogereau ("Jerusalem Collection," 363) notes that in 1 Cor 16:1–4 Paul calls his collection a λογεία, a term used to refer to "any kind of voluntary, or compulsory, money collection." Safrai and Tomson ("Paul's 'Collection'," 139) draw on this technical use of the term to state that "Paul is using administrative language to indicate a special campaign." They believe that it entails that Paul's undertaking needs to be distinguished from the general religious duty termed "almsgiving," well attested in the New Testament and subsequent Christian sources, and originates from Jewish employment. Following Mitchell, Ogereau ("Jerusalem Collection," 364) argues that it is when the Corinthians' enthusiasm to give has subsided that Paul termed his collection "a divine privilege or gift, in which they can participate voluntarily and out of love."

129. Becker, *Paul's Usage of* χάρις, 93.

130. Ibid., 208, 206.

which imagery fits the Old Testament cultic offerings. But this association requires caution to avoid both the oversimplification and the overspiritualization of Paul's understanding of Christian giving. Failure to strike this balance would lead one "to rob the act of giving, and the gifts themselves, of their material significance."[131]

Concerning the Macedonians' commitment, Paul also notes that they were dedicated to him (ἑαυτοὺς ἔδωκαν πρῶτον τῷ κυρίῳ καὶ ἡμῖν). This statement leads to the suggestion that Paul considered his own apostolic ministry to be intrinsically connected to God's work among the Macedonian believers.[132] It is worth noting that for Paul the three types of dedication are inseparable: self-dedication to the Lord Jesus, attachment to Paul in his ministry, and the giving of their wealth to the collection.[133] Paul's confidence that Titus was the right person to send to Corinth was not only based on the fact that it was he who had started the collection there, but also and above all because he had managed to bring the Corinthians to repentance from their opposition to Paul and gained their trust and respect (2 Cor 7:5–16).[134] Titus granted Paul's request with enthusiasm (v. 17). He had started (προενήρξατο)[135] the collection in Corinth, and Paul urges him to carry it to completion (ἵνα . . . οὕτως καὶ ἐπιτελέσῃ εἰς ὑμᾶς καὶ τὴν χάριν ταύτην). It is difficult to imagine that Titus started the collection when he delivered the "painful" letter as Witherington maintains.[136] Rather, it is conceivable that he did so shortly after the delivery of 1 Corinthians.[137] Betz situates Titus' activity before the composition of 1 Corinthians, but admits that the gaps present in the text prevent us from giving a certain answer to this question.[138] In any case, it is clear that 2 Corinthians 8:6 anticipates the long discourse on the recommendation of Titus and the

---

131. Ibid., 206.
132. Martin, *2 Corinthians*, 252.
133. Talbert, "Money Management," 363.
134. Harris, *Second Epistle*, 570.
135. Ibid., 570. This verb is used only in this verse and in v. 10 in the New Testament. It is totally absent from pre-Christian Greek including the LXX, and means to "make a beginning beforehand." It indicates that Titus had started the collection before the time Paul was writing 2 Cor, and more specifically the previous year (ἀπὸ πέρυσι) in v. 10.
136. Witherington III, *Conflict and Community*, 332.
137. Harris, *Second Epistle*, 571.
138. Betz, *2 Corinthians 8 and 9*, 55.

delegates of the churches that Paul is sending to Corinth for the sake of the collection (8:16–24). By sending Titus to resume the collection, Paul carefully makes it clear that he is not personally handling money in order not to lay himself open to his detractors' criticism.[139]

3.2 The Corinthians Exhorted to Complete the Collection (2 Cor 8:7–12)

Verse 7: Ἀλλ' ὥσπερ ἐν παντὶ περισσεύετε, πίστει καὶ λόγῳ καὶ γνώσει καὶ πάσῃ σπουδῇ καὶ τῇ ἐξ ἡμῶν ἐν ὑμῖν ἀγάπῃ, ἵνα καὶ ἐν ταύτῃ τῇ χάριτι περισσεύητε.

Now as you excel in everything – in faith, in speech, in knowledge, in utmost eagerness, and in our love for you – so we want you to excel also in this generous undertaking.

Here Paul touches on the point about which the Corinthians are passionate: their excellence in spiritual matters. As in 8:2 the verb περισσεύειν, used intransitively, means: to abound, to be in abundance.[140] It is part of Paul's favorite vocabulary. Among its thirty-nine occurrences in the New Testament, twenty-seven are found in Paul's letters. Although it may have been the claim of the Corinthians that they had abounded in faith (ἐν πίστει),[141] speech (ἐν λόγῳ), knowledge (ἐν γνώσει), zeal (ἐν σπουδῇ) and love (ἐν ἀγάπῃ),[142] Paul does not discuss this.[143] In 1 Corinthians 1:5 he agrees with them about their spiritual accomplishments. Paul writes that in Christ they have been enriched in everything, this being demonstrated through their power of speech and knowledge (ὅτι ἐν παντὶ ἐπλουτίσθητε ἐν αὐτῷ, ἐν παντὶ λόγῳ καὶ πάσῃ γνώσει). In Paul λόγος means preaching,

---

139. Witherington III, *Conflict and Community*, 414.
140. Kohlenberger III et al., *Exhaustive Concordance*, 791.
141. Harris, *Second Epistle*, 574. Harris correctly understands πίστις as referring to "personal trust in the Lord," in other words saving faith, and not to the spiritual gift to perform miracles (1 Cor 12:9–10; 13:2). Martin (*2 Corinthians*, 262) agrees with this interpretation, whereas Betz (*2 Corinthians 8 and 9*, 57) argues that the term indicates faithfulness in general, regarded as a virtue in Greek society.
142. Harris, *Second Epistle*, 574.
143. Martin, *2 Corinthians*, 261.

eloquence, word, and the ability to preach (1 Thess 1:5, 6; 2:13; 2 Thess 3:14; 1 Cor 1:15, 18; 2:4; 15:2; 2 Cor 1:18; 8:7; 11:6; Rom 15:18; etc.).[144]

The concept of knowledge used by Paul is known in the Greek world and in Judaism. In secular literature, the verb γινώσκειν from which the noun γνῶσις derives, carries a range of meanings:[145] to understand, perceive by senses, to get personal acquaintance, reflect through a logical process. Therefore, knowledge can be existential or theoretical; while its object can be either a concrete object or an abstract idea. In the LXX, the verb γινώσκειν and its cognates render the word group of the Hebrew root יָדַע which has a wide variety of meanings as well.[146] It can mean: to notice, experience, observe (Gen 3:7; 41:31); to distinguish between; to know through a learning process (Prov 30:3); to have familiarity with a person or thing (Prov 2:6; Eccl 8:17); to get the ability to do things (Isa 47:11); to have a personal relationship with somebody (Deut 34:10). The knowledge of God fits in the latter meaning and is always connected to God's self-revelation.

The word γνῶσις is found sixteen times in 1 and 2 Corinthians.[147] Together with the term λόγος (speech, eloquence) they form a crucial claim made by the Corinthians. When Paul states that the Corinthians have been enriched in their knowledge, he remains in the line of Judaism that claims that the knowledge of God can be attained thanks to his revelation. This is confirmed by the fact that Paul adds that the testimony of Christ had been confirmed among the Corinthians and that they consequently acquired spiritual gifts as they earnestly waited for the coming of the Lord Jesus (1 Cor 1:6–7). As in 1 Corinthians 8:1 this knowledge indicates that one knows "the true being of God."[148] But if such knowledge leads one to be puffed up and disregard the weak who do not have it, it must be rejected because it lacks love (1 Cor 8:7–9).

As for the excellence in love, I have discussed the problem of textual criticism posed by this verse. I have made my choice for ἐξ ἡμῶν ἐν ὑμῖν

---

144. Carrez, *La deuxième épitre*, 182.
145. Brown, *New International Dictionary*, 392.
146. Ibid., 395.
147. Martin, *2 Corinthians*, 262.
148. Brown, *New International Dictionary*, 403.

ἀγάπη. Paul is alluding to "the Corinthians' love for Christ and for fellow believers" which Paul's preaching of the gospel has produced in their lives[149] On the basis of all the spiritual qualities in which the Corinthians have an excellent ranking, Paul appeals for a similar performance in the grace of giving. In other words, Paul wants the Corinthians to show that their love is really practical. This means their participation in the collection which, as in the previous verse, is presented as a "generous undertaking" (NRSV), "gracious deed," or "benefaction."[150]

> Verse 8: Οὐ κατ' ἐπιταγὴν λέγω ἀλλὰ διὰ τῆς ἑτέρων σπουδῆς καὶ τὸ τῆς ὑμετέρας ἀγάπης γνήσιον δοκιμάζων.
>
> I do not say this as a command, but I am testing the genuineness of your love against the earnestness of others.

Paul continues his *parenesis* by explaining his approach in dealing with the Corinthians concerning the collection. He says that he is not giving an injunction as an apostle. In 8:10 he indicates that he is giving an advice (γνώμην) to complete the collection. The question to be raised here is why Paul refrains from giving a command in this matter. One possible answer would be that it would have compromised the principle of the voluntary nature of Christian giving (8:3; 9:5, 7), and exposed Paul to criticism of being domineering (1:24). As a consequence, the motivation of the collection as a gift would have raised suspicions among the Corinthians. Betz, who sees in 2 Corinthians 8:1–15 a piece of deliberative rhetoric, argues that Paul complies with rhetorical convention in which commands are excluded. Moreover, following the practice of fundraising of his times, Paul knew that "a collection of this sort depends by nature on the voluntary cooperation of the contributors."[151] But it is also possible to think that Paul's tactically chosen strategy reflects his awareness of the precarious ground on which he was operating. The fresh reconciliation achieved required of him

---

149. Harris, *Second Epistle*, 574. The phrase τῇ ἐξ ἡμῶν ἐν ὑμῖν ἀγάπῃ is not easy to translate. Since the preposition ἐκ indicates origin, and ἐν location, it means "the love that derived from us and now resides in you."

150. Thrall, *2 Corinthians*, vol. 2, 530.

151. Betz, *2 Corinthians 8 and 9*, 59.

much prudence.¹⁵² Instead of commanding, Paul invokes the Macedonians' example to push the Corinthians to emulate that experience.¹⁵³ In so doing they will demonstrate the genuineness of their love (τὸ τῆς ὑμετέρας ἀγάπης γνήσιον δοκιμάζων).¹⁵⁴ The Macedonians' commitment to the Lord and to Paul's ministry has convinced him of the genuineness of their love (8:2–5). Therefore, the apostle sets it as a benchmark, and wants the Corinthians to prove that they "share the same quality, both of love and zeal" as claimed in 7:7, 12.¹⁵⁵ And this will be demonstrated only by the completion of the collection. Against Betz who argues that Paul is promoting a contest among rivals,¹⁵⁶ Harris rightly points out that the apostle is "encouraging friendly imitation among equals."¹⁵⁷ In 1 Corinthians 13 Paul has already spelled out the nature of Christian love. He indicated that love must be the motivation of any Christian activity. Even the distribution of one's possessions, however admirable this might be, loses its value once it is not done out of love (v. 3). Although I do not follow the rhetorical approach in this study, Witherington's remark is to the point. He maintains that Paul uses comparison to implicitly accuse or criticize his readers. Thus, Paul suggests that unlike their fellows in Macedonia, "the Corinthians have

---

152. Martin, *2 Corinthians*, 262. As in 1 Cor 7:6, 26 Paul resorts to the same stylistic strategy, the "permissive style" as Martin says.

153. In other words, Paul says that he refrains from commanding, "but he is using rhetoric to gently twist their arms, saying that this is a matter of testing *their* eagerness and love . . . as the painful letter has tested their genuineness" (Witherington III, *Conflict and Community*, 420).

154. Harris, *Second Epistle*, 576. The adjective γνήσιος initially referred to "the natural or legitimate son as opposed to the adopted or illegitimate." Figuratively, it means "regular," "genuine." As for the verb δοκιμαζείν, it carries the idea of putting to proof, approving by test, discovering to be appropriate through examination; with the expectation that the result will be positive.

155. Martin, *2 Corinthians*, 262.

156. Betz, *2 Corinthians 8 and 9*, 48–49. Joubert (*Paul as Benefactor*, 174) holds the same line of interpretation. Consistent with his attempt to interpret Paul's collection in the framework of social exchange, he argues that the agonistic culture of the ancient Mediterranean informed Paul's rhetoric in this passage: "Paul thus deliberately creates an *implicit rivalry* between these two beneficiaries in the reciprocal relationship with Jerusalem by emphasizing that the Macedonians did *everything* according to the book. They received God's grace, and in response, gave themselves to him and to Paul. The Macedonians then contributed to the collection beyond their material means. This placed them in the favourable position as would-be benefactors of Jerusalem."

157. Harris, *Second Epistle*, 577.

been recalcitrant."[158] Paul may then be trying to use the Corinthians' sense of self-respect as an internal motivation to complete the collection.

> Verse 9: γινώσκετε γὰρ τὴν χάριν τοῦ κυρίου ἡμῶν Ἰησοῦ Χριστοῦ, ὅτι δι' ὑμᾶς ἐπτώχευσεν πλούσιος ὤν, ἵνα ὑμεῖς τῇ ἐκείνου πτωχείᾳ πλουτήσητε.

> For you know the generous act of our Lord Jesus Christ, that though[159] he was rich, yet for your sakes he became poor, so that by his poverty you might become rich.

The conjunction γάρ introduces the motivation for the Corinthians to resume the fundraising for the poor believers in Jerusalem. Paul has already mentioned the Macedonians' zeal and the amount of material assistance they have gathered which exceeded his expectations in view of

---

158. Witherington III, *Conflict and Community*, 412.

159. An alternative to the translation of the participle ὤν has been suggested (Barclay, "Because He Was Rich," 338–344). Barclay notes that the translation of ὤν in a concessive way "though he was rich" does not express the paradox that 2 Cor 8–9 contains. He thus sets out to read 2 Cor 8:9 in a way that reflects a paradox "that relates its economic metaphor to the financial terms of its context, and that draws a tight and close parallel between the Christ-event and the expected behavior of believers, both as expressions of one and the same χάρις" (ibid., 338). He explains that the participle ὤν should be read in a causative way rather than in a concessive sense. Thus, the phrase πλούσιος ὤν would be rendered "because he was rich." Barclay observes that the same reading is also possible in some passages where it is commonly given a causal meaning such as in 1 Cor 9:19 and; Phil 2:6 (ibid., 339). In the case of 2 Cor 8:9 he writes the following: "it was precisely because of his wealth and as an expression of it, that Christ made himself poor" (ibid., 340). Barclay argues that Christ's wealth consists in his generosity and not in what he possessed. He shows that this agrees with what is said about the Macedonians whose wealth consisted in their ἁπλότης, generosity as the result of χάρις and not in what they possessed. In the same vein, Christ's χάρις manifested his wealth through his poverty (i.e. his incarnation which involved "utter humiliation, vulnerability and weakness all the way to the cross" [ibid., 341]). However, Barclay admits that Paul also uses the enrichment metaphor in different ways, not only with a paradoxical sense as presented above. The apostle says that the Corinthians are also made rich with a variety of charismata (1 Cor 1:4–7) and that they have already been enriched (1 Cor 4:8). In 2 Cor 6:10 Paul claims that he makes many rich; which clause can denote different things. Barclay concludes that although both the concessive and the causal senses of the participle ὤν are grammatically possible and can draw support from parallel expressions elsewhere in the Pauline writings, "the context of 2 Cor 8–9, with its consistently paradoxical uses of the term 'wealth', suggests that the better reading of the verse would be to take the participle as causal, rather than concessive" (ibid., 343). In my view, Barclay's analysis is insightful but is not convincing in some respects. To limit the Corinthians' enrichment in 2 Cor 8–9 to generosity since that is what is required of them in the context of the collection is somehow superficial (ibid., 343). Moreover, Barclay's interpretation does not clarify the difference between Christ's wealth (generosity) and his poverty (incarnation).

their financial situation (vv. 1–5, 8). The apostle has also praised the Corinthians' initial enthusiasm in their participation in the collection, and their excellence in spiritual matters (v. 7). In verse 9 Paul reaches the peak of his motivation to prompt the action of his Corinthian converts (i.e. Christ's voluntary self-giving for the benefit of others).[160] The Corinthians shared with Paul this knowledge about God's salvation in Christ, summarized in "the Christological and soteriological concept of grace."[161] The Corinthians' knowledge of this doctrine is expressed by the indicative present γινώσκετε (you know). The latter cannot be an imperative because of γάρ which follows it; otherwise we would expect οὖν.[162] In 8:1 Paul has also appealed to the Corinthians' knowledge to introduce his *parenesis* discourse based on the Macedonians' example.

In the phrase γινώσκετε γὰρ τὴν χάριν τοῦ κυρίου we have a subjective genitive. It emphasizes the nature and attitude of Christ, and not the idea of possession.[163] In this verse, χάρις holds "the theological weight of a divine attribute, namely, love in action, expressed on sinners and reaching out to help the undeserving."[164] Thus, the Lord's action can be correctly called a "generous act" (NRSV). The example of Christ is introduced here as "the ultimate incentive for wholehearted participation, the supreme and purest motivation" for the collection.[165] The generous act of Jesus is manifested in his self-giving: ὅτι δι' ὑμᾶς ἐπτώχευσεν πλούσιος ὤν, ἵνα ὑμεῖς τῇ ἐκείνου πτωχείᾳ πλουτήσητε. The parallelism between the χάρις τοῦ θεοῦ which was displayed in the generosity of the Macedonians (v. 1) and their self-giving (v. 4), and the χάρις τοῦ κυρίου (Χριστοῦ) demonstrated in his self-impoverishment is striking. The enrichment of the Corinthians is spiritual in nature and not material, and consists in their full receiving of God's salvation – that is, the forgiveness of sins (5:19), reconciliation with God (5:18), and the reception of the Spirit (1:22; 5:5).[166] This spiritual

---

160. Harris, *Second Epistle*, 578.
161. Betz, *2 Corinthians 8 and 9*, 61.
162. Harris, *Second Epistle*, 578.
163. Ibid.
164. Martin, *2 Corinthians*, 263.
165. Harris, *Second Epistle*, 577.
166. Ibid., 579. However, Barclay ("Because He Was Rich," 342) contends that Christ's enrichment of the Corinthians does not entail that they acquire spiritual or material

meaning of the wealth acquired by the Corinthians may indicate that what is said about Christ (ἐπτώχευσεν[167] πλούσιος ὤν) has the same connotation. It refers to "the plenitude of divinity in Christ."[168] For J. P. Becker, Paul indicates in 2 Corinthians 8:9 that Christ's χάρις "can be accumulated unto wealth, and it can be spent unto poverty – *actual* wealth and *actual* poverty."[169] He concludes that "Paul is calling the Corinthians to risk financial impoverishment – a circumstance which would involve the actual forfeiture of precious resources."[170] Becker explains that the Lord's impoverishment in χάρις could have the significance to the Lord that Paul implies only if χάρις is "finite and precious"; and he thinks it is so in the apostle's mind.[171] This reading is questionable in various respects. Paul does not say that Christ's impoverishement consisted in a kind of diminution of his χάρις. Futhermore, the view that Paul is calling the Corinthians to financial impoverishment is contradicted by what he explicitly says in 8:13 that he does not "mean that there should be relief for others and pressure on you." But Becker makes an important point about the incarnation of Christ which can be seen as an indirect critique of the Corinthians who claim to be spiritual (1 Cor 14).[172] It is through his incarnation, an "aromatic" ministry as Becker says, that Christ administered his χάρις to humans. This ministry culminated in his passion through which he ultimately glorified God and enriched his disciples (Phil 2:6–11; 2 Cor 8:9). The imitation of Christ for the Corinthians, says Becker, would consist in passing to action, the very thing they can achieve only "somatically."[173]

---

goods, but that like Christ they become rich in generosity. He finds that the two ἵνα clauses in 8:7 and 9:8 point to this meaning since in both cases the ultimate goal of enrichment or abundance is not that the believers may increase possessions, but that they may give more.

167. The verb πτωχεύω which is found six times in the LXX is a *hapax legomenon* in the New Testament (Panikulam, *Koinonia in the New Testament*, 52). The term πλοῦτος and its derivatives occur often in Paul and are used to denote glory (Rom 9:23; Eph 1:16), goodness (Rom 2:4), mercy (Eph 2:4), or divine grace.

168. Panikulam, *Koinonia in the New Testament*, 52.

169. Becker, *Paul's Usage of* χάρις, 233–234.

170. Ibid., 223–224.

171. Ibid., 224.

172. Ibid., 231–232.

173. Ibid., 232. But Becker (ibid., 235) exaggerates when he argues that if 2 Cor 8:9 is taken on its own – without interpreting it in light of Phil 2:6–11 – although even Becker has not succeeded in doing so – Paul's appeal would probably appear to have no religious or

By Jesus's self-impoverishment (ἐπτώχευσεν πλούσιος ὤν),[174] some think that Paul is talking of Jesus's taking on "the specific socioeconomic state of poverty" despite his spiritual riches.[175] Betz sees in this verse only an allusion to "Christ's sacrifice."[176] For Carrez, the phrase refers to Christ's incarnation and earthly life as a whole,[177] the "Christ's event" in Barclay's words.[178] This view is defensible because the aorist of stative verbs is generally ingressive (pointing to the act of entering that state), although it can also be constative. Therefore, ἐπτώχευσεν comprehends "Christ's incarnation, life, and death-resurrection in a single glance as "becoming poor," as "self-impoverishment" with πτωχεία referring to that same sequence of events as 'poverty'."[179] The richness and poverty of Christ do not denote material wealth and destitution but the renunciation of heavenly glory to assume the human condition. In 2 Corinthians 6:10 Paul demonstrates how Christ's example has impacted on his own life and ministry[180]: ὡς πτωχοὶ πολλοὺς δὲ πλουτίζοντες, (as poor, yet making many rich). Paul chose to live as a poor person, working with his hands for subsistence (1 Cor 4:11; Phil 4:11–12; 2 Cor 11:9; 1 Thess 2:9; 2 Thess 3:7–8; Acts 18:3; 20:34). However, through his ministry the Corinthians have been enriched (1 Cor 1:5). As we read in Ephesians 3:8, the apostle was aware that "this grace was given, that I should preach among the Gentiles the unsearchable riches of Christ." Ultimately, it is vital to realize that Paul's point is not to be sought in the Lord's economic status, but in Christ's self-giving

---

theological overtones. He contends that Paul, "perhaps even crudely, apotheosizes giving and monetizes χάρις." Consequently, Becker adds, instead of calling the Corinthians to be Christ-like in altruism, he may be exhorting them to be Christ-like in having the propensity to work.

174. The belief of the early church in the pre-existent Christ, who deliberately accepted self-debasement, is present in Phil 2:6–11 and Heb 10:5–7. But J. D. G. Dunn rejects the interpretation of 2 Cor 8:9 and these two passages in this line: Dunn, *Christology in the Making*, 122–135.

175. Witherington III, *Conflict and Community*, 420.

176. Betz, *2 Corinthians 8 and 9*, 47.

177. Carrez, *La deuxième épitre*, 183.

178. Barclay, "Because He Was Rich," 331.

179. Harris, *Second Epistle*, 580. This interpretation agrees with Paul's view that salvation is brought about by the death and resurrection of Jesus (Rom 5:10; Gal 6:14). It is noticeable that the point made in 2 Cor 8:9 is broader than John 1:14 (incarnation itself) and Phil 2:7 (incarnation, life, and exaltation of Christ in vv. 9–11).

180. Ibid., 484–485.

for the benefit of the believers, in this case the Corinthians.[181] Although Barclay does not defend the incarnational interpretation of Christ's becoming poor in 2 Corinthians 8:9, he makes an important point concerning the soteriological meaning of the event. In his view, it implies Christ's engaging in "a relationship in which his generosity is expressed in what he shared, and not only in what he gave up or gave away."[182] As noted earlier, Barclay sees that what Christ shares with the Corinthians is his generosity.

However, James D. G. Dunn argues that Jesus's richness is "his communion with God," whereas his poverty refers to "his desolation on the cross" (Mark 15:34).[183] He concludes that it is more appropriate to see in 2 Corinthians 8:9 a variation of Adam Christology. He holds that the incarnational interpretation of this verse does not fit in with Paul's theology because whenever the apostle uses Adam language, he refers to Jesus' resurrection.[184] In Dunn's view, the contrast between the first and the last Adam resides in the fact that the first ended his adventure in death, a return to the dust out of which he had been made; whereas the last (Christ) defeated death through his resurrection. But both stand as heads of a long line of descendants whose destiny follows the footprints of the prototype.

Nonetheless, the fact that Paul describes Christ's work in terms of the last Adam – and emphasizes that he came after the first and earthly Adam (1 Cor 15:45–46; Rom 5:12–19) – does not preclude him from firmly stating that "there is one God, the Father, of whom are all things, and we for Him; and one Lord Jesus Christ, through whom are all things, and through whom we live" (1 Cor 8:6). Although it is not possible to discuss all the Pauline texts studied by Roukema which argue for Paul's belief in the pre-existence of Jesus Christ, his conclusion at this juncture is convincing. When Paul associates Jesus with the creation of the world, he surmises his pre-existence. Moreover, the identification of Christ with the rock from which the Israelites drank their "spiritual drink" (1 Cor 10:4)

---

181. Martin, *2 Corinthians*, 263–264.
182. Barclay, "Because He Was Rich," 432.
183. Dunn, *Christology in the Making*, 122. Phil 2:6–11 and Heb 10:5–7, which are seen by many as pointing to the early church belief in the pre-existent Christ, who deliberately accepted self-debasement, are equally thought to reflect different stages in the development of the Adam Christology.
184. Ibid., 107–108.

indicates that Jesus was believed to be pre-existently traveling with this people.[185] It turns out that there is no surprise that in 2 Corinthians 8:9 Paul's reference to Christ's becoming poor denotes his view of the incarnation of the pre-existent Christ. Since Paul does not explain this belief, we can assume that he takes for granted the fact that his readers know it well. This is more important if we see how for instance he discusses at length the traditional doctrine of the resurrection of the dead in 1 Corinthians 15. When this point of doctrine, which was accepted at an early stage by the first Christians, became problematic at Corinth, Paul dealt with it as an urgent and essential issue for the Christian faith.

By this reference to Christ's self-giving, Paul is not urging the Corinthians to impoverish themselves in order to enrich the poor in Jerusalem, nor is he suggesting that they should lead an ascetic life.[186] Rather, he encourages the Corinthians to emulate the example of "selflessness of the Lord"[187] displayed by the Macedonians, and which reflects God's generosity.[188] This christological example points out "the close connection between Christology and ethics with respect to the Jerusalem collection."[189] Following Betz,[190] Perkins says that unlike the Jewish temple tax and other religious offerings at a worship place, Paul's collection is not meant to support cultic activities. Rather, it turns out "to be a new venture whose orientation is social, a voluntary gift of charity by the Gentile churches"[191] for the sake of their fellow Christians in Jerusalem. Besides its connection with God's grace, which makes it a religious enterprise, Paul's collection displays another religious dimension in its reference to Christ's example.[192] By referring to the Macedonians' and Christ's selflessness, Paul invites the reader to realize that Christian giving focuses on the welfare of others "without any malevolent and selfish intent,"[193] and thus presents his collection as a critique of the

---

185. Roukema, *Jesus, Gnosis and Dogma*, 22.
186. Harris, *Second Epistle*, 580–581.
187. Nickle, *Collection*, 120.
188. Harris, *Second Epistle*, 581.
189. Downs, *Offering of the Gentiles*, 135.
190. Betz, *Galatians*, 102.
191. Perkins, "Taxes," 193.
192. Ibid., 194.
193. Kamalakar Jayakumar, "System of Equality," 250.

selfish practices of patronage and benefaction within Greco-Roman society. For J. P. Becker, instead of "burdening the Corinthians with Christ's self-sacrifice," Paul presents to them a sort of incentive "assuring them that their investment of χάρις will pay dividends in kind with those which Christ reaped from his investment (9:10–11)."[194] In his view, the same argument undergirds Philippians 2:6–11. However, it appears unwarranted here to apply this commercial analogy to Paul's characterization of Christ's self-giving. It is as if Christ calculated beforehand the benefits of his undertaking; which seems not to be Paul's idea in his treatment of the collection. Perhaps Harrison is right that Paul introduced Jesus's example as an alternative model of beneficence within the Christian communities "to eliminate inevitable tensions and misunderstandings."[195] Such a climate was promoted by the rampant culture of public benefaction, characteristic of human and divine relationships in the Mediterranean basin of Paul's time, which went with rivalry, competition and the expectation of returns in material form or social recognition. In fact, Paul proved to be innovative and counteractive as he came up with the idea that divine χάρις instigates human benevolence; which view was quite "unusual in Greco-Roman religion."[196]

> Verse 10: καὶ γνώμην ἐν τούτῳ δίδωμι· τοῦτο γὰρ ὑμῖν συμφέρει, οἵτινες οὐ μόνον τὸ ποιῆσαι ἀλλὰ καὶ τὸ θέλειν προενήρξασθε ἀπὸ πέρυσι
>
> And in this matter I am giving my advice: it is appropriate for you who began last year not only to do something but even to desire to do something.

As in verse 8 where Paul refrained from prescribing what the Corinthians ought to do, he now indicates that he just wants to give them advice. In fact, the motivation *par excellence* given in verse 9 (i.e. the example of Christ's self-giving), makes commands unnecessary in this matter.[197] By reminding the Corinthians that they were not only the first to give some contribution

---

194. Becker, *Paul's Usage of* χάρις, 106.
195. Harrison, *Paul's Language of Grace*, 255.
196. Ibid., 285. Harrison admits that philosophers could speak of humans imitating the benevolence of the gods but notes that this is different from Paul's depiction of God's grace and its effect.
197. Harris, *Second Epistle*, 581.

but also to decide to participate in the project (οἵτινες οὐ μόνον τὸ ποιῆσαι ἀλλὰ καὶ τὸ θέλειν προενήρξασθε ἀπὸ πέρυσι), Paul compels them to engage in a sort of self-assessment. In 1 Corinthians 16:1–4 it is probable that they asked Paul about the collection, and the apostle advised them to follow the instructions he had given to the churches in Galatia. The Corinthians started to implement it, but their work came to a halt. This was most likely due to the strong influence of radical Jewish Christians on the Corinthian congregation since they had challenged Paul's authority as an apostle.[198] It is possible that the temporal indication (ἀπὸ πέρυσι) refers back to the Corinthians' initiative mentioned in 1 Corinthians 16:1–4.[199] Paul's tact should be noticed here. He does not even mention the possible reasons for the interruption of the collection, but leaves the Corinthians to think about it and decide accordingly. Is it possible that Paul may be avoiding raising issues that could revive the tensions between him and the Corinthians? This is possible given that their reconciliation has been recently achieved and the situation is still fragile. Paul refrains from any authoritarian attitude towards this congregation. But even so, once reminded of the earlier special position they enjoyed in the promotion of the collection (προενήρξασθε), the Corinthians can hardly remain indifferent, lest they agree to drag behind others. They were the first both to show their intent to participate in the collection and to start its implementation: οὐ μόνον τὸ ποιῆσαι ἀλλὰ καὶ τὸ θέλειν προενήρξασθε ἀπὸ πέρυσι.

> Verse 11: νυνὶ δὲ καὶ τὸ ποιῆσαι ἐπιτελέσατε, ὅπως[200] καθάπερ ἡ προθυμία τοῦ θέλειν, οὕτως καὶ τὸ ἐπιτελέσαι ἐκ τοῦ ἔχειν.
>
> Now finish doing it, so that your eagerness may be matched by completing it according to your means.

At this point Paul draws a logical conclusion from the statement of verse 10. He seems to tell the Corinthians that it does not make sense to be the first to decide to participate in the project and even begin to implement it,

---

198. Safrai and Tomson, "Paul's 'Collection'," 148, 161.

199. Carrez, *La deuxième épitre*, 184. The same expression is used in 2 Cor 9:2. The identification of the time indicated by this expression depends on the reconstruction of Paul's correspondence with the Corinthians.

200. Harris, *Second Epistle*, 584. After ὅπως the subjunctive of εἰμί or γίνομαι is implied.

but fail to complete it.[201] Paul argues that there should be a correspondence between the Corinthians' completion of the collection project and their initial eagerness to participate in it. In keeping with their ambition for excellence, the Corinthians would logically bring to completion this collection. In this verse Paul uses two forms of the verb ἐπιτελέω, which he has already used in verse 6 about Titus's efforts in the collection, to express his appeal to the Corinthians to complete their offering. We have an imperative (τὸ ποιῆσαι ἐπιτελέσατε)[202] and an articular infinitive (τὸ ἐπιτελέσαι).

Concerning individual contribution to the collection, Paul adds an important specification: one must give according to what one possesses (ἐκ τοῦ ἔχειν).[203] In doing so, he gives room to personal judgement in the subject matter. Worth noting is Paul's use of the word προθυμία to express the necessity to complete this act of generosity. Among the five times the term occurs in the New Testament, four are found in 2 Corinthians in relation to the collection (8:11, 12, 19; 9:2). The word means an "exceptional interest in being of service, willingness, readiness, goodwill."[204] Acts 17:11 uses it in the sense of zeal. Applied to the Corinthians (2 Cor 8:11, 12; 9:2), it emphasizes their eager desire which is beyond a simple agreement to the collection project. By emphasizing that the Corinthians should each give according to their own means, and alluding to their original eagerness to participate in the collection, Paul tactically tries to persuade them to actively and cheerfully complete it. Once again, the apostle's statement demonstrates that he is aware of the sensitiveness of the situation in the Corinthian congregation. He does not want to appear to be taking advantage of the fresh repentance of his converts from their opposition to him (7:9, 11).[205]

> Verse 12: εἰ γὰρ ἡ προθυμία πρόκειται, καθὸ ἐὰν ἔχῃ εὐπρόσδεκτος, οὐ καθὸ οὐκ ἔχει.

---

201. Carrez, *La deuxième épitre*, 184.

202. This is the only formal imperative used by Paul in 2 Cor 8–9.

203. Betz, *2 Corinthians 8 and 9*, 37, 65. The expression is found only here in the New Testament and can mean "out of what you have," or "in proportion to what you possess." The preposition ἐκ with the meaning "in accordance with" is known in Greek.

204. Danker et al., *Greek-English Lexicon*, 870.

205. Martin, *2 Corinthians*, 265.

> For if the eagerness is there, the gift is acceptable according to what one has – not according to what one does not have.

Paul continues his advice as to how to contribute by showing that the value of the contribution is not to be sought in the amount given. He wants the Corinthians to understand that the willingness and giving in proportion to one's wealth remain the two valid criteria for the gift to be acceptable (εὐπρόσδεκτος).[206] And here Paul has certainly in mind the idea that it is God who evaluates one's work.[207] Paul sees that there may be a temptation to be driven by enthusiasm and give what is beyond one's means, or that one may undertake to borrow money in order to give a contribution.[208] It is even possible that out of enthusiasm or misreading of Paul's praise for the Macedonians, one may decide to contribute to the collection at the expense of some other crucial duties such as taking care of one's family.[209] This is why he insists on spelling out the wrong interpretation of the matter that must be prevented: οὐ καθὸ οὐκ ἔχει. In this case he wants the Corinthians not to misunderstand his previous mention of the Macedonians' example, as if he was expecting them to give beyond their means (8:1–5, 8, 10).[210] It is quite clear that Paul remains consistent with

---

206. Harris, *Second Epistle*, 585–586. Betz (*2 Corinthians 8 and 9*, 66) observes that in Antiquity it was a rule that the sacrificial gift had to be proportionate to one's wealth in order to be acceptable to the deity. In this, Paul conformed to the religious thought prevailing in his times.

207. Cf. 1 Pet 2:5; 1:17. However, in Rom 15:31 Paul is concerned that his collection should be acceptable to the Christians in Jerusalem.

208. Witherington III, *Conflict and Community*, 421.

209. *La Bible Vie nouvelle: Avec notes d'étude* makes an interesting actualizing comment on 2 Cor 8:12. It explains that the sense of sacrifice expected from Christians when they practice charity does not mean that they have to sacrifice the rights of those who are under their care. Rather, it requires a sense of duty on the part of the giver: "Pratiquer la libéralité dans un esprit de sacrifice requiert un certain sens des responsabilités. Nous sommes appelés à nous montrer généreux, mais pas en ignorant les besoins fondamentaux de ceux dont nous avons la charge. Donnons d'une manière qui implique des sacrifices pour nous, mais sans priver notre famille du soutien financier que nous lui devons": *La Bible Vie nouvelle*. In a different context but related to sacral giving, the gospels have preserved a tradition in which Jesus is remembered to have warned about the practice of declaring one's property as a gift consecrated to God, κορβᾶν, as a strategy for the owner to evade responsibilities towards parents (Mark 7:11-13). Once the property was declared κορβᾶν, the owner could not use it to take care of parents in their old age. Jesus condemned this pernicious strategy to use a religious practice as a pretext to violate God's commandment to honor one's parents (Gaertner, "Corban," 279).

210. Harris, *Second Epistle*, 585.

his earlier practical advice in 1 Corinthians 16:2 in which he indicated that the Corinthians' donations had to be set aside on a weekly basis and in proportion to one's earnings.

3.3 The Purpose of the Collection (2 Cor 8:13–15)

> Verses 13–14: οὐ γὰρ ἵνα ἄλλοις ἄνεσις, ὑμῖν θλῖψις, ἀλλ᾽ ἐξ ἰσότητος· ¹⁴ἐν τῷ νῦν καιρῷ τὸ ὑμῶν περίσσευμα εἰς τὸ ἐκείνων ὑστέρημα, ἵνα καὶ τὸ ἐκείνων περίσσευμα γένηται εἰς τὸ ὑμῶν ὑστέρημα, ὅπως γένηται ἰσότης,
>
> I do not mean that there should be relief for others and pressure on you, but it is a question of a fair balance between ¹⁴your present abundance and their need, so that their abundance may be for your need, in order that there may be a fair balance.

After having indicated the right way to determine the amount of contribution to give (i.e. according to what one has and out of willingness), Paul explains the purpose of the collection. In a negative statement, he first says what the collection is not designed for: οὐ γὰρ ἵνα ἄλλοις ἄνεσις, ὑμῖν θλῖψις. If the participation in the collection is not a well-matured action on the part of the giver, it may result in a disaster whereby the giver becomes vulnerable. The word θλῖψις indicates here that one may find oneself in financial hardships accompanied by sorrow and regret, instead of feeling joy and fulfillment at the work done. Second, Paul uses a positive statement to show the purpose of his collection: ἀλλ᾽ ἐξ ἰσότητος, as a matter of a fair balance or equality. The concept of ἰσότης was used in different domains in ancient Greece: mathematics, law, philosophy, and politics. It was a principle regulating not only "unity and solidarity in the state,"[211] but also interpersonal dealings.[212] It expresses "the sense of equality, fairness, and impartiality, in relation to justice (δικαιοσύνη/τὸ δίκαιον) and the law (νόμος)."[213] Therefore, when Paul advocates ἰσότης, "he presupposes the

---
211. Stählin, "Ἴσος, ἰσότης, ἰσότιμος," 346.
212. Ibid., 346–347.
213. Ogereau, "Jerusalem Collection," 365.

Corinthians' commitment to the well-known principle of equality and fair dealing . . . and in particular their awareness of the commonality, friendship, and solidarity in Christ that bound Gentile and Jewish Christians together."[214]

Paul explains how the principle of equality should characterize the relationship "between the relatively prosperous Corinthians and the poor within the Jerusalem church."[215] Those who are enjoying abundance of wealth (περίσσευμα) should feel the responsibility to provide for the needs (ὑστέρημα) of those in economic difficulties. But the only purpose of this exchange should be the establishment of equality in the sense of solidarity. This view agrees with Paul's conception of the church as a body in which all parts have equal concern for one another (1 Cor 12:26). It is true that this passage refers to the local congregation, but the same thought can be extended to the relations among Christian communities. Thus, Paul is not expecting the Corinthians to engage in a kind of renunciation or asceticism, but to consciously share what they have with those who are in need.[216] This is clearly expressed by the Pauline word ἄνεσις (relief).[217] However, Martin proposes a different interpretation which sees an eschatological meaning in 2 Corinthians 8:14.[218] He argues that this verse is to be understood in the light of Romans 9–11. In his view, the expression ἐν τῷ νῦν[219] καιρῷ, "at the present time," also used in Romans 3:26; 8:18; 11:5, refers to the present age in which God justifies "the ungodly" thanks to their faith in Jesus. This era is characterized by the offer of salvation to the Gentiles through a law-free gospel preached by Paul. Moreover, Martin claims that the Corinthians' abundance (περίσσευμα) in the present time can under no circumstances mean material prosperity, but refers to spiritual enrichment (1 Cor 1:7). He contends that the περίσσευμα of the saints in Jerusalem thus means the future reconciliation of all Israel

---

214. Harris, *Second Epistle*, 590.
215. Ibid., 588.
216. Carrez, *La deuxième épitre*, 185.
217. Paul also uses it in 2:13; 7:5; and in 2 Thess 1:7.
218. Martin, *2 Corinthians*, 267.
219. Harris, *Second Epistle*, 590. The adverb νῦν is used as an adjective.

with God.[220] The reconciled Israel will enrich the Gentiles "by accelerating the close of the age" (Rom 11:5).[221] Martin assumes that this view is possibly voiced in 2 Corinthians 8:4. However, this reading is questionable.[222] Paul is talking about equality between the Corinthians and the Jerusalem congregation and not between the Gentiles and the Jews in general. In the same way, the Corinthian material aid is directed to a specific group (the Jewish Christians in Jerusalem) and not to Israel as a whole. It is therefore unwarranted to assert that Paul has in mind this view of the salvation history. The text "simply refers to those occasions when the Corinthians have a surplus of goods and the Jerusalem believers are in need."[223] Moreover, the text of Exodus 16:18 quoted in verse 15 as a justification of equality has no eschatological connotations in early Judaism.[224] If Paul thought that the περίσσευμα of the saints in Jerusalem is related to the messianic era, he would have invoked one of the many Old Testament texts appropriate for such an eschatological context.

Other views to be considered here are those presented by Betz and Joubert. For Betz, although the Jerusalem church is economically poor, it is spiritually rich. The Corinthians' want resides in their failure to complete the collection. He argues that the successful completion of the collection by the Corinthians will mean that the Jerusalem church will have helped the Corinthians to fill in their spiritual gap.[225] But Betz does not explain in which way the Jerusalem congregation will have played this role. It must be noted that in Paul's statements, this church is presented only as a

---

220. Martin, *2 Corinthians*, 267.
221. Ibid., 269.
222. Thrall, *Critical and Exegetical Commentary*, vol. 2, 542.
223. Harrison, *Paul's Language of Grace*, 306.
224. However, Joubert (*Paul as Benefactor*, 143) confidently asserts that Exod 16:18 has "obvious connotations with the Messianic era in Jewish apocalyptic circles" (*Syrian Apocalypse of Baruch*. 29.8; *Sibylline Oracles*. 7.149). In my view, this claim is difficult to accept. Even the huge collection of rabbinic sources of Strack and Billerbeck, *Kommentar zum Neuen Testament*, 523, does not give any messianic interpretation of Exod 16:18. It must be noted that Joubert invokes these texts to support the view that the collection, especially in its aim of creating equality, has to be understood "within the era of salvation inaugurated by the Christ-event." This is true but the proof from the messianic interpretation of Exod 16:18, which may have influenced the Christian reading of this passage in Paul's time, is unwarranted.
225. Betz, *2 Corinthians 8 and 9*, 68, 69.

recipient of the Corinthians' aid. Joubert also esteems that the Jerusalem Christians will enrich the Corinthians in a spiritual sense. He argues that since 2 Corinthians 9:12–14 envisions the Jerusalem response for the collection in terms of spiritual benefits, 2 Corinthians 8:14 should be read in the same perspective.[226]

However, Paul may have in mind the possibility that the Jerusalem Christians will return material benefits to the Corinthians. The reciprocal giving expressed in verse 14 as being equality (ὅπως γένηται ἰσότης)[227] most naturally refers to the same economic dimension of life as in the previous verse.[228] Thrall notes that the use of καί after ἵνα implies "the equivalence of ideas in two clauses."[229] Perhaps our knowledge of the course of events in the sixties during the Jewish war with Rome, its destructive effects on the Jerusalem church may make it difficult for us to agree with this reading. But if we bear in mind that Paul did not have this knowledge, our view may change. Nothing indicates that Paul may not have thought that in the future the economic conditions could change in Jerusalem and Corinth due to different factors which would place Jerusalem in better economic conditions.[230] It is important to note that Paul mentions such a reversal in the economic situation of the two congregations as a possibility, but does not make a statement asserting that it will definitely happen. In other words, Paul is realistic and aware of the contingencies of human existence. This is substantiated by the use of the subjunctive in this sentence:

---

226. Joubert, *Paul as Benefactor*, 142.

227. The word occurs only five times in the LXX and in Pseudepigraphical literature (Job 36:29; Zech 4:7; Letter of Aristeas 1:263; Ps.-Phoc. 1:137; Ps. Sol. 17:41), and apart from 2 Cor 8:13–14 only once in the New Testament (Col 4:1): Ogereau ("Jerusalem Collection," 364–365).

228. Harris, *Second Epistle*, 590, n. 11. Witherington III (*Conflict and Community*, 420) holds the same view: Paul "suggests that a relationship of giving and receiving would be set up by their gift, so that if and when the time came that the Jerusalem congregation had a surplus, then they could reciprocate by helping the Corinthians."

229. Thrall, *Critical and Exegetical Commentary*, vol. 2, 540, n. 239.

230. Ibid., 542: "If Christian poverty was sometimes the result of persecution, he could have envisaged a time when the Jerusalem church might be free of it whilst the Corinthians were suffering. Again, poverty might result from poor harvests: the Corinthians might be affected whilst the inhabitants of Judaea were not. The theoretical prospect of future aid from Jerusalem to Corinth might well seem realistic. It remains possible that this is what Paul had in mind."

τὸ ἐκείνων περίσσευμα γένηται εἰς τὸ ὑμῶν ὑστέρημα (their abundance may be for your need).

It is also worth noting the fact that unlike in Romans 15:25–27, Paul says nothing about the role of the Jerusalem Christian community as the mother church and the Jewish people in general in redemption history.[231] The centrality of Jerusalem in salvation history which occurs elsewhere in the New Testament does not feature in Paul's treatment of the collection in the Corinthian correspondence. All these observations may confirm Dunn's view that the pastoral dimension of the collection was the most determinant in Paul's thought. He believes that this fundraising campaign "was simply an act of Christian compassion – a highly practical expression of concern for fellow believers in need" which realized Paul's perception of the church as the body of Christ, and this at an international scale.[232] Correlatively, the possibility of the reciprocal giving mentioned in 2 Corinthians 8:14 should be understood as an expression of Paul's view that his collection aimed among other things at raising awareness of mutual interdependence among early Christians, especially between Jewish and Gentiles Jesus followers. In this respect, Harrison's view that Paul's usage of the concept of grace enabled him to redefine the Greco-Roman reciprocity system which could have been operating in the minds of the Corinthians

---

231. The theological theme "redemption history" is supposed to find its origin in the German theologian J. C. K. von Hofmann who, around the middle of the nineteenth century, sought to demonstrate from the Scriptures that God's communion with human beings developed steadily throughout history. He interpreted the Scriptures in light of the principle of "Prophecy and Fulfillment," and "viewed Christ as the center of history and the beginning of its completion" (Roukema, "Herman Ridderbos," 262). Furthermore, Hofmann asserted that the Christian believer takes part in this redemption history by the experience of being born again (ibid., 262). Roukema notes that the view that there exists a divine plan of salvation which unfolds from Creation to the Consummation was held much earlier by Irenaeus of Lyons around the year 180. For his part, Oscar Cullmann held the view that redemption history or salvation history is the heart of New Testament teachings (ibid., 266). Cullmann's idea was favored by Herman Ridderbos who argued that the New Testament must be exposited in a redemptive-historical perspective (ibid., 270–272). By this he meant that God has promised the coming of his kingdom in human history, and that this promise was partially fulfilled in the coming of Christ. Ridderbos also pointed out that Christ did not teach that the end of history would occur after his resurrection. On the contrary, said Ridderbos, Christ envisaged some time for the church that would partake in this partial realization of the promise as it waits for its consummation.

232. Dunn, *Beginning from Jerusalem*, 944.

should be considered here.²³³ Through his theology of grace, Paul wanted both parties involved in the collection to regard themselves as beneficiaries of God's grace, tied together by the reciprocal obligation of love and by the recognition of the Jews' priority in salvation history. But as noted earlier, it seems to me that this last point about the Jews' primacy is difficult to defend on the basis of 2 Corinthians 8–9.

> Verse 15: καθὼς γέγραπται· ὁ τὸ πολὺ οὐκ ἐπλεόνασεν, καὶ ὁ τὸ ὀλίγον οὐκ ἠλαττόνησεν.
>
> As it is written, "The one who had much did not have too much, and the one who had little did not have too little."

For Paul the principle of equality introduced in the previous verse finds support in the Scriptures. The quotation is taken from Exodus 16:18 in the context where God himself gave the manna to Israel.²³⁴ The text of the LXX quoted by Paul with slight variations runs as follows: καὶ μετρήσαντες τῷ γομορ οὐκ ἐπλεόνασεν ὁ τὸ πολύ καὶ ὁ τὸ ἔλαττον οὐκ ἠλαττόνησεν ἕκαστος εἰς τοὺς καθήκοντας παρ' ἑαυτῷ συνέλεξαν (And they measured by the gomor. The one with much did not have excess, and the one with less did not have too little. Each person collected for those appropriate at his own home). About this text, Philo states that God "devised new and strange forms of benefaction" to teach Israel to be patient in unfavorable circumstances with hope for a better future.²³⁵ His interpretation reflects the belief in God's providence. God remains the provider for his people. This is why for Philo, the instruction to collect the food for one day, except for the day before the Sabbath, shows that God's intention was to always "bestow gifts ever new."²³⁶ Josephus for his part sees the restrictions imposed on the collection of manna as God's way to limit the zeal of the strong in collecting it. God did so to protect the weak from being deprived of food.²³⁷

---

233. Harrison, *Paul's Language of Grace*, 313.
234. Harris, *Second Epistle*, 593.
235. Philo, *Mos.* 1.199 (Colson, LCL).
236. Philo, *Mos.* 1.204 (Colson, LCL).
237. Josephus, *Ant.* 3.29–30.

It is conceivable that Paul and his readers, especially the Jewish Christians, may have known of such different but not mutually exclusive interpretations of the manna experience. The fact that Paul makes brief reference to the manna account without any explanation implies at least that the Corinthians were familiar with this story. Paul singles out only the purpose of God's regulating the collection of food (i.e. the divinely established equalizing aspect).[238] However, the whole story profoundly informs Paul's thought. Like Philo, Paul is aware that in his grace God provides for his people. For Israel, God himself established equality among the people. But the Christian communities, which benefit from God's beneficence in Christ, have to realize this equality through a reasonable sharing of wealth as it is given to them in time and space.[239] It is possible that Paul used the manna experience to implicitly urge the Corinthians not to fear that by giving to others they would suffer shortage of financial means. In the case of the Israelites, those who tried to collect more grains of manna to store for the following days toiled in vain, because the provisions stank and were therefore thrown away. By this example Paul may be telling the Corinthians that the purpose of Christian life is not to be sought in the accumulation of wealth but in sharing with others what one has. Furthermore, by stressing the principle of equality set by God, Paul is not far from Josephus who maintains that God protected the weak among the Israelites by regulating the collection of manna.

Paul's use of Exodus 16:18 in the context of the collection perhaps reveals Paul's concern for social inequalities in Greco-Roman society and may suggest that there is a pressing need for the restoration of "a certain balance between need and surplus."[240] This view may be supported by the notion of ἰσότης introduced here in the context of the collection. 1 Corinthians 11:17–22 suggests that inequalities were becoming apparent in the early church.[241] Evidently, when Paul associates ἰσότης with κοινωνία in the treatment of the collection, he gives to his relief project a

---

238. Carrez, *La deuxième épitre*, 186.
239. Harris, *Second Epistle*, 594.
240. Ogereau, "Jerusalem Collection," 366.
241. Ibid., 377.

"socio-economic dimension."[242] However, Ogereau overstretches Paul's thought when he claims that the apostle's use of the concepts of ἰσότης and κοινωνία in connection with the collection shows that he nurtured the ambition to reform "the structural inequalities of Graeco-Roman society" on a large scale.[243] Furthermore, as J. P. Becker aptly remarks, it is worth noting that in Exodus 16 ἰσότης does not come about through κοινωνία.[244] On the contrary, it is God who oversaw the daily collection of the manna and led the whole process to its expected outcome. The implication of this for the understanding of 2 Corinthians 8:12–15 is that God is supernaturally involved in Paul's collection, influencing its outcome for all parties involved in it (i.e. fair balance). This conclusion about the supernatural hand of God in the collection is arrived at by Binz Antony. He observes that the noun θεός occurs seventy-nine times in 2 Corinthians, ten of which are found in chapter 8 and 9, in the nominative (2 Cor 9:7, 8), accusative (9:13), genitive (8:1, 5; 9:14), and the dative (8:16; 9:11, 12, 15). He infers that in this passage "God is presented as facilitating something to be accomplished in the human world, which causes human gratitude to God."[245]

Worth noting is also the fact that Paul does not try to defend the practice of tithing.[246] Nor does he resort to any other fixed regulations on almsgiving abundantly enunciated in the Old Testament. This omission probably means that the apostle of the Gentiles holds to the principle of the voluntary character of Christian giving.

---

242. Ibid., 373.

243. Ibid., 377: "Paul's rhetorical appeal to ἰσότης and κοινωνία rather suggests that he had very concrete objectives in mind. His intentions seem to have extended beyond the mere alleviation of poverty by means of charitable giving. Indeed, he appears to have aimed at reforming the structural inequalities of Graeco-Roman society that were also becoming apparent in the early church . . . by fostering socio-economic ἰσότης between Jews and Gentiles and by establishing a global, socially and ethnically inclusive κοινωνία among them."

244. Becker, *Paul's Usage of* χάρις, 111.

245. Antony, "He Who Supplies Seed," 306.

246. Witherington III, *Conflict and Community*, 421, n. 38.

3.4 The Delegates, Their Commendations and Mission (2 Cor 8:16–9:5)

Verses 16–17: Χάρις δὲ τῷ θεῷ τῷ δόντι τὴν αὐτὴν σπουδὴν ὑπὲρ ὑμῶν ἐν τῇ καρδίᾳ Τίτου, ¹⁷ ὅτι τὴν μὲν παράκλησιν ἐδέξατο, σπουδαιότερος δὲ ὑπάρχων αὐθαίρετος ἐξῆλθεν πρὸς ὑμᾶς.

But thanks be to God who put in the heart of Titus the same eagerness for you that I myself have. For he not only accepted our appeal, but since he is more eager than ever, he is going to you of his own accord.

Paul opens this section with a thanksgiving to God. It is possible to see a conceptual link between this new section (v. 16) and verse 15. The same God who provided the Israelites with manna in the desert "gave Titus a zealous devotion for the Corinthians; Titus' σπουδή, like the Israelite's manna, was supernaturally supplied."[247] But a stronger connection may be found earlier, in 8:1. The same God who gave the Macedonians the ability to engage in the collection (8:1) enabled Titus to be willing to work among the Corinthians. Titus' trustworthiness and commendable relationship with the Corinthians have already been affirmed by Paul in 2 Corinthians 7:6–16 and 8:6.[248] It is notable that in 2 Corinthians 8:16 Paul attributes Titus' zeal for the Corinthians to divine activity[249] rather than seeing it as a simply natural ability. Paul bursts out in thanksgiving to God for his gracious intervention in Titus' life. The term χάρις carries here the meaning of thanks or gratitude. In two other instances in this letter, Paul uses the same phrase (χάρις τῷ θεῷ) to express his gratitude to God for his "graceful intervention" in his ministry (2:14; 9:15).[250] Here in 8:16 Paul has another reason to thank God: he has realized that Titus' eagerness for the Corinthians "is the same (τὴν αὐτὴν σπουδὴν) as his own."[251] But Martin

---

247. Harris, *Second Epistle*, 597.
248. Downs, *Offering of the Gentiles*, 139.
249. Ibid.
250. Harris, *Second Epistle*, 597–598.
251. Martin, *2 Corinthians*, 273.

thinks that Paul's joy is motivated by the fact that Titus is ready to return to Corinth to consolidate what has already been done in the implementation of the collection.[252] This view is in fact implied in that presented above which emphasizes that Paul is grateful to God because Titus is animated by the same zeal as his own. Paul's zeal for the Corinthians in the present verse aims at helping them to complete the collection according to their initial eagerness.

Titus' zeal for the Corinthians was not a superficial, emotional reaction, but an inward disposition: ἐν τῇ καρδίᾳ Τίτου. The word καρδία, heart, was relatively rare in pagan writings but is frequently used in the LXX and other Jewish literature.[253] The Old Testament,[254] Judaism[255] and early Christianity[256] as well as Greek tragedy[257] shared the view that the heart is the inner part of a human being, the seat of will, plans and decisions.[258] It is important to note that elsewhere in the Pauline writings it is said that God reveals the secrets of the heart (1 Cor 14:25), exerts his action on it (Eph 1:18), and encourages it (Col 2:2). Paul says thus that God inspires Titus' heart with zeal or enthusiasm.[259] This idea is also reflected in Philippians 2:13 where Paul affirms that it is God who creates in the believers the will and the ability to do his will.

Titus' zeal (σπουδή) is directed at the Corinthians. Paul has earlier said that both the Corinthians and the Macedonians too have σπουδή (7:11–12; 8:7, 8). As noted earlier, the phrase τὴν αὐτὴν σπουδὴν ὑπὲρ ὑμῶν used about Titus indicates the 'same zeal' that moves Paul to seek the welfare of the Corinthians. Furnish points out that Paul tactfully says that Titus is zealous for the Corinthians and not for the completion of the collection

---

252. Ibid., 273.
253. Danker et al., *Greek-English Lexicon*, 508.
254. Exod 35:5; 36:2; 1 Kgs 21:3; Jer 23:20.
255. T. Levi 13:1; T. Jos. 10:5.
256. 2 Cor 9:7; Luke 21:14; Acts 5:3; Jas 4:8; Matt 5:8.
257. Sophocles Antigone 1105 reads καρδίας δ' ἐξίσταμαι τὸ δρᾶν, . . . (Baumgärtel and Behm, "καρδία," 608); Seneca could write "nihil esse grato animo honestius" ("Nothing is more honorable than a grateful heart": *Ben.* 6.10.2 (Basore, LCL); *Ep.* 81.5–6, 30 (Gummere, LCL); quoted by Betz, *2 Corinthians 8 and 9*, 105, n. 124.
258. Baumgärtel and Behm, "καρδία," 606–607, 610; Danker et al., *Greek-English Lexicon*, 509; Betz, *2 Corinthians 8 and 9*, 105.
259. Harris, *Second Epistle*, 598.

itself although this idea is implicit in 8:6.[260] This resonates with Paul's statement in 2 Corinthians 12:14: "Now for the third time I am ready to come to you. And I will not be burdensome to you; for I do not seek yours, but you."

We are told that Titus's activity was a convergence of two factors: he received an appeal from Paul (μὲν παράκλησιν ἐδέξατο) to return to Corinth to help the congregation bring the collection to completion. This appeal is referred to in 8:6 as Paul's "upshot of the enthusiasm of the Macedonians to the relief project (8:1–5)."[261] Paul's appeal would not have yielded any fruits if there was not Titus' own eagerness (σπουδαιότερος δὲ ὑπάρχων αὐθαίρετος) to return to Corinth.[262] One may wonder how to reconcile the idea that Paul appealed to Titus to return to Corinth and the view that the latter did so of his own accord.[263] Harris notes that the phrase μὲν . . . δὲ may have the meaning "to be sure . . . but."[264] For Paul Barnett, Paul's appeal found Titus already with the zeal to return to Corinth.[265] In Nickle's view, Paul is underscoring Titus' enthusiastic response to his appeal.[266] At any rate, two important things are communicated to the Corinthians: Titus himself made a decision to return to Corinth, "yet he was also coming in response to Paul's suggestion and therefore with the apostle's full support."[267] The use of the epistolary aorist here[268] indicates that Titus is about to return to Corinth.

---

260. Furnish, *II Corinthians*, 433.

261. Harris, *Second Epistle*, 599.

262. It seems that Paul did refrain from forcing his co-workers to do something against their will. In a different context, although he was strongly urged by Paul to go to Corinth with other brothers, Apollos was quite unwilling to do so (1 Cor 16:12). But Paul hoped that "our brother Apollos" would go there when he has the opportunity.

263. The same word αὐθαίρετος is used by Paul to speak of the Macedonians who gave their contribution to the Jerusalem collection without any pressure put on them (8:3).

264. Harris, *Second Epistle*, 599.

265. Barnett, *Second Epistle*, 228.

266. Nickle, *Collection*, 18.25.

267. Harris, *Second Epistle*, 599.

268. The epistolary aorist expresses an "action that is contemporaneous or future at the time of writing but will be past when the letter is read" (Ibid., 600, n. 9). The same aorist tense is used in 8:18, 22 and 9:3. Some commentators see the same use in 8:17 and 9:5. Others consider all these verbs to be preterit aorists, expressing past actions.

Verses 18–19: συνεπέμψαμεν δὲ μετ' αὐτοῦ τὸν ἀδελφὸν οὗ ὁ ἔπαινος ἐν τῷ εὐαγγελίῳ διὰ πασῶν τῶν ἐκκλησιῶν, ¹⁹ οὐ μόνον δέ, ἀλλὰ καὶ χειροτονηθεὶς ὑπὸ τῶν ἐκκλησιῶν συνέκδημος ἡμῶν σὺν τῇ χάριτι ταύτῃ τῇ διακονουμένῃ ὑφ' ἡμῶν πρὸς τὴν αὐτοῦ τοῦ κυρίου δόξαν καὶ προθυμίαν ἡμῶν,

With him we are sending the brother who is famous among all the churches for his proclaiming the good news; ¹⁹ and not only that, but he has also been appointed by the churches to travel with us while we are administering this generous undertaking for the glory of the Lord himself and to show our eagerness to help.

Titus, whom Paul calls his brother in 2:13, is sent with another brother whose identity is not disclosed. As noted in 8:1 the term brother not only means a fellow Christian but also a co-worker in early Christianity. It seems that the latter connotation of this term is more emphasized than the former in the current verse. About this unnamed brother, Paul says that he is praised throughout all the churches for his work for the gospel (ὁ ἔπαινος ἐν τῷ εὐαγγελίῳ διὰ πασῶν τῶν ἐκκλησιῶν). Moreover, this brother has been appointed by the churches to travel with Paul in the handling of the collection (χειροτονηθεὶς ὑπὸ τῶν ἐκκλησιῶν συνέκδημος ἡμῶν σὺν τῇ χάριτι ταύτῃ τῇ διακονουμένῃ ὑφ' ἡμῶν). The verb συνπέμπω used here means that Paul is dispatching "this additional emissary as Titus's companion in travel and also as his colleague."[269]

Concerning the commendation of this brother, the phrase ἐν τῷ εὐαγγελίῳ may indicate that he was praised "in the sphere of" or "in the matter of" or "in connection with" the gospel.[270] Thus, it is difficult to know whether his praise resulted from his preaching or from his spreading of the gospel.[271] Against Harris who argues that the expression διὰ πασῶν τῶν ἐκκλησιῶν may include all Pauline congregations or even all Christians,

---

269. Ibid., 600.
270. Ibid., 601.
271. Ibid. Witherington's translation (*Conflict and Community*, 422) is that the brother was praised "in the gospel"; which may mean that this brother's praise was due to his preaching of the gospel or that he was mentioned in the early oral kerygma. But he opts for the former meaning.

it seems to me natural to say that the brother was praised throughout all the Macedonian churches that Paul talked about earlier (8:1–5). In any case, "his fame indicates that he is more than a local congregational leader" as observes Furnish.[272] As for the names of this brother and that of the second one mentioned in verse 23, I will not expand on this matter about which certainty cannot be achieved. Furthermore, this question has no influence on the interpretation of the passage. Suffice it to say that the views according to which these two so commendable delegates ended up losing their renown in Corinth and their names were subsequently deleted from this letter[273] or that Paul omitted their names to promote Titus's primacy are not convincing. Rather, it may be right to consider that the apostle omitted their names because they were more or less unknown to the Corinthians and that he expected Titus to introduce them to the church up there.[274]

As noted earlier, besides his praise throughout all the churches, this brother is said to have been appointed by the churches. The passive aorist participle χειροτονηθείς is "an absolute participle"[275] which stands for the finite verb ἐχειροτονήθη. This phenomenon is not infrequent in 2 Corinthians (5:12; 6:3; 7:5; 9:11, 13; 10:4, 15; 11:6).[276] Χειροτονέω originally meant to raise the hand as an expression of agreement in a vote.[277] It acquired later the sense of selecting people for specific tasks. The same verb could also mean to nominate. It is in this sense that it is used in the present verse regarding the unnamed brother. The verb implies that the appointee is invested with a certain authority by the churches which commissioned him for "a specific task, namely acting as Paul's traveling companion and assistant (συνέκδημος)" in delivering the offering to Jerusalem.[278]

---

272. Furnish, *II Corinthians*, 434.
273. Ibid., 436.
274. Harris, *Second Epistle*, 601–602.
275. Ibid., 602.
276. Ibid., 602, n. 24.
277. Lohse, "χείρ, χειραγωγέω, 437. The verb χειροτονέω is totally absent from the LXX. It is also used in Acts 14:23, where it does not mean that the elders were elected by the congregation, since they were rather appointed by Paul and Barnabas. The cognate substantive χειροτονία shows up once in Isa 58:9 with the sense of "pointing with the finger." But it does not occur in the New Testament.
278. Harris, *Second Epistle*, 603.

It is difficult to know the number of the churches that appointed this brother. As for their identification, it is more probable that these congregations were Macedonian since it seems that Paul was in Macedonia when he wrote 2 Corinthians (cf. 7:5), and this church had succeeded in collecting their aid for Jerusalem. Thus the Macedonian church was in a good position to send a delegate who could perhaps use the experience from his home congregation to help Titus and the Corinthians to complete their collection.[279]

As in 1 Corinthians 16:3 and 2 Corinthians 8:6–7 the collection is termed a χάρις, "charitable work" (CJB), a "gracious work" (NAS), an "offering" (NIV), a "gift" (NKJV), "entreprise généreuse" (BFC), "libéralité" (FBJ), "oeuvre de bienfaisance" (LSG) or "oeuvre de générosité" (TOB). By means of a telic preposition (πρὸς) Paul goes on to indicate the twofold purpose of his relief fund: πρὸς τὴν αὐτοῦ τοῦ κυρίου δόξαν καὶ προθυμίαν ἡμῶν. First and more importantly, the collection aims at honoring the Lord. The collection will promote the Lord's glory maybe because its success "would prompt people to praise God" as expressed in 9:11–13.[280] The emphatic use of the pronoun αὐτοῦ between the two occurrences of ἡμῶν conveys the idea that Paul's motivation in organizing the collection "was not self-centered; it was a desire for the Lord's own glory that impelled his action."[281] The second aim of the collection mentioned by Paul, closely connected with the first, is his desire to demonstrate his goodwill, willingness, or readiness to serve the Jerusalem church through assistance to its poor members.

Verses 20–21: στελλόμενοι τοῦτο, μή τις ἡμᾶς μωμήσηται ἐν τῇ ἁδρότητι ταύτῃ τῇ διακονουμένῃ ὑφ᾽ ἡμῶν· ²¹προνοοῦμεν γὰρ καλα[282]V οὐ μόνον ἐνώπιον κυρίου ἀλλὰ καὶ ἐνώπιον ἀνθρώπων

---

279. Ibid.
280. Ibid., 604.
281. Ibid., 604–605.
282. Unlike in Rom 12:17 (προνοούμενοι καλὰ ἐνώπιον πάντων ἀνθρώπων) which refers to what is good in general, 2 Cor 8:21 draws attention "to honest and honorable action in financial matters rather than simply the performance of praiseworthy acts" (Harris, *Second Epistle*, 608).

We want to avoid anyone from blaming us about this generous gift that we are administering, 21 for we intend to do what is right, not only in the Lord's sight but also in the sight of others.

In these two verses, Paul digresses from the commendation of the delegates to explain the mission of the delegation (i.e. to avoid blame for financial improprieties). The verb στέλλω, which occurs in the LXX and in the New Testament only in the middle voice, means "to keep one's distance, keep away" from someone (Mal 2:5; 3 Macc 1:19; 2 Thess 3:6).[283] It can also mean "to shun," "avoid, try to avoid" something.[284] The direct object τοῦτο indicates what Paul is trying to avoid by the dispatch of the three emissaries. The middle verb μωμάομαι, which is used only here and in 2 Corinthians 6:3 in the New Testament corpus, means "to find fault with, criticize, censure, blame" someone.[285] Thus, Paul avoids being blamed for "this generous gift," ἐν τῇ ἁδρότητι ταύτῃ. As Furnish points out, Paul takes seriously Cicero's advice to avoid any "suspicion of self-seeking" in the management of public affairs.[286] It is significant that Paul calls his collection a ἁδρότης which, in relation to money, conveys the sense of an important amount.[287] This choice of terminology can signify two important things. First, Paul expected that the Corinthians would give lavishly as did the Macedonians (8:2). Second, Paul was aware "that the larger the sum of money collected, the greater the possibility that he would be suspected of embezzlement."[288] We see here Paul's awareness that as a manager of the whole relief project his responsibility also

---

283. Danker et al., *Greek-English Lexicon*, 942.

284. Ibid., 943.

285. Ibid., 663.

286. Cicero, *Off.* 2.21.75 (Miller, LCL), quoted by Furnish, *II Corinthians*, 434.

287. Becker (*Paul's Usage of* χάρις, 242, 243) writes that it is most likely that Paul uses the word ἁδρότης in the sense of "vital force." Becker puts it in relation to χάρις, the matter at stake in 2 Cor 8–9 as he says. He concludes that Paul is indicating that χάρις is "a discrete power of God, in an objective and tangible sense." This is consistent with his view that this term has invariably the same meaning in all its occurrences. However, I think that it is better to say that as Paul uses the word χάρις with various meanings in this passage; he also finds different terms to designate his collection: as χάρις or as ἁδρότης. It is true that the meaning of the latter is not clear enough, perhaps because of its rarity in Greek and its unique occurrence in the Bible (2 Cor 8:20).

288. Harris, *Second Epistle*, 606–607.

entails transparency. His precautions in this matter are all the more motivated by the presence of opponents in the Corinthian congregation. From what Paul says in 2 Corinthians 12:16–19, it seems that he is striving to counter his detractors, who may be saying that he is trying to trick the Corinthians through the collection, despite his earlier commitment to a free-of-charge ministry.

Whether this implicit accusation is from the Corinthians themselves or from the opponents who intruded the church there is not at stake here.[289] Witherington argues that the invective came from intruders, but also that some Corinthians had probably managed to convince the congregation that Paul considered them to be an inferior church. The reason for this accusation may have been that the apostle had decided to take money from the Philippians and not from the Corinthians.[290] Witherington notes that 2 Corinthians 10–13, in which Paul opposes his adversaries, is not addressed to the Corinthian Christians, "but against the false apostles."[291] Paul's refusal of material help seemingly irritated the rich members of the Corinthian church (1 Cor 9:12; 2 Cor 11:7–15; 12:14–18), and even jeopardized the validity of his ministry.[292] According to the practice of the time, philosophers and itinerant teachers were paid for their teaching, or financially supported by wealthy members of the society. However, unlike other apostles, Paul and Barnabas denied themselves such a privilege. Rather, they preferred to work to earn a living (1 Cor 9:3–6). By doing so, Paul refused to get entangled in the social practices of patronage and benefaction

---

289. Downs (*Offering of the Gentiles*, 139) notes that considering "the likelihood that Paul had earlier faced severe criticism from some members of the Corinthian community on account of his financial policies – with accusations focused specifically on the apostle's handling of the collection fund – his decision to dispatch this delegation is entirely understandable."

290. Witherington III, *Conflict and Community*, 418.

291. Ibid., 411: "The Corinthians themselves are not Paul's opponents, and thus there is no reason to think that Paul was whistling in the dark when he spoke of having some confidence in them. 7:11 makes it clear that they are impressionable and that the painful letter had had it proper impact. But they are still also under the influence of the false *apostoloi*. All is not well in Corinth by any means, but the chief cause of this is external. Paul seems to think that the majority, but by no means all, are largely on his side (cf. ch. 2) and will still listen to and heed his advice. It is with this hope and confidence that he writes chaps. 8–9. It is difficult to get the balance right in evaluating the degree of alienation from and attachment to the apostle that the Corinthians had" (ibid., 411–412, n. 3).

292. Carrez, *La deuxième épitre*, 35.

which would have placed him in an inappropriate type of reciprocity with some wealthy Corinthians.[293] Such a binding relationship would have assigned him to a particular place and deprived him of his freedom to minister to all people from different social statuses. In 2 Corinthians 12:14–15 Paul makes it clear that he does not want to depend on the Corinthians in financial matters. This, apparently, in the eyes of the Corinthians, deprived him of the right to claim the title of apostle.[294] Moreover, such an attitude could be interpreted as a lack of love for the giver, in this case the Corinthians. Paul denied that this was the case (2 Cor 11:11). He thus gave the true motivation for his attitude. Not only did he avoid being a burden to the Corinthians (11:9), but also he wanted to "cut off the opportunity from those who desire an opportunity to be regarded just as we are in the things of which they boast" (11:12). Although he found this practice legitimate and would enjoy it (1 Cor 9:12), Paul decided to preach the gospel free of charge (1 Cor 9:18). In a nutshell, 2 Corinthians 8:20 implies that Paul's words and actions are part and parcel of "the demonstration of his innocence and honesty" in the management of the collection.[295]

To reinforce his commitment to precautionary strategy and transparency in the management of his collection, Paul says expressly that he takes pains to do what is good not only before the Lord but also in human sight. It is possible that Paul has in mind the sage's exhortation from Proverb 3:4

---

293. Witherington III, *Conflict and Community*, 417. According to E. A. Judge, quoted by Witherington III (ibid., 418), to refuse a gift was not easier at all, since it gave rise to harsh enmity (Judge, "Social Identity," 214). But Witherington III (*Conflict and Community*, 419) rightly remarks that Paul's refusal of gifts has to be qualified: "He does not refuse to accept traveling expenses (1 Cor 16:6; 2 Cor 1:16), nor does he always refuse *missionary* support of his gospel work when he is away from the group supporting him (cf. Phil 4:16; 2 Cor 11:19). Perhaps the Philippians understood, but some Corinthians did not, that the giving and receiving between Paul and his converts had to be on a basis that did not turn him into someone's client. Paul was also not reluctant to accept Christian hospitality, even from a well-to-do Christian and even in Corinth, so long as the wrong sorts of strings were not attached (cf. Rom 16:23)."

294. Safrai and Tomson ("Paul's 'Collection'," 176) point out that ancient society was familiar with the practice of compensation for public services rendered by the elite. This could take the form of financial goods or privileges, power and social recognition. In this context, if a class fails to secure appropriate compensation for its functions, "it is not an elite, even if its services to society are essential." Applied to Paul's situation, one may surmise that his refusal of material compensation from the Corinthians could undermine his social dignity in their eyes.

295. Witherington III, *Conflict and Community*, 412.

in the LXX (καὶ προνοοῦ καλὰ ἐνώπιον κυρίου καὶ ἀνθρώπων: And think of what is noble in the sight of the Lord and of people). Like the sage, Paul gives priority to God's approval. Human appraisal, which is also important, is subordinated to divine appreciation of human conduct. Ideally, both should go together but this order must be observed strictly.[296] In 1 Corinthians 10:33 Paul shows that he was very sensitive to the appreciation of his work by others, especially in his dealings with the Corinthians in general: "just as I try to please everyone in everything I do, not seeking my own advantage, but that of many, so that they may be saved."

> Verse 22: συνεπέμψαμεν δὲ αὐτοῖς τὸν ἀδελφὸν ἡμῶν ὃν ἐδοκιμάσαμεν ἐν πολλοῖς πολλάκις σπουδαῖον ὄντα, νυνὶ δὲ πολὺ σπουδαιότερον πεποιθήσει πολλῇ τῇ εἰς ὑμᾶς.
>
> And with them we are sending our brother whom we have often tested and found eager in many matters, but who is now more eager than ever because of his great confidence in you.

Paul leaves his digression and returns to practical issues concerning the delegates. He announces the dispatch of a second emissary together with Titus. As in 8:18, when Paul introduces the first unnamed brother, he means that the second unnamed messenger is also his co-worker in ministry. Concerning his credentials, this brother has proven to be diligent in many matters, presumably relating to the management of funds.[297] The verb δοκιμάζω[298] is used here in the sense of "to determine genuineness of something, put to test, examine."[299] It can also convey the sense of "to draw a conclusion about worth on the basis of testing, prove, approve."[300] In this case, emphasis is laid on the result of the whole process of examination. In 8:2 Paul used the cognate substantive δοκιμή to refer to the Macedonians

---

296. In Acts 4:19–20, Luke's narrative indicates that the apostles, summoned by the Sanhedrin to refrain from proclaiming the Christian faith, decided to obey to God rather than to men.

297. Martin, *2 Corinthians*, 277.

298. According to Harris (*Second Epistle*, 609), ἐδοκίμασεν must be viewed as a "summary or constative aorist comprehending all the occasions and ways in a single glance" that Paul used to verify this brother's devotion to ministry.

299. Danker et al., *Greek-English Lexicon*, 255.

300. Ibid.

as having undergone a great ordeal. Here in verse 22 this brother is said to have proved to be "eager in many matters." Like the envoy mentioned in 8:18, the name of this brother is not revealed. Although Paul does not state here that this brother of 8:22 was appointed by the churches, verse 23 leads to this conclusion because both brothers are termed "messengers of the churches."

The second qualification of the second messenger of the churches is that he is now very earnest in his determination to work among the Corinthians because of the confidence he has in them: νυνὶ δὲ πολὺ σπουδαιότερον πεποιθήσει πολλῇ τῇ εἰς ὑμᾶς. Nothing is said about the circumstances which promoted this brother's confidence in the Corinthians. Following Windisch, Furnish suggests that, like Paul, the brother probably gained this confidence thanks to Titus's positive report when he returned from Corinth.[301] But it is difficult to know when and how this brother learned about Titus' report concerning Corinth since he was not Paul's companion before he was appointed by the churches for the collection project. However, there is no need to follow Furnish when he suggests that the fact that this brother is mentioned second and without specific tasks implies that "his role in Titus' mission was regarded as of less importance" than that of the other brother mentioned previously.[302] In my view, Paul found it redundant to repeat the same tasks for this brother. It is quite natural to see the two brothers sent with Titus as having the same mission of certifying the integrity of the collection. More importantly, this brother, together with the former, are said to be the churches' messengers and the glory of Christ (v. 23). As noted earlier, Paul has interrupted his commendations for the envoys started in verse 16 and passes on to the explanation of the mission of the delegation (vv. 20–21). Thus, he separates the two brothers to be sent along with Titus. In any case, Paul's statement in verse 22 is that the messenger "felt sure that the forthcoming mission to Corinth would be successful and that the believers there would give liberally to the relief fund."[303] In this case, Paul's commendation of the messengers serves to urge the Corinthians to live up to this expectation.

---

301. Furnish, *II Corinthians*, 436.
302. Ibid.
303. Harris, *Second Epistle*, 610.

Verse 23: εἴτε[304] ὑπὲρ Τίτου, κοινωνὸς ἐμὸς καὶ εἰς ὑμᾶς συνεργός· εἴτε ἀδελφοὶ ἡμῶν, ἀπόστολοι ἐκκλησιῶν, δόξα Χριστοῦ.

As for Titus, he is my partner and co-worker among you; as for our brothers, they are messengers of the churches, the glory of Christ.

Paul summarizes his commendations and goes on to clarify the position of these delegates among the Corinthians. Titus is referred to as Paul's κοινωνός (companion, partner) and εἰς ὑμᾶς συνεργός (fellow worker for you).[305] Concerning the two brothers sent along with Titus, Paul reiterates that they are messengers of the churches (ἀπόστολοι ἐκκλησιῶν). But in Paul's view, these brothers are no simple delegates, but the reflection of Christ's glory (δόξα Χριστοῦ). Harris is right in saying that Paul is once again here "exercising forethought and taking a precautionary measure, anticipating issues that may arise when the delegation reaches Corinth."[306] Titus, Paul's appointee (vv. 16–17, 23a), was leading the delegation, part of which were the other two brothers appointed by the churches (v. 18, 22). This may be substantiated by the fact that Paul calls him κοινωνὸς ἐμὸς καὶ εἰς ὑμᾶς συνεργός. This designation (κοινωνὸς ἐμός) indicates close partnership or cooperation between Titus and Paul in the ministry in general, and specifically in the collection project among the Corinthians (εἰς ὑμᾶς συνεργός). Furnish correctly points out that this distinction between Titus and the other two brothers is marked out by the use of the singular pronoun for the former (κοινωνὸς ἐμός) and the plural for the latter (ἀδελφοὶ ἡμῶν).[307] The designation of the two brothers as ἀπόστολοι ἐκκλησιῶν does not have the meaning of a ministerial mandate conferred to the Twelve and Paul (Matt 10:2; 1 Cor 9:1; 15:5, 7), but has the broader sense of envoys of the churches. However, this distinction does not lessen their

---

304. Harris (ibid.) observes that the expression εἴτε ... εἴτε ("whether ... or," "if ... if") is not followed by a finite verb, thus leaving an ellipsis. Therefore, it can be translated by "if [someone asks]" or "if [there is any question]."

305. Witherington III (*Conflict and Community*, 422) is right to say that Paul indirectly considers the Corinthians as his fellow workers through Titus, his apostolic representative.

306. Harris, *Second Epistle*, 610.

307. Furnish, *II Corinthians*, 437.

value in Paul's view. Rather, Paul states clearly that they are δόξα Χριστοῦ, Christ's glory. This last qualification may mean that the brothers lived an exemplary Christian life and carried out a ministry that promoted Christ's glory. Therefore, Down's view that Paul's depiction of the two unnamed emissaries as δόξα Χριστοῦ "relativizes their importance in relation to the glory which is due to Christ" must be rejected.[308] On the contrary, Paul is saying that the two unnamed brothers, too, deserve honor although they are not vested with the same credentials and authority as Titus, his personal representative. Otherwise, Paul would have given a similar notice to Titus's accreditation in relation to Christ's glory. Furthermore, the apostle would never think that there could be any of his messengers or himself who might compare to Christ's glory. All in all, Paul's summary of commendations here serves as a good preparation and support for his request to the Corinthians in verse 24.

Verse 24: τὴν οὖν ἔνδειξιν τῆς ἀγάπης ὑμῶν καὶ ἡμῶν καυχήσεως ὑπὲρ ὑμῶν εἰς αὐτοὺς ἐνδεικνύμενοι εἰς πρόσωπον τῶν ἐκκλησιῶν.

Therefore openly before the churches, show them the proof of your love and of our reason for boasting about you.

After his commendations for his supporting group in the administration of the collection at Corinth, Paul returns to the point of chapter 8 (i.e. an appeal to the Corinthians to complete their contributions for Jerusalem). I will not expand on the explanation of the participial form of the verb ἐνδείκνυμι here. Paul employs it in this verse to indicate the action to be performed by the Corinthians. Suffice it to say that the participle ἐνδεικνύμενοι functions here as an imperative under the influence of a Semitic idiom,[309] as in Romans 12:9–17.[310] Paul makes two points in his appeal to the Corinthians. First, the apostle wants his Corinthian converts to show the proof of the love which they have and which he commended earlier in 8:7. Whether Paul has in mind the love the Corinthians have for

---

308. Downs, *Offering of the Gentiles*, 139, quoting O'Mahony, "Pauline Persuasion," 130.
309. Metzger, *Textual Commentary*, 513–514.
310. Thrall, *Critical and Exegetical Commentary*, vol. 2, 555–556.

these three emissaries, for Paul himself, for Christ or for the disadvantaged members of the Jerusalem church is not specified here. In Harris's view, there is no reason to be limitative in this matter.[311] Martin thinks that Paul wants the Corinthians to warmly receive these delegates, which will confirm his boasting about the Corinthians to the Macedonians.[312] But Furnish's remark is more convincing.[313] Paul's discourse is not an exhortation to love these delegates, nor is it a general appeal to love (cf. 1 Cor 16:14). Rather, the apostle is reminding the Corinthians of what he said in 8:7–15 (i.e. that they should fulfill their promise of contributions to the collection for Jerusalem).

The second point that Paul makes to the Corinthians is that he expects them to show the proof of his boasting or pride about them. Perhaps, Paul is indirectly telling the Corinthians that he had been boasting about their love and their eagerness to participate in the collection. But it is also possible to understand ἡμῶν καυχήσεως as referring to Paul's pride in the Corinthians (CJB, NIV), "la fierté que nous avons de vous" (TOB). In this case, Paul's pride about the Corinthians does concern the whole life of the congregation as a living community.

Paul says that this proof of the Corinthians' love and the validity of Paul's pride are to be demonstrated εἰς αὐτούς (i.e. most naturally to the three envoys).[314] Since these messengers will be acting on behalf of the Macedonian churches that most probably commissioned them, the attitudes and actions of the Corinthians will be in full view of these sending churches (εἰς πρόσωπον τῶν ἐκκλησιῶν). Moreover, since the news about the Corinthians' attitude and acts during the delegates' stay in their midst will probably reach other Christian congregations, the phrase εἰς πρόσωπον τῶν ἐκκλησιῶν should not be restricted to the Macedonian congregations. Above all, Paul is reminding the Corinthians that the successful conclusion of the collection will be a tangible proof of their love for the Jerusalem church.[315]

---

311. Harris, *Second Epistle*, 614.
312. Martin, *2 Corinthians*, 279.
313. Furnish, *II Corinthians*, 438.
314. Harris, *Second Epistle*, 614.
315. Ibid., 615.

9:1: Περὶ μὲν γὰρ τῆς διακονίας τῆς εἰς τοὺς ἁγίους περισσόν μοί ἐστιν τὸ γράφειν ὑμῖν.

Now concerning the ministering to the saints, it is superfluous for me to write to you.

Paul does not continue with the point about the delegates but starts talking about a different matter. As I noted in the discussion of the literary integrity of 2 Corinthians 8–9 in chapter 2, Paul uses the expression περὶ μὲν γὰρ not to introduce a new subject, but to come back to 8:24 in order to give further explanation.[316] As in 8:4, Paul terms the collection project a "ministering to the saints" (ἡ διακονία εἰς τοὺς ἁγίους). He says that it is superfluous to write again about it, yet he expounds on it (9:2–15). Paul is using here a rhetoric device which actually enables him to emphasize the subject of the collection.[317]

Verse 2: οἶδα γὰρ τὴν προθυμίαν ὑμῶν ἣν ὑπὲρ ὑμῶν καυχῶμαι Μακεδόσιν, ὅτι Ἀχαΐα παρεσκεύασται ἀπὸ πέρυσι, καὶ τὸ ὑμῶν ζῆλος ἠρέθισεν τοὺς πλείονας.

for I know your eagerness, which is the subject of my boasting about you to the people of Macedonia, saying that Achaia has been ready since last year; and your zeal has stirred up most of them.

Paul reminds the Corinthians of their original eagerness to contribute to the relief fund for Jerusalem. But he gives more than a reminder here. In the first place, he states that he knows (οἶδα) their eagerness, goodwill or willingness (τὴν προθυμίαν ὑμῶν). The apostle wants to assure them that he takes their commitment seriously. Moreover, he is implicitly telling

---

316. Stowers, *"Peri men gar,"* 346. But Betz (*2 Corinthians 8 and 9*, 90) argues that the presence of μέν indicates that the conjunction γάρ points to what follows and that it has no connection with what precedes.

317. Harris, *Second Epistle*, 618. Heb 11:32–38 is the best example of the use of this figure of thought in the New Testament. Betz (*2 Corinthians 8 and 9*, 90–91) esteems that Paul's rhetorical style here shows that he is aware that the collection has become a boring subject for the readers though he cannot refrain from writing about it again. Furnish (*II Corinthians*, 438) understands that what Paul finds superfluous to write about is the Corinthians' "goodwill toward the collection." In Furnish's view, Paul rather deems it necessary to write about the current delegation he is about to commission to Corinth.

them that they need to consider it with the same seriousness.[318] Paul indicates that he boasts to the Macedonians (καυχῶμαι Μακεδόσιν) about the Corinthians' eagerness. It is worth noting that Paul uses the present tense. This implies two things at least:[319]

- Paul is in Macedonia when he writes 2 Corinthians and continues to boast about the Corinthians.
- When 2 Corinthians was being written, the collection was still in progress in Macedonia; otherwise Paul's boasting to stir the Macedonians to action would not make sense.

The second important thing that Paul mentions to the Corinthians is that their zeal (τὸ ὑμῶν ζῆλος) to contribute to the collection, which was shared by the churches in Achaia,[320] prompted the Macedonians' action. Paul clarifies that his boasting is about the Achaeans' zeal to translate their eagerness (προθυμία) into action through the relief fund. The verb ἐρεθίζω usually means to arouse or provoke in a negative way; thus, to irritate or embitter (Col 3:21).[321] In 2 Corinthians 9:2 it denotes the idea of giving an encouraging example. It thus has the meaning of to "stir up," "to rouse to action."[322] We are told that the Corinthians' zeal stirred up τοὺς πλείονας. οἱ πλείονες, a substantivated comparative, indicates here that "the majority" or "most"[323] of the Macedonians were roused to action by the Corinthians'

---

318. The Corinthians' προθυμία has been previously mentioned three times: 8:11, 12, 19.

319. Harris, *Second Epistle*, 621. Betz (*2 Corinthians 8 and 9*, 91), who must have overlooked Paul's use of the present tense, argues that Paul boasted to the Macedonians during his recent visit to Macedonia (2 Cor 1:15–16; 2:13; 7:5).

320. Apart from the church in Cenchreae (Rom 16:1), we know nothing about other Christian congregations in Achaia. But 2 Cor 1:1 implies that there were some other congregations outside of Corinth and Cenchreae. Nor do we know about the progress of the implementation of the collection in Achaia except in Corinth. Therefore, when Paul uses the term the Achaeans, he has in mind the whole Roman province. Similarly, the designation "Macedonians" covers all the congregations established in the Roman province of Macedonia, namely Thessalonica, Philippi, and Berea. It is unlikely that the apostle uses the term Achaia to designate only Corinth, just to mention one region beside another (i.e. Macedonia).

321. Danker et al., *Greek-English Lexicon*, 391.

322. Furnish, *II Corinthians*, 426.

323. Danker et al., *Greek-English Lexicon*, 848; Harris, *Second Epistle*, 621. οἱ πλείονες has the same meaning in 2 Cor 2:6.

zeal.[324] By bringing in the Macedonians' experience, Paul is using comparison as a strategy to arouse among the Corinthians the sense of honor which will bring them to resume their contribution.[325] Paul's point is full of irony. The Macedonians, who were stimulated by the Corinthians' example, have now made important progress in gathering their contributions to the collection. But the Corinthians, who were first to show an eager intention (ἡ προθυμία τοῦ θέλειν, 8:11) to participate in the collection and start it (8:10), are languishing.

> Verses 3–5: ἔπεμψα δὲ τοὺς ἀδελφούς, ἵνα μὴ τὸ καύχημα ἡμῶν τὸ ὑπὲρ ὑμῶν κενωθῇ ἐν τῷ μέρει τούτῳ, ἵνα καθὼς ἔλεγον παρεσκευασμένοι ἦτε, ⁴μή πως ἐὰν ἔλθωσιν σὺν ἐμοὶ Μακεδόνες καὶ εὕρωσιν ὑμᾶς ἀπαρασκευάστους καταισχυνθῶμεν ἡμεῖς, ἵνα μὴ λέγω ὑμεῖς, ἐν τῇ ὑποστάσει ταύτῃ. ⁵ἀναγκαῖον οὖν ἡγησάμην παρακαλέσαι τοὺς ἀδελφούς, ἵνα προέλθωσιν εἰς ὑμᾶς καὶ προκαταρτίσωσιν τὴν προεπηγγελμένην εὐλογίαν ὑμῶν, ταύτην ἑτοίμην εἶναι οὕτως ὡς εὐλογίαν καὶ μὴ ὡς πλεονεξίαν.

And I am sending the brothers in order that our boasting about you may not prove to have been empty in this case, so that you may be ready, as I said you would be; lest somehow, if some Macedonians come with me and find that you are not ready, we would be humiliated – not to say you – in this undertaking. So I thought it necessary to urge the brothers to go on ahead to you, and arrange in advance for this generous gift that you have promised, so that it may be ready as a generous gift and not as one grudgingly given.

---

324. This implies that there was a minority that was not stimulated to action by the Corinthians' zeal.

325. As in his comments on 8:1-5, Joubert (*Paul as Benefactor*, 174–175, 190) argues here as well that Paul uses an "agonistic" strategy to persuade the Corinthians to complete the collection in a spirit of competition with the Macedonians, their "rivals." But it is better to see in these two instances Paul's strategy to encourage "friendly imitation among equals" (Harris, *Second Epistle*, 577).

Paul returns to the issue of his delegates. As noted earlier, ἔπεμψα should be construed as an epistolary aorist.³²⁶ Paul is about to send the brothers to Corinth. These men are evidently the same as the three brothers whose commendations are provided in 8:16–23; these are Titus and the two unnamed brothers.³²⁷ This is why Paul introduces them here without explanation. After this introduction of the delegates, Paul goes on to give the reasons for their mission in Corinth (v. 3). In the first place, he wants to prevent his boasting about the Corinthians (8:24) from being found void in this case of the collection (τὸ καύχημα ἡμῶν τὸ ὑπὲρ ὑμῶν κενωθῇ ἐν τῷ μέρει τούτῳ). The second motive is that the apostle strives to make the Corinthians ready before his pending visit, as he has been boasting they would be (ἵνα καθὼς ἔλεγον παρεσκευασμένοι ἦτε).³²⁸ In other words, Paul wants the Corinthians' good intentions to be followed by proper actions.³²⁹ In relation to the Corinthians' unpreparedness for the completion of the collection and its possible consequences, Paul expresses the third reason for sending the delegates ahead of him to Corinth. The apostle is concerned that he and the Corinthians may be humiliated (v. 4). If Paul comes with some Macedonians, who know well how he has been boasting about the Corinthians' zeal, they will discover that the situation is totally different from what they were told. The apostle is thus anticipating a visit to Corinth in the company of some delegates from Macedonia (v. 4).³³⁰ If the Corinthians fail to complete the collection before Paul arrives, the Macedonian delegates will discover (εὕρωσιν) that the Corinthians are not ready (ἀπαρασκευάστους), and Paul will "be not merely embarrassed

---

326. But Betz (*2 Corinthians 8 and 9*, 94), Martin (*2 Corinthians*, 284) and others understand it as a preterit.

327. Betz (*2 Corinthians 8 and 9*, 93) argues that Titus was not a member of the group mentioned here. He also thinks that these delegates are different from those introduced in chapter 8.

328. παρεσκευασμένοι ἦτε, a periphrastic subjunctive with ἵνα hardly found in the New Testament (see also 1:9), is here formed by the perfect participle middle with the subjunctive of εἰμί. As a perfect, it expresses "a continuous, settled state of readiness" and thus literally means "(so that) you may be in a state of having prepared yourselves" (Harris, *Second Epistle*, 624).

329. Furnish, *II Corinthians*, 438.

330. ἐάν used with an aorist subjunctive expresses a real possibility (Witherington III, *Conflict and Community*, 426).

but actually shamed or disgraced (καταισχυνθῶμεν ἡμεῖς)."³³¹ For it will become evident that Paul's constant boasting (ἔλεγον, v. 3) that they would have completed their collection was unwarranted.

Paul's fears expressed above raise a question on his earlier statement that Achaia (including Corinth) has been ready since a year ago ('Αχαΐα παρεσκεύασται ἀπὸ πέρυσι) (v. 2). One wonders whether Paul exaggerated the extent of their readiness in order to prompt a quick action among the Macedonians.³³² According to 8:10, the Corinthians were the first to express the previous year their eager desire to participate in the collection. They also took the lead in giving their donations: οὐ μόνον τὸ ποιῆσαι ἀλλὰ καὶ τὸ θέλειν προενήρξασθε ἀπὸ πέρυσι. What they need to do now is to complete their contributions (8.11). It means that Paul had been boasting to the Macedonians about the Achaeans' eagerness to participate in the collection. This eagerness was a first important step because it showed that the Achaeans, including the Corinthians, fully endorsed Paul's project. But this step had to be followed by others in order to complete this generous undertaking. However, the crisis provoked by Paul's opponents must have disrupted the good preparations that had already started in Corinth. The restoration of good relations between the apostle and the Corinthians allows him to rely on them again (7:16). Moreover, Paul can trust that the Corinthians have not abandoned their original commitment towards the funding project. But he also needs to make sure that everything is done before he arrives (9:3–4).³³³ Thus the perfect παρεσκεύασται, with the temporal qualification "since last year" (ἀπὸ πέρυσι), should rightly be rendered "Achaia has been ready" (NRSV). The Corinthians have been ready

---

331. Harris, *Second Epistle*, 625.
332. Ibid., 620. For Betz (*2 Corinthians 8 and 9*, 92, 139–140), the reference to Achaia's preparedness does not include Corinth. In his view, this is also an indication that chapter 9 was a separate letter sent to Achaia. However, it is possible that Paul prefers to refer to the Christians of the whole Roman province of Achaia which includes also Corinth, its capital city (Harris, *Second Epistle*, 619).
333. A similar view is also shared by Thrall (*Critical and Exegetical Commentary*, vol. 2, 566) though she esteems that chapter 9 belongs to a different letter to the Corinthians written shortly after that of chapter 1–8. She notes that when Paul starts the letter of chapter 9 he reminds the Corinthians that when he visited them before the crisis, they were following his instructions given in 1 Cor 16:1–2. It is about this situation that Paul has been boasting to the Macedonians and hopes that the crisis "will not have changed the situation." But the apostle still has some doubts reflected in 9:3–4.

to give since they got practical instructions about the arrangement of their contributions (1 Cor 16:1) and the help of Titus in this matter (2 Cor 8:6).³³⁴ All in all, Paul is saying that the Achaeans have been ready to participate. He is not saying that they have all the money for the collection "ready" for delivery to Jerusalem.³³⁵

It is important to realize how Paul avoids offending the Corinthians. In the first place, he uses the two particles μή πως, to mark "a negative perspective expressing misgiving."³³⁶ Used with an aorist subjunctive as is the case here in 9:4, these particles mean "lest somehow" and indicate that the realization of Paul's fear of shame is hypothetical.³³⁷ Secondly, although he actually thinks that the Corinthians would also be absolutely put to shame, he prefers to speak primarily of himself (ἡμεῖς) and adds them as a parenthetical thought (ἵνα μὴ λέγω ὑμεῖς, "not to say you").³³⁸ This shame would mean that Paul's credibility as an apostle and the Corinthians' as believers would be jeopardized in the matter of the collection.³³⁹ To avoid such a discredit, Paul has thought it necessary (ἡγησάμην)³⁴⁰ to send the three brothers to help the Corinthians make ready (προκαταρτίσωσιν) their donation to the collection for Jerusalem as they had promised previously (v. 5). Although it is possible to understand the verb προκαταρτίζω in its neutral meaning of getting things ready in advance,³⁴¹ or making arrangements in advance,³⁴² the Corinthians' "propensity for disorderliness" (1 Cor 14:33, 40) allows one to understand it in the sense of rectifying things beforehand.³⁴³ Thus, since Paul's and the Corinthians' honor are at

---

334. Harris, *Second Epistle*, 621.

335. Ibid., 620.

336. Danker et al., *Greek-English Lexicon*, 901.

337. Harris (*Second Epistle*, 625) notes that the word order μή πως ἐάν and not μὴ ἐάν πως means that πως relates to καταισχυνθῶμεν.

338. Harris, *Second Epistle*, 625.

339. Furnish, *II Corinthians*, 439.

340. Although ἡγησάμην may be seen as an epistolary aorist, it is also possible to construe it as a preterit. In the latter case, the thought of sending the brothers had taken place in Paul's mind and had been welcomed by these delegates (Harris, *Second Epistle*, 627).

341. Betz, *2 Corinthians 8 and 9*, 87.

342. Thrall, *Critical and Exegetical Commentary*, vol. 2, 563.

343. Harris, *Second Epistle*, 627–628.

stake, the collection becomes here an important link between the apostle and his converts who had been alienated from him.[344]

The apostle designates his collection as a ὑπόστασις. This word can mean "confidence," which would agree with 8:20–23 where Paul refers to his earlier boasting about the Corinthians and which in 9:4 is at risk of being jeopardized. Against Thrall and other scholars who translate it as "plan," J. P. Becker opts for "substance" and contends that we have here an allusion to χάρις.[345] But as explained in my treatment of the critical apparatus of the verse at stake here, nothing precludes us from rendering it by "undertaking."[346] Paul indicates the nature of the contribution he expects from the Corinthians. The apostle twice calls the collection an εὐλογία.[347] This noun derives from the verb εὐλογέω which means "to speak well" both in the sense of to make a fine speech or "to speak well of someone" or a god, "to eulogise" "to praise," "to extol."[348] The verb is also employed to say that "the gods honour a man and grant him benefits."[349] However, the notion of "blessing" by gods plays a limited role in classical Greece.[350] In the LXX ευλογ- word group designates a blessing bestowed to human beings by God or by their fellows (Gen 27:12, 35, 36, 38, 41; 39:5; Exod 32:29; Lev 25:21; Num 23:11; Deut 11:26, 27; etc.).[351] The term εὐλογία very occasionally designates a gift offered by one person to another as a "blessing" (Gen 33:11; 2 Kgs 5:15). In the New Testament, the ευλογ- word group usually takes up much of the Old Testament notion of blessing.[352] God or Jesus blesses people (Rom 15:29; Eph 1:3; Heb 6:7, 14; Mark 10:16; Luke 24:50, 51) and the latter praise God (Luke 1:64; 2:28; 24:53; Jas 3:9).

---

344. Witherington III, *Conflict and Community*, 426.
345. Becker, *Paul's Usage of* χάρις, 129-130.
346. Danker et al., *Greek-English Lexicon*, 1040.
347. Paul employs the same term in 1 Cor 16:1 to indicate the collection.
348. Danker et al., *Greek-English Lexicon*, 408.
349. Beyer, "εὐλογέω, εὐλογητός," 755.
350. Ibid. The gods are viewed as "men's helpers and defenders" who may also punish them. But no specific acts of blessing are ascribed to the gods.
351. Danker et al., *Greek-English Lexicon*, 407–408.
352. Beyer, "εὐλογέω, εὐλογητός," 761–763; Safrai and Tomson ("Paul's 'Collection'," 146–147) show that in the LXX the Hebrew word ברכה which means both "praises" and "wealth" or "bounty" is translated by εὐλογία whose meaning in general Greek is "speaking well," "eulogy"and "praises."

The same word group also refers to human interrelationships (Matt 5:44; Luke 2:34; 6:28; Rom 12:14; 1 Cor 4:12; 1 Pet 3:9). Thus, the collection will be a blessing on the Christians in Jerusalem.[353] Romans 15:27 reflects Paul's broader view of his collection as a Gentile εὐλογία (material blessing) towards the Jerusalem Christians in gratitude for spiritual blessings they received from them. Since the notion "of blessing connotes the idea of bounty," εὐλογία can be understood as a "generous gift, bounty."[354] Such a "bountiful gift" is actually voluntarily given (NRSV) and is thus a blessing to its recipient.[355] For Paul, the generous character of the collection (i.e. as a planned response beforehand), may easily appear if it is ready before he comes.[356]

Paul reminds the Corinthians that the collection he is requesting them to complete is in effect nothing but what had been previously promised (τὴν προεπηγγελμένην εὐλογίαν ὑμῶν) not by him to Jerusalem, "but by the Corinthians to him."[357] Paul is thus convinced – and he wants the Corinthians to take it seriously – that any verbal commitment made voluntarily is in reality a binding promise.[358] This view is emphasized by the use of the perfect participle (προεπηγγελμένην) to indicate that the act of promising is a past event but "with present effect"[359] (i.e. with present validity). However, Paul warns the Corinthians that their contribution must

---

353. Bruehler, "Proverbs, Persuasion and People," 212.

354. Danker et al., *Greek-English Lexicon*, 409. In 8:20 Paul uses the term ἁδρότης (abundance, lavishness) to refer to his relief project.

355. Betz (*2 Corinthians 8 and 9*, 96) translates the word as a "gift of blessing." He notes that in Hellenism "the gift of blessing" is in effect that "of generosity and liberality." It is opposed to greediness, seen as a serious offence to public morality. Greediness is thus "the obsessive attempt to hold fast to what one possesses at any cost, and to acquire still more." Betz argues that Paul's insistence on the nature of the collection as a gift of blessing here reflects his worry that the Corinthians, who are still struggling to have it completed, may have lost sight of its "spiritual purpose" in the course of time.

356. Martin, *2 Corinthians*, 285.

357. Harris, *Second Epistle*, 628.

358. Ibid.

359. Duff, *Elements*, 179.

not be a πλεονεξία,³⁶⁰ "a gift that is grudgingly granted by avarice"³⁶¹, "a scanty contribution given grudgingly."³⁶² This would be the opposite of the sincerity of heart and selflessness exemplified by the Macedonians and above all by Christ. To put it differently, Paul refers to two contrasted "attitudes of giving": with generosity or with miserliness; and not to two ways of getting a gift either "by voluntary act or by extortion."³⁶³

---

360. Delling, "πλεονέκτης, πλεονεκτέω, πλεονεξία," 266, 267. The word group was not solely used with reference to material wealth but could be extended to other issues. It denotes the idea of "having more," "receiving more," and "wanting more." πλεονεξία could for instance mean an obsession for power. In ethical discourses πλεονεξία is formally seen as "excess" and usually means "greed," "insatiability" in relation to food and pleasures; and finally one's act that encroaches on the things that belong to others. In this context, the verb πλεονεκτέω, exclusively found in the Pauline writings where it occurs five times, means "to seize the goods of others," "to seek something by force," "to do violence to." The substantive πλεονεξία appears ten times in the New Testament among which six are found in the Pauline corpus (Rom 1:29; 2 Cor 9:5; Eph 4:19; 5:3; Col 3:5; 1 Thess 2:5; 2 Pet 2:3, 14).

361. Danker et al., *Greek-English Lexicon*, 824. As noted earlier, a greedy person can use violence in order to acquire more wealth. He/she will also hold fast to what he/she possesses and will always show an eager desire to have more. If this person happens to give, he/she does it reluctantly or grudgingly because he/she views what he/she gives to others as a loss. Since Paul is speaking about giving and not acquiring money, it is better to translate ὡς πλεονεξίαν in the present phrase, as a gift "grudgingly given" (NRSV) and not "greediness" (Betz, *2 Corinthians 8 and 9*, 96).

362. Harris, *Second Epistle*, 630.

363. Ibid. Betz (*2 Corinthians 8 and 9*, 97) agrees that Paul contrasts two attitudes towards wealth and notes that the general practice of gift exchange in Antiquity is at the background of the apostle's thought here. He also observes that in that same context, prosperity was thought to result from "divine generosity." Concerning the two contrasted attitudes towards wealth, he makes an instructive comment: "A gift of blessing is given in response to blessings received, while greed represents a failure to respond in kind, owing to one's failure to receive anything as a gift." This awareness that what one has is a gift from God is expressed in 1 Cor 4:7. Thus, greediness is equated with stubborn ingratitude. Becker (*Paul's Usage of* χάρις, 131, 132) also points to the attitude of the giver but in a different perspective. He explains that Paul probably had in mind the competitive giving spirit which was pervasive in Greco-Roman culture. Following Harrison (*Paul's Language of Grace*, 314), he writes that there could have existed unexpressed tensions between the Macedonians and the Corinthians resulting from the fact that Paul had accepted the material gifts of the former while refusing the latter's ones. Becker says that the patronage practice and what it implied in terms of status and power for the benefactor could have given rise to the spirit of competition between both Christian communities. In his conclusion, he proposes to translate πλεονεξία as *"self-serving one-upmanship."*

3.5 God Reciprocates the Generosity of a Cheerful Giver (2 Cor 9:6–10)

V. 6: Τοῦτο δέ, ὁ σπείρων φειδομένως φειδομένως καὶ θερίσει, καὶ ὁ σπείρων ἐπ' εὐλογίαις ἐπ' εὐλογίαις καὶ θερίσει.

And what I say is this:[364] the one who sows sparingly will also reap sparingly, and the one who sows bountifully will also reap bountifully.

Paul starts a new discourse with an illustration of the statement he made previously about the correct way of giving.[365] The expression τοῦτο δέ refers back to verse 5b: ταύτην ἑτοίμην εἶναι οὕτως ὡς εὐλογίαν καὶ μὴ ὡς πλεονεξίαν (so that it may be ready as a voluntary gift and not as one grudgingly given) by way of explanation. Paul uses a metaphor borrowed from the farmer's practice of sowing and reaping. It is clear that the adverb φειδομένως ("sparingly" or "meagerly") and its contrast ἐπ' εὐλογίαις ("bountifully,"[366] "generously," "liberally"[367]) are related to εὐλογία in verse 5.[368] It is very important to keep in mind that the Greek expression carries the notion of blessing which is lost in our modern translations.[369] Thus ἐπ' εὐλογίαις refers to a way of bestowing a gift to benefit the recipient.[370]

---

364. This is the NRSV translation with some adaptations. Since in 1 Cor 7:29 and 15:50 Paul uses the full expression τοῦτο δέ φημί "What I say is this," it is correct to supply this ellipsis with φημι, or λέγω in the present verse (Furnish, *II Corinthians*, 440). Furthermore, the particle δέ is transitional (and), not adversative (but).

365. Martin (*2 Corinthians*, 289) and Betz (*2 Corinthians 8 and 9*, 102) argue that the expression τοῦτο δέ points to what follows and translate it respectively "now mark this," "consider the following."

366. Danker et al., *Greek-English Lexicon*, 409, 1051. Philo, *Leg.* 3.210 (Colson and Whitaker, LCL) uses this expression with a connotation of blessing: πολλὰ γὰρ εὐλόγιστα δρῶσί τινες ἀλλ'οὐκ ἐπ' εὐλογίαις "for there are some people who do many things that are of the nature of benedictions, when their underlying character is not fraught with blessing." Philo insists here on "the necessity of the right motive for a right action."

367. Witherington III (*Conflict and Community*, 424) translates "upon blessing." Thus, he who sows "upon blessing gets a blessed return." Betz (*2 Corinthians 8 and 9*, 103) rightly observes that the adverb φειδομένως (sparingly) is related to πλεονεξίαν (greed) in v. 5.

368. Becker, *Paul's Usage of χάρις*, 256. Therefore, Becker's interpretation which suggests that what is sowed and reaped is χάρις proves misleading.

369. Betz, *2 Corinthians 8 and 9*, 103.

370. Harris, *Second Epistle*, 633.

In Galatians 6:7–8 Paul uses the same agricultural axiom to express the consequences of one's moral conduct. The indicative future θερίσει refers to the end of time. The harvest expected according to this text is either φθορά (destruction or corruption) or ζωὴ αἰώνιος (eternal life). But in 2 Corinthians 9:6b the general principle of farming is applied to the Corinthian context without eschatological overtones. We will see that the harvest to be reaped from the Corinthians' liberal contributions is summarized in verses 7–14. It includes the relief of needs among the poor Jerusalem Christians and intercessional prayers by the recipients.[371] It seems that unlike in Galatians 6:7–8, where Paul's point is "what" one sows, the point in the Corinthian situation is "how much."[372] Apparently, the apostle wants to say that the harvest is proportionate to the seed sown.[373] Paul's thought may be that a meager donation by the Corinthians would give rise to some harvest, "but his desire and aim was for a sizable gift that would produce a correspondingly substantial harvest of benefits for both givers and recipients."[374]

However, Bart Bruehler argues that the translation of ἐπ' εὐλογίαις by "bountifully" is infelicitous.[375] He contends that φειδομένως indicates the negative way of giving and may indicate giving in a miserly manner.[376] As for ἐπ' εὐλογίαις, which retains the notions of "goodwill and kindness," he observes that it depicts an act of giving that is done "blessingly" and thus really is a blessing to the recipients.[377] Bruehler emphasizes that the Greco-Roman ethicists of Paul's time such as Seneca[378] insisted on the attitude of the giver and the benefit the recipient gains from the gift. Their concern was never the benefit that one would gain from the gift bestowed

---

371. Ibid., 633–634.
372. Furnish, *II Corinthians*, 447. But Furnish notes that this may be true if the saying is taken by itself. For him, the context of the latter calls for a different view. Considering 2 Cor 8:13–15 and the fact that it is difficult for most of the Corinthians to give much now, Paul's point may be that "God will provide the means to be generous, that one can sow *liberally* (which also means freely and cheerfully, v. 7a) in the confidence that God will bestow a liberal harvest." This view is amply discussed in the subsequent paragraphs.
373. Harris, *Second Epistle*, 634.
374. Ibid.
375. Bruehler, "Proverbs, Persuasion and People," 214.
376. Ibid., 213.
377. Ibid., 213–214.
378. Seneca, *Ben.* 1.1.8; 2.1.2.

on others. In Bruehler's view, Paul's thought is "how you give largely determines the effect and results of your gift."[379] However, it must be noted that Seneca is not totally uninterested in the benefit which the giver gains from the gift bestowed as Bruehler pretends. It is true that Seneca's basic principle is that beneficence brings joy to the giver and that it is a totally altruistic and virtuous act.[380] At the same time, it appears that he does not rule out social approval as an incentive and reward for benefaction. This is clear in Seneca's insistence on the fact that the giver expects gratitude in return from the recipient: "And so, if you wish the benefactions that you bestow to be rewarded with gratitude, you will be concerned to have them come undiminished to those to whom they were promised."[381] For this reason, he emphasizes the necessity of discernment on the part of the giver while bestowing benefits.[382] The "ideal recipient" needs to be upright, sincere, mindful, grateful, not a stealer, not greedily attached to his own, and kind to others.[383] Moreover, Bruehler does not pay much attention to the context from which Paul's quotation is taken (Prov 11:24 LXX) which carries the idea of the benefit returning to the giver. Bruehler is correct to suggest that Paul may be applying Deuteronomy 15:10 to the collection.[384] Surprisingly, Bruehler fails to note that the second half of Deuteronomy 15:10 clearly speaks of the blessings on the one who takes care of the poor. Deuteronomy 15:1–18 contains divine injunctions as to how the poor must be treated in the sabbatical year, and the promise that those who comply with them will be blessed. Paul appears to agree with this Old Testament belief. In 2 Corinthians 9:11 he states clearly that the Corinthians will be enriched by God so that they continue to excel in every kind of liberality. One may recognize that Paul does not emphasize only the good way of giving (which blesses the recipient); he also makes it clear that God will reciprocate such a sincere and generous giving. But the

---

379. Bruehler, "Proverbs, Persuasion and People," 214.
380. Seneca, *Ben.* 1.6.1; 1.1.9.
381. Seneca, *Ben.* 2.4.3 (Basore, LCL).
382. Seneca, *Ben.* 1.1.2.
383. Seneca, *Ben.* 4.11.1.
384. Bruehler, "Proverbs, Persuasion and People," 214.

apostle does not advocate a self-centered giving in which the giver first calculates the benefits to be gained from God in terms of material prosperity.[385]

However, it is hard to imagine that Paul could expect the poor believers to give substantial contributions.[386] Generosity is not merely about the size of the gift given, but also the inner disposition out of which it is granted. Seneca remarks that some people "become generous" only because they lack courage to withhold their gift.[387] Thus, the adverb φειδομένως (sparingly) is always in relation to what one has (8:11–12), and not to what others have nor to the needs of the recipients. In this way there is no opposition between Paul's insistence on the qualitative aspect of the Corinthians' contributions (8:11–12) and his implied interest in the quantitative dimension of their donations in chapter 9. Two important principles are interrelated here: to show an eager desire to give and to give in accordance with one's means. Once both conditions are met, one who gives will do so joyfully (9:7).[388]

What Paul says in verse 6 functions as a truth borrowed from proverbial wisdom shared by the Corinthians. Thus the apostle does not find it necessary to make further comments on it. And this is true of the whole section (vv. 6–14). The use of the general principle of sowing and reaping to say that one's moral actions have good or bad consequences appears in the pre-Pauline Jewish and Greco-Roman traditions.[389] The use of the

---

385. Concerning the purpose of giving, Bruehler ("Proverbs, Persuasion and People," 215) correctly notes: "The goal is not giving in order to receive, but giving in order to bless."

386. Martin (*2 Corinthians*, 289) observes that the use of ἐπ' εὐλογίαις as "denoting manner may be colloquial" and that "the plural noun indicates abundance." He is also right to note that Paul's appeal does not stress the motive of reward and that it is not the issue of amount that is at stake, but a sincere involvement (8:12).

387. Seneca, *Ben.* 2.1.2 (Basore, LCL).

388. Harris, *Second Epistle*, 634.

389. Betz, *2 Corinthians 8 and 9*, 98–100. The main component of these thoughts was that the farmer's "sowing and reaping" constituted a religious undertaking. The intervention of the divine in the farmer's efforts is attested in the ancient world. Given the unpredictable factors related to nature, the weather, the quality of the soil and seed, the outbreak of diseases and attacks by insects, the farmer's work demonstrated his risk-taking as well as "his trust in the divine each time he cast the seed." Jer 12:13 says that God disturbs crops because he is angry with his people. In Mic 6:15 we read that God would not let his people enjoy their harvest to punish them for their injustices. In the New Testament Paul says that God is involved in the shaping of the body of a seed-grain sown in the soil (1 Cor 15:36–38). In 1 Cor 3:7 Paul points out that God's action in making the seed grow is much more important than the acts of sowing and watering (Betz, *2 Corinthians 8 and 9*, 98–99).

agrarian metaphor was a usual way for the ancient people to give moral lessons. Cicero writes that the saying *"Ut sementem feceris, ita metes"* (As you sow, you shall reap) is used to say that one will receive the same treatment as one has treated someone else.[390] Job 4:8 reads καθ' ὃν τρόπον εἶδον τοὺς ἀροτριῶντας τὰ ἄτοπα οἱ δὲ σπείροντες αὐτὰ ὀδύνας θεριοῦσιν ἑαυτοῖς (For instance, I saw those who plow wrongs, and those who sow them reap torments for themselves). In the book of Sirach 7:3 the sage gives this advice to his son: υἱέ μὴ σπεῖρε ἐπ' αὔλακας ἀδικίας καὶ οὐ μὴ θερίσῃς αὐτὰ ἑπταπλασίως (Do not sow in the furrows of injustice, and you will not reap them sevenfold).[391]

There is no precise parallel to 2 Corinthians 9:6 either in Greco-Roman literature or in Jewish Scriptures. However, it is probable that Paul has in mind the Jewish wisdom tradition from Proverb 11:24 LXX[392] where the wise man writes:[393] εἰσὶν οἳ τὰ ἴδια σπείροντες πλείονα ποιοῦσιν εἰσὶν καὶ οἳ συνάγοντες ἐλαττονοῦνται: There are those who by distributing their livelihood increase it, and there are others who gather, yet have less.[394] It has also been suggested that Paul was influenced by Proverb 22:8[395]: ὁ σπείρων φαῦλα θερίσει κακά πληγὴν δὲ ἔργων αὐτοῦ συντελέσει (He who sows what is cheap will reap what is bad and will complete the impact of his deeds). This may be correct since Paul continues in verse 7 to quote from Proverb 22:8a (LXX, a Greek addition to the Hebrew text): ἄνδρα ἱλαρὸν καὶ δότην εὐλογεῖ ὁ θεός (God blesses a cheerful and generous man).

Verse 7: ἕκαστος καθὼς προῄρηται τῇ καρδίᾳ, μὴ ἐκ λύπης ἢ ἐξ ἀνάγκης· ἱλαρὸν γὰρ δότην ἀγαπᾷ ὁ θεός.

---

390. Cicero, *De or.* 2.65.262 (Sutton and Rackham, LCL).

391. Other Jewish and Christian passages reflect the same wisdom: Job 31:8; Ps 126:5; Prov 11:18; 22:8; Eccl 11:6; Jer 12:13; Hos 8:7; Gal 6:7–8.

392. This hint is suggested by the NA28.

393. Betz (*2 Corinthians 8 and 9*, 104) rejects this view for two main reasons. First, the Masoretic Text and the LXX are different in wording though their content and their context are similar. Second, Paul's text is different from the two Old Testament texts in wording. Betz concludes that Paul may have drawn his quotation from oral tradition in which this proverb was in circulation under different versions.

394. Vv. 25–26, 28 speak of the attitude towards wealth.

395. Gale, *Use of Analogy*, 163; quoted by Harris, *Second Epistle*, 634.

May each person give as he has decided in his heart, not reluctantly or under compulsion, for God loves a cheerful giver.

Paul gives another exhortation to the Corinthians to give their contributions to the collection in a proper way (i.e. joyfully). After ἕκαστος, "each person," a verb like δίδωμι has to be supplied. Since in 2 Corinthians 8–9 Paul generally prefers to give advice rather than commands (8:8, 10), it is better to supply here the aorist optative δῴη: "May each person give."[396] As he does in 1 Corinthians 16:2, Paul uses ἕκαστος to emphasize the personal commitment of the Corinthians as they contribute to the relief fund that will, however, be delivered as a communal offering.[397] Paul repeats the view that donations to the relief fund are voluntary (cf. 8:3, 8) by reminding the Corinthians that one should give according to what they have decided in their hearts (προῄρηται τῇ καρδίᾳ). It is important to note that the apostle uses the perfect tense in this verse (προῄρηται). This may imply that Paul has in mind that, like other churches in Achaia, the Corinthians had made a certain decision about their contribution when they became acquainted with this project a year ago as stated in 9:1 (ὅτι Ἀχαΐα παρεσκεύασται ἀπὸ πέρυσι). In other words, Paul is indirectly requesting the Corinthians to fulfill what they had decided at that time before their work came to a halt. Paul notes that this decision about giving has been made τῇ καρδίᾳ (in one's heart). I noted in 8:16 that the heart is seen as the "seat of physical, spiritual and mental life" and that human will and its decisions originate from there.[398] The heart is also "the working place" of God's Spirit (Gal 4:6; 2 Cor 3:2–3; Rom 5:5).[399] It is thus correct to say that Paul's insistence on the heart as the location of one's intentions and decisions as well as the use of the verb προαιρέω serve to emphasize the volitional nature of the collection.[400] Paul thinks that the Corinthians' gift must not be the result of a sudden emotion, but rather something that one has reflected on

---

396. Lietzmann, *An die Korinther I/II*, 138, followed by Harris, *Second Epistle*, 635.
397. Harris, *Second Epistle*, 635.
398. Danker et al., *Greek-English Lexicon*, 508, 509.
399. Joubert, *Paul as Benefactor*, 194.
400. Bruehler, "Proverbs, Persuasion and People," 215. The verb προαιρέω in the middle voice means "to reach a decision beforehand, choose (for oneself), commit oneself to, prefer." In this context ἕκαστος καθὼς προῄρηται τῇ καρδίᾳ can be translated "as he has made up his mind" (Danker et al., *Greek-English Lexicon*, 865).

beforehand. To put it differently, true giving should result from personal conviction.[401]

Paul gives two other negative connotations of giving that the Corinthians should avoid: to give ἐξ λύπης (literally with "grief, sorrow, affliction," thus reluctantly)[402] or to give ἐξ ἀνάγκης ("under pressure").[403] In Deuteronomy 15:10 we have the same exhortation to give cheerfully to the poor: "Give liberally and be ungrudging when you do so, for on this account the LORD your God will bless you in all your work and in all that you undertake." In a different context where judges are admonished to avoid favoritism (Exod 23:3), Philo insists that God has filled his precepts to Israel "with injunctions to show pity and kindness."[404] He adds that the same God does not tolerate arrogant attitudes but rewards those who provide for the needs of their neighbors. Philo indicates that those who show kindness to the poor do not actually regard abundant possessions as their property, but as something to be shared with the poor. He finally asserts that it is only in showing kindness to his neighbor that man can much resemble God.[405]

To reinforce his exhortation to give generously and freely, Paul provides evidence from Scripture: ἱλαρὸν γὰρ δότην ἀγαπᾷ ὁ θεός. Paul's wording is however slightly different from Proverb 22:8a LXX that he quotes. The LXX exhortation reads as follows: ἄνδρα ἱλαρὸν καὶ δότην εὐλογεῖ ὁ θεός (God blesses a cheerful and generous man). Paul's use of ἀγαπᾷ instead of εὐλογεῖ has received much attention from scholars. Various reasons for this alteration have been given. Some believe that Paul wants to avoid the idea that God would reciprocate the Corinthians' generosity with material things. Thus Paul wished his readers to understand that it is the recipient who is blessed through the gift received and not the giver.[406] In this context ἀγαπάω conveys the idea of "to be well pleased, or content with,"[407] to

---

401. Martin, *2 Corinthians*, 289.
402. Danker et al., *Greek-English Lexicon*, 604–605.
403. Ibid., 61.
404. Philo, *Spec.* 4.72 (Colson, LCL).
405. Philo, *Spec.* 4.73.
406. Bruehler, "Proverbs, Persuasion and People," 215.
407. Ibid.

approve or to value.[408] Others argue that Paul was trying to exhort the Corinthians to long for God's love rather than for material prosperity as a motive for generous giving; it has also been suggested that Paul may have been influenced by Proverb 22:11.[409] In my view, the difference between ἀγαπάω and εὐλογέω in the current verse should not be overestimated. For instance, in Luke 6:27–28 both verbs are used almost in a synonymous parallelism: Ἀλλὰ ὑμῖν λέγω τοῖς ἀκούουσιν· ἀγαπᾶτε τοὺς ἐχθροὺς ὑμῶν, καλῶς ποιεῖτε τοῖς μισοῦσιν ὑμᾶς,²⁸ εὐλογεῖτε τοὺς καταρωμένους ὑμᾶς, προσεύχεσθε περὶ τῶν ἐπηρεαζόντων ὑμᾶς. ("But I say to you that listen, Love your enemies, do good to those who hate you,²⁸ bless those who curse you, pray for those who abuse you"). Paul emphasizes here that God approves of a generous giver and this approval materializes in "special blessings" upon him.[410] However, one should avoid the view that Paul thinks that giving "should result from a desire to gain God's favor," as claims Harris.[411] This may be contrary to Paul's thought that those who have been benefitted by God's grace should give freely by way of gratitude. No one is a cheerful giver by nature; it is only when one realizes that what one has is a gift from God that one can become a cheerful giver.[412] In other words, Paul is saying that God's love for believers is not the reward for their generous gift, but a motivating force for such human charity.[413]

> Verse 8: δυνατεῖ δὲ ὁ θεὸς πᾶσαν χάριν περισσεῦσαι εἰς ὑμᾶς, ἵνα ἐν παντὶ πάντοτε πᾶσαν αὐτάρκειαν ἔχοντες περισσεύητε εἰς πᾶν ἔργον ἀγαθόν.
>
> And God is able to provide you with every blessing in abundance, so that by always having enough of everything, you may abound in every good work.

---

408. Furnish, *II Corinthians*, 441, n. 7. See this meaning in Wis 7:28; Sir 4:14; Prov 22:11 (LXX).

409. Betz, *2 Corinthians 8 and 9*, 107.

410. Harris, *Second Epistle*, 636.

411. Ibid., 637.

412. Betz, *2 Corinthians 8 and 9*, 111. 1 Cor 4:7 reflects the same awareness that all gifts are from God.

413. Antony, "He Who Supplies Seed," 310.

Paul has already said that the benefit that one will get from one's contribution will be determined by what one gives (v. 6). Now, in verse 8 he is more explicit and gives another reason why the Corinthians should give their contributions generously to the relief fund: God is able to make every χάριν abound towards the Corinthians. In the phrase δυνατεῖ δὲ ὁ θεὸς (God is able), it is possible to see a reference to "the specific idea of God's power" as in Romans 4:21 (καὶ πληροφορηθεὶς ὅτι ὃ ἐπήγγελται δυνατός ἐστιν καὶ ποιῆσαι: being fully convinced that God was able to do what he had promised); 11:23 (δυνατὸς γάρ ἐστιν ὁ θεὸς πάλιν ἐγκεντρίσαι αὐτούς, for God has the power to graft them in again).[414] God is able to grant the Corinthians πᾶσαν χάριν. The question is how to understand the term χάρις. Our different versions of the Bible reflect this difficulty. Some of them translate χάρις by the very common meaning of "grace" (NKJV), which is confusing. Becker, who adopts the same rendering, explains that the grace that is supplied to the Corinthians will produce a greater measure of grace and result in self-sufficiency. Becker concludes that it seems that the apostle is telling the Corinthians that his collection is "actually an excellent investment opportunity" in the sense that they offer money but receive in return what is most valuable, God's grace. In his view, Paul is depicting χάρις in 2 Corinthians 9:1–12 as "something which is both objective and quantifiable."[415] By contrast, Harris is right to indicate that the term has rather the meaning of εὐλογία and can be correctly translated by "blessing"[416] (NRSV), "benefit"[417] or "gracious gift" (CJB). It is clear that in this context the word χάρις refers to all sorts of benefits, spiritual and material, that God can grant his people. Becker sees here an indication that χάρις displays what he constantly calls "pneusomatic" aspects.[418] The qualifier πᾶσαν used with χάριν supports this inclusive sense of the term. Therefore, it is not possible to restrict its meaning either to material prosperity or to spiritual blessings.

---

414. Furnish, *II Corinthians*, 441n. 8.
415. Becker, *Paul's Usage of χάρις*, 248, 249.
416. Harris, *Second Epistle*, 637.
417. Furnish, *II Corinthians*, 441n. 8.
418. Becker, *Paul's Usage of χάρις*, 249–255.

The purpose of God's action in pouring out every kind of χάριν is clearly spelled out: ἵνα ἐν παντὶ πάντοτε πᾶσαν αὐτάρκειαν ἔχοντες περισσεύητε εἰς πᾶν ἔργον ἀγαθόν (so that by always having enough of everything, you may abound in every good work). The substantive αὐτάρκεια denotes "independence" and generally means "sufficiency."[419] We find this sense in Stoicism and Cynicism. For Stoics and Cynics, αὐτάρκεια meant "the self-sufficiency and contentment of the person who was self-supporting and independent of other people and of circumstances."[420] Thus, αὐτάρκεια implied the ability to resist any disturbance caused by emotion.[421] The substantive αὐτάρκεια is totally absent from the LXX, but its cognate adjective αὐτάρκης occurs there several times and can mean "sufficient" (Prov 30:8), "sufficient in oneself" or "self-supporting" (Sir 40:18), "without excess" (Sir 34:28), and "despotic" (4 Macc 9:9)[422] The related verb αὐταρκέω appears in Deuteronomy 32:10 with reference to God's providence reflected in his provision of food and instruction to Israel.[423] In this passage it carries a meaning which is slightly opposed to the basic sense of αὐτάρκεια noted above since it means to grant the necessary provisions or maintain. In 2 Corinthians 9:8 the word αὐτάρκεια[424] means the "state of having what is adequate, sufficiency," and thus the state of having "enough of everything."[425] It is not correct to restrict this sufficiency to material things, as does Witherington.[426] Rather, it covers material and spiritual needs (ἐν παντί).[427] It is important to note that Paul emphasizes that the Corinthians' sufficiency does not come from their "self-discipline" as was the case for the Stoics and Cynics, but from God who provides the believers with the basic

---

419. Danker et al., *Greek-English Lexicon*, 152.
420. Joubert, *Paul as Benefactor*, 195.
421. Longenecker, *Remember the Poor*, 75.
422. Lust, Eynikel and Hauspie, *Greek-English Lexicon*, 95.
423. Harris, *Second Epistle*, 638.
424. The term is found only here and in 1 Tim 6:6 with the sense of contentment as opposed to πλεονεξία (insatiability, avarice, covetousness). Its cognate αὐτάρκης, content, is a New Testament *hapax* (Phil 4:11).
425. Danker et al., *Greek-English Lexicon*, 152.
426. Witherington III, *Conflict and Community*, 427.
427. Bruehler, "Proverbs, Persuasion and People," 216. Martin (*2 Corinthians*, 290) argues that Paul's thought is that God will grant the givers "both the desire to share and the necessary ability to do so."

necessities and even a surplus (Phil 4:11–13).[428] For the apostle, one can attain "self-sufficiency" as long as one sees and uses material wealth "as part of God's grace" and not as "the result of a purely human achievement."[429]

For Paul, the God-given αὐτάρκεια among the Corinthians does not aim at self-enjoyment, or at "their total independence from others in terms of their financial and spiritual needs."[430] On the contrary, it will lead them to interact with other people.[431] This is what Paul means when he writes that the Corinthians' sufficiency will enable them to abound or excel in every good work (πᾶν ἔργον ἀγαθόν).[432] It is worth noting that Paul uses a present subjunctive to express this purpose of the Corinthian αὐτάρκεια: ἵνα . . . περισσεύητε. It implies that Paul expects the Corinthians to engage in every good deed as a continuous action, a way of living. The phrase πᾶν ἔργον ἀγαθόν refers to the deeds that are accomplished by humans and that exhibit the moral character of those who accomplish them.[433] In the context of the collection, it is quite sure that the phrase πᾶν ἔργον ἀγαθόν includes the collection and other forms of care for the needy. In Paul's view, the very nature of the divine grace is that "it overflows from any situation or vessels into which it has been bestowed" to affect others.[434] By putting God and others at the center of the believer's life, Paul redefines the notion of αὐτάρκεια. The apostle highlights "the communitarian dimension of the human family," and especially the communal essence of the Christian faith over and against the sacralization of individuals.[435]

---

428. Furnish, *II Corinthians*, 448.

429. Betz, *2 Corinthians 8 and 9*, 110.

430. Joubert, *Paul as Benefactor*, 196.

431. Furnish, *II Corinthians*, 448.

432. The expression πᾶν ἔργον ἀγαθόν (every good work) is frequently used in the Pastorals (1 Tim 5:10; 2 Tim: 2:21; 3:17; Titus 1:16; 3:1) but rarely in other Pauline letters (Col 1:10; 2 Thess 2:17): Harris, *Second Epistle*, 639, n. 35. It also appears in 1 Clem. 2.7; 33.1; 34.4.

433. Danker et al., *Greek-English Lexicon*, 390. For Joubert (*Paul as Benefactor*, 196), Paul's message to the Corinthians can be summarized as follows: "They once more need to become fully aware of the nature of God's blessings in their lives in order to turn into grateful beneficiaries who would joyfully adhere to the principles laid down in verse 7."

434. Antony, "He Who Supplies Seed," 311.

435. Ibid., 312.

Verse 9: καθὼς γέγραπται· ἐσκόρπισεν, ἔδωκεν τοῖς πένησιν, ἡ δικαιοσύνη αὐτοῦ μένει εἰς τὸν αἰῶνα.

As it is written, "He has dispersed abroad, he has given to the poor; his righteousness endures forever."

Paul finds in Psalm 111 LXX the confirmation of his previous statement in verse 8. In Paul's quotation, the identification of the subject of the two verbs (ἐσκόρπισεν, ἔδωκεν) has divided many scholars. But it is quite clear that God is the subject in verses 8a and 10. Some relate the two aorists to the Corinthians.[436] For them, the point is that once they have received God's beneficence, the Corinthians will excel in every good work (v. 8b). Nevertheless, there are good reasons to see God as the subject of these verbs as in verses 8a and 10.[437] Although Psalm 111:9 LXX speaks unambiguously of the righteous man, one may suspect that Paul has altered the sense of this text to make it fit in with its new setting. Paul uses the same "hermeneutical strategy" in 2 Corinthians 9:10 as I will demonstrate below.[438] Whereas in Isaiah 55:10 LXX the action of giving seed to the sower and bread for food is ascribed to the earth, in Paul's quotation (9:10) the same activity is attributed to God.[439] Similarly, in 2 Corinthians 9:9 Paul has altered the sense of Psalm 111:9 LXX by changing the subject of the verb ἐσκόρπισεν. Whereas for the LXX it is the righteous man who

---

436. Thrall (*Critical and Exegetical Commentary*, vol. 2, 583) and Harris (*Second Epistle*, 640) argue that the implied subject of 9:9 is the Corinthians. The main reason is that except for the last verse, Ps 111 LXX quoted by Paul is entirely devoted to the deeds of the righteous man and not to God. This is true. The psalmist speaks of the blessings that will come upon the righteous man and his descendants (vv. 1-2). Prosperity, victory and continual remembrance are promised to him (vv. 3-8). The righteous man is characterized by astounding generosity towards the needy (9). It is said that his δικαιοσύνη lasts forever (v. 9). On the contrary, the wicked man will be frustrated (v. 10). Other arguments are also given as pieces of evidence for this interpretation: ἐσκόρπισεν refers back to ὁ σπείρων in v. 6; ἔδωκεν looks back to the implied idea of giving in v. 7, while the phrase τοῖς πένησιν relates to the poor (οἱ πτωχοί) among the saints in Jerusalem (Rom 15:26). In the same vein, the righteousness which is individualized in v. 9 (ἡ δικαιοσύνη αὐτοῦ) becomes corporate and is applied to the Corinthians in v. 10 (δικαιοσύνη ὑμῶν). See also Bruehler, "Proverbs, Persuasion and People," 217, n. 24 for the same view.

437. Georgi, *Remembering the Poor*, 98; Betz, *2 Corinthians 8 and 9*, 111–112; Witherington III, *Conflict and Community*, 427; Antony, "He Who Supplies Seed," 312.

438. Downs, *Offering of the Gentiles*, 142.

439. The idea that God is the one who literally provides or germinates seed is occasionally found in Scriptures: Gen 26:12; Ps 65:9; Isa 55:10–11; 62:8 (Betz, *2 Corinthians 8 and 9*, 112, n. 173).

scatters his wealth and gives to the needy, in 2 Corinthians 9:10 it is God who does so. Unlike in many other biblical narratives where the scattering activity denotes a negative situation – sometimes God is against his enemies – in the present passage it does produce a positive effect.[440] In this context, God's δικαιοσύνη means his faithfulness to his covenant and to all his promises to his people.[441] His δικαιοσύνη μένει εἰς τὸν αἰῶνα (endures forever). Therefore, the Corinthians can rely on God's faithfulness not only while contributing to the collection but also thereafter. If this interpretation is correct, verse 9 gives evidence to the idea that God is able to pour material and spiritual blessings upon the Corinthians (v. 8a).[442] Otherwise, it is difficult to imagine that the phrase ἡ δικαιοσύνη αὐτοῦ μένει εἰς τὸν αἰῶνα (his righteousness endures forever) applied to human beings can fit in Paul's overall theology.

> Verse 10: ὁ δὲ ἐπιχορηγῶν σπόρον τῷ σπείροντι καὶ ἄρτον εἰς βρῶσιν χορηγήσει καὶ πληθυνεῖ τὸν σπόρον ὑμῶν καὶ αὐξήσει τὰ γενήματα τῆς δικαιοσύνης ὑμῶν.
>
> He who supplies seed to the sower and bread for food will supply and multiply your seed and increase the harvest of your righteousness.

Paul returns to and develops the idea expressed in verse 8 to the effect that God provides for the needs of the Corinthians to enable them to constantly perform every good deed. In a broader sense, the agrarian imagery used by Paul in this verse summarizes the content of the whole section of verses 6–10.[443] The apostle strives to dissipate any fears among the Corinthians that they may face shortage after giving generously their

---

440. Antony, "He Who Supplies Seed," 313: 2 Sam 22:15; Wis 17:3; Ezek 5:1-17; Zech 13:7-9; Matt 12:30; Luke 11:23; John 16:32.

441. In previous chapters of 2 Cor the word δικαιοσύνη is infrequently used in different contexts. The new covenant is termed ἡ διακονία τῆς δικαιοσύνης (the ministry of justification) as opposed to ἡ διακονία τῆς κατακρίσεως (the ministry of condemnation). In 5:21 it is said that in Christ the believers have been made δικαιοσύνη θεοῦ (the righteousness of God). In 6:7 Paul speaks of τὰ ὅπλα τῆς δικαιοσύνης (the weapons of righteousness), whereas 6:14 (regardless of the question of its authenticity) tells us about the sharp contrast existing between δικαιοσύνη (righteousness) and ἀνομία (lawlessness or evil).

442. Betz, *2 Corinthians 8 and 9*, 11–112; Furnish, *II Corinthians*, 448–449.

443. Downs, *Offering of the Gentiles*, 142.

contributions to the collection.[444] Concerning the phrase ἐπιχορηγῶν σπόρον τῷ σπείροντι καὶ ἄρτον εἰς βρῶσιν Betz remarks that a threefold provision is implied: seed to sow in the present year, seed for the next year's sowing, and bread for present consumption.[445] The subject of ἐπιχορηγῶν is the same as in verses 8a and 9 (i.e. God). He is presented as the one who supplies abundantly seed and food to the farmer (sower). Paul draws from the agricultural experience to support his statement about God's provision by quoting Isaiah 55:10 with some alterations. In the LXX the text runs as follows:[446]

> ὡς γὰρ ἐὰν καταβῇ ὑετὸς ἢ χιὼν ἐκ τοῦ οὐρανοῦ καὶ οὐ μὴ ἀποστραφῇ ἕως ἂν μεθύσῃ τὴν γῆν καὶ ἐκτέκῃ καὶ ἐκβλαστήσῃ καὶ δῷ σπέρμα τῷ σπείροντι καὶ ἄρτον εἰς βρῶσιν . . .

> For as rain or snow comes down from heaven and will not return until it has soaked the earth and brought forth and blossomed and given seed to the sower and bread for food . . .

In Isaiah 55 the prophet is calling upon the people of Israel, those who are in spiritual want, to come to God. Verses 8–9 say that God's thoughts are far different from those of humans. Verse 10 shows that the divine Word will inevitably have an effect. By way of demonstration, the prophet uses an example taken from daily life and showing God's gracious intervention. The prophet affirms that the sower's efforts in plowing the soil become productive only because of the fall of precipitation. Paul's point in this comparison is that what the earth does in producing seed and bread is comparable to what God himself does for the giver. God will provide the Corinthians

---

444. Joubert, *Paul as Benefactor*, 197. Bruehler ("Proverbs, Persuasion and People," 222) contends that in this section Paul seems to be addressing the Corinthian Christians in financial difficulties, whereas vv. 12–14 are directed to those living in financial comfort. But we should be careful here because on the one hand the rich may also be very worried about losing their wealth by giving their donations to the relief fund. On the other hand, as the Macedonians' example shows, the poor may very well display generosity and joy while giving.

445. Betz, *2 Corinthians 8 and 9*, 113.

446. As can be observed, Paul introduces two changes in the text of the LXX. First, he replaces sπέρμα with σπόρον. But both words are synonyms. Second, Paul alters the original text to tally with his affirmation about God's providential care. Whereas in the LXX the action of giving seed to the sower and bread for food is ascribed to the earth, in Paul's quotation (9:9) the same activity is attributed to God.

with the necessities in order for them to give freely to those in need. Paul uses three consecutive future indicatives to assure the Corinthians of God's provision. χορηγήσει (he will supply), πληθυνεῖ (he will multiply), αὐξήσει (he will increase). God will multiply their resources as they commit themselves to giving generously to the collection for Jerusalem.[447] The σπόρον that will be supplied to the Corinthians and multiplied by God refers to the material resources they need to contribute to the collection.[448] This idea of God's expanding the provision of the giver resonates with Proverb 11:24a:[449] "There are those who by distributing their livelihood increase it." It is important to realize that it is God who provides "the initial seed" to sow as well as bread for food for the sower.[450] Elsewhere Paul expresses the same idea that it is God who gives to the believers the goodwill to do what is good (Phil 2:3). Consequently, the idea that givers receive God's benefits for their generosity is not seen by Paul as a reward, as if some prior bargain had been struck between them and God.[451] For Paul, it is God who provides all the resources needed to perform the act of giving.

The third affirmation made by Paul about God's involvement in the Corinthians' giving is that he will "increase the harvest" of the Corinthians' righteousness (αὐξήσει τὰ γενήματα τῆς δικαιοσύνης ὑμῶν). Paul alludes here to Hosea 10:12 LXX:

---

447. Antony, "He Who Supplies Seed," 313–134. Many Old Testament references depict God as the multiplier: Gen 1:22, 28; 8:17; 9:1, 7; 17:6, 20; 28:3, etc.

448. Betz, *2 Corinthians 8 and 9*, 114.

449. Harris, *Second Epistle*, 643.

450. Bruehler, "Proverbs, Persuasion and People," 217.

451. Harris, *Second Epistle*, 637: "The twofold biblical principle is 'bless others, because you have been blessed by God' (cf. Deut. 15:4); 'bless others, in order to be blessed by God' (e.g. Deut. 14:28–29; 15:10, 18; Prov 22:9; cf. 1 Pet 3:9)." According to Paul, human beings do not earn or deserve harvest; they rather receive it from God. Therefore, "if God's blessing results from generous giving, as Deut. 15:10 so emphatically asserts, it is also true that it is God who implants in humans the χάρις of προθυμία, the 'grace' of the 'willingness to give' (cf. 8:11–12)" (Furnish, *II Corinthians*, 447). In Rom 4:4 Paul points out a sharp contrast between what one earns as a reward and what is received as a divine gift. As Paul deals with the basis of justification, he cites the example of Abraham in Gen 15:6 and explains that the latter's complete trust in God was counted for righteousness on his part (Rom 4:3). He then concludes that works do not play any role in justification since God's justifying decision is not earned but rather received freely from God.

σπείρατε ἑαυτοῖς εἰς δικαιοσύνην τρυγήσατε εἰς καρπὸν ζωῆς
φωτίσατε ἑαυτοῖς φῶς γνώσεως ἐκζητήσατε τὸν κύριον ἕως
τοῦ ἐλθεῖν γενήματα δικαιοσύνης ὑμῖν.

Sow for yourselves unto justice; reap unto the fruit of life; enlighten yourselves with the light of knowledge; seek the Lord until the produce of justice comes upon you.

The prophet accuses his people of having abandoned their God to embrace idolatry (10:1–2), and having relied on their power (10:13). He thus launches an invitation to the inhabitants of Juda and Israel to sow εἰς δικαιοσύνην (righteousness, justice) whose harvest will be life. Otherwise, they will face God's punishment (10:9–10, 14–15). This means that they must change their ways and place their confidence in God rather than in their idols and their military power. However, nothing indicates that the prophet is tackling social injustices among the people.

Perhaps, Paul is interested in the farming vocabulary rather than in the meaning that the term δικαιοσύνη has in Hosea 10:12. Paul indicates that God will increase the harvest (γενήματα) which springs up from the Corinthians' δικαιοσύνη.[452] Here δικαιοσύνη[453] is almost equated with generosity.[454] Then the phrase τὰ γενήματα τῆς δικαιοσύνης encapsulates the content of verses 6–11.[455] Moreover, it reiterates the key concept of δικαιοσύνη mentioned in verse 9 in relation to God. Thus the close relationship between God's righteousness in 9b and the Corinthians' is

---

452. Harris, *Second Epistle*, 643: τῆς δικαιοσύνης is a subjective genitive, "produced by/springing (up) from righteousness." But Bruehler ("Proverbs, Persuasion and People," 217–218) understands it as "a genitive of apposition (or an epexegetical genitive)" which can be translated "the harvest which is your righteousness."

453. Here δικαιοσύνη bears the meaning it carries in Matt 6:1; i.e. acts of kindness and piety including almsgiving (Bruehler, "Proverbs, Persuasion and People," 217). It is an act "which meets the demands of the law in regard to social responsibility for others" (Dunn, *Beginning from Jerusalem*, 943). Dunn insists on the fact that Paul uses other terms from Jewish social ethic which set his collection in the framework of Israel's covenant. The apostle calls the Corinthians to do "what is good" (καλὰ, 2 Cor 8:21); he writes that God expects them to "abound in every good work" (ἵνα ... περισσεύητε εἰς πᾶν ἔργον ἀγαθόν, 2 Cor 9:8); and speaks of the Corinthians' "obedience" (ὑποταγή) to their confession of the gospel of Christ (2 Cor 9:13). However, Dunn warns that this supplementary Jewish concern does not undermine Paul's conviction that his enterprise was primarily motivated by God's grace in Christ (Dunn, *Beginning from Jerusalem*, 944).

454. Witherington III, *Conflict and Community*, 427.

455. Harris, *Second Epistle*, 643.

clarified here: "God's righteousness provides for human righteousness by establishing its economic basis."[456] The Corinthians are provided with the means to exercise their righteousness through their attendance to the needs of the poor in the Jerusalem church. The harvest of the Corinthians' righteousness comprehends "God's material and spiritual" benefits for generous giving (vv. 8–11),[457] the relief of the needy (v. 12a), and prayers of thanksgiving and intercession" from the Jerusalem Christians (vv. 12b–14).[458] 2 Corinthians 9:10 tells about the dependability of God as a solid reason to give generously.

3.6 The Outcomes of the Collection and Doxology (2 Cor 9:11–15)

Verse 11: ἐν παντὶ πλουτιζόμενοι εἰς πᾶσαν ἁπλότητα, ἥτις κατεργάζεται δι' ἡμῶν εὐχαριστίαν τῷ θεῷ.

You will be enriched in every way in order to show every kind of generosity, which will produce thanksgiving to God through us.

Paul is now about to conclude his appeal to the Corinthians to give their contributions to the collection. In verse 11 Paul says that they will

---

456. Betz, *2 Corinthians 8 and 9*, 114.

457. In line with the Jewish thought of his time, Paul views the Corinthians' assistance to the needy in Jerusalem as the expression of δικαιοσύνη that God expects from his people. I noted in chapter one that in early Judaism, as attested by the LXX, righteousness was often equated with almsgiving (Dan 4:27; Sir 3:14, 30; 7:10; 12:3; 40:17).

458. Harris, *Second Epistle*, 633–634. But Nickle (*Collection*, 137) argues that Paul was not speaking of "an increase in funds"; but was trying to assure the Corinthians that "their involvement in the collection would be used by God to produce an abundant harvest in connection with the proclamation of the gospel of redemption among Israel." In the same way, thinks Nickle, their thanks would not be motivated by the relief fund received, "but much more, through its witness to the salvation of the Gentiles, their mission to convert Israel would prosper." As can be seen, Nickle expands on his overall thesis about the eschatological meaning of Paul's collection. His thought is that Paul's collection has to be interpreted in the light of the old Jewish traditions regarding the Gentiles flooding into Jerusalem with their gifts. However, I argued in the first chapter of this study that this association can hardly be proved in Paul's writings and that this eschatological reading of the collection must be abandoned.

constantly be enriched (πλουτιζόμενοι).⁴⁵⁹ The phrase ἐν παντὶ preceding πλουτιζόμενοι indicates that the Corinthians' enrichment "incorporates both economic and spiritual blessings" just like the πᾶσαν χάριν in verse 8a.⁴⁶⁰ God's purpose in enriching the Corinthians is that they demonstrate every sort of generosity (εἰς πᾶσαν ἁπλότητα). Paul repeats here, in a different way, what he mentioned in verse 8b: ἵνα ἐν παντὶ πάντοτε πᾶσαν αὐτάρκειαν ἔχοντες περισσεύητε εἰς πᾶν ἔργον ἀγαθόν (so that by always having enough of everything, you may abound in every good work). In both cases (vv. 8b and 11), without deviating from his concern about the present contribution to the Jerusalem collection, Paul thinks beyond it and considers "future opportunities to share with others the resources provided by God."⁴⁶¹ The apostle expects that the Corinthians' diverse generosity will produce thanksgiving among the Jerusalem Christians. The phrase δι' ἡμῶν (through us)⁴⁶² means that the Christians in Jerusalem will thank God for the gift they received through Paul.⁴⁶³ In a context where benefactors would expect to receive public praise for their deeds, it is noteworthy that Paul insists twice that εὐχαριστία will be rendered to God (vv. 11, 12),

---

459. Note the present participle which expresses a continuous action. In accordance with the verbs in v. 10 (χορηγήσει καὶ πληθυνεῖ . . . αὐξήσει), the participle πλουτιζόμενοι stands for an indicative future too. Betz (*2 Corinthians 8 and 9*, 115) maintains that this participle is related to δι' ἡμῶν εὐχαριστίαν and translates it as "we are wealthy."

460. Harris, *Second Epistle*, 645. Betz (*2 Corinthians 8 and 9*, 115, 116) has the same interpretation and observes that Paul's thought here is consistent with what he says about the Corinthians in 1 Cor 1:5 and in 2 Cor 8:7. Thus, as far as material wealth is concerned, Paul does not view it as "spiritually corrupting." Rather, he finds it "good and acceptable if it leads to generosity." See also Thrall, *Critical and Exegetical Commentary*, vol. 2, 585.

461. Harris, *Second Epistle*, 645. Joubert (*Paul as Benefactor*, 197) notes that Paul is saying that following their generous and free giving, the Corinthians will experience "the miracle" eventuated by God's grace in their lives and they will have "even more to give in the future." But the concept of miracle introduced by Betz here overstretches Paul's statement.

462. Furnish (*II Corinthians*, 443, n. 11) maintains that Paul probably has in mind the accompanying group that will be with him in the delivery of the collection. Betz (*2 Corinthians 8 and 9*, 116) argues that this plural includes all those who followed Paul's instructions in the collection project. However, it is most probable that Paul uses here the literary plural as he frequently does in this passage (8:1, 4, 5, 6, 18, 19, 20, 21, 22; 9:3, 4, 5).

463. Betz, *2 Corinthians 8 and 9*, 116, 117. But Betz's idea that the expression emphasizes that the offering of this gift was to Paul's credit and promoted his righteousness before God must be rejected.

since it is thanks to his grace that the collection project has been achieved.[464] This view is consistent with what Paul says about his own ministry in 2 Corinthians 4:15: "For everything is for your sake, so that grace, having enlarged its scope through the growing numbers, may cause the thanksgiving to increase to the glory of God."[465] It is thus correct to conclude that the apostle subverts the principle of the Greco-Roman benefaction by emphasizing that honor and praise are due to God, the ultimate benefactor, and not to his human agents.[466]

> Verse 12: ὅτι ἡ διακονία τῆς λειτουργίας ταύτης οὐ μόνον ἐστὶν προσαναπληροῦσα τὰ ὑστερήματα τῶν ἁγίων, ἀλλὰ καὶ περισσεύουσα διὰ πολλῶν εὐχαριστιῶν τῷ θεῷ.
>
> for the rendering of this service not only supplies the needs of the saints but also overflows with many thanksgivings to God.

Paul introduces the explanation of his argument in verse 11 by the use of ὅτι. He points out two outcomes of the Corinthians' ἁπλότης (generosity): the relief of the needs of the saints in Jerusalem and thanksgivings to God. In the first place Paul calls the collection ἡ διακονία τῆς λειτουργίας.[467] The word διακονία has here the general meaning of the act of performing a certain activity or task; a "service," "ministering," "rendering." The term λειτουργία and its cognates originally bear a wholly secular meaning. In politics λειτουργία indicated the fulfillment of political duties in the city as distinct from fiscal tasks. Wealthy citizens would accomplish by obligation or voluntarily specific tasks of public interest such as feeding people and the payment of military expenses.[468] With time the term developed from its technical political sense to refer to any public service, and later on it acquired a popular meaning and designated any type of private service one could render to others. This included the services of a slave to his master, a worker to his taskmaster, a friend to another, the services of a father to his

---

464. Downs, *Offering of the Gentiles*, 143. Judaism strongly emphasizes the view that thanksgiving is a highly religious obligation (Betz, *2 Corinthians 8 and 9*, 117, n. 220).
465. Thrall, *Critical and Exegetical Commentary*, vol. 1, 321, 344–347.
466. Downs, *Offering of the Gentiles*, 143–144.
467. Strathmann, "λειτουργέω, λειτουργία, λειτουργός," 215.
468. Ibid., 216-217.

son, or the services an organ renders to the whole body.[469] In the LXX and Hellenistic Judaism λειτουργία is almost always used as a technical term for cultic activities (Exod 37:19; Deut 18:5; Num 8:22; 16:9; 2 Chr 31:2; 36:16; Josephus, *Antiquitates Judaicae* 3.107; *The Jewish War* 1.39; 6.299; Philo, *De Somniis* 1.214; *De Sacrificiis Abelis et Caini* 1.132).[470] This religious meaning is taken up in the New Testament (Luke 1:23; Heb 8:6; 9:21; Phil 2:17).[471] The word λειτουργία is also used in its secular and popular sense to speak of Epaphroditus' services to the apostle Paul (Phil 2:30).[472] In 2 Corinthians 9:12 it is possible that Paul wants the reader to keep the civic and religious meanings of the term.[473] It is interesting that in Romans 13:6 civic community rulers are called God's λειτουργοί in the sense of "public servants" to whom all citizens including Christians have to pay taxes.[474] The expression ἡ διακονία τῆς λειτουργίας ταύτης can naturally be construed as meaning "the rendering of this service" (RSV, NRSV), "the administration of this service" (KJV, NKJV).

The apostle expects that the collection, seen as a λειτουργία, will address the needs of the saints in Jerusalem and cause them to worship God. Moreover, as we will see, the collection is expected to lead the recipients to say intercessional prayers for the givers (v. 14). In other words, Paul does not see his collection project as a purely philanthropic undertaking. It also has a religious significance. However, Down appears to overstate the religious aspect of Paul's collection when he argues that by calling his collection a λειτουργία, the apostle wants the Corinthians "to understand their contribution as a priestly service offered to God."[475] Such a restrictive

---

469. Ibid., 217.

470. Ibid., 221. Besides his agreement with the LXX in his use of the term, Philo also employs it metaphorically to indicate the spiritual worship of God: *Post.* 185.

471. Danker et al., *Greek-English Lexicon*, 591. In Rom 15:27, Paul uses the related verb seemingly with a secular meaning (Strathmann, "λειτουργέω, λειτουργία, λειτουργός, λειτουργικός," 227).

472. Danker et al., *Greek-English Lexicon*, 591.

473. Witherington III, *Conflict and Community*, 428. See also Bruehler, "Proverbs, Persuasion and People," 220: "Therefore, λειτουργία reinforces not only the charitable aspect of the collection, but also its religious significance since the Corinthians' gift would become an impetus for worship in Jerusalem."

474. Wright, "Introduction," 721.

475. Downs, *Offering of the Gentiles*, 145.

view of Paul's collection does not appreciate correctly the fact that Paul was seriously concerned by the plight of the poor Christians in Jerusalem and hoped that his collection would relieve them.

As noted above, two purposes of the collection are spelled out in 9:12. First, the collection will supply the needs of the Jerusalem church (ἐστὶν προσαναπληροῦσα τὰ ὑστερήματα τῶν ἁγίων). In Rom 15:27 Paul states clearly that the Gentiles have a moral obligation to reciprocate the spiritual blessings they have received through the gospel preached to them from Jerusalem, by sharing with the saints in Jerusalem their material wealth (εὐδόκησαν γὰρ καὶ ὀφειλέται εἰσὶν αὐτῶν· εἰ γὰρ τοῖς πνευματικοῖς αὐτῶν ἐκοινώνησαν τὰ ἔθνη, ὀφείλουσιν καὶ ἐν τοῖς σαρκικοῖς λειτουργῆσαι αὐτοῖς). However, I pointed out earlier that this motif is totally absent from Paul's conceptualization of his collection in the Corinthian correspondence. The second result expected from the collection in Paul's thought is the abundant thanksgivings which will spring from the Jerusalem church as a result of their receiving this relief fund. As was the case in verse 11, it is important to note that the thanksgivings will be directed to God and not to the givers nor to Paul as God's main agent in this project. Harris argues that the construction οὐ μόνον . . . ἀλλὰ καί indicates that the supply of the needs of the saints in Jerusalem is subsidiary to the act of thanking God, the theological function of the collection.[476] But this reading is not convincing. Rather, Paul's intention was to emphasize that the ordinary purpose of such a donation was to supply the needs of destitute people.[477] Through this giving of thanks to God, the Christians in the Jerusalem church will show that they recognize that God is the "ultimate source" of the relief fund.[478]

Verses 13–14: διὰ τῆς δοκιμῆς τῆς διακονίας ταύτης δοξάζοντες τὸν θεὸν ἐπὶ τῇ ὑποταγῇ τῆς ὁμολογίας ὑμῶν εἰς τὸ εὐαγγέλιον τοῦ Χριστοῦ καὶ ἁπλότητι τῆς κοινωνίας εἰς αὐτοὺς καὶ εἰς

---

476. Harris, *Second Epistle*, 650.
477. Betz, *2 Corinthians 8 and 9*, 118.
478. Harris, *Second Epistle*, 650: "In other words, by doing what God expects from them, they will not only experience αὐτάρκεια on a material level, but also in terms of their relationship with God. Giving money to those in need is not an inferior spiritual undertaking. It forms part of an encompassing involvement in the lives of others. But more importantly, through the sharing of their possessions, they are actually giving to God as the indirect object of their benefactions, who in turn will reciprocate in an encompassing way."

πάντας, ¹⁴ καὶ αὐτῶν δεήσει ὑπὲρ ὑμῶν ἐπιποθούντων ὑμᾶς διὰ τὴν ὑπερβάλλουσαν χάριν τοῦ θεοῦ ἐφ' ὑμῖν.

Because of the approved character of this ministry, they will glorify God for your obedience to your confession of the gospel of Christ and for the generosity of your sharing with them and with everyone, ¹⁴ and as they pray for you they will long for you because of the surpassing grace of God that rests upon you.

Paul understands that "everyone is blessed so that God is glorified in praise and thanksgiving."[479] He explains the reason for the saints in Jerusalem to praise God by the use of διά.[480] The word δοκιμή can mean "proof" or "evidence."[481] It implies that something has been tested and thus approved. Hence, δοκιμή may be easily rendered by "approval" and not "testing,"[482] or better, "the approved character"[483] or the genuineness of something. Paul says that because of this high quality of the gift from the Corinthians (i.e. the service rendered out of true generosity motivated by love [8:8]), the Jerusalem Christians will praise God. The verb δοξάζω[484] means to enhance one's reputation, to praise, to honor, to extol.[485] It is unlikely that the participle δοξάζοντες has the same subject as ἔχοντες in 9:8 and πλουτιζόμενοι of 9.11 (i.e. the Corinthians as suggests Antony).[486] It is quite clear that from verse 12 Paul focuses on the saints in Jerusalem whom he expects to give many thanks to God for the gift from Corinth. Therefore, it is natural to conclude that it is the saints in Jerusalem who will praise God.[487] Because of the genuineness of the service of the collection, they will acknowledge and proclaim that God deserves honor and praise.

---

479. Antony, "He Who Supplies Seed," 314.

480. The preposition δια, with genitive occasionally means "because of": Danker et al., *Greek-English Lexicon*, 225.

481. Harris, *Second Epistle*, 651.

482. Martin, *2 Corinthians*, 293.

483. Danker et al., *Greek-English Lexicon*, 256.

484. Betz, *2 Corinthians 8 and 9*, 120: the participles used in vv. 13–14 should be construed as descriptive rather than imperative.

485. Danker et al., *Greek-English Lexicon*, 258.

486. Antony, "He Who Supplies Seed," 314.

487. Thrall, *Critical and Exegetical Commentary*, vol. 2, 588.

By the preposition ἐπί Paul indicates the twofold occasion for which praise will be given to God. In the first place, the Jerusalem Christians will recognize that the Corinthians' participation in the collection is an expression of their obedience to the confession[488] of the gospel of Christ (ἐπὶ τῇ ὑποταγῇ τῆς ὁμολογίας ὑμῶν εἰς τὸ εὐαγγέλιον τοῦ Χριστοῦ). The second reason for the Jerusalem Christians to praise God is that they will see in the donation the Corinthians' generosity (καὶ ἁπλότητι τῆς κοινωνίας εἰς αὐτοὺς καὶ εἰς πάντας). The collection for the poor in Jerusalem is expected to be a tangible proof that the Corinthians have aligned themselves with their confession of the gospel of Christ. In other words, participation in the collection will demonstrate that the Corinthians' deeds match their profession of faith in the gospel of Christ. In this context, it is important to note that for Paul, concern for the needy is part and parcel of the gospel preached by and concerning Christ (τὸ εὐαγγέλιον τοῦ Χριστοῦ).[489] Thus, for Paul, Jesus Christ must be remembered as the one whose heart was deeply moved by the plight of the poor (Luke 6:38). The consequence of this recognition is far-reaching. If Paul's expectation that the Jerusalem Christians recognize that the Corinthians have genuinely adhered to the gospel of Christ materializes, they will also acknowledge their full incorporation in the church, the body of Christ.[490] Following Munk, Safrai and Tomson feel that "a strategic purpose of the collection was to embody the unity of the church of Christ consisting of Jews and gentiles and to express the link with Jerusalem while the gospel spreads throughout the world."[491] At the same

---

488. Danker et al., *Greek-English Lexicon*, 709. The word ὁμολογία means the "expression of allegiance as an action," "statement of allegiance," "confession." For Betz (*2 Corinthians 8 and 9*, 122–124), the word refers here to a legal document ("the contractual agreement") accompanying a donation expressing the giver's intention to enter into a partnership with the recipient. But he acknowledges that there is no trace of such a document. Furthermore, Betz's translation ("the submission [expressed] by the contractual agreement for the [benefit of] the gospel of Christ") is excessive and is consistent with his general tendency to interpret the collection mainly in light of socio-political dealings of the time.

489. The expression τὸ εὐαγγέλιον τοῦ Χριστοῦ is also used in 2:12 to indicate the content of Paul's preaching. In Rom 10:8–17 Paul points out that this gospel is "preached, believed and confessed" (Furnish, *II Corinthians*, 445, n. 13).

490. Nickle, *Collection*, 129.

491. Safrai and Tomson, "Paul's 'Collection'," 150. They explain that in Galatians and 2 Corinthians, Paul probably could not express this motivation clearly since he wished "to strike the balance between his basically positive relationship with the Jerusalem church and

time, Paul's collection from the Gentiles to the mother church would demonstrate that his law-free gospel is viable.[492] Since this gospel was preached to the Corinthians by Paul, adhesion to it also implies the reaffirmation of "allegiance to Paul" on the part of the Corinthians.[493] Furthermore, bearing in mind that 2 Corinthians testifies to a situation in which Paul was facing serious opposition from judaizing missionaries concerning his authority as an apostle, the successful completion of his collection could challenge them severely.[494] On the side of the Jewish Christians in Jerusalem, their hoped-for acknowledgement of the Corinthians' compliance with the gospel preached to them would mean indirectly that they fully recognize Paul's apostolic ministry to the Gentiles.[495] Therefore, Safrai and Tomson are right to maintain that in 2 Corinthians 8–9 Paul strives to rescue not only his collection project but also his whole apostolate in Corinth.[496] Similarly, it is possible to say that Paul indirectly expresses through his collection to the poor within the mother church in Jerusalem the centrality of the latter in the unfolding of God's salvation plan.[497] Paul expects that the

---

its getting compromised by the intervention of radicalized Judaeo-Christians." For his part, Dunn (*Beginning from Jerusalem*, 944) feels that rather than seeing in Paul's collection an expression of the unity of the early church, it is more appropriate to regard it as an attempt to restore the disrupted unity following several controversies and opposition which the apostle's mission to the Gentiles had been facing from his Jewish counterparts. In addition to the expression of Christian compassion as an act of righteousness, and an attempt to restore the unity of Jews and Gentiles, Dunn expounds the eschatological function of the collection discussed in the introduction of this research (*Beginning from Jerusalem*, 945–946): the realization of the prophetic hope that the Gentiles would flood in Jerusalem bearing their presents to the Lord, and the view that it would provoke Israel to jealousy by the Gentiles' acceptance of the gospel, which would at the same time lead the former to conversion. Moreover, Dunn suggests that Paul's collection could be seen as a Christian equivalent to the Temple tax, expressing the centrality of Jerusalem and the mother church there. He concludes that for Paul, "the collection was simply a recognition of mutual interdependence even among believers in countries far apart (Rom 15:26), and a particular acknowledgment by Gentile believers of the spiritual blessings they had received through their participation in the heritage of Israel (15:27)" (Dunn, *Beginning from Jerusalem*, 946). He suspects that this ambiguity surrounding the collection was a major reason for Paul's apprehension about its possible failure (Rom 15:31).

492. Safrai and Tomson, "Paul's 'Collection'," 148.
493. Martin, *2 Corinthians*, 294.
494. Safrai and Tomson, "Paul's 'Collection'," 148, 158.
495. Martin, *2 Corinthians*, 294.
496. Safrai and Tomson, "Paul's 'Collection'," 148.
497. In his article on the centrality Jerusalem, Van Houwelingen ("Jerusalem, the Mother Church," 13, 14) writes that the latter, the location of the mother church, has been

completion and successful delivery of the collection will lead the Christian Jerusalemites to thank God for the Corinthians' generosity (ἁπλότητι τῆς κοινωνίας εἰς αὐτοὺς καὶ εἰς πάντας). Unlike in Romans 15:26 where the word κοινωνία has the meaning of "contribution," it is better to render it here by "sharing." This sharing of material resources is not restricted to the saints in Jerusalem but is extended to everyone (καὶ εἰς πάντας). This includes other fellow Christians and those non-Christians who are in need. Such generous acts are not necessarily performed as a corporate collection. Indeed, the view that Christians should do good even to the unbelievers is expressed by Paul in Galatians 6:10. The apostle's expectation is that the Jerusalem church will appreciate the "generous spirit" which moves the Corinthians.[498]

As noted earlier, in verse 12 Paul's attention shifts from the Corinthian church as the giver of the collection, to the Jerusalem Christians as the recipients. The apostle expects that the latter will give thanks to God as the ultimate benefactor (v. 12), and glorify him (v. 13). Moreover, their gratitude will move them to say intercessional prayers for the Corinthians (v. 14). Whereas the usual term to refer to prayer is προσευχή, the word δέησις indicates an "urgent request to meet a need, exclusively addressed to God,"

---

considered a holy city by Jews, Christians and Muslims, although it has also been a place of conflict. He states that for Christians in particular, as in the Old Testament, Jerusalem was the focal point of God's presence among his people, the city of the great king David (Matt 5:35). He highlights that Jerusalem was the place of Jesus' crucifixion, and where the power of his Spirit was sent to his disciples and created the first Christian community. Moreover, it is in that city that the gospel of the living Lord was proclaimed and from there spread across the world through oral proclamation and writings. Houwelingen also writes that Jerusalem has been promised a remarkable future in the sense that it will be a city uniting heaven and earth (ibid., 20). In this respect, the Jerusalem church is rightly called the mother church which extends beyond the holy city itself, because its members are also present in Judea, Samaria, and Galilee (Acts 1:8). Worth of mention is also the fact that the church in Jerusalem followed closely the rise of the second Christian community, the Antiochene congregation (Acts 11), "the daughter church" according to Houwelingen's terminology (ibid., 21–22). In his opinion, the church that was birthed by the work of the Holy Spirit at Pentecost with its roots in Jerusalem gradually extended to the whole world, becoming a spiritual universal Christian community (ibid., 25).

498. Martin, *2 Corinthians*, 294. However, there is no evidence of the Corinthians raising money for other churches.

an "entreaty,"[499] an earnest petition or supplication.[500] The phrase αὐτῶν δεήσει presents a syntactical difficulty.[501] Among the various options proposed to solve this problem, the most satisfactory seems to be that which takes ἐπιποθούντων as a case of "the looser use of the genitive absolute in NT Greek," set in apposition with αὐτῶν, and standing for a future finite verb: "they will long."[502] As for δεήσει, it is construed as a modal dative denoting "attendant circumstances": "as they pray."[503] Ultimately, Paul understands that from a Christian point of view, the prayer of thanksgiving includes praise rendered to God (v. 13, δοξάζοντες τὸν θεὸν) and intercession for the sake of others (v. 14, αὐτῶν δεήσει ὑπὲρ ὑμῶν).[504]

The expected longing prayer of the Jerusalem Christians for the Corinthians is justified by what follows the preposition διά, because. It will be prompted by the fact that the Jerusalem church will have fully realized that God's surpassing grace is operating among the Corinthians (διὰ τὴν ὑπερβάλλουσαν χάριν τοῦ θεοῦ ἐφ᾽ ὑμῖν) as it was among the Macedonians (8:1).[505] This χάρις has been given by God to the Corinthians and it has driven them to wholeheartedly share their material resources with the needy within the Jerusalem church. By χάρις it is most probable that Paul is referring to God's inspiring and enabling the Corinthians to attend to the material needs of the poor Christians in Jerusalem through the collection. Paul is thus convinced that the service to the poor is one of the expressions of divine grace in the life of a believer. And ultimately, correct giving to the poor gives rise to gratitude and worship, the proper response to God's blessing.[506]

---

499. Danker et al., *Greek-English Lexicon*, 213.

500. Both terms are used together in Eph 6:18 to encourage believers to address their requests to God: Διὰ πάσης προσευχῆς καὶ δεήσεως προσευχόμενοι ἐν παντὶ καιρῷ ἐν πνεύματι (Pray in the Spirit at all times in every prayer and supplication).

501. Bruehler ("Proverbs, Persuasion and People," 220) mistakenly sees δεήσει as a finite verb. But no dictionary offers it.

502. Thrall, *Critical and Exegetical Commentary*, vol. 2, 592.

503. Ibid.

504. Betz, *2 Corinthians 8 and 9*, 120–121. The same is also true of Judaism. Betz relates that the *berakhah* comprised three parts: "praise, thanksgiving, and petition." The same three components are also typical of the *birkat ha-mazon* recited at the table after meals.

505. Ibid., 126.

506. Bruehler, "Proverbs, Persuasion and People," 221.

The verb ἐπιποθέω means to have a strong desire for something," "long for, desire."[507] In the Pauline letters, the verb and its cognates express an eager desire to see someone (Rom 1:11; 15:23; 2 Cor 7:7, 11; Phil 1:8; 2:26; 1 Thess 3:6; 2 Tim 1:4).[508] Thus, it is normal that the Jerusalem Christians would long to see the Corinthians after receiving their generous gift.[509] This longing to see them presupposes the desire to express gratitude to them for the collection received. Thus, one can say that Paul's view that praise and honor are due to God from whom all benefactions originate does not exclude the possibility for the recipients of a gift to express their gratitude to the ones who have bestowed it. Paul himself thanks the Philippians for the material support they granted him several times in his ministry and God for his riches in Christ (Phil 4:10–20). Paul's attitude here matches his own commitment to do what is good both before the Lord God and before men (2 Cor 8:21). But a deeper motivation for the longing on the side of the Jerusalem church may be to engage in a long-lasting fellowship with the Corinthians with whom they are bound through God's grace in Christ.[510]

Verse 15: Χάρις τῷ θεῷ ἐπὶ τῇ ἀνεκδιηγήτῳ αὐτοῦ δωρεᾷ.

Thanks be to God for his indescribable gift!

Paul has already explained to the Corinthians that God's providential care to the cheerful giver is a good reason for them to complete their contributions to the relief fund for Jerusalem (vv. 6–11). Being confident that the Corinthians will eventually fulfill what they have promised in this regard (v. 5), the apostle expresses his hope that the Jerusalem Christians will praise God for the gift received (vv. 12–13). He also expects eagerness from them to offer prayers of intercession to God on behalf of the Corinthians and a longing to see them as a way of gratitude for the gift received (v. 14). Now Paul ends his discourse with a doxology: χάρις τῷ θεῷ. In the present verse χάρις has the meaning of "thanks."[511] But this is no simple thanks. Rather,

---

507. Danker et al., *Greek-English Lexicon*, 377.

508. Martin, *2 Corinthians*, 294; Harris, *Second Epistle*, 657.

509. Harris, *Second Epistle*, 658.

510. Thrall, *Critical and Exegetical Commentary*, vol. 2, 593.

511. However, Becker (*Paul's Usage of* χάρις, 67, 68, 69, 139–140) rejects the idea of such distinctions in meaning. He argues that all the occurrences of the term have to be treated "as equal in weight" so that one apprehends "both the breadth of and the

it is a deep expression of gratitude. Whereas elsewhere in 2 Corinthians the apostle praises God for his merciful assistance in his apostolic ministry (2:14) and for Titus' eagerness to serve among the Corinthians (8:16), Paul now addresses his thanks to God for his indescribable gift (ἐπὶ τῇ ἀνεκδιηγήτῳ[512] αὐτοῦ δωρεᾷ).[513] This δωρεά is from God (αὐτοῦ) and is ἀνεκδιήγητος, indescribable; it goes beyond the human ability to describe things. It is noteworthy that after a long discourse on human giving, Paul reminds his readers that God is the giver *par excellence*.[514] The collection can only be "but a small part" of God's gift.[515] However, Paul does not explain what this δωρεά consists in. With this qualification ἀνεκδιήγητος, it is hardly conceivable that δωρεά in the present verse means the collection. One may be tempted to relate it to the χάρις τοῦ θεοῦ which was at work among the Macedonians and which Paul believed will move the Corinthians to give their contributions to the collection (v. 14).[516] J. P. Becker contends that this gift may be "the blessedness of being the *earthen*

---

commonality in Paul's usage of the word in this passage." While he agrees with Harris on the *inclusio* bracketed by χάρις in 2 Cor 8–9, Becker disagrees with the view that its end be placed in 2 Cor 9:14. According to him, this *inclusio* of 2 Cor 8:1–9:15 emerges clearly from the text once one becomes aware that Paul's usage of χάρις is "pneumasomatically comprehensive and semantically univocal." He indicates that in 8:1 χάρις proceeds from God to the believer, whereas in 9:15 it is returned to God from the believer. He insists that both trajectories are "complementary and balanced," and that this suggests that "they are part of a larger schemata – for one picks up where the other leaves off." He finds support in Dunn (*Christ and the Spirit*, 707–708) who expresses the same idea though in a different vocabulary. In Becker's view, Paul understands χάρις as "a gift, the gift that provides salvation, and the gift that empowers believers to live the Christian life." In my view, there is good reason to assert that this does not exclude the fact that a word can have various meanings as is the case for χάρις in our text.

512. This adjective is a New Testament *hapax*.

513. Outside this letter, Paul uses the same phrase χάρις τῷ θεῷ to give thanks to God (1 Cor 15:57 [τῷ δὲ θεῷ χάρις τῷ διδόντι ἡμῖν τὸ νῖκος διὰ τοῦ κυρίου ἡμῶν Ἰησοῦ Χριστοῦ, But thanks be to God, who gives us the victory through our Lord Jesus Christ]; Rom 6:17 [χάρις δὲ τῷ θεῷ ὅτι ἦτε δοῦλοι τῆς ἁμαρτίας ὑπηκούσατε δὲ ἐκ καρδίας εἰς ὃν παρεδόθητε τύπον διδαχῆς, But thanks be to God that you, having once been slaves of sin, have become obedient from the heart to the form of teaching to which you were entrusted]; 7.25 [χάρις δὲ τῷ θεῷ διὰ Ἰησοῦ Χριστοῦ τοῦ κυρίου ἡμῶν, Thanks be to God through Jesus Christ our Lord]). Antony ("He Who Supplies Seed," 308, 309) writes that in both letters to the Corinthians Paul thanks God for the achievement of something which is beyond human capabilities, "yet the divine initiative becomes operative through the human medium."

514. Martin, *2 Corinthians*, 295.

515. Betz, *2 Corinthians 8 and 9*, 128.

516. Furnish, *II Corinthians*, 452.

vessels for this power of God (4:7) – the beatitude of realizing the *purpose* [...] of the Christian enterprise in one's own person (8:1 – 9:14)."[517] It is thus possible that Paul has in mind God's gift in a much broader sense. The word δωρεά appears 11 times in the New Testament 5 of which are found in the Pauline letters, and 4 in Acts.[518] In some of these occurrences this gift is well explained. Acts 10:45 speaks of ἡ δωρεὰ τοῦ ἁγίου πνεύματος (the gift of the Spirit) to the Gentiles. Nonetheless, the broader context of 2 Corinthians 8–9 does not lend any support to the idea that Paul alludes to this gift in his doxology. Rather, Paul has probably in mind the gift of salvation through the work of Christ (ἡ χάρις τοῦ θεοῦ καὶ ἡ δωρεὰ ἐν χάριτι τῇ τοῦ ἑνὸς ἀνθρώπου Ἰησοῦ Χριστοῦ) in Romans 5:15 as opposed to death brought about by the fall of the first Adam (Rom 5:12–14, 16–18). In the context of the collection Paul may be indirectly referring back to the self-giving of Christ that he has presented as the leading motivation for Christian generosity (8:9) and not to the collection.[519] It is remarkable that Paul's discourse on the collection is started and closed with the term χάρις.[520]

Conclusion

The exegetical analysis of 2 Corinthians 8–9 has pointed out that Paul uses the concept of χάρις in its various meanings to stimulate the Corinthians to resume their collection for Jerusalem. The Macedonians' enthusiastic contribution to the collection is seen as the result of God's χάρις (8:1), and as an example to be emulated by the Corinthians (8:8). From the Macedonians' amazing example, Paul passes to the self-impoverishment of Jesus Christ, depicted also as χάρις, a generous act for the benefit of the Corinthians (8:9). The collection itself is called χάρις in the sense of a generous undertaking (8:6, 7, 19), a generous gift (9:5) while participation in it is seen as χάρις, a privilege (8:4). Moreover, reference is made to God's bestowing πᾶσαν χάριν (9:8) in the sense of material and spiritual resources

---

517. Becker, *Paul's Usage of* χάρις, 143.
518. Neirynck and Van Segbroeck, *New Testament Vocabulary*, 95.
519. Harris, *Second Epistle*, 660.
520. Bruehler, "Proverbs, Persuasion and People," 221; Becker, *Paul's Usage of* χάρις, 143.

to cheerful givers. Therefore, serving the poor through the collection is an expression of God's χάρις in the life of a believer (9:14); it is an aspect of righteousness on the part of the latter (9:10). The Jerusalem Christians will hopefully reciprocate this χάρις, gratitude by means of thanksgivings addressed to God and intercessional prayers for the Corinthians. Similarly, Paul, who expressed χάρις to God for Titus's work among the Corinthians (8:16), invites the Corinthians and other Achaean churches to join him in worship to God for his surpassing gift of salvation (9:15).

Paul spells out to the Corinthians five motivations for them to give to his collection for Jerusalem:

- Divine grace produces generosity within the believer's life as manifested among the Macedonian Christians (8:1).
- The imitation of the Lord Jesus Christ whose self-impoverishment is a generous act which benefitted the Corinthians (8:9).
- The belief in the possibility that in the future the Corinthians would benefit from the generosity of the Jerusalem church in case of a reversal in economic conditions (8:13–15).
- The conviction that God will continue to provide for the needs of joyful givers (9:6–11).
- Dynamic fellowship expected from the collection: it will relieve the needs of the poor Christians in Jerusalem and drive the Jerusalemite Christians into longing and intercessional prayers for the Corinthians and worship to God (9:12–14).

Having these motivations in mind, Paul indicates that one must give according to one's ability, personal decision and with joy (8:11–12; 9:7). In this way, he clears up the possibility of misunderstanding his previous mention of the Macedonians who gave beyond their means, as if he was encouraging the Corinthians to do the same. Paul sticks to his earlier practical instruction in 1 Corinthians 16:2 when he commanded them to collect their donations on a weekly basis and in proportion to one's earnings. To ensure the integrity of management of the collection, Paul deems it wise to associate a three-man group (8:16–9:5). This delegation will assist the Corinthians in the arrangement of their offering for a successful completion before the apostle's pending visit. This shows that for the sake of the success of his fundraising campaign, Paul sets up a strong network of collaborators to manage it with him.[521]

All in all, Paul's usage of χάρις in his exhortation for the collection enables him to show that his project is not a purely humanitarian undertaking. Apart from the obvious relief of needs to be achieved among the Jerusalem church, the apostle expects the collection to set in motion a dynamic of fellowship not only among the people involved in it, but also between them and God. In this way, he redefines the notion of αὐτάρκεια (sufficiency) by putting God and others at the center of the believer's life. The apostle of the Gentiles highlights the communal essence of the Christian faith. By depicting the God who speaks through the Scriptures as the one who reciprocates "economic generosity"[522] for those who take care of the poor, Paul wants his readers to fully count on God's faithfulness to his promises. But divine provisions are not seen as a reward for the good done because the initial resources needed to give to the needy are provided by God (9:10).

In the following chapter I will examine how the text of 2 Corinthians 8–9 has been interpreted by some prominent figures from the patristic time to the Reformation. Attention will be given to the motivations of Christian giving.

---

521. Safrai and Tomson, "Paul's 'Collection'," 140.
522. Longenecker, *Remember the Poor*, 276.

CHAPTER 4

2 Corinthians 8–9 from Late Antiquity to the Reformation Period

After the exegetical analysis of 2 Corinthians 8–9, I want to look at its reception history from late Antiquity to the Reformation. The main aim of this investigation is to point out to what extent the concept of grace, which is central to Paul's thoughts in this passage, is taken into consideration in various readings handed down to us. In the same vein, I will investigate how these ancient readers explain the motivations of Christian generosity and the attitude towards possessions. Attention will also be paid to the concept of reward and the question of the ways of giving alms. Another issue that will be addressed is to what extent care for the poor is perceptible in homilies and commentaries on 2 Corinthians 8–9 steming from that period.

Before the end of the second century, the use of 2 Corinthians in written sources is almost exclusively limited to allusions.[1] However, E. M. Becker correctly argues that this does not mean that the letter was not known and read in churches. Its early quotations are found in Irenaeus († c. 200), Tertullian († c. 220), Clement of Alexandria († c. 220), and Origen († c. 254).[2] The knowledge of this letter is substantiated by its attestation in the second-century collections of Christian writings (i.e. Marcion's canon, the Muratorian canon, and P^{46}. Cyril of Alexandria [† c. 444] wrote a commentary on individual verses). John Chrysostom (c. 349–407) produced a combined commentary and homilies, while Theodoret of Cyrus (c.

---

1. Becker, *Letter Hermeneutics*, 151.
2. Ibid., 158.

393–466) and Ambrosiaster (late fourth century) wrote full commentaries on this epistle. A running commentary, authored by Pelagius (c. 354–418?),[3] was mistakenly attributed to Jerome (c. 345–420).[4]

In the Middle Ages, many complete commentaries on 2 Corinthians were produced.[5] Among others we can mention here Claudius of Turin, Raban Maur, Haimo of Auxerre, Hatto of Vercelli, Lanfranc of Bec, Bruno of Cologne, Herve of Bourg-Dieu, Gilbert de la Porrée, Robert of Melun, Peter Lombard or Stephen Langton, Hugues of Saint-Cher, John of La Rochelle, Thomas Aquinas, Guerric of Saint-Quentin, Peter of Tarentaise, Nicholas of Gorran. In the Reformation period John Calvin and Melanchthon wrote full commentaries on this epistle.[6]

As stated in the general introduction of this research, I will focus on the authors of whom we have full commentaries on 2 Corinthians and translations in English or French, and whose influence on Christian thought in general has more or less been established. These include John Chrysostom, Theodoret of Cyrus, Ambrosiaster, Thomas Aquinas and John Calvin.

4.1 John Chrysostom

Ordained a priest in 386 by Flavian who had succeeded Melitius, Chrysostom pursued his "career as preacher, exegete, and moralist."[7] He carried out his preaching activity in Antioch until he was appointed Patriarch of Constantinople on 26 February 398 to replace Nectarius who had died the previous year.[8] We learn that once appointed to this patriarchate, Chrysostom had to curb expenses since his predecessor had wasted church money. Moreover, he "opened hospitals, and alleviated the misery of the poor" and initiated important reforms within the clergy.[9] John used different strategies to secure resources to assist the needy.[10] He

---

3. McKenna, "Pelagius and Pelagianism," 61.
4. Dahan, "Introduction," II; Murphy, "Jerome, St.," 757.
5. Dahan, "Introduction," II.
6. Ibid.
7. Harkins, "John Chrysostom," 945–946.
8. Ibid., 496.
9. Ibid.; Mayeur et al., *Histoire du Christianisme* II, 486–488.
10. Mayeur et al., *Histoire du Christianisme* II, 487.

tirelessly exhorted his congregants to generosity. He would encourage the widows to give or to will their possessions to the church. He did not even hesitate to sell some ornamental church valuables to reach out to the destitute. Richard Finn rightly notes that almsgiving was central to the early fourth century church.[11] Regarding John Chrysostom, he remarks that in his treatise on the bishop's duty, John insisted that the bishop's obligations towards the destitute did not consist merely in the distribution of alms, but in first "collecting together the church's riches through the good will of the flock he rules over."[12] And this insistence on almsgiving by the bishop was to acquire enough resources for charitable work in the church. John Chrysostom was remarkably interested in charitable actions. It is therefore not surprising that the text of Matthew 25:31–46 takes up a considerable place in his thought.[13] This passage underlines the central role of concrete social actions to relieve the needy in the final judgement by the Son of Man.

While in Antioch between 386 and 397, Chrysostom produced and preached his homilies on 1 and 2 Corinthians, but their exact date of composition and delivery cannot be established.[14]. Chrysostom's homilies appear to be "poorly structured, roving from point to point and filled with repetitions, but they have an interior, spiritual unity."[15] However, there is no trace of Arian controversy in Chrysostom's homilies on 2 Corinthians 8–9. In fact, Antioch knew a long period of disruption not only by Arians but also by dissensions among the pro-Nicene bishops.[16] Since 362, there were three bishops in Antioch: the Arian Euzoios and the two rivals Paulinus and Meletius within the orthodoxy. It is also difficult to tell to what extent rivalry between Paulinus and Meletius affected our preacher. In one instance (Homily 18),[17] Chrysostom deplores that in his congregation people are so widely separated from one another, unable to realize that the church

---

11. Finn, *Almsgiving*, 35–88.
12. Ibid., 36, quoting Chrysostom, *Sac.* 3.12.
13. Roldanus, "Le chrétien," 231.
14. Quasten, *Golden Age,* 433, 445.
15. Harkins, "John Chrysostom," 497.
16. Mayeur et al., *Histoire du Christianisme* II, 362; Downey, "Antioch," 522.
17. Chrysostom's comments on 2 Cor 8:1–6 conclude his Homily 16 which begins with 7.13. Homily 17 deals with 2 Cor 8:7–17 whereas Homily 18 covers 2 Cor 8:16–24. Homily 19 is concerned with 2 Cor 9:1–9; Homily 20 being about 2 Cor 9:10–15.

is one body.[18] He thus ends his sermon with a pressing and tireless call for complementarity. Leaders are strongly exhorted to cast down arrogance and pride, and learn to listen to their subordinates whoever they are, and consider their counsels.

4.1.1 The Benefits of God's Grace, Mutuality and the Dangers of Wealth

Worthy of mention is how Chrysostom emphasizes the use of the term χαρίς in his sermons on 2 Corinthians 8–9. He notes that Paul calls the Macedonians' participation in the collection χαρίς in order to not only make the Corinthians humble, but also and above all to raise the spirit of emulation among them.[19] In Chrysostom's view, Paul wants the Corinthians to understand that what the Macedonians accomplished was not the outcome of human prowess, but first of all the result of divine influence. Chrysostom notes that Paul chooses his words purposely to describe the collection in order to exalt it: τὴν χάριν καὶ τὴν κοινωνίαν τῆς διακονίας, the grace and the fellowship in the ministering to the saints. As he says, since Paul knew that the Corinthians were ambitious of spiritual gifts, he called the collection χάρις in order that they might seek it eagerly.[20] Moreover, John explains that the apostle wanted them to recognize that God is the ultimate author of all these things.[21]

Chrysostom sees 2 Corinthians 8:9 as "the head and crown" of Paul's persuasion thanks to its reference to the Lord's χάρις.[22] He argues that the apostle wants the Corinthians to consider the greatness of this χάρις both in its "extent and nature"; and in doing so they will grudge nothing of their possessions.[23] The father explains that this χάρις, manifested through the self-impoverishment of Jesus Christ, means his becoming a human being in flesh and all that he suffered. He explains that the Lord's self-empting yielded riches for believers which comprise the experience of godliness, purification of sins, justification, sanctification and so many things already

---

18. Chrysostom, *Hom. 2 Cor.* 18.3.77–86 (PG 61:528; NPNF I, 12:366).
19. Chrysostom, *Hom. 2 Cor.* 16.2.11–16 (PG 61:513; NPNF I, 12:356).
20. Chrysostom, *Hom. 2 Cor.* 16.3.8–10 (PG 61:514; NPNF I, 12:357).
21. Chrysostom, *Hom. 2 Cor.* 20.2.1–7 (PG 61:538; NPNF I, 12:372–373).
22. Chrysostom, *Hom. 2 Cor.* 17.1.34–35 (PG 61:517; NPNF I, 12:360).
23. Chrysostom, *Hom. 2 Cor.* 17.1.38–42 (PG 61:517–518; NPNF I, 12:360).

given and those to come.[24] However, Chrysostom shows that God's grace does not exclude human will. He emphasizes the full cooperation between Titus's eagerness to engage in the collection and God's grace.[25] It is in this way that he reconciles the two statements that Titus was exhorted by Paul to go to Corinth and that he went there of his own accord (2 Cor 8:17). Thus, the χάρις administered by Paul and his companions in 2 Cor 8:19 comprises both the preaching of the gospel and the collection. In Chrysostom's terms, the collection is sacred money.[26] He relates this to Acts 6:3 concerning the election of the seven reliable men who would be entrusted with the daily distribution of food.

Chrysostom shows that God's χάρις also meets the needs of the giver. He understands that in 2 Corinthians 9:8 Paul prays for the Corinthians: δυνατεῖ δὲ ὁ θεὸς πᾶσαν χάριν περισσεῦσαι εἰς ὑμᾶς, "And God is able to provide you with every blessing in abundance."[27] John emphasizes the fact that Paul does not ask God merely to provide his χάρις to the Corinthians, but to make it abound and enable them to abound in liberality. He admires the apostle's "philosophy" here and remarks that Paul prays for "all sufficiency" and not for riches nor for abundance (Οὐ πλοῦτον εὔχεται οὐδὲ Περισσείαν, ἀλλὰ πᾶσαν αὐτάρκειαν).[28] And since Paul does not pray for "superfluity" (τὸ περιττόν), another way for Chrysostom to refer to riches, Paul does not expect the Corinthians to contribute of their "want" because he was aware of their weakness.[29] However, Chrysostom rejects the idea that one who serves the Lord cannot go through hardships. He explains that the widow of Zarephath who fed Elijah did not have a single thought that if the man who came to her was a prophet, he wouldn't have begged for food.[30]

In Chrysostom's thoughts God's χάρις also eventuates interconnectedness between the giver and the receiver. He explains that the apostle termed

---

24. Chrysostom, *Hom. 2 Cor.* 17.1.48–52 (PG 61:518; NPNF I, 12:360).
25. Chrysostom, *Hom. 2 Cor.* 18.1.21–32 (PG 61:523; NPNF I, 12:363).
26. Chrysostom, *Hom. 2 Cor.* 18.1.73–84 (PG 61:524; NPNF I, 12:364).
27. Chrysostom, *Hom. 2 Cor.* 19.2.98–102 (PG 61:532; NPNF I, 12:369).
28. Chrysostom, *Hom. 2 Cor.* 19.3.13–14 (PG 61:532; NPNF I, 12:369).
29. Chrysostom, *Hom. 2 Cor.* 19.3.14–18 (PG 61:532–533; NPNF I, 12:369).
30. Chrysostom, *Hom. 2 Cor.* 19.4.31–34 (PG 61:533; NPNF I, 12:370–371).

the collection a κοινωνία to teach the Corinthians that they not only give, but also receive.[31] Chrysostom remarks that besides the thanks addressed to God for the things received, the saints in Jerusalem will pray to God seeking to see the Corinthians. He notes that their desire is not based on money. Rather, they seek to witness the χάρις that has been granted to the Corinthians. It is fitting that John emphasizes the idea of interdependency among people. In his view, it reflects God's will.[32]

Another point which deserves our attention here is Chrysostom's praise for poverty and his aversion towards material wealth. He asserts that it is worthless to desire to become rich, because the need of possessions keeps increasing endlessly.[33] He maintains that righteousness in the sense of beneficence to the poor cannot come to us "along with wealth," but that it is only "through it" that it becomes present.[34] Chrysostom points out that lust for possessions and righteousness are incompatible and that one cannot try to make them cohabitate. With sarcastic irony, he rejects the search for autonomy through accumulation of riches by saying that whoever wants to get exceedingly independent of everyone should "pray for poverty."[35] He explains that a poor man depends on others only for food and clothing. But the rich man always needs others for the safety of his wealth and his honor as well.

4.1.2 The Justification for Christian Generosity

Chrysostom shows much interest in almsgiving. When Paul says that he can rely on the Corinthians (2 Cor 7:16), Chrysostom understands that he means that their past good works make them more ready to give their alms. It is also remarkable in the whole chapter that Chrysostom uses the word ἐλεημοσύνη, alms, to indicate the collection. But as I observed in the first chapter, the term covers any kind deed done for the benefit of the needy. By the example of the widow who assisted the prophet Elijah and

---

31. Chrysostom, *Hom. 2 Cor.* 16.3.10–11 (PG 61:514; NPNF I, 12:357).
32. Chrysostom, *Hom. 2 Cor.* 17.3.43–44 (PG 61:521; NPNF I, 12:362–363).
33. Chrysostom, *Hom. 2 Cor.* 17.2.101–104 (PG 61:521; NPNF I, 12:361–362).
34. Chrysostom, *Hom. 2 Cor. Paul* 19.4.78–89 (PG 61:536; NPNF I, 12:371).
35. Chrysostom, *Hom. 2 Cor.* 17.3.1–7 (PG 61:521; NPNF I, 12:362).

who is mentioned in Luke 4, Chrysostom emphasizes in his comments on 2 Corinthians 9:9 that the Lord of the prophets requests alms.[36]

The second motivation for almsgiving given by Chrysostom is his strong belief in reward. The father frequently uses the terms μισθός and ἀντίδοσις to talk about reward or recompense as a motivation for Christian almsgiving. He explains that the reward for good works certainly results from accomplishing rather than receiving what is good.[37] He finds in 2 Corinthians 9:6 Paul's invitation to the Corinthians to think first about recompense through the metaphor of sowing and harvesting, and learn that one receives more than what one gives.[38] He rebukes those who fear that their wealth will diminish if they give alms. Such people, in his view, do not know that their wealth is being multiplied in heaven, and consequently look for worldly recompense. In Homily 17, Chrysostom sees that Paul's exhortation to the Corinthians to complete the good work also implies that they will receive "the reward" which is the result of good deeds (2 Cor 8:11).[39] But Chrysostom shows that the expectation of reward is not the most important motivation for good deeds. He notes that human beings like emulating others. Chrysostom illustrates this by referring to the fact that Paul cites the example of the Macedonians and the Lord's to stimulate the Corinthians to action. He then indicates that although the Lord's example in 2 Corinthians 8:9 could truly have had a huge impact on the Corinthians, it is the expectation of reward which stirred them up the most.[40] For Chrysostom, this happened because the Corinthians were weak. Nevertheless, our preacher does not explain whether the Corinthians were anticipating recompense in the present life or in the hereafter. In the conclusion of Homily 19 Chrysostom exhorts his hearers to shun hell and welcome heaven in order to gain freedom in the present life and obtain the kingdom of God. This is possible through both the grace of our Lord Jesus Christ and love towards human beings.[41] In this context, love is syn-

---

36. Chrysostom, *Hom. 2 Cor.* 19.4.24-25 (PG 61:534; NPNF I, 12:370).
37. Chrysostom, *Hom. 2 Cor.* 16.4.10-11 (PG 61:516; NPNF I, 12:358).
38. Chrysostom, *Hom. 2 Cor.* 19.2.75-78 (PG 61:532; NPNF I, 12:369).
39. Chrysostom, *Hom. 2 Cor.* 17.1.78-80 (PG 61:518; NPNF I, 12:360).
40. Chrysostom, *Hom. 2 Cor.* 19.1.42-45 (PG 61:529; NPNF I, 12:367).
41. Chrysostom, *Hom. 2 Cor.* 19.4.63-68 (PG 61:535–536; NPNF I, 12:371).

onymous with generosity expressed through almsgiving. It is clear that for Chrysostom, the exercise of charity cooperates with grace to open the way to the kingdom of heaven. Although he does not explicitly identify recompense with admission into God's kingdom, this notion seems to be at the back of his exhortation.

In Homily 20, which deals with 2 Corinthians 9:10–15, Chrysostom reinforces his belief in reward. He notes that the phrase ἐσκόρπισεν, ἔδωκεν τοῖς πένησιν, ἡ δικαιοσύνη αὐτοῦ μένει εἰς τὸν αἰῶνα refers to a spiritual recompense (πνευματικῆς ἐστιν ἀμοιβῆς) whereas πληθύναι τὸν σπόρον ὑμῶν expresses a temporal return (σαρκικῆς ἀντιδόσεως).[42] He indicates that in verse 10 Paul harks back to the spiritual consideration of recompense through his phrase αὐξῆσαι τὰ γενήματα τῆς δικαιοσύνης ὑμῶν, "May he increase the harvest of your righteousness." He rephrases Paul's statement as follows: If God provides for the needs of those who sow in the soil and grants abundance those who feed the body, much more will he provide his care to "those who till the soil of heaven" and attend to the needs of the soul.[43] Chrysostom insists that the apostle does not express this truth "in the way of inference," "but in the form of a prayer" in verse 10.[44] It is important to realize that Chrysostom uses the Majority text which has the aorist optatives χορηγῆσαι, πληθύναι, and αὐξῆσαι instead of the indicatives χορηγήσει, πληθυνεῖ, and αὐξήσει. I discussed this textual question in the second chapter of this study. Chrysostom also emphasizes Paul's statement about the multiplying of the seed and the increasing of the fruits of righteousness by saying that they imply giving with liberality. At the same time, says John, Paul uses it to tell the Corinthians to seek only what is necessary for their life. John finds support for the latter view in Paul's saying that God gives to the sower "bread for food" (v. 10).[45] However, Chrysostom seems to contradict himself in the interpretation of the term σπόρος, seed. He had previously indicated that πληθύναι τὸν σπόρον ὑμῶν expresses "a temporal recompense" (σαρκικῆς ἀντιδόσεως),[46] but now he

---

42. Chrysostom, *Hom. 2 Cor.* 20.1.4–8 (PG 61:535; NPNF I, 12:372).
43. Chrysostom, *Hom. 2 Cor.* 20.1.15–19 (PG 61:536; NPNF I, 12:372).
44. Chrysostom, *Hom. 2 Cor.* 20.1.20–24 (PG 61:536; NPNF I, 12:372).
45. Chrysostom, *Hom. 2 Cor.* 20.1.27–30 (PG 61:536–537; NPNF I, 12:372).
46. Chrysostom, *Hom. 2 Cor.* 20.1.7–8 (PG 61:536; NPNF I, 12:372).

argues that the Corinthians' σπόρος that is to be multiplied is spiritual (πληθύναι τὸν σπόρον ὑμῶν τουτέστι, τὸν πνευματικόν) and concerns alms bestowed with largess (Οὐδὲ γαρ ἁπλῶς αἰτεῖ, ἀλλὰ τὴν μετὰ δαψιλείας).[47]

Gratitude to God is another reason for almsgiving in John's view.[48] He explains that Paul, together with the Corinthians, gives thanks to God in 2 Corinthians 9:15 because they all recognize him as the ultimate agent behind the collection. The father thinks that the word δωρεά, gift, used by Paul in this verse most probably refers to all the benefits that God, through his coming into the world, has offered to it abundantly. John concludes that the only response to such a great benefit granted to men will be to make every effort to lead a virtuous life and to give alms. The fourth motivation for almsgiving mentioned by John is that our need for others makes it an obligation.[49] It is only in this way that believers can make sense of Paul's statement that they are ambassadors of Christ (2 Cor 5:20) and God's servants through whom the appeal to reconciliation is made to the world.

The redemptive function of alms is another important motivation for almsgiving in John's discourse. He uses a sacrificial language to show the value of alms. His thoughts find their climax in the view that alms atone for sins. He argues that this view is reflected in Paul's statement in 2 Corinthians 9:9 about the righteousness that endures forever. Our preacher understands that almsgiving makes the giver righteous because it consumes sins like fire.[50] For this reason, he says that the merciful man's garment does not consist in luxurious clothing, but in loving-kindness.[51] Such a person is the realization of Psalm 103:4 where it is said that God crowns his people with pity and mercies. For Chrysostom, this garment is holier than that of priests in the Old Testament. Therefore, the merciful man offers his sacrifice not on altars made of material things, but of "reasonable souls" (διὰ ψυχῶν λογικῶν)[52] (i.e. the members of the church that

---

47. Chrysostom, *Hom. 2 Cor.* 20.1.38–41 (PG 61:537; NPNF I, 12:372).
48. Chrysostom, *Hom. 2 Cor.* 20.2.1–25 (PG 61:538; NPNF I, 12:373).
49. Chrysostom, *Hom. 2 Cor.* 17.3.1–64 (PG 61:520; NPNF I, 12:361).
50. Chrysostom, *Hom. 2 Cor.* 19.3.37–39 (PG 61:533; NPNF I, 12:369).
51. Chrysostom, *Hom. 2 Cor.* 20.2.64–3.23 (PG 61:539–540; NPNF I, 12:374).
52. Chrysostom, *Hom. 2 Cor.* 20.3.4 (PG 61:539; NPNF I, 12:374).

Chrysostom terms the body of Christ). He tells his audience that whenever they see a poor believer, they should consider him an altar.[53] To the one who cares for a beggar for instance, God will be propitious; and that person will attain the promised good things.

In the first chapter of this study, I noted that this belief in the redemptive power of alms is attested in the LXX, namely in Ben Sira and Tobit. In the Christian tradition, it is remarkable that Chrysostom inherited this teaching from the apostolic fathers.[54] For instance, 2 Clem. 16.4 says that repentance and almsgiving merit remission of sins. This belief emerges from *Polycarp*, *Ignatius*, the *Two Ways*, *Barnabas*, the *Didache*, and the *Shepherd of Hermas*.[55]

4.1.3 The Special Place of the Poor in Chrysostom's Thought

Chrysostom's concern for the poor is strongly reflected in his treatment of 2 Corinthians 8–9. He uses a theologically dense terminology to characterize their special value. When he explains that in our diverse social statuses, professions, and trades we always need one another, he ascribes a special place to the poor man.[56] The latter is the most useful because of the prominent role he plays in our salvation. Chrysostom writes that we find in this person someone to whom to bestow our possessions.

---

53. Chrysostom, *Hom. 2 Cor.* 20.3.61–66 (PG 61:540; NPNF I, 12:374).

54. Garrison, *Redemptive Almsgiving*, 76–108.

55. After Chrysostom, this special function of alms is also attested in Pope Leo the Great (400–461) in a closely related perspective: Murphy, "Leo I, Pope, St.," 474. In a mid-fifth century series of sermons (6–11) to raise funds from his wealthier parishioners for the poor and prisoners in the city of Rome, Leo draws much on 2 Cor 8–9. This indicates that in late ancient Christianity charity for the poor had developed into "a full-grown system" under the direct management of bishops. Leo explains that charitable collections were established by the holy Fathers and supports this view by 2 Cor 9:7 where Paul instructs that one has to give willingly and according to one's means: Leo the Great, *Sermon* 7.1 (CCSL 138), 36. For Leo this is a Christian duty (*Sermon* 8.1); and like Chrysostom he maintains that we see the person of Christ in the destitute (*Sermon* 9.2). In his opinion, this identification of the poor person with Christ is confirmed by Paul when he speaks of the self-impoverishment of the Lord (2 Cor 8:9): Leo the Great, *Sermon* 7.1 (CCSL 138), 36, 41. After saying that the present time is a time of sowing and that the gathering of harvest will take place on the day of the final judgement (*Sermon* 10.3, cf. 2 Cor 9:6), Leo draws inspiration from Sir 29:15 to tell his parishioners that their alms themselves will intercede for them.

56. Chrysostom, *Hom. 2 Cor.* 17.3.43-44 (PG 61:521; NPNF I, 12:361–363).

Εἰ γὰρ μὴ πένητες ἦσαν, τὸ πλέον ἂν ἀνετράπη τῆς ἡμετέρας σωτηρίας, οὐκ ἐχόντων που καταβαλεῖν τὰ χρήματα. Ὥστε καὶ ὁ δοκῶν ἁπάντων ἀχρηστότερος εἶναι πένης, οὗτος ἁπάντων ἐστὶ χρησιμώτερος.

For if there were no poor, the greater part of our salvation would be overthrown, in that we should not have where to bestow our wealth. So that even the poor man who appears to be more useless than any is the most useful of any.[57]

Chrysostom goes further in the depiction of the poor. I noted previously that he terms them living altars on which the merciful man offers his sacrifices to God.[58] Chrysostom's consideration for the poor finds its climax in his identification of Christ with the hungry and the needy.[59] All this explains why for Chrysostom care to the poor must be a permanent duty for a Christian believer.

4.1.4 The Ways of Giving

John indicates that in 2 Corinthians 8:2 Paul insists not on the amount given by the Macedonians but on their commendable inner disposition. The father contrasts πλοῦτος τῶν δοθέντων, "the richness of the gift" with πλοῦτος τῆς ἁπλότητος, "the riches of their liberality."[60] This inner attitude in giving is clearly emphasized by Chrysostom in his comments on 2 Corinthians 8:5 where it is mentioned that the Macedonians gave beyond Paul's expectations. In the eyes of our preacher, the expression οὐ καθὼς ἠλπίσαμεν, not merely as we expected, refers both to the amount they gave and to their afflictions.[61] In John's view, genuine almsgiving is voluntary and is directed to the needy, which produces joy in the giver.[62] He insists that the adverbial expression ἐπ' εὐλογίαις, "bountifully," used by the apostle in that metaphor in 2 Corinthians 9:6, is stronger than δαψιλῶς, "generously," "abundantly," because the former carries the notion

---

57. Chrysostom, *Hom. 2 Cor.* 17.2.90-93 (PG 61:520; NPNF I, 12:361).
58. Chrysostom, *Hom. 2 Cor.* 20.3.61-66 (PG 61:540; NPNF I, 12:374).
59. Chrysostom, *Hom. 2 Cor.* 16.4.5-9 (PG 61:516; NPNF I, 12:358, 362).
60. Chrysostom, *Hom. 2 Cor.* 16.2.68-86 (PG 61:514; NPNF I, 12:357).
61. Chrysostom, *Hom. 2 Cor.* 16.3.13–14 (PG 61:514; NPNF I, 12:357).
62. Chrysostom, *Hom. 2 Cor.* 16.4.5–9 (PG 61:516; NPNF I, 12:358).

of gladness that Paul develops in 2 Corinthians 9:7 and that he supports by a quotation from Scripture.⁶³ This quotation says that God loves a cheerful giver. In Chrysostom's opinion, although this Old Testament text refers to a generous giver, δαψιλής,⁶⁴ Paul uses it to express the sense of giving with eagerness,⁶⁵ τὸ μετὰ προθυμίας διδόναι.⁶⁶

Concerning the amount to be given, Chrysostom marvels at Paul's extraordinary wisdom in his use of the Macedonians' zeal and the qualification of the contribution as acceptable in 2 Corinthians 8:12. He observes that Paul asked the Corinthians to do according to what one possesses and leaves the Macedonians' example to do its work. In effect, asserts Chrysostom, Paul was aware that emulation stimulates people much more than exhortation does.⁶⁷ Furthermore, he argues that the word εὐπρόσδεκτος used by Paul in 2 Corinthians 8:12 to qualify one's contribution implies what is required by God. But John explains that the apostle softened this notion by leaving the Corinthians at liberty to decide because he trusted the efficiency of the example he had cited to them. However, for Chrysostom this does not imply that the apostle did not want the Corinthians to literally emulate the Macedonians' example. On the contrary, Paul was hindered by the Corinthians' weakness.⁶⁸ The quotation used in 2 Corinthians 9:9 is understood by Chrysostom as an argument employed by Paul for his exhortation to bountifulness. In his view, the word ἐσκόρπισεν, he has dispersed abroad, simply means a plentiful giving.⁶⁹ The righteousness which lasts forever is love shown to people.

Chrysostom insists on the fact that the Christians ought to give profusely. Commenting on Paul's instruction that the Corinthians' collection should be ready as a voluntary gift and not as a gift grudgingly given (2 Cor 9:5), he explains that the apostle speaks of the "quickness," "liberality" and "eagerness" (πρὸς τῷ περὶ τάχους διαλέγεσθαι καὶ δαψιλείας

---

63. Chrysostom, *Hom. 2 Cor.* 19.2.75–78 (PG 61, 532; NPNF I, 12:369).
64. Liddell and Scott, *Greek-English Lexicon*, 371.
65. My translation. Chambers (1889, NPNF I, 12:369) has "giving with readiness"
66. Chrysostom, *Hom. 2 Cor.* 19.2.93–96 (PG 61:532; NPNF I, 12:369).
67. Chrysostom, *Hom. 2 Cor.* 17.1.88–89 (PG 61:519; NPNF I, 12:360).
68. Chrysostom, *Hom. 2 Cor.* 17.2.6–9 (PG 61:519; NPNF I, 12:361).
69. Chrysostom, *Hom. 2 Cor.* 19.3.29–37 (PG 61:533; NPNF I, 12:369).

καὶ προθυμίας)⁷⁰ that should characterize the Corinthians in their contributing to the collection.⁷¹ Chrysostom indicates that when Paul depicts the Macedonians' giving, he also points out the same three things; they gave much, gladly and quickly. He goes on to teach that there exists an opposition between φιλοτιμία, generous zeal,⁷² and προθυμία, eagerness. But here Chrysostom's line of thought is tortuous. It seems that he is underscoring the necessity of preparation and a well-thought plan for the one who is to give alms. Perhaps, in his opinion, the one animated by φιλοτιμία gives much but this generosity can result in sorrow if one did not reflect on it beforehand. But another, motivated by προθυμία, may give less and does not experience sorrow thereafter.⁷³ John admires the way Paul handles this issue wisely in the case of the Corinthians. In his view, since the apostle wants the Corinthians to give a substantial amount but out of free will, he avoids prescribing a certain amount to be given. John explains that the apostle did not say that "it is better to give a little and of free choice, than much of necessity; because he wished them to contribute both much and of free choice" (Οὐ γὰρ εἶπεν, ὀλίγον βέλτιον δοῦναι καὶ μετὰ προαιρέσεως, ἢ πολὺ μετὰ ἀνάγκης ἐπειδὴ καὶ πολὺ, καὶ μετὰ προαιρέσεως ἠβούλετο αὐτοὺς εἰσενεγκεῖν).⁷⁴ John sees that Paul expresses this in 2 Corinthians 9:5 by telling the Corinthians that their contribution should be ready as an εὐλογία rather than a πλεονεξία. Thus, the father understands that in this context the word εὐλογία indicates a large amount.⁷⁵ At the same time he argues that it carries the notion of blessing.⁷⁶ Both meanings are used in this context. Without giving further explanation, John says that Paul's exhortation presents those who give μὴ μετὰ ἀνάγκης, not out of compulsion, as εὐλογίας πεπληρωμένους τοὺς παρέχοντας, people filled with blessing. In his view, by exhorting the Corinthians to complete the collection, Paul and his delegates want to be the "cause of blessing" to them

---

70. I adopt here the translation provided by the NRSV and used in the exegetical part of this study.
71. Chrysostom, *Hom. 2 Cor.* 19.2.33–36 (PG 61:531; NPNF I, 12:368).
72. Danker et al., *Greek-English Lexicon*, 1060.
73. Chrysostom, *Hom. 2 Cor.* 19.2.47–51 (PG 61:531; NPNF I, 12:368).
74. Chrysostom, *Hom. 2 Cor.* 19.2.53–56 (PG 61:531; NPNF I, 12:368).
75. Chrysostom, *Hom. 2 Cor.* 19.2.56–58 (PG 61:531; NPNF I, 12:368).
76. Chrysostom, *Hom. 2 Cor.* 19.2.59–64 (PG 61:532; NPNF I, 12:369).

(ἀλλ'ὥστε αἴτιοι γενέσθαι ὑμῖν εὐλογίας).[77] John understands πλεονεξία as synonymous with ἀνάγκη, compulsion, used in 2 Corinthians 9:7. This is clear when John quotes Paul's clause (ἵνα προέλθωσιν προκαταρτίσωσιν τὴν εὐλογίαν ὑμῶν ἑτοίμην εἶναι ὡς εὐλογίαν, μὴ ὡς πλεονεξίαν) and immediately adds that Paul tells the Corinthians what their gift is supposed to be and thereafter what it should not look like (i.e. τοῦ μὴ μετὰ ἀνάγκης, given out of compulsion).[78] For John, by μὴ ὡς πλεονεξίαν, Paul indicates that he does not want the Corinthians to see him as one taking their offering by force (Μὴ νομίσετε, φησὶν, ὅτι ὡ'ς πλεονεκτοῦντες αὐτὴν λαμβάνομεν).[79] He goes on to say that πλεονεξία is associated with unwillingness and is thus opposed to εὐλογία; because no one gives a blessing with sorrow (οὐδεὶς γὰρ εὐλογίαν δίδωσι μετὰ λύπης). Worthy of note is Chrysostom's affirmation that God judges the value of alms not by the amount given, but by the inner disposition, literally "the extent of the substance" of the giver (τῇ δυνάμει τῆς οὐσίας τοῦ διδόντος).[80] This means to give whether or not out of one's superfluities (τὸ περιττόν).

Concerning the frequency of almsgiving, Chrysostom teaches that giving to the needy must be a permanent duty, the only excuse being when one has nothing to give.[81] He goes on to castigate speculation on grain, and finds it a shameful contradiction to Jesus's example of self-impoverishment.

4.2 Theodoret of Cyrus

Theodoret's sensibility to the poor's plight cannot pass unnoticed. His background of a rich Christian family did not prevent him from a fascination with monastic asceticism, which led him to become a monk after the death of his parents.[82] We learn that he distributed his entire heritage to the needy before he joined the monastic life at Nicerte.[83] He continued with his ascetic orientation even after his consecration as bishop of Cyr in

---

77. Chrysostom, *Hom. 2 Cor.* 19.2.66–67 (PG 61:532; NPNF I, 12:369).
78. Chrysostom, *Hom. 2 Cor.* 19.2.58–59 (PG 61:532; NPNF I, 12:369).
79. Chrysostom, *Hom. 2 Cor.* 19.2.65–66 (PG 61:532; NPNF I, 12: 369).
80. Chrysostom, *Hom. 2 Cor.* 19.4.72–74 (PG 61:536; NPNF I, 12:371).
81. Chrysostom, *Hom. 2 Cor.* 17.3.64–75 (PG 61:521; NPNF I, 12:362).
82. Canivet, "Theodoret of Cyr," 878.
83. Pásztori-Kupán, *Theodoret of Cyrus*, 4.

423.[84] During his office he used his revenue for public and social welfare. Apart from the construction of "an aqueduct, public bridges, baths and porticoes," Theodoret "introduced skilled craftsmen and medical personnel to look after the people."[85] Furthermore, he pleaded with the leaders of the locality to alleviate the fiscal burden weighing down the population. In his writings Theodoret warned his readers against the power of material riches and urged them to take care of the poor. His commentary on the Pauline letters is dated by many historians to the mid-440s.[86] Theodoret's commentaries on Paul's letters to the Corinthians are relatively concise in comparison with John Chrysostom's.[87] They betray the influence that Chrysostom had on Theodoret who grew up in the same city of Antioch. Indeed, at the age of six, Theodoret could listen to Chrysostom's sermons.[88]

4.2.1 God's Grace and Its Effects

Theodoret notes that Paul exhorts the Corinthians to take care of the saints.[89] Although the term faith does not appear in Paul's text, he says that Paul describes the genuine faith of the Macedonians in 2 Corinthians 8:1. He adds that the Macedonians' abundance in generosity was the expression of this sincere faith. He goes on to indicate that Paul "called possession of good things *grace of God*, not to exclude the independence of their free will but to bring out that with divine assistance it was possible to assemble the riches of virtue."[90] It is clear that Theodoret sees the risk of misunderstanding Paul's notion of grace as if it meant that the decision to participate in the collection was imposed on the Macedonians by God's grace. In his view, there is cooperation between the divine action and the human will to accomplish what he calls virtue. Concerning the χάρις of sharing in the ministry to the saints requested by the Macedonians as Paul says

---

84. Canivet, "Theodoret of Cyr," 878.
85. Pásztori-Kupán, *Theodoret of Cyrus*, 5.
86. Theodoret of Cyrus, *Commentary*, 279.
87. The limitations imposed on this research do not allow us to explore Theodoret's dogmatic works, especially his involvement in Christological controversies which marked his time such as Apollinarianism, Nestorianism, and Monophysitism.
88. Pásztori-Kupán, *Theodoret of Cyrus*, 4.
89. Theodoret of Cyrus, *Comm. in omnes S. Pauli Epistolas* 8.1 (PG 82:421), 279.
90. Theodoret of Cyrus, *Comm. in omnes S. Pauli Epistolas* 8.1 (PG 82:421), 279.

in 2 Corinthians 8:4, Theodoret explains that the collection was actually profitable both to the Macedonians and the believers in Jerusalem.[91] But he does not explain here in what way the former were to benefit from their contributing to the collection. Yet this becomes clear in his interpretation of the phrase πᾶσαν χάριν used in 2 Corinthians 9:8. For him, Paul means spiritual things, all "the riches of divine gifts."[92] The father comes back to this advantage when he notes that the Christians in Jerusalem might be able to relieve the Corinthians' needs from their abundance (2 Cor 9:13–15).[93]

4.2.2 Motivations, Ways of Giving and the Danger of Possessions

Theodoret highlights the idea that God is the provider for the believers.[94] Like Chrysostom, he maintains that in 2 Corinthians 9:8–11 Paul prays for the Corinthians. In Theodoret's view, the apostle associates prayer with exhortation to express his belief that God alone is able to provide everyone with good things abundantly. Theodoret understands that as God cares for the seed sown until it provides food for people (v. 10), he expects us to give the needy the necessities of life. It is remarkable that in his commentary on 2 Corinthians 8–9, Theodoret does not expound on the idea of caring for the poor as does John Chrysostom. This is partly due to the fact that unlike Chrysostom's homilies, his commentary is more concise as noted previously.[95]

Love for God is also at the heart of giving in Theodoret's view. The father notes that it is this love that motivated the Macedonians' commendable zeal for the collection. In his view, another motivation for Christian generosity is that the giver hopes to receive spiritual things, all "the riches of divine

---

91. Theodoret of Cyrus, *Comm. in omnes S. Pauli Epistolas* 8.3–4(PG 82:424), 279–280.
92. Theodoret of Cyrus, *Comm. in omnes S. Pauli Epistolas* 9.8–9 (PG 82:432), 284.
93. Theodoret of Cyrus, *Comm. in omnes S. Pauli Epistolas* 8.13–15 (PG 82:425), 281.
94. Theodoret of Cyrus, *Comm. in omnes S. Pauli Epistolas* 9.8–9, 10-11 (PG 82:432), 284.
95. Theodoret of Cyrus, *Comm. in omnes S. Pauli Epistolas* 9.8–9 (PG 82:432), 284. Theodoret uses the term "the saints" to designate the members of the Christian church as do Paul and other New Testament writers after him. Moreover, it is interesting that Theodoret notes that the saints in Jerusalem will perceive the Corinthians' generosity not only to the Christian believers in Jerusalem, but also their beneficence to other saints living everywhere.

gifts," and possible reciprocation of assistance.⁹⁶ The language of reward is rare in Theodoret's discourse. The idea that in the future the Macedonians' abundance will supply the Corinthians' needs is given an additional interpretation. The father indicates that the best reward to be expected by the Corinthians would consist in joining the saints in endurance.⁹⁷

Concerning the way of giving, Theodoret notes that in 2 Corinthians 8:10–12 Paul wants the Corinthians to understand that God measures the offering by the capacity of the giver; he takes interest in "the quality of free will" rather than in quantity.⁹⁸ In his reading of 2 Corinthians 9:5, Theodoret writes that throughout his discourse Paul never calls the collection a philanthropic deed, but "only a gift, fellowship, alms"⁹⁹ (Οὐδαμοῦ φιλανθρωπίαν ὠνόμασε τὴν μετάδοσιν, ἀλλὰ χάριν, καὶ κοινωνίαν, καὶ εὐλογίαν). He concludes that the apostle expected the contribution to the collection to be done joyfully because he knew well that the extortioner is irritated whereas the generous giver is glad. Since Paul had given everyone the freedom to decide the measure of one's giving, he found it important to give a further exhortation through the farming metaphor in 2 Corinthians 9:6. In Theodoret's view, Paul calls generosity seed (τὸ σπόρος) in order to express its variegated fruits.¹⁰⁰ A bit further, while commenting on verses 12–13, he explains that the results of the Corinthians' generosity consist in the relief of the saints' needs and praises to God. He remarks that Paul challenged miserly givers by indicating that the harvest is proportionate to the amount of the sowing; yet once again the apostle returned to his principle of free will in 2 Corinthians 9:7 in which he spoke of God's love for the cheerful giver.¹⁰¹ Theodoret writes that elsewhere, in Romans, Paul speaks of the one who gives out of mercy and joyfully.¹⁰² He concludes that from a satisfied soul springs the offering of money.

---

96. Theodoret of Cyrus, *Comm. in omnes S. Pauli Epistolas* 8.13–15 (PG 82:425), 281.
97. Theodoret of Cyrus, *Comm. in omnes S. Pauli Epistolas* 8.13–15 (PG 82:425), 281.
98. Theodoret of Cyrus, *Comm. in omnes S. Pauli Epistolas* 8.12 (PG 82:425), 281.
99. Theodoret of Cyrus, *Comm. in omnes S. Pauli Epistolas* 9.5 (PG 82:429), 283.
100. Theodoret of Cyrus, *Comm. in omnes S. Pauli Epistolas* 9.6 (PG 82:432), 283, 284.
101. Theodoret of Cyrus, *Comm. in omnes S. Pauli Epistolas* 9.6 (PG 82:432), 283.
102. Theodoret of Cyrus, *Comm. in omnes S. Pauli Epistolas* 9.7 (PG 82:432), 283: Rom 12:8.

Like Chrysostom, Theodoret is aware of the danger of possessions. This is clear from his reading of 2 Corinthians 8:13–15. He argues that the Lord defines "perfection" as contempt for material wealth and as voluntary poverty.[103] The story of the rich young man in Matthew 19:16–22 is adduced to demonstrate how Jesus taught that this life should be detached from material goods. However, Theodoret notes that Paul, who was instructed in this teaching about perfection, refrained from giving the Corinthians high standards. Rather, he adjusted the laws to "the limitations of their good will," by asking them to share their surplus.[104] Theodoret contends that the experience of the manna invoked by Paul testifies to God's establishing the principle of fair balance. Theodoret explains that Paul prayed for the Corinthians to be granted "the riches of the divine gifts," purposively calling them πᾶσαν χάριν, "every grace," to show that "contempt for money" produces righteousness which lasts forever.[105] He adds that the apostle reinforced this view by a quotation from Scripture which affirms that God provides for human needs (2 Cor 9:10).

4.3 Ambrosiaster

The name Ambrosiaster was coined in the sixteenth century by Erasmus to designate the Christian writer who produced the earliest complete commentary on the entire Pauline corpus.[106] This work had been mistakenly attributed to Bishop Ambrose of Milan (fourth century). This anonymous author, who is believed to have been a clerk in the Roman Church, was influential at Rome throughout the late fourth century. Another work, a collection of 127 *Quaestiones Veteris et Novi Testamenti*, traditionally attributed to Augustine is believed to stem from the same author. His anonymous identity makes difficult any further investigation into his interest or achievements in relieving the needy.

---

103. Theodoret of Cyrus, *Comm. in omnes S. Pauli Epistolas* 8.13–15 (PG 82:425), 281.
104. Theodoret of Cyrus, *Comm. in omnes S. Pauli Epistolas* 8.13–15 (PG 82:425), 281.
105. Theodoret of Cyrus, *Comm. in omnes S. Pauli Epistolas* 9.8–9 (PG 82:432), 284.
106. Crehan, "Ambrosiaster," 346; De Bruyn et al., "Translation," https://arts.uottawa.ca/cla-srs/sites/arts.uottawa.ca/cla-srs/files/debruyn.translation.ambrosiaster_0.pdf.

4.3.1 Different Meanings of Gratia

Ambrosiaster explains that the *gratia* received by the Macedonians (2 Cor 8:1) consisted in their accepting "the word of faith" with devotion.[107] This faith is a confidence for "the hope promised to them" which enabled them to endure afflictions and rejoice.[108] Ambrosiaster notes that in 2 Corinthians 9:8 Paul says that the same divine power that brought the Corinthians to conversion will cause them to perform every good deed by God's *gratia*.[109] Moreover, the collection itself is a *gratia* in which Paul in 2 Corinthians 8:6 believed that Titus could play an important role among the Corinthians.[110]

4.3.2 The Use of Possessions and Care for the Needy

The question about the attitude towards wealth and the way of giving in Ambrosiaster deserves our attention. This father draws on Paul's statement in 2 Corinthians 9:10 and explains that all things are God's property.[111] God multiplies these things, allows human beings to enjoy them, and commands that a portion of them be used to relieve the needy. It is in this way that Ambrosiaster notes that in 2 Corinthians 8:2 Paul speaks of the Macedonians' *devotio* to God. He points out that they were materially poor but their souls were rich. This spiritual wealth is demonstrated by their ministering to the saints "with a pure conscience."[112] He notes that they sought to please God and not men; God being the only one who knew what they were able to achieve in this respect. For Ambrosiaster, the Macedonians were eager to contribute beyond what their situation allowed because they wholly surrendered to God (2 Cor 8:3). He notes that in all this they displayed sincerity and devotion.

Ambrosiaster's interpretation of 2 Corinthians 8:14 is worth mentioning here as far as the attitude towards wealth is concerned.[113] In his understanding, Paul says that at a time when the Christians in Jerusalem are confronted with deep poverty they should completely abandon worldly

---

107. Ambrosiaster, *Ad Corinthios secunda* 8.1 (CSEL 81, 2, 256.18); 236.
108. Ambrosiaster, *Ad Corinthios secunda* 8.2 (CSEL 81 2, 256.20); 236.
109. Ambrosiaster, *Ad Corinthios secunda* 9.8 (CSEL 81, 2, 267.21–24); 242.
110. Ambrosiaster, *Ad Corinthios secunda* 8.6 (CSEL 81, 2, 258.16–17); 237.
111. Ambrosiaster, *Ad Corinthios secunda* 9.10 (CSEL 81, 2, 269.16–19); 243.
112. Ambrosiaster, *Ad Corinthios secunda* 8.2 (CSEL 81, 2, 256–257.27–31); 236.
113. Ambrosiaster, *Ad Corinthios secunda* 8.14 (CSEL 81, 2, 261.1–13); 238.

affairs to focus on religious activities (i.e. to study the Scriptures and intercede for others). However, Ambrosiaster does not say that believers must not possess material wealth. He notes that those believers who gain material wealth from different activities or inheritance are expected to assist the saints. In the future, when these saints are at ease and those who ministered to them are in want, they will repay the assistance received. He indicates that through the collection the saints (the church in Jerusalem) are made debtors (*debtores*) to those who sent them assistance. To emphasize the value of this solidarity, Ambrosiaster quotes Matthew 25:40 where Jesus says that assistance to the least of people is actually directed to himself.

For Ambrosiaster, three main questions have to be asked to determine the right way of giving (2 Cor 9:8).[114] The first deals with the amount to be given; the second is related to the amount one possesses; the third question asks in which spirit one is about to give. He concludes that giving correctly is to give as much as one can. For such a giver, says Ambrosiaster, God will surely provide for material things needed for them to continue the deeds of generosity.[115] Without stating clearly that material wealth is bad, Ambrosiaster expresses a negative view on it. Commenting on 2 Corinthians 9:11, he notes that there are some people who choose what is better and despise worldly possessions to commit themselves entirely to God's things.[116] For these people God appoints rich people to provide for their food and clothing.

The notion of true conversion is related to Christian giving in Ambrosiaster. In his comments on 2 Corinthians 8:5 Ambrosiaster refers the phrase *et non sicut speravimus*, "and this, not merely as we expected," to the Macedonians' conversion: *semet ipsos dederunt primum Domino*, "they gave themselves first to the Lord."[117] In his view, Paul says that they gave themselves to God beyond his expectations. In their contributing to the collection they were not trying to corrupt Paul so that he would not pay attention to their vices and thus deflect his authority. Later on when he comments on 2 Corinthians 8:7, he indicates that the Corinthians' eagerness

---

114. Ambrosiaster, *Ad Corinthios secunda* 9.8 (CSEL 81, 2, 268.9–10); 242.
115. Ambrosiaster, *Ad Corinthios secunda* 9.8 (CSEL 81, 2, 268.13–17); 242.
116. Ambrosiaster, *Ad Corinthios secunda* 9.11 (CSEL 81, 2, 269.21–270.6–9); 243.
117. Ambrosiaster, *Ad Corinthios secunda* 8.5 (CSEL 81, 2, 257.23–258.4); 237.

to minister to the saints proves that "they have mended their ways."[118] In Ambrosiaster's view, the same understanding is reflected in 2 Corinthians 8:8 when the apostle writes that he is not giving a command. He explains that what Paul is asking the Corinthians is not merely to send money to the needy. Rather, he is exhorting them to demonstrate that they are upright before God and other people.[119] Ambrosiaster understands that the same view about the right attitude before God underlies Paul's exhortation in 2 Corinthians 8:10 where he says that he is giving his advice to the Corinthians.[120] He explains that the apostle wants them to consider their wealth and give according to their ability. In this way, notes Ambrosiaster, they will stay away from the pretense which consists in being pleasing to men but accomplishing nothing for God.[121]

Ambrosiaster insists on Paul's care for the poor. He sees that this consciousness is reflected in 2 Corinthians 8:20 when the apostle says that he is preventing anyone from blaming him about the collection. For Ambrosiaster, Paul fears that he might be seen as being negligent regarding the assistance to the poor or the saints, or acting slowly in this matter.[122] In his comments on 2 Corinthians 9:9, Ambrosiaster indicates that Paul quotes Psalm 111 (LXX) as another example of concern for the poor to incite the Corinthians to abound in every good work.[123] He esteems that the act of taking pity on the poor, *misericordia*, is termed righteousness, *iustitia* in this context. For Ambrosiaster, this *misericordia/ iustitia* results from the conviction that God gives good things to all without any discrimination. He concludes that the righteous person shares his wealth with the needy so that the latter might not seem to be deprived of God's beneficence. Ambrosiaster's sensitivity to the plight of the poor is also seen in the way he reads Paul in 2 Corinthians 9:12–15.[124] He observes that Paul is saying that those who receive money from a charitable offering are no longer subject

---

118. Ambrosiaster, *Ad Corinthios secunda* 8.7 (CSEL 81, 2, 258.25–27); 237.
119. Ambrosiaster, *Ad Corinthios secunda* 8.8 (CSEL 81, 2, 259.3–6); 237.
120. Ambrosiaster, *Ad Corinthios secunda* 8.8 (CSEL 81, 2, 259.24–28); 238.
121. Ambrosiaster, *Ad Corinthios secunda* 8.8 (CSEL 81, 2, 259.24–28); 238.
122. Ambrosiaster, *Ad Corinthios secunda* 8.20 (CSEL 81, 2, 262.24–263.6); 239.
123. Ambrosiaster, *Ad Corinthios secunda* 9.9 (CSEL 81, 2, 268.20–269.11); 242.
124. Ambrosiaster, *Ad Corinthios secunda* 9.12–15 (CSEL 81, 2, 270.1–271.20); 243–244.

to beggary but to the service of God whom they recognize as the one who actually feeds them. Ambrosiaster concludes that those who help the needy in this way make their gifts to God. But these gifts are also God's because it is he who commands people to offer them.

4.3.3 The Language of Retribution

The notion of reward, *fructus* or *retributio*, comes up several times in Ambrosiaster mainly in relation to Christian giving. But he uses it in other instances as well. Concerning the Macedonians (2 Cor 8:4), he says that they valued more the promises for the future than immediate returns in their lifetime.[125] He argues that this promised hope remains the stimulus that lies behind the collection as a service to the poor.[126] As for Paul (2 Cor 8:4), Ambrosiaster maintains that he finally accepted the Macedonians' contribution lest he might "lose his reward out of kindness towards them."[127] In his comments on 2 Corinthians 8:6, Ambrosiaster insists once again on the concept of reward.[128] He says that Titus has been rewarded for his earlier exhortations and can now persuade the Corinthians to give their assistance to the saints. But he does not explain in what this reward consisted. It is possible that he has in mind the fact that Paul praises Titus in chapter 7. As for the Corinthians who are mending their faults as Ambrosiaster says, they would receive the reward of their generosity. Ambrosiaster explains that it is probably for this reason that Paul in 2 Corinthians 8:12 insists on the fact that one should give according to one's means.[129] He is afraid that if he compels them to give beyond what they are capable of, they would later be resentful and thus lose their reward in the future. However, Ambrosiaster states that in 2 Corinthians 9:6 Paul speaks of sowing sparingly because he finds that the Corinthians are like misers who deliberate much after they have promised to give a long time ago.[130] For Ambrosiaster, since misers "regret having promised anything," they must be forced to give.[131] He goes

---

125. Ambrosiaster, *Ad Corinthios secunda* 8.4 (CSEL 81, 2, 257.17–20); 237.
126. Ambrosiaster, *Ad Corinthios secunda* 9.15 (CSEL 81, 2, 271.18–20); 244.
127. Ambrosiaster, *Ad Corinthios secunda* 8.4 (CSEL 81, 2, 257.17–20); 237.
128. Ambrosiaster, *Ad Corinthios secunda* 8.6 (CSEL 81, 2, 258.12–20); 237.
129. Ambrosiaster, *Ad Corinthios secunda* 8.12 (CSEL 81, 2, 260.3–7); 238.
130. Ambrosiaster, *Ad Corinthios secunda* 9.6 (CSEL 81, 2, 267.2–11); 241–242.
131. Ambrosiaster, *Ad Corinthios secunda* 9.6 (CSEL 81, 2, 267.2–3); 241.

on to indicate that a bountiful sower is the one who acts joyfully, being confident that they will receive reward in the future.

The same notion of reward is to be read in 2 Corinthians 9:7,[132] notes Ambrosiaster. God rewards only the person who acts wholeheartedly as if he was depositing for himself his treasure in God's presence. He concludes that a rich person who assists the needy in accordance with God's will receives a double reward for one sowing, "both for the present and for the future."[133] His resources are multiplied to enable him to continue his practice of good deeds; and ultimately he will receive the reward from God in the world to come. But whoever gives to the needy without simplicity of heart is simply losing as says the Lord, notes Ambrosiaster quoting Matthew 6:2.

4.4 Thomas Aquinas

Thomas Aquinas (c. 1225–1274)[134] is "the most important and influential scholastic theologian and philosopher."[135] This is why of all the medieval commentaries mentioned earlier I will discuss only his. Thomas's commentary on 2 Corinthians is one of his works which shows his interest in the interpretation of Scripture rather than in a hasty application to his contemporaries through a moralizing discourse.[136] It is remarkable, for instance, that when he speaks of alms in this commentary, he does not hint at the Mendicant Orders, especially the Dominicans, with regard to their strategies to address the problem of poverty among their members. He

---

132. Ambrosiaster, *Ad Corinthios secunda* 9.7 (CSEL 81, 2, 267.14–19); 242.
133. Ambrosiaster, *Ad Corinthios secunda* 9.11 (CSEL 81, 2, 270.2–12); 243.
134. Weisheipl, *Friar Thomas d'Aquino*, 4.
135. Wallace, Weisheipl and Johnson, "Thomas Aquinas, St.," 13.
136. Dahan, "Introduction," III. But this does not imply that Thomas Aquinas rejects the traditional view of the four senses of the Scriptures. As observes M. Dubois, Thomas is regarded in the Roman Catholic tradition as the most prominent theologian of this hermeneutical tradition. In the very first question of his *Summa Theologica* (Ia, q.1, a.10) he makes this point but insists that the spiritual meaning must be rigorously based on the literal sense of any biblical text. He explains that the spiritual meaning comprises three levels: the allegorical sense unfolds in the New Testament prefigured in the Old; the moral reveals how the Scriptures become a rule of life; while the anagogical points to what the Scriptures signify in relation to eternal realities in the world to come (Dubois, "Mystical and Realistic Elements," 39–40, 43).

produced exegetical, homiletical, liturgical and philosophical writings.[137] He is mostly known for his *Summa contra gentiles* (c.1258–1264) and his *Summa Theologiae* (1265–1274) also called the *Summa Theologica* or the *Summa*. The former is a synthesis of the main Catholic teachings produced to be used by Dominican missionaries in Spain whose activity involved heated debates with cultivated Muslims and Jews. The *Summa Theologica*, Aquinas' main work, was destined for theology students. There is no evidence that Thomas may have been involved in practical activity to relieve the poor. However, it is beyond doubt that his theological and philosophical writings reflect his concern for the needy. This becomes clear when we consider the fact that his *Summa* contains two treatises on charity and its consequences.[138] For instance, while he affirms the superiority of the soul over the body and that one must give priority to one's neighbor's spiritual needs, he admits that in a concrete case corporal considerations may take preference. Correlatively, Thomas states that practicing philosophical debates is higher than bestowing charity. But he concedes that "what a man dying of hunger needs is to be fed, not to be instructed."[139] He finds support in Aristotle who, in his discussion on how to decide what is more worthy of choice, says that "to be a philosopher is better than to make money" but that the former is not preferable for the needy.[140] Thomas understands that Aristotle meant that "*it is better to give a poor man money [...] than to philosophize to him.*"[141] It is remarkable that Thomas held charity in high esteem. Moreover, in his philosophical works he wrote about society and global trade, which confirms his interest in economic justice.[142]

4.4.1 Gratia, Genuine Generosity and Its Benefits

Thomas Aquinas explains that Paul asks the Corinthians to give alms (*eleemosynas*) to increase their merits (*ut merita ipsorum crescant*).[143] By the term

---

137. Wallace, Weisheipl, and Johnson, "Thomas Aquinas, St," 24–28.
138. T. Aquinas, *Summa Theologiae* 34; *Summa Theologiae* 35.
139. T. Aquinas, *Summa Theologiae* 34, 247.
140. Aristotle, *Posterior Analytics. Topica* III, 2.118a 10 (Tredennick and Forster, LCL).
141. T. Aquinas, *Summa Theologiae* 34, 247.
142. Michael, "St. Thomas Aquinas," http://www2.gcc.edu/dept/econ/ASSC/Papers2013/ASSC2013-HaganMichael.pdf.
143. T. Aquinas, *Ad Corinthios II*, 8. *Lectio* 1, 473 (S. de Saint-Eloy), 196.

merit, Thomas understands that the Corinthians' generosity is "worthy of receiving a reward" from God.[144] He says that Paul does this in the time of *gratia*; the time in which alms are meritorious (*tempore gratiae, tunc enim eleemosunae meritoriae sunt*).[145] This means that the elect, by divine grace, accomplish in the state of grace good acts in the form of alms which merit God's reward.[146] He understands that the *gratia* that has been given to the Macedonians is a divine free gift (i.e. generosity through alms [*eleemosynarum largitionem*]). In his view, Paul calls this generosity *gratia* because all good that we accomplish stems from God's *gratia*.[147] Thomas cites Ephesians 3:8 to show that Paul is aware that he also has been given the same *gratia* to minister to the Macedonians. He says that the *gratia* given to the Macedonians concerns their endurance in afflictions and their generosity through almsgiving.[148] He emphasizes that the Macedonians asked Paul to participate in the collection and explained to him why they wanted to be given this favor (*gratia*).[149] Thomas indicates that giving alms is a type of *gratia*, and that Paul expects Titus to help the Corinthians abound in it as they do in other spiritual gifts.[150] With regard to Christ, Thomas Aquinas

---

144. Sullivan, "Merit," 510. It is not possible to discuss here the doctrine of merit as it has been debated in the history of Christian thoughts. Neither is it the purpose of this study to explore Thomas's teaching on this point. Some general remarks will suffice here. Sullivan (ibid., 511–512) notes that Thomas Aquinas insists on the fact that man, justified by God's grace, can practice to perform good acts which deserve divine reward. In *ST* I.23 art.5 Thomas explains that although "merit" means "a voluntary human act that deserves a reward from God," a person cannot merit salvation (Nieuwenhove and Wawrykow, *Theology of Thomas Aquinas*, 203). On the contrary, the point is that "God has ordered good acts to be done in the state of grace to eternal life as meritorious of eternal life." Besides the reward of merit consisting in eternal life, Aquinas notes that whereas it is impossible for one to merit for oneself the first grace which works conversion, one can earn it for another if it is God's will. Here Aquinas refers to the believer's prayer. He explains that such a prayer for one's salvation or that of another person may yield positive results if God has ordained to use it to further one's own or someone else's salvation. Moreover, those who are in grace receive "a secondary reward for the good acts that merit heaven"; and this reward consists in "growth in and firmer possession of the habitual grace given to the elect in their conversion" (Nieuwenhove and Wawrykow, *Theology of Thomas Aquinas*, 205). It means perseverance in the state of grace given to the elect by God.

145. T. Aquinas, *Ad Corinthios II*, 8. *Lectio* 1, 473 (S. de Saint-Eloy), 196.
146. Nieuwenhove and Wawrykow, *Theology of Thomas Aquinas*, 204.
147. T. Aquinas, *Ad Corinthios* II, 8. *Lectio* 1, 473-474 (S. de Saint-Eloy), 196.
148. T. Aquinas, *Ad Corinthios* II, 8. *Lectio* 1, 474 (S. de Saint-Eloy), 196.
149. T. Aquinas, *Ad Corinthios* II, 8. *Lectio* 1, 474 (S. de Saint-Eloy), 198.
150. T. Aquinas, *Ad Corinthios* II, 8. *Lectio* 1, 474 (S. de Saint-Eloy), 199.

writes that *gratia* has been bestowed upon human beings. He explains that it is this grace that led the Son of God to take on himself the punishment that was reserved for us. According to Thomas, the Lord Jesus's grace consists in the fact that he made himself indigent. He insists that Christ became poor in material possessions but remained rich spiritually.[151] As for Paul and his companions (2 Cor 8:19), Thomas understands that the *gratia* administered by them is nothing but the work entrusted to the apostle and Barnabas as his companion in Acts 13:2. In Thomas' view, this work accomplished for the Lord's glory consisted in the preaching of the gospel and the collection of alms.[152]

On the one hand, Thomas Aquinas points out the necessary relation between correct giving and repentance. He indicates that the apostle commends the Macedonians' generosity because they gave themselves to God before they offered their possessions.[153] He insists that this order must be maintained in the matter of giving. In his view, the Macedonians meet this condition. This view is implied by Thomas's interpretation of 2 Corinthians 8:5 when Paul says that the Macedonians gave beyond his expectations. For Thomas, the apostle means that they did not give to redeem their sins (*pro culpis redimendis*).[154] On the other hand, Thomas disagrees with a reading that implies that alms from sinners should not be received. For him, it is only when sinners give their alms with the intention to remain in their sins that they must not be accepted.[155]

Thomas Aquinas argues that in 2 Corinthians 9 Paul takes pains to show the Corinthians how to give correctly (i.e. promptly [*prompte*],[156] abundantly [*abundanter*], and joyfully [*hilariter*]) because in chapter 8 he exhorted them to give their alms to the saints.[157] In Thomas's view, Paul ex-

---

151. T. Aquinas, *Ad Corinthios* II, 8. *Lectio* 2, 476 (S. de Saint-Eloy), 200–201. Thomas makes a distinction between *indiget*, indigent, the person who has nothing at all and is in want; and *pauper*, poor, one who has a little for subsistence.

152. T. Aquinas, *Ad Corinthios* II, 8. *Lectio* 3, 478-479 (S. de Saint-Eloy), 206–207.

153. T. Aquinas, *Ad Corinthios* II, 8. *Lectio* 1, 474-475 (S. de Saint-Eloy), 198.

154. T. Aquinas, *Ad Corinthios* II, 8. *Lectio* 1, 475 (S. de Saint-Eloy), 198.

155. T. Aquinas, *Ad Corinthios* II, 8. *Lectio* 1, 475 (S. de Saint-Eloy), 198.

156. For this he quotes Prov 3:8 which forbids the postponement of help to the needy when one is able to give it right away.

157. T. Aquinas, *Ad Corinthios* II, 9. *Lectio* 1, 480 (S. de Saint-Eloy), 209–210.

presses this when he says that he wants the Corinthians to be ready (*parati*, the Vulgate's translation of παρεσκευασμένοι) before he comes (2 Cor 9:3). He indicates that Paul's mention of the Macedonians' arrival exhorts the Corinthians to give promptly. As for the apostle's clause that he thought it necessary to send the brothers ahead of him, Thomas notes that it points to giving abundantly. He explains that these brothers had the task of helping the Corinthians to make ready their promised contributions (*repraeparent repromissam benedictionem hanc*) as Paul says in 2 Corinthians 9:5.[158] It is clear that Thomas follows the Vulgate which translates here the term εὐλογία by *benedictio*, blessing. He argues that the Corinthians' alms are called blessing because they are a source of eternal blessing. He affirms that God blesses the giver.[159] For Thomas Aquinas, this gift-blessing implies abundance as opposed to miserliness (*id est, abundanter, et non quasi avaritiam, id est, parce*). He indicates that through the sowing metaphor (2 Cor 9:6) Paul gives the reason why the Corinthians should give important contributions. Thomas understands that Paul says that whoever gives a small amount in this world will receive less in the world to come. But whoever gives much, literally in blessing, will receive an important retribution from God (*Dei largam retributionem*). However, Thomas Aquinas maintains that this abundance of retribution applies only to those who give (sow) in a good way. He quotes 1 Corinthians 15:41 which says that "star differs from star in glory" to indicate that although all those who give correctly will receive abundant reward, there will be some differences; not in terms of substance but in degrees. For Thomas there may be differences in the reward conferred to the saints (Christians) in the present life (*praemium accidentale*), but this does not affect at all the substantial recompense that one will receive in the life hereafter (*praemium substantiale*). He illustrates this difference among the saints in the present life with a reference to 1 Corinthians 8:15 where Paul quotes Exodus 16:8: "The one who had much did not have too much, and the one who had little did not have too little." Thomas pushes this paradox further when he says that *aliquando*

---

158. T. Aquinas, *Ad Corinthios* II, 9. *Lectio* 1, 480 (S. de Saint-Eloy), 211.
159. T. Aquinas, *Ad Corinthios* II, 9. *Lectio* 1, 480–481 (S. de Saint-Eloy), 211.

aliquis parce dat, et cum magna charitate et abundanter metet, "it happens that one gives little but with great charity, and so will reap abundantly."[160]

Thomas Aquinas explains that Paul's exhortation to give as one has decided in one's heart means that the apostle wants the Corinthians to give joyfully.[161] He explains that Paul justifies this view by saying that God loves a cheerful giver (2 Cor 9:7). In Thomas's opinion, Paul says that giving as one has deliberated in one's heart means to give voluntarily and not out of necessity (*Ut unusquisque voluntarie det, non coacte*).[162] He indicates that the apostle exposes here two factors which oppose human free will (i.e. coercion and sorrow). The Corinthians' gift will be the result of coercion or necessity, if they give because of Paul's commandment. They may feel sorrow if they give their contributions only because they fear that they may suffer confusion if they are found unprepared. But the Corinthians' joy in giving should stem from their love for the saints in Jerusalem, notes Thomas Aquinas. He has already referred to the correct way of giving in his comments on 2 Corinthians 8:12 where Paul says that one should give according to one's possessions. For Thomas, Paul says that he does not have the intention to force the Corinthians to give beyond their means, but that he is certain that their prompt will to contribute to the collection will push them to give more than they could afford.[163] To emphasize Paul's advice to the Corinthians, Thomas cites Tobit 4:8: "If you have many possessions, make your gift from them in proportion; if few, do not be afraid to give according to the little you have." He observes that the giver's inward disposition is crucial since unlike human beings, God looks at the heart.[164]

Thomas explains that when Paul says that God loves a cheerful giver (2 Cor 9:7), he means that God approves and rewards (*Deus approbat et remunerat*) such a giver. For Thomas, it is certain that God multiplies alms given by believers. He bases his affirmation on Paul's statement in

---

160. T. Aquinas, *Ad Corinthios* II, 9. Lectio 1, 481 (S. de Saint-Eloy), 211: "Tous 'moissonnent' abondamment quant à la récompense substantielle, mais avec parcimonie par rapport à la récompense accidentelle, qui différencie les saints [...] Car il arrive qu'on donne peu mais avec une grande charité, on moissonne alors avec abondance."

161. T. Aquinas, *Ad Corinthios* II, 9. Lectio 1, 481 (S. de Saint-Eloy), 211–212.

162. T. Aquinas, *Ad Corinthios* II, 9. Lectio 1, 481 (S. de Saint-Eloy), 212.

163. T. Aquinas, *Ad Corinthios* II, 8. Lectio 2, 477 (S. de Saint-Eloy), 202.

164. T. Aquinas, *Ad Corinthios* II, 9. Lectio 1, 481–482 (S. de Saint-Eloy), 212–213.

2 Corinthians 9:8 that "God is able to provide you with every blessing in abundance." He indicates that, in other words, the apostle tells the Corinthians that they do not have to fear to give because they are afraid to find themselves in indigence and regret their good deed.[165] He remarks that "every blessing" which God will supply to the Corinthians consists in spiritual and material riches since Paul states that they will be enriched in all things (2 Cor 9:11).[166] In his comments on 2 Corinthians 9:10 where Paul says that God is the one who provides the seed and bread to the farmer, Thomas remarks that Paul wants the Corinthians to realize that even what they have and from which they give their alms stems from God. This awareness should thus enable them to give voluntarily out of love for God.[167] He goes on to explain that the apostle assures the Corinthians that they will always receive from God enough to meet their own material needs and to give alms joyfully.[168] For Thomas, with the same promise that the Corinthians will always receive enough in order to give alms, the apostle prevents them from taking abundant wealth as the purpose of their life. At the same time, says Thomas, the apostle wants the Corinthians not to think that one must possess spiritual riches and live in idleness, without making good use of them. For the latter instruction, Thomas explains that Paul writes precisely *abundetis in omnem simplicitatem*, so that you abound in simplicity. In Thomas's understanding, this means that the Corinthians are expected to give abundantly with simplicity of heart, such that a generous gift proceeds from material possessions whereas simplicity stems from spiritual riches (*ut largitio procedat ex divitiis temporalibus, simplicitas autem ex spiritualibus*).[169]

Thomas's belief in the benefit of almsgiving on the part of the giver is once more noticeable in his comments on 2 Corinthians 8:10 where Paul

---

165. T. Aquinas, *Ad Corinthios* II, 9. *Lectio* 2, 482 (S. de Saint-Eloy), 214.
166. T. Aquinas, *Ad Corinthios* II, 9. *Lectio* 2, 482, 483 (S. de Saint-Eloy), 214–215, 216.
167. T. Aquinas, *Ad Corinthios* II, 9. *Lectio* 2, 482 (S. de Saint-Eloy), 215.
168. T. Aquinas, *Ad Corinthios* II, 9. *Lectio* 2, 483 (S. de Saint-Eloy), 216.
169. T. Aquinas, *Ad Corinthios* II, 9. *Lectio* 2, 483 (S. de Saint-Eloy), 216: "Mais de crainte qu'on ne croit pas qu'il faille mettre sa fin dans l'abondance des richesses temporelles, ou qu'on doive posséder les richesses spirituelles dans l'oisiveté et sans les mettre à profit..."

says that he gives the Corinthians advice in the matter of the collection.[170] Thomas indicates that the one who practices piety through almsgiving gains a spiritual advantage, whereas the receiver of alms gets only a material gift. Quoting 1 Timothy 4:8 he emphasizes the usefulness of piety in everything. He explains that as spiritual things are much more precious than material goods, in the area of almsgiving the benefits of the giver are preferable to the ones of the recipient.

Thomas shows that God's *gratia* creates interconnectedness between the Corinthians and the saints in Jerusalem. Because of God's *gratia* spread among the Corinthians, the saints will long to see the Corinthians in eternity (*in aeterna beatitudine*).[171] It is surprising that Thomas limits this longing for a meeting to the hereafter. However, he notes that the collection brings about spiritual interrelatedness between the Corinthians and the Christians in Jerusalem. He argues that the "fair balance" mentioned by Paul as the aim of the collection means that the riches that the Corinthians give to the poor Christians in Jerusalem will be proportionate to the riches the former receive from the latter's intercessional prayers.[172]

4.4.2 Poverty Praised and Concern for the Poor

Thomas's interpretation of Paul's thought on the Macedonians' poverty (2 Cor 8:2) is telling. First of all, following the Vulgate, he has translated the term ἁπλότης by *simplicitas*, simplicity. In the third chapter of this study, I observed that in the Pauline epistles ἁπλότης can have this meaning in other instances (2 Cor 11:3; Eph 6:5; Col 3:22). But I maintained that in 2 Corinthians 8:2 it has the meaning of generosity.[173] Thus, Thomas understands that the Macedonians' deep poverty overflowed in wealth of simplicity. He explains that the Macedonians' complete devotion to God resulted in contempt for possessions. He supports this view by a quotation from Proverb 11:3 (Vulgate) which says that *simplicitas iustorum diriget eos*, "the simplicity of the upright will guide them." Thomas Aquinas argues that people are prompt to give enough either because they have abundant

---

170. T. Aquinas, *Ad Corinthios* II, 8. *Lectio* 2, 476 (S. de Saint-Eloy), 201.
171. T. Aquinas, *Ad Corinthios* II, 9. *Lectio* 2, 484 (S. de Saint-Eloy), 217–218.
172. T. Aquinas, *Ad Corinthios* II, 8. *Lectio* 2, 477–478 (S. de Saint-Eloy), 204.
173. Harris, *Second Epistle*, 563.

possessions or because they have contempt for wealth.[174] He explains that a rich person's abundance and a poor person's contempt for wealth will finally have the same effect.

Thomas Aquinas insists on the fact that in 2 Corinthians 8:9 Paul gives the example of Christ to incite the Corinthians to almsgiving.[175] He explains that the incarnated Christ remained spiritually rich but made himself indigent in worldly possessions (i.e. more than poor because he was deprived of everything and was in want). For Thomas, Christ cherished material poverty. He adds that we have to do the same in order to become rich in spiritual things.[176] He supports this view by a quotation from James 2:5 about divine election of the poor in material things. Later on, Thomas Aquinas will come back to this view when he comments on 2 Corinthians 8:13 where Paul says that his intention is not to make the saints live comfortably whereas the Corinthians themselves suffer want. He goes on to say that in fact it is better for one to give everything to the needy and, as a consequence, live in afflictions for Christ's sake.[177] Thomas conceded that it is by condescendence that Paul advised the Corinthians to give according to what one had because he was aware of their weakness.

Thomas's concern for the poor deserves mention here. He notes that the scriptural quotation used by Paul in 2 Corinthians 9:9 says explicitly to whom we have to give; that is to the indigent (*indigentibus*).[178] He explains that the verb *dispersit* (ἐσκόρπισεν, He has dispersed abroad), has humans as a subject and indicates that we must not give our entire alms to one poor person. On the contrary, notes Thomas, we have to distribute it among indigents. It seems to him that this clause refers back to the previous verse to say that God provides the givers with every blessing because they have dispersed their benefits to the poor.[179] In Thomas's view, Paul's clause "his righteousness endures forever" carries two possible meanings. It may mean

---

174. T. Aquinas, *Ad Corinthios* II, 8. *Lectio* 1, 474 (S. de Saint-Eloy), 197.
175. T. Aquinas, *Ad Corinthios* II, 8. *Lectio* 2, 475–476; (S. de Saint-Eloy), 200–201.
176. T. Aquinas, *Ad Corinthios* II, 8. *Lectio* 1, 476 (S. de Saint-Eloy), 200.
177. T. Aquinas, *Ad Corinthios* II, 8. *Lectio* 2, 477 (S. de Saint-Eloy), 202–203.
178. T. Aquinas, *Ad Corinthios* II, 9. *Lectio* 2, 482 (S. de Saint-Eloy), 215.
179. T. Aquinas, *Ad Corinthios* II, 9. *Lectio* 2, 482 (S. de Saint-Eloy), 215.

that the giver's will to give continues to grow, or that the reward of his justice remains forever.[180]

4.5 John Calvin

Calvin (1509–1564)[181] is the reformer most prolific in the interpretation of the Scriptures. He commented on all the books of the Bible except Revelation. In William D. Chamberlain's view, Calvin was even the greatest interpreter of the Bible of his time which was characterized by a significant advance in biblical interpretation with much interest in "the actual, practical significance" of Scripture for people's daily living.[182] Thus, the study of his work is worthwhile in this research. Calvin's commentaries on the Corinthians were written around the year 1546, a turbulent time for Calvin and the nascent Protestantism in general. Charles V of Spain continued to be a real threat to the Protestant movement whereas Calvin himself was confronted with intense personal opposition from his Geneva environment. It is remarkable that despite the pressures of such a troubled context and his engagement in lecturing, preaching and civil responsibilities, Calvin's writings display the marks of clarity and a finished work.[183] With his continuous attention to the historical context of the Bible and the grammatical analysis of biblical texts in their original language, Calvin could not accommodate the allegorizing interpretation of Scripture which had been privileged for many centuries.

Calvin involved himself in social affairs as a result of his theological principles. As notes André Biéler, Calvin's concern for the poor and the weak in general is rooted in his deep conviction that human life is a supreme gift of God and therefore sacred.[184] The second theological principle that guides him is that God is the sole owner of the universe. At creation, he gave the earth to man so that the latter might enjoy its benefits and rationally ensure an economy of abundance to benefit others too. However,

---

180. T. Aquinas, *Ad Corinthios* II, 9. *Lectio* 2, 482 (S. de Saint-Eloy), 215.
181. Olin, "Calvin, John," 887.
182. Chamberlain, "Introduction," 2.
183. Ibid., 1.
184. Biéler, *La pensée économique*, 351–356.

since man in his fallen state is still tempted by laziness, selfishness, greed, and cupidity, Calvin considered that the State should act as a regulator of society in protecting private property and ensuring that the fruits of the earth benefit all members of society.[185] Thus, the institutional organization of charity is of paramount importance in the thought of Calvin.[186] When he was in Geneva, "he and his friends provided for the continuing stream of Protestant refugees from Roman Catholic areas by offering them food and shelter" in the city.[187] This hospitality grew into a social welfare institution known as the *Bourse française* (the French Fund for poor foreigners) whose mandate was to care for those who came to settle in Geneva to live according to the Reformation principles.[188] During his exile

---

185. Ibid., 378–382.

186. One can then understand why he insisted on creating a solidarity fund to be supplied jointly by the church members and the State (ibid., 152–156). In the same vein, Calvin strengthened official social medicine for those who could not afford health care. He even went further in helping the poor by laying particular emphasis on the education and re-education of all social groups to enable individuals to be in control of their own destiny for through work one values oneself and makes oneself useful to the community. At this point, Calvin takes up Luther's doctrine of profession as a calling from God, *Beruf* in German: Weber, *L'éthique protestante*, 197. Another area in which Calvin defends the cause of the poor concerns financial activities (Biéler, *La pensée économique*, 455–469). He notes that a free loan is a tangible sign of a good understanding of God's grace. Our reformer makes a clear distinction between "le prêt de consommation" (the consumer loan) assigned to help the needy and therefore unproductive for the debtor and "le prêt de production" (production loan) also called "prêt d'entreprise" (business loan) which generates benefits for the lessee. According to Calvin, it is only for the latter that compensation/interest may legitimately be required of the borrower. But in this case also a loan becomes reprehensible if it is granted at an excessive interest rate. Calvin goes further in his protection of the poor by saying that "whoever invests in business the money that he was supposed to allocate to the solidarity fund is equally a usurer" (Biéler, *La pensée économique*, 472).

187. Olson, *Calvin and Social Welfare*, 11.

188. As notes Olson (ibid., 12), the Reformers maintained the view that almsgiving is central to Christianity as the medieval church also had held to it firmly. However, they rejected soteriological perceptions attached to it and provided it with a new theological understanding: "The reformers had undermined the medieval recognition of giving alms to the poor as a worthy act counting toward the remission of the temporal punishment for sin that otherwise would need to be purged in Purgatory. Protestants emphasized charity as a response of love to God and one's neighbor . . . The haphazard aspects of traditional almsgiving in Geneva were minimized by encouraging people to channel their benevolence regularly through a fund administered through deacons who would ensure that the welfare would be distributed systematically, comprehensively, and compassionately. The *Bourse française* was an important part of that system of welfare because it was dedicated to foreigners in a city popular to refugees."

at Strasbourg (1538–1541), he took charge of a Christian community for French Protestant refugees.[189]

4.5.1 Gratia in Relation to Christian Generosity in 2 Corinthians 8–9

Calvin indicates that Paul ascribes to God's *gratia* the Macedonians' involvement in the collection (8:1) in order to cause emulation among the Corinthians.[190] He explains that although everyone admits that helping the needy is a commendable virtue, not everyone sees it as a gain or divine grace. On the contrary, people are inclined to think that what they give is lost.[191] But for Paul, says Calvin, assisting the poor has to be acknowledged as a special privilege. He goes on to explain that the Macedonians received a twofold *gratia*.[192] It consisted in a joyful endurance which they displayed in afflictions and in the act of giving a part of their slender resources to the needy believers. He concludes that we are expected to show liberality even in extreme poverty.[193]

Calvin explains that the term *gratia* used in 2 Corinthians 8:4 to recommend alms can have different interpretations.[194] But he thinks that by Paul's clause δεόμενοι ἡμῶν τὴν χάριν καὶ τὴν κοινωνίαν τῆς διακονίας τῆς εἰς τοὺς ἁγίους, "begging us earnestly for the privilege of sharing in this ministry to the saints," we must understand that we need to imitate our Father in heaven who freely grants us all good things. This imitation will consist in doing good to others. In Calvin's estimation, by doing so, one becomes a dispenser of God's *gratia*. He considers that although Paul does not explain why he refers to Jesus Christ's *gratia* in 2 Corinthians 8:9, it is quite clear that the apostle is exhorting us to beneficence.[195]

The reformer explains that God's *gratia* grants the believers a double benefit (2 Cor 9:8).[196] He remarks that the apostle gives this promise to the

---

189. Olin, "Calvin, John," 889.
190. Calvin, *Ad Corinthios II* 8.1, 134.18–20 (trans. Smail), 106.
191. Calvin, *Ad Corinthios II* 8.1, 134.20–23 (trans. Smail), 106–107.
192. Calvin, *Ad Corinthios II* 8.1, 134.25–26 (trans. Smail), 107.
193. Calvin, *Ad Corinthios II* 8.2, 135.15–17 (trans. Smail), 107.
194. Calvin, *Ad Corinthios II* 8.4, 136.17–23 (trans. Smail), 108.
195. Calvin, *Ad Corinthios II* 8.9, 139.4–7 (trans. Smail), 110.
196. Calvin, *Ad Corinthios II* 9.8, 153.31–33 (trans. Smail), 123.

Corinthians when he says that δυνατεῖ δὲ ὁ θεὸς πᾶσαν χάριν περισσεῦσαι εἰς ὑμᾶς, "And God is able to provide you with every blessing in abundance." For Calvin, the first benefit the Corinthians should expect consists in receiving what they need for their own living. The second advantage will be that they will have enough resources to assist the needy. Calvin argues that Paul uses the term αὐτάρκεια to mean the "amount that the Lord knows to be profitable to us, for it is not always to our good to be filled to satiety."[197] This amount may be more or less providing that we do good to other people. The reformer underlines that since men are naturally miserly and inclined to distrust, Paul speaks of God's reciprocating the alms to bring the Corinthians to understand that what they give will certainly turn to their own advantage.[198] And this is to be expected not only in heaven but also in the present life, comments Calvin.[199]

Calvin notes that the same twofold benefit of God's blessing upon the believers is mentioned by the apostle in 2 Corinthians 9:10: sufficiency for themselves and resources to relieve the needy.[200] The reformer is aware that the Greek manuscript presents two different readings in this verse. While he agrees that the variant which reads future verbs χορηγήσει καὶ πληθυνεῖ ... καὶ αὐξήσει (He will supply and multiply...and increase) would be suitable, Calvin prefers the other which he calls the infinitive (χορηγῆσαι καὶ πληθῦναι...καὶ αὐξῆσαι).[201] He observes that the infinitive sometimes replaces the optative to express a wish. However, I recall from the second chapter of this study that these forms are nowadays interpreted as aorist optatives. Calvin's view is that Paul prays for the Corinthians: "And may he that supplies seed to the sower and bread for food, supply and multiply your seed for sowing, and increase the fruits of your righteousness." It is remarkable that Calvin brings in the concept of *gratia* in this context of 2 Corinthians 9:10 though the word χάρις is absent from Paul's clause. He argues that Paul rejects the view that the sower reaps the fruit of his

---

197. Calvin, *Ad Corinthios II* 9.8, 153.31–35 (trans. Smail), 123.
198. Calvin, *Ad Corinthios II* 9.8, 153.16–30 (trans. Smail), 122–123.
199. Calvin, *Ad Corinthios II* 9.6, 152.19–23 (trans. Smail), 121.
200. Calvin, *Ad Corinthios II* 9.10, 156.4–6 (trans. Smail), 124.
201. Calvin, *Ad Corinthios II* 9.10, 155.8–156.3 (trans. Smail), 124, 123.

toil through the harvest.²⁰² He notes that the apostle maintains that God is the one who provides the seed and food to the farmer: ὁ δὲ ἐπιχορηγῶν σπόρον τῷ σπείροντι καὶ ἄρτον εἰς βρῶσιν. Calvin explains that this provision demonstrates God's *gratia* as did the manna which was granted to the Israelites (Deut 8:16).

4.5.2 Christian Generosity and Reward

In his introductory remarks on 2 Corinthians 8–9 Calvin points out that Paul exhorts the Corinthians to actively collect alms (*eleemosynas*) to relieve the needs of the Christians in Jerusalem.²⁰³ He says that Paul had promised to take care of this concern (Gal 2:10) following the apostles' instruction. Commenting on 2 Corinthians 8:10 Calvin refers to Martial's wisdom recommending generosity: *quas dederis, solas semper habebis opes*, "Only the wealth you give away will always be yours."²⁰⁴ And he explains that the reason behind this thinking is that "what is given to friends is safe from risk."²⁰⁵ However, he rejects the idea that our giving to the needy should be stimulated by the hope of any kind of return as a way of compensation (*compensatio*). Calvin emphasizes that even though people should fail to recognize the good we did to them, and that we may appear to have lost our resources bestowed to them, God expects us not to give up our generosity. He argues that the believer's advantage lies in the fact that, as says Proverb 19:17, what is given to the poor is actually lent to God. Calvin asserts that this is important inasmuch as God's blessing is much more precious than earthly possessions.²⁰⁶ Thus, almsgiving should be an unceasing exercise, like perennial waters in a Christian's life. Calvin explains that this is intimated by Paul when he cites Psalm 112:9 in 2 Corinthians 9:9 about the pious man whose righteousness (i.e. his good deeds), would last for ever: *dispersit dedit pauperibus iustitia eius manet in aeternum*, ἐσκόρπισεν, ἔδωκεν τοῖς πένησιν, ἡ δικαιοσύνη αὐτοῦ μένει εἰς τὸν αἰῶνα, "He has dispersed abroad, he has given to the poor; his righteousness endures forever."²⁰⁷

---

202. Calvin, *Ad Corinthios II* 9.10, 155.1–7 (trans. Smail), 123.
203. Calvin, *Ad Corinthios II* 8, 134 (trans. Smail), 106.
204. Martial, *De Spectaculis Liber* 5, 42 (Shackleton Bailey, LCL).
205. Calvin, *Ad Corinthios II* 8.10, 139.24–25 (trans. Smail), 111.
206. Calvin, *Ad Corinthios II* 8.10,139. 25–30 (trans. Smail), 111.
207. Calvin, *Ad Corinthios II* 9.9, 154.6–11 (trans. Smail), 123.

It is worthwhile to remark that for Calvin the scattering of gifts to the poor worded by the psalmist has the pious man rather than God as subject.[208] He adds that this view of continuous almsgiving is also expressed by Paul in Galatians 6:9.

Although Calvin rejects the view that the Christians' generosity may be motivated by the expectation of any sort of divine compensation as I noted earlier, he admits that believers will assuredly receive benefits with "large interest" (*cum largo foenore*) from their almsgiving.[209] He makes this point in his comments on 2 Corinthians 9:6. For Calvin, the fear of losing through almsgiving has to be constantly dissipated from our minds by Paul's doctrine that the amount of harvest corresponds to the sowing: "The more liberal you are to your neighbours, the more liberal you will find the blessing that God pours forth on you."[210] In the same vein, Calvin rejects any restrictive interpretation of what the apostle teaches in the sowing metaphor in 2 Corinthians 9:6. In his view, the harvest has to be understood as indicating both spiritual and material benefits: *Caeterum messis tam de spirituali mercede vitae aeternae, quam terrenis benedictionibus, quibus Deus prosequitur homines beneficos, exponi debit*, "The harvest, however, should be explained as referring to the spiritual recompense of eternal life, as well as to the earthly blessings, which God confers upon the beneficent."[211] As for the reward the Corinthians are to expect from the saints in Jerusalem,

---

208. Calvin, *Commentary on the Book of Psalms,* vol. 4; translated from the original Latin, and collated with the author's French version by J. Anderson (1949), 328–329. It is remarkable that Calvin insists on the fact that the righteous do not bestow their charity randomly. Rather, he observes, they give it with much care to specifically relieve the needs of the needy, rather than making unnecessary spending for ostentatious purposes. Calvin explicitly indicates that Paul quotes the psalmist in 2 Cor 9:9 to teach us that it is very easy "for God to bless us with plenty, so that we may exercise our bounty freely, deliberately, and impartially" (ibid., 329). As for the righteousness which endures for ever, he writes that this statement is capable of two interpretations. It might mean that the unrestrained ambition of the unbelievers to give away their wealth does not deserve to be called a virtue. The other meaning may be that God "preserves the glory of that righteousness which is due to their liberality," by providing more and more benefits to them either in terms of power or prosperity. That Calvin equates here δικαιοσύνη, *iustitia*, righteousness with beneficence becomes clearer in his treatment of 2 Cor 9:10.

209. Calvin, *Ad Corinthios II* 9.6, 152.7–14 (trans. Smail), 121.
210. Calvin, *Ad Corinthios II* 9.6, 152.24–25 (trans. Smail), 121.
211. Calvin, *Ad Corinthios II* 9.6, 152.19–22 (trans. Smail), 121.

Calvin maintains that it consists in benevolence expressed through gratitude and earnest prayers addressed to God for their sake (2 Cor 9:14).[212]

4.5.3 Alms as a Due to the Poor

It is important to note here that Calvin highlights that the poor have a right to be assisted. He expresses this view in his comments on 2 Corinthians 9:1 where the apostle calls the collection a "ministering to the saints," ἡ διακονία εἰς τοὺς ἁγίους. Calvin concedes that the term διακονία is not well suited to designate the assistance to the poor because a more splendid word is needed to refer to liberality. He argues that Paul used διακονία, however, to say what believers "owe to their fellow-members" in the same church, the body of Christ as Calvin remarks.[213] And negligence towards the saints who are in want "is more than just unkindness" since it amounts to defrauding them of their due.[214] Thus, Calvin indicates that Paul's phrase τὰ γενήματα τῆς δικαιοσύνης "the fruits of righteousness" (2 Cor 9:10) designates a charitable work or the duty of love, *officium caritatis*.[215] As notes Elsie A. Mckee, the word *caritas* is very important in Calvin's thought and cannot be simply equated with the English 'charity'.[216] On the contrary, caritas summarizes the second table of the Ten Commandments which regulate our relation to others. In this sense, observes Mckee, "*caritas* is the fruit of faith that justifies, the evidence of repentance and regeneration."[217] It finds expression mostly "in giving or sharing, ranging from the concrete form of alms . . . through hospitality, to the less tangible mutual communication of vocation."[218] One realizes that Calvin agrees with John Chrysostom and Theodoret of Cyrus that δικαιοσύνη, *iustitia*, righteousness, in 2 Corinthians 9:10 means beneficence, *beneficientia*. However, he hastens to indicate that this is only one aspect, but not the least, of the whole concept of righteousness; whoever despises it is unrighteous,

---

212. Calvin, *Ad Corinthios II* 9.14, 157.21–25 (trans. Smail), 125.
213. Calvin, *Ad Corinthios II* 9.1, 150.11–14 (trans. Smail), 120.
214. Calvin, *Ad Corinthios II* 9.1, 150.14–18 (trans. Smail), 120.
215. Calvin, *Ad Corinthios II* 9.10, 156.8–14 (trans. Smail), 124.
216. McKee, *John Calvin*, 42.
217. Ibid., 242.
218. Ibid., 248.

iniquos.²¹⁹ It is evident that Calvin indirectly alludes to the other meaning which the concept of righteousness has elsewhere in Paul. For instance, the reformer explains that Romans 3:21 speaks of God's righteousness. He argues that in his mercy, God communicates this righteousness to a human being and that the latter receives it only by faith, without the aid of works.²²⁰

4.5.4 The Ways of Giving

Calvin's comments on 2 Corinthians 8:11 tackle the question of the way of giving. He argues that Paul's view that one must give according to one's ability aims at removing all human pretexts for not giving. For him, Paul gives the reason why each should give according to one's means: "God looks not at the amount but at the heart."²²¹ For Calvin, Paul's clause in 2 Corinthians 8:12 εἰ γὰρ ἡ προθυμία πρόκειται, καθὸ ἐὰν ἔχῃ εὐπρόσδεκτος, "For if the eagerness is there, the gift is acceptable according to what one has" means nothing but the disposition of heart. The reformer concludes that the intention of the one who offers a small gift from slender means "is just as valuable in God's eyes as" that of a rich person who makes a large gift out of his or her abundant wealth.²²² Calvin thinks that the idea that God is pleased with our willingness to give whether we are rich or poor also transpires in 2 Corinthians 8:13: οὐ γὰρ ἵνα ἄλλοις ἄνεσις, ὑμῖν θλῖψις, "I do not mean that there should be relief for others and pressure on you." Our reformer goes further on to say that we owe to God all our being and all that we possess. However, remarks Calvin, God is merciful and allows us to give only what we are able to and he is satisfied with it.²²³ Thus, on the one hand, Calvin castigates those of his time that he calls fanatics, who advocate asceticism. These people claim that alms can be acceptable to God only if people have given away their possessions to form a community of goods.²²⁴ On the other hand, Calvin formally declares that a curse will fall upon miserly rich people together with the riches they hoarded at

---

219. Calvin, *Ad Corinthios II* 9.10, 156.17–18 (trans. Smail), 124.
220. Calvin, *Ad Romanos* 3.21 (trans. Owen), 134.
221. Calvin, *Ad Corinthios II* 8.11, 140.21–22 (trans. Smail), 112.
222. Calvin, *Ad Corinthios II* 8.11, 140.22–26 (trans. Smail), 112.
223. Calvin, *Ad Corinthios II* 8.13, 141.9–15 (trans. Smail), 112.
224. Calvin, *Ad Corinthios II* 8.13, 141.18–22 (trans. Smail), 112.

the expense of the indigent believers, in the same way it went in the story of manna.[225]

For Calvin, although Paul was eager to persuade the Corinthians to give large contributions in order to aid the saints sufficiently, he refrained from forcing them to act to that end. He understands that this explains why the apostle insisted that people were to give as they had decided in their heart (2 Cor 9:7).[226] McKee says that Calvin frequently alludes to 2 Corinthians 9:7 especially with regard to alms but also in relation to the attitude of giving.[227] Liberality, *simplicitas*, is expected from the deacons who administer (Rom 12:8), while individuals who take care of the poor have to demonstrate joy, *hilaritas*, as they carry out their duty.[228] Calvin's interpretation of 2 Corinthians 9:11 is worthy of mention here as far as true giving is concerned. He argues that when Paul says that the Corinthians will be enriched εἰς πᾶσαν ἁπλότητα, "in order to show every kind of generosity," he infers that true liberality means to rely on divine providence and to give joyfully one's resources as God directs.[229]

Calvin uses a sacrificial terminology to talk about true giving. He maintains that "alms are a sacrifice" to God.[230] He adds that to be pleasing to God, a sacrifice must be voluntarily offered. In his view, this resonates with Paul's statement that God loves a joyful giver (2 Cor 9:7). Calvin observes that the Greek term λειτουργία applied to the collection in 2 Corinthians 9:11 was used to mean a sacrifice or "a publicly assigned office."[231] From this philological consideration the reformer asserts that all those who contributed to the collection for the saints offered an acceptable sacrifice to God or fulfilled an obligatory service; Paul being the minister.[232] However, Calvin does not go further to say that almsgiving atones for sins as does John Chrysostom.

---

225. Calvin, *Ad Corinthios II* 8.15, 144.5–11 (trans. Smail), 114.
226. Calvin, *Ad Corinthios II* 9.7, 152.30–153.4 (trans. Smail), 122.
227. McKee, *John Calvin*, 249, n. 70.
228. Ibid., 250.
229. Calvin, *Ad Corinthios II* 9.11, 156.19–27 (trans. Smail), 124.
230. Calvin, *Ad Corinthios II* 9.7, 153.11-13 (trans. Smail), 122.
231. Calvin, *Ad Corinthios II* 9.11, 156.35-157.1 (trans. Smail), 125.
232. Calvin, *Ad Corinthios II* 9.11, 157.1-7 (trans. Smail), 125.

4.6 Summary

In this chapter, I have explored different interpretations handed down to us from late Antiquity to the Reformation period. This investigation was selective and guided by three main questions: to what extent did the concept of grace, which is central to Paul's thoughts in 2 Corinthians 8–9, catch the attention of the authors studied in this chapter? What are the motivations of Christian generosity and the right attitude towards possessions according to these authors? To what extent is care for the poor perceptible in these ancient readings of our passage?

John Chrysostom identifies different meanings conveyed by the term χάρις in 2 Corinthians 8–9. He says that the Macedonians' involvement in the collection is called χάρις to teach the Corinthians humility and exhort them to emulation. This also means that what the Macedonians accomplished was not the outcome of human efforts, but first of all the result of divine influence. But God's χάρις does not exclude human will. The full cooperation between Titus' eagerness to engage in the collection and God's grace is an example. Χάρις also qualifies Christ's attitude and heart in his incarnation, which generates the deep experience of salvation and its benefits now and in the world to come. This χάρις, which is ultimately from God, produces abundant material resources necessary for the believers' own life and from which they can give alms. Thus, God's χάρις creates a profound fellowship between those who give alms and their recipients. This fellowship actually generates interdependence among them. Through the collection, the Corinthians are taught that they give from their material resources and receive intercessional prayers from the Christians in Jerusalem. By χάρις John also understands Paul's and his companions' preaching of the gospel and the administration of the collection.

John gives us different motivations for almsgiving. First of all, God himself requests alms to feed his people. The hope for reward, gratitude to God for all the benefits to believers through Jesus's incarnation, interdependency among people as a status devised by God, and the atoning function of alms are the other strong reasons for Christian generosity. As for the way of giving, John insists on the fact that one should give abundantly and voluntarily. It seems to this father that considering the Corinthians' weakness, Paul made a concession and allowed them to give according to their possessions. But at the same time John lays emphasis on the fact that God judges the value of alms not on the basis of their amount, but on that of the giver's inner disposition. Almsgiving must be a continual practice for a Christian. Material wealth must not be hoarded but distributed to the poor. Correspondingly, Chrysostom glorifies asceticism. He indicates that it is worthless to desire to become rich, because the need of possessions is never satisfied. Lust of possessions and righteousness are incompatible. The poor play an important role in our salvation because we bestow our alms upon them.

In Theodoret's commentary on 2 Corinthians 8–9, it is remarkable that the father points out that the Macedonians' zeal in the collection is called χάρις to show that with divine assistance humans can achieve virtuous deeds. He avoids here the risk of misunderstanding Paul's notion of grace as if it meant that the Macedonians were imposed by divine grace to participate in the collection. Sharing in the collection is in fact a χάρις, a privilege since the Corinthians were to expect spiritual benefits which are also the various riches of divine χάρις. Like Chrysostom Theodoret is aware of the danger of possessions. He understands perfection as contempt for material wealth and voluntary poverty. He views that Paul exhorts the Corinthians to contempt for money, which produces everlasting righteousness. Theodoret also indicates that the apostle teaches the Corinthians that God alone is able to provide everyone with good things abundantly. Also, as God cares for the seed sown until it gives food to people, he expects the Christians to give the needy the necessities of life. Theodoret notes that love for God motivated the Macedonians for the collection. Another reason for the Corinthians to give generously is that they could expect spiritual things from divine χάρις, and assistance from the saints' abundance when they are in need. But the best reward the Corinthians were to hope for consisted in joining the saints in endurance. It is remarkable that the language of retribution is rare in Theodoret.

Concerning the way of giving, Theodoret points out that God measures the offering by the capacity of the giver. Therefore, giving must be voluntary and performed in a joyful spirit. The farming metaphor according to which the harvest is proportionate to the amount of the sowing was used by Paul to challenge miserly givers. On this point Theodoret does not deviate from John who insists that this sowing imagery is an invitation to give abundantly.

For his part, Ambrosiaster indicates that the *gratia* received by the Macedonians consisted in their accepting "the word of faith" with devotion. It is also by the same *gratia* that the Corinthians came to conversion and were expected to perform every good deed. Moreover, the collection itself is a *gratia* in which Paul believed that Titus was to play a prominent role among the Corinthians.

For Ambrosiaster, the conviction that all things are God's property commands correct almsgiving. Human beings are allowed to enjoy them and give a portion of them to the needy. Three main questions have to be asked to determine the right way of giving. The first deals with the amount to be given; the second is related to the amount one possesses; the third question asks in which spirit one is about to give. All in all, giving correctly means to give as much as one is able to. The hope for reward is another motivation for Christian generosity. This reward consists in returns in the present time and recompense in the hereafter as well. God rewards only those who act wholeheartedly as if they were depositing for themselves their treasure in God's presence. Their resources are multiplied to enable them to continue their practice of good deeds; and ultimately they will receive the reward from God in the world to come. Ambrosiaster shows a relatively negative view on material wealth. Although he does not state clearly that earthly wealth is bad, he thinks that there are some people who choose what is better and despise worldly possessions to commit themselves entirely to God's things. For these people God appoints rich people to provide for their food and clothing.

Ambrosiaster insists on Paul's care for the poor. He explains that the apostle handles the collection with extreme attention because he fears that he might be seen as being negligent regarding the assistance to the poor or the saints in Jerusalem, or acting slowly in this matter. Moreover, he observes that in Paul's opinion, those who receive money from a charitable offering are no longer subject to beggary but to the service of God whom they recognize as the one who actually feeds them. It is fitting that Ambrosiaster concludes that those who help the needy in this way make their gifts to God. But these gifts are also God's because it is he who commands people to offer them.

In his treatment of 2 Corinthians 8–9 Thomas Aquinas argues that the *gratia* that the Macedonians have been granted is a divine free gift which comprehends endurance in afflictions and generosity through almsgiving. In his view, Paul calls this generosity *gratia* because all good that we accomplish stems from God's *gratia*. Thus, giving alms is a type of *gratia* like other spiritual gifts. *Gratia* also refers to the collection of alms and the preaching of the gospel carried out by Paul and his collaborators.

This *gratia* through almsgiving merits reward from God. Divine recompense covers both spiritual things and material possessions. And since God multiplies alms, one must give correctly (i.e. promptly, abundantly and joyfully). Almsgiving should be a permanent practice because it is a genuine expression of piety and must be directed to the indigent. Surrender to God must precede our almsgiving. However, alms from a sinner should be accepted if the individual does not display the intention to remain in sin. Like John Chrysostom and Theodoret, Thomas praises material poverty. Complete devotion to God results in contempt for possessions. For this reason, it is better for one to give everything to the needy and, as a consequence, live in afflictions for Christ's sake. But considering human weakness, one should give according to one's possessions.

The last author I considered is Calvin. It is highly remarkable that the term *gratia* permeates his thought in his treatment of the collection in 2 Corinthians 8–9. He insists that Paul terms his collection God's *gratia* because all that we are and possess comes from God. Thus, almsgiving is the imitation of God, our Father in heaven, who liberally provides us with all good things. Calvin explains that this provision demonstrates God's *gratia* as did the manna which was granted to the Israelites in the desert. Therefore, unlike the common idea that helping the needy is a commendable virtue, assisting the poor has to be reckoned as a special privilege, a *gratia*. All believers are expected to show liberality even when confronted with extreme poverty. In other words, almsgiving should be an unceasing exercise in a Christian's life. In the context of 2 Corinthians 8–9, almsgiving is so important inasmuch as it is an aspect of righteousness. Negligence of it amounts to defrauding the poor of their due.

Although beneficence should not be motivated by the expectation of recompense, to those who engage in true almsgiving, Calvin believes that a double reward is promised: provisions for their own living, and enough resources to assist the destitute. He explains that God alone is said to know the right amount needed for all people to meet their own needs and do good to others. This reward is also double inasmuch as it concerns eternal life and enrichment in terms of possessions in the present life.

While we owe our being and our possessions to God, Calvin emphasizes that we are allowed to give only what we are able to. However, this freedom must be taken so seriously that Calvin does not hesitate to declare that a curse will fall upon miserly rich people together with the riches they treasured. It is fitting that for Calvin, true liberality means to rely on divine providence and to give joyfully one's resources as God directs. With such a positive disposition of heart, almsgiving becomes a sacrifice pleasing to God. But no atoning function is attached to it in Calvin's thought.

Conclusion

My reading of 2 Corinthians 8–9 in the third chapter of the present study using the grammatico-historical analysis has confirmed the centrality of the concept of χαρίς, *gratia*, grace in this passage. This awareness also transpires in the selected authors I studied as far as the reception history of this text is concerned. Moreover, I have shown that the philanthropic aspect of Paul's collection in 2 Corinthians 8–9 becomes evident once one applies the tools of grammatico-historical analysis to this passage. The ancient readers of this text also note with a varying degree of emphasis the fact that the collection attests Paul's concern for the poor. These questions of the fundamental function of the concept of grace and the highly charitable aspect of Paul's collection in 2 Corinthians 8–9 need to be addressed when I will be dialoguing with the prosperity gospel proponents over the use of the same text in their call for generous giving. At the same time, it is crucial to ask whether the prosperity gospel, which insists on the donation of various forms of offerings, shows any traces of the view that alms are meritorious as Thomas thought; or that they hold atoning powers as believed John Chrysostom.

Indeed, the belief in recompense in the present time and in the hereafter is confessed by all the authors I have analyzed in the present chapter. It is remarkable that this theme is one of the main principles of the prosperity gospel. The view that God reciprocates a sincere giver's alms is welcomed to different degrees by the ancient authors studied in this thesis. They draw this teaching from Paul's reference to the metaphor of sowing and reaping in 2 Corinthians 9:6–11. For some, this reward consists in the multiplication of material resources during one's lifetime and spiritual blessings now and in the hereafter. For others, the emphasis is very much on the second aspect of recompense (i.e. spiritual benefits in the present life and in eternity). Aversion to material possessions is integral to this viewpoint. There is no need to say that this belief in recompense is at home in the prosperity gospel circles. Interestingly, the prosperity gospel teachers favor the reading which sees material blessings stemming from material generous giving. This question will be addressed from different vantage points when I discuss later in the final chapter the use of 2 Corinthians 8–9 by some teachers of prosperity in sub-Saharan Africa. Since the prosperity gospel is one of the main features of African Pentecostalism, it is worthwhile to explore the main tenets of the latter as a global phenomenon and a particularly influential expression of Christianity in the Majority World. This will be the focal point of the next chapter.

CHAPTER 5

Pentecostalism in Sub-Saharan Africa: An Overview

In this chapter I will focus on Pentecostalism as a global movement which has significantly reconfigured African Christianity. In the following pages, I will make a brief presentation of Pentecostalism as a global religious phenomenon and its use of the Bible. The present chapter will thus serve as an interpretive framework of the prosperity gospel which is prominent in African Pentecostalism.[1]

5.1 Pentecostalism as a Global Movement

Pentecostalism as a global movement and its role in the growth of Christianity in the Majority World in general and in Africa in particular has been assessed by many specialists in the field in recent years.[2] The very

---

1. In the following development, the designation African Pentecostalism refers to all forms of the movement in sub-Saharan Africa regardless of whether they were started by Africans or Western missionaries.

2. I am aware of the ambiguities which the terms North/West, South/Global South carry as reflected in current scholarship (Jenkins, *New Christendom*, 4-5). In the 1950s when emerging African and Asian nations decided to form a grouping distinct from the capitalist West and communist East, they declared themselves to be the non-aligned Third World. But this designation soon lost its ideological connotation of "prosperous neutrality" to mean socio-economic misery. For some analysts it was clear that the division was not in fact based on political but on economic realities. When the Cold War was at its height in 1980, the Brandt Commission depicted the world as faced with a crisis in which both the Global North (Europe, North America, and Japan) and Global South were engaged. In this context the South referred to the remaining nations regardless of their location on the globe. Obviously, the term was more related to a limited access to financial means than to a geographical location. Worth mentioning is that a country like South Korea was included in this category despite its economic development. Today, many other countries

rapid growth of Pentecostalism in a broader context marked by the new vitality of different religions and sects – and this in sharp contrast with "the death of God" and the extinction of spirituality prognosticated many years ago by theologians and sociologists respectively has struck Harvey Cox. He thinks that religion is being reshaped in the twenty-first century and that "a religious renaissance," another kind of "great awakening" is taking place in our time on a global scale.[3] Many a scholar has attempted to define this movement.[4] In this chapter I follow Allan Anderson and Asamoah-Gyadu in their use of "Pentecostalism" to refer to the variegated denominations and movements that emphasize the experience of the activity of the Holy Spirit and the practice of the gifts that he entrusts to believers and which

---

from this group such as India, Brazil, South Africa, Mexico, Argentina, Saudi Arabia, Malaysia, Singapore, and Indonesia have become economically influential in the global market. This implies that this economic prosperity has improved to varying degrees the living conditions of their inhabitants. The ambiguities of the terms North/West, South/Global South are compounded by the fact that some countries in the West are facing an economic crisis today. This complex situation entails that there are more and more Third World/South people in the West/North and vice versa. Despite these ambiguities and for the sake of brevity, I will use the categories the North/the West and the Majority World to mean respectively Western Europe and North America on the one hand, and Africa, Asia and Latin America on the other. Moreover, it is arguable that African, Asian and Latin American theologies and spirituality in their diversity represent an important expression of the Christian faith distinct from the historical Eastern and Western traditions.

3. Cox, *Fire From Heaven*, xiv, xvi, 83, 82. Cox strives to "show why, after a mere ninety years, what began as a despised and ridiculed sect is quickly becoming both the preferred religion of the urban poor and the powerful bearer of a radically alternative vision of what the human world might one day become." In his view, the success of Pentecostalism as a "restorationist" movement is due to the fact that it has enabled innumerable people to retrieve, on a quite personal level, three dimensions of elemental spirituality that he terms "primal speech," "primal piety," and "primal hope." In this case, primal speech or "language of the heart" refers to the phenomenon of "ecstatic utterance" or glossolalia known as "speaking in tongues" or "praying in the spirit" in Pentecostal terminology. Primal piety is about the reappearance in Pentecostalism of "trance, vision, healing, dreams, dance, and other archetypal religious expressions." By the third dimension, primal hope, Cox points to the millennial teaching according to which Pentecostalism emphasizes that a radically new era is about to dawn.

4. C. Währisch-Oblau argues that Pentecostals are the historically older denominations, well established with church structures. These insist on the doctrine of the baptism in the Holy Spirit whose initial evidence is speaking in tongues and remains an essential feature of this tradition. As for Charismatics, she notes that they are "historically newer movements which stress non-denominationalism, the gifts of the Holy Spirit, prosperity teaching and spiritual warfare" (Währisch-Oblau, *Missionary Self-Perception*, 46).

are manifested in their lives and church liturgy.[5] The term "charismatic" will be sometimes introduced for more clarity. Both scholars recognize that defining this movement remains a daunting task which risks reductionism.[6] Statistics, which must be interpreted with much caution, indicate that there were about 600 million Pentecostals and other charismatic Christians worldwide in 2010 and 612 million in 2012, representing up to a quarter of world Christianity estimated at two billion in 2008.[7] Anderson observes that world Christianity itself, however, has remained approximately a third of the world's population since 1900.[8]

This rapid growth of Pentecostalism, according to Anderson, has resulted in a shift of the center of gravity of Christianity from the North to the South as far as the number of Christians is concerned.[9] Most of these

---

5. Anderson, *Introduction to Pentecostalism*, 6; Asamoah-Gyadu, *Contemporary Pentecostal Christianity*, 1, 6.

6. Anderson, *Introduction to Pentecostalism*, 157; Anderson, "Varieties, Taxonomies, and Definitions," 17–20. Anderson classifies Pentecostals into four categories: (1) Classical Pentecostals who are virtually denominational. They emanated from the revival and missionary movements of the early twentieth century. (2) Older charismatic movements in older mainstream denominations including Catholic charismatics. (3) Older Independent and charismatic churches founded in China, Asia and sub-Saharan Africa. (4) Neo-Pentecostal and Neo-charismatic churches which are generally seen as "Charismatic independent churches." These bear the influence of both classical Pentecostalism and the charismatic movement. However, Ogbu Kalu (*African Pentecostalism*, 69–71) suggests that there should be a distinction between the classical African Independent Churches which arose during the colonial time and those which developed later. He stresses that the difference between some of these types of charismatic Christianity cannot be explained simply by the passing of time. For his part Asamoah-Gyadu (*Contemporary Pentecostal Christianity*, 10) maintains three groupings, namely New Pentecostal Churches, Renewal movements within non-Pentecostal mainstream denominations and a third one which seems to be lacking in Anderson's characterization of the movement and needs probably to be distinguished from the rest. This comprises trans-denominational Pentecostal fellowships such as "the Full Gospel Businessmen's Fellowship International and Women Aglow movements." Such lay movements promote active church membership.

7. Ogbu Kalu, *African Pentecostalism*, 1, 3.

8. Synan, *Holiness Pentecostal Tradition*, ix–x, 281, 296; Anderson, *Introduction to Pentecostalism*, 5. But L. Sanneh writes that by 2005, the number of Christians in Africa "had increased to roughly 393 million, which is just below 50 percent of Africa's population." He observes that this trend of growth is expected to continue, making Christianity one of "the fastest growing religions," and even "the principal religion of the peoples of the world." (Sanneh, *Disciples of all Nations*, xx, xix). I leave this debate aside here to focus on the subject matter of the present study.

9. However, it is important to note that power structures in world Christianity have not undergone the same change. The West still holds the keys of the decision-making structures in world Christianity, partly because of its economic hegemony.

Pentecostal and charismatic Christians live in Africa, Latin America and Asia.[10] The African continent hosts now more than four times as many Christians as it had in 1970.[11] One estimate indicates that Christians of a charismatic persuasion represent 13.7 percent of Africa's population.[12] Whereas this steady growth has to do with various demographic variables, it can be argued that the spread of Pentecostalism played a prominent role in this change. It remains true that "much of the growth of African Christianity has occurred through conversion, where the influence of Pentecostalism is strongest."[13] Moreover, it is significant that today more than half of the Zimbabwean population is said to belong to Pentecostal churches; South Africa's population registers 40 percent, Kenya would have over a third; while the Democratic Republic of Congo, Nigeria, Ghana and Zambia each count over a quarter of the population.[14] And as Cephas Omenyo's book reveals, the charismatic movement has risen in mainstream churches as well.[15]

Therefore, Asamoah-Gyadu is right to write that it is no longer possible to talk relevantly about African Christianity without referring to Pentecostalism.[16] This important contribution of the Majority World in the configuration of world Christianity has led Anderson to call Pentecostalism "a new reformation of the church" and "the African Reformation of the twentieth century which has fundamentally altered the character of African Christianity, including that of the older mission churches."[17] On a global scale, precisely as far as culture is concerned as a medium of communicating beliefs, the decisive role of Africa in world Christianity is a fact. Lamin Sanneh correctly notes that whereas Christianity continues to be "a Western religion, . . . its future as a world religion is now being decided and

---

10. Sanneh, *Disciples of all Nations*, xxii, 275; Jenkins, *New Christendom*, 4–6; Anderson, *Introduction to Pentecostalism*, 4–5, 10.

11. Asamoah-Gyadu, *Contemporary Pentecostal Christianity*, 9.

12. Ibid., xiv.

13. Anderson, *Introduction to Pentecostalism*, 198–220; Asamoah-Gyadu, *Contemporary Pentecostal Christianity*, xiv; Kalu, *African Pentecostalism*, xii.

14. Anderson, *Introduction to Pentecostalism*, 114.

15. Omenyo, *Pentecost outside Pentecostalism*.

16. Asamoah-Gyadu, *Contemporary Pentecostal Christianity*, 3.

17. Anderson, *Introduction to Pentecostalism*, 15, 115.

shaped by the hands and in the minds of its non-Western adherents, who share little of the West's cultural assumptions."[18]

The commonly held view that Pentecostalism originated from the USA has been seriously challenged in recent scholarship. Nevertheless, the leading role that the Azusa Street revival in Los Angeles, led by William J. Seymour in 1906, played in its spreading worldwide remains undeniable.[19] Missionaries were sent to over twenty-five countries over the world, as far as China, India, Japan, Egypt, Liberia, Angola and South Africa. However, other revival movements with charismatic manifestations did occur in Africa, Asia and Latin America and even in North America with no direct contact with the Azusa Street revival movement; and some even preceded it. It is in this context that different movements known as African Independent Churches rose. In the case of Rwanda, the *World Christian Encyclopedia* mentioned in 1982 the Kimbanguist Church as the only African Independent Church in the country; it had been operating there since 1965.[20] The same source reads that this church counted five hundred members in mid-1970.[21] After the civil war (1990–1994) which culminated in the genocide against Tutsi (1994), the situation changed drastically. New Pentecostal and charismatic churches burgeoned throughout the

---

18. Sanneh, "Changing Face of Christianity," 4.

19. Anderson, *Introduction to Pentecostalism*, 36, 206, 207–210; Kalu, *African Pentecostalism*, viii, 11–22.

20. Spijker, "Les nouvelles communautés," 47. He rightly explains that two main reasons can justify the situation of Rwanda. The East African revival in the 1930s that originated in Rwanda developed as a charismatic movement within the Anglican church and other Protestant churches. The proponents of this revival remained in their respective churches whose leaders were tolerant. Another reason is that the Rwandan government between 1960 and 1994 prevented religious sectarianism by applying a strict policy regarding church planting. It usually required the approval of a new church by the Protestant Council of Rwanda (*Conseil Protestant du Rwanda, CPR*), which was unlikely to be easy in a context of religious competition. The recommendation from the Roman Catholic Church, the stream of Christianity then predominantly present in the country, was also required (Gatwa, "God in the Public Domain," 328–329). The repatriation from a long exile of thousands of former refugees opened a new era in the religious constellation of Rwanda. Thousands among these former refugees used to an open ecclesiology and flexible liturgy found it difficult to join existing denominations. This gave rise to the emergence of new independent charismatic churches.

21. Barrett, *World Christian Encyclopedia*, 590, 589.

country.[22] In 1997 more than a hundred of such churches were identified.[23] A recent publication on the history of Christianity in Rwanda shows that no fewer than three hundred have been registered.[24]

It is remarkable that much of African Pentecostalism started from within, and in some cases Western missionaries were invited in by Africans to escape the hostility of colonial regimes. Later, their intervention was called upon as a way of securing the prestige of being part of a worldwide movement which can give not only ministerial training, but also funding.[25] Conversely, in the colonial period missionaries sometimes deplored the failure of colonial regimes to subdue autochthonous movements of this kind.[26] Today, the number of Pentecostal and new charismatic churches continues to increase in Africa with much appeal "to younger, educated and urban people,"[27] West Africa being "one of the hot spots of the world" as far as the growing influence of Pentecostalism is concerned.[28] A larger number of these new churches sprang up in "the context of interdenominational and evangelical campus and school Christian organizations like Scripture Union."[29]

Pentecostalism lays much emphasis on "health and wealth" in this continent ravished by poverty.[30] In Ogbu Kalu's view, this wave of renewal movements that developed in Africa since the second half of the twentieth century and became much stronger from the 1970s onwards

---

22. Renewal movements spread rapidly across most mainstream Protestant churches in the 1990s. One estimate indicates that in 1995 they counted 1,237,000 members, 51 percent of whom were Pentecostals, 41 percent charismatic Christians, and 8 percent adherents of African Independent Churches (Barrett, Kurian and Johnson, *World Christian Encyclopedia*, 630).

23. Spijker, "Les nouvelles communautés," 48.

24. Gapapa, "Les nouveaux mouvements religieux," 46–49.

25. Kalu, "Globecalisation' and Religion," 222; Anderson, *Introduction to Pentecostalism*, 113; Kalu, *African Pentecostalism*, 41.

26. Kalu, *African Pentecostalism*, viii.

27. B. Meyer writes that these churches are significantly influential "both in rural and urban areas and to members of all classes." They especially attract "young and middle-aged people of both sexes for whom success in life is not a mere dream and who have started to prosper, often by being involved in international trade." (Meyer, "Make a Complete Break," 319-320).

28. Anderson, *Introduction to Pentecostalism*, 9, 43, 131, 127.

29. Ibid., 132.

30. Asamoah-Gyadu, *Contemporary Pentecostal Christianity*, xi.

is the "third response" of Africans to the form of Christianity brought by Western missionaries.[31] It is mostly characterized by its utilization of sub-Saharan African cosmology, and specifically addresses the question of spiritual powers that concerns African people.[32] As I noted earlier, sub-Saharan Africa reflects a huge diversity in every respect but people also have many things in common which allow some generalization. People there share the cosmological view that the universe is monistic, inhabited by visible and invisible beings which exist in physical and spiritual modes respectively and in constant interaction. The invisible beings include god(s), ancestors, spirits, and children to be born. Any disturbance of the necessary balance in relationships within this complex interaction of beings is thought to occasion every sort of crisis in individuals, groups, communities and nature. In this context, the dead continue to exist among them but in a different state, spiritual. They are believed to influence positively or negatively people's lives. These beliefs have not been swept away by the often brutal strategies of Western colonialists and Christian missionaries to "civilize" Africans. So, appropriate ways to deal with spiritual beings have always been a real concern for Africans.[33] In 2004 Gunilla Nyberg Oskarsson's fieldwork led her to the conclusion that the remarkable growth of Pentecostalism in the south of Burundi between 1935 and 1960 is partly explained by its partial recognition of traditional perceptions regarding the presence and power of evil spirits, as well as its spiritual provisions to deal with them.[34] In her research on Ewe

---

31. Kalu, *African Pentecostalism*, 10, 24, 26, 28, 32-39. The first response was Ethiopianism in the 1860s. This movement, says Kalu, was a quest for an African expression of Christianity against the "representation of African values, cultures, and the practice of the Christian faith" characterized by the hegemonic mentality of Western missionaries and the total exclusion of Africans in the shaping of this new religion. The second response came from the African Independent Churches that sprang up at the end of the nineteenth and the start of the twentieth century as a result of the split from the missionary churches whose integration into the African cultural and religious context was judged superficial. These churches emphasized "prayer, miraculous healing, indigenous symbolism and liturgy, and African agency in Christian matters"; Spijker, "Les nouvelles Communautés," 54.

32. Kalu, *African Pentecostalism*, 178, 189.

33. Mutombo-Mukendi, "Le nouveau culte," 86–93.

34. Nyberg Oskarsson, *Le mouvement pentecôtiste*, 290–293. The other two factors of growth indicated by Oskarsson are the relationships of mutual assistance which characterized Pentecostal communities, and the zeal of Pentecostals to bring their relatives into their new community of faith.

Christianity in Ghana, whose results may apply to other parts of Africa, Birgit Meyer discovered that traditional gods and spirits have been equated with demons in Christianity in general. These demonic gods and spirits are held responsible for the many existential hindrances that people are confronted with.[35] Meyer explains that Pentecostals go further in the exploitation of this belief. References to the devil and demons occupy a central place in Pentecostal discourses and precise rituals have been devised to deal with them.[36] Some members of Pentecostal churches reported that they had quit mainstream Protestant churches because they do not take the challenge of the devil and demons seriously.[37] From the above, it is right to conclude that one of the major factors which explain the rapid expansion of Pentecostalism is its ability to adapt itself to different cultural contexts through forms of liturgy that give room to emotions and integrate vital elements of ancient religious traditions such as healing and deliverance practices to meet people's everyday concerns.[38] More precisely, the influence of this movement at the start of the twentieth century was due to its "additional emphasis" on the power of the Holy Spirit – the valorization of "the experiential element of Christianity" – in addition to other theological themes such as the authority of the Bible, the central role of the cross in salvation, regeneration, and holiness shared by other Evangelicals.[39] In fact, it is commonly agreed that charismatic experiences intensify "the religious or spiritual life of people."[40]

However, as noted earlier, Pentecostalism is far from being homogeneous. There are many Pentecostal denominations, most of which are independent from those founded in the West at the beginning of the twentieth century.[41] The diversity within Pentecostalism manifests itself

---

35. Asamoah-Gyadu, *Contemporary Pentecostal Christianity*, 44.
36. Meyer, *Translating the Devil*, xvii.
37. Ibid., xviii.
38. Asamoah-Gyadu, *Contemporary Pentecostal Christianity*, xii; Anderson, *Introduction to Pentecostalism*, 189.
39. Asamoah-Gyadu, *Contemporary Pentecostal Christianity*, 2.
40. Brown, *Introduction*, 532.
41. Asamoah-Gyadu, *Contemporary Pentecostal Christianity*, xi–xii; Anderson, *Introduction to Pentecostalism*, 1–6.

in doctrines, liturgies, structures, rituals and so on.[42] Anderson argues that it would probably be appropriate to speak of "Pentecostalisms."[43] In his view, "the most universal characteristic of the many varieties of Pentecostalism and perhaps the main reason for its growth in the developing world" is healing prayer which it strongly believes in and practices.[44] Healing is credited to the encounter with the Holy Spirit. All Pentecostals agree on this personal experience with the Spirit which transforms and empowers believers for service. It needs to be noted that the understanding of the working of the Holy Spirit is related to the person and work of Jesus Christ. Asamoah-Gyadu terms this "Pneumatical Christology," which he reads in John 14:18.[45] Pentecostal pneumatology is therefore Christological in the sense that the Spirit empowers the believers to serve God and humanity for the glory of Christ.[46] And this service through spiritual gifts is carried out "beyond human ability."[47] All Pentecostals see healing as "good news for the disadvantaged."[48] Through healing prayer, God's immanence is experienced by believers in a tangible way. Asamoah-Gyadu speaks of the "interventionist" character of theology in general and of prayer in particular in Pentecostalism.[49] Healing prayer is extremely important in a context like Africa where Christians and non-Christians believe in witchcraft and in the view that the universe is inhabited not only by human beings but also by "the devil and by a host of spirit forces that are ever attentive to us."[50] On the negative side, Pentecostalism worldwide has been characterized by schisms since

---

42. Anderson, *Introduction to Pentecostalism*, 1–6; "Varieties, Taxonomies, and Definitions," 14–16.

43. Anderson, "Varieties, Taxonomies, and Definitions," 14.

44. Anderson, *Introduction to Pentecostalism*, 30.

45. Asamoah-Gyadu, *Contemporary Pentecostal Christianity*, 13.

46. Anderson, *Introduction to Pentecostalism*, 197. Kalu (*African Pentecostalism*, 6) stresses the Christological characteristic of Pentecostalism. The movement emphasizes the encounter with "Christ as Savior, healer, sanctifier (who baptizes with the Holy Spirit), and the sustainer of hope of glory. He is the soon-coming-king."

47. Kalu, *African Pentecostalism*, 7.

48. Anderson, *Introduction to Pentecostalism*, 179, 188, 202.

49. Asamoah-Gyadu, *Contemporary Pentecostal Christianity*, 6, 42–43.

50. Sanneh, "Changing Face of Christianity," 7; Kalu, *African Pentecostalism*, 176–178.

its inception at the start of the twentieth century within the Azusa Street movement between Charles Parham and Joseph Seymour.[51] Very often, schisms are instigated by the emergence of renewal movements based on Pentecostalism's valorization of "the intuitive and emotional through the revelations and freedom of the Spirit rather than following a slavish biblical literalism."[52]

The engagement of African Pentecostals with social issues has also been explored in current scholarship. Anderson observes that although "many, if not most Pentecostals demonize social problems and seek spiritual solutions rather than structural ones," it is remarkable that they are, particularly in the Majority World, increasingly becoming aware of and involved in diversified socio-political actions.[53] In Rwanda, for instance, Gatwa writes that in the aftermath of the genocide against Tutsi in 1994 a message calling for the engagement with the social challenges of the country was badly missing and was perceived as irrelevant by many Christians, especially those of charismatic persuasion. However, he notes that for some years, there has been a perceptible change among the new Pentecostal churches in general because of their contacts with various ecumenical gatherings, and the pressure of social constraints of the country. They are now performing social actions either to fulfill a call or a precise revelation or a vow made to God. They achieve this in opposition to the established churches whose social actions have grown too secular in the eyes of the new Christian denominations.[54] This move within Pentecostalism is in fact determined by its proclivity to appeal to "marginalized and working-class people," and its worldview that fuses the spiritual and physical realms.[55] However, Anderson admits that

---

51. Anderson, *Introduction to Pentecostalism*, 61, 69–70.

52. Ibid., 308.

53. Anderson, *Introduction to Pentecostalism*, 284; Kalu, *African Pentecostalism*, 135–136. On page 199, Kalu observes that political engagement needs to be understood in its broader sense rather than being limited to "overt activities such as political protest, party politics, and electoral process." For Kalu (*African Pentecostalism*, 222), in Pentecostalism, the political space "consists of discourse and activity on extraction and allocation of resources and services, providing the individual and community with spiritual and material benefits that the state promised but failed to provide."

54. Gatwa, "God in the Public Domain," 331.

55. Anderson, *Introduction to Pentecostalism*, 281, 284, 295; Asamoah-Gyadu, *Contemporary Pentecostal Christianity*, xiii.

"many Pentecostal leaders are still to be convinced of the need to be more involved in social protest, and that this will not deflect them from their central 'spiritual' focus."[56]

The relationship between contemporary African Pentecostalism and globalization with its use of mass media modern technology is evident.[57] This is particularly seen through the astounding spread of "health and wealth" teaching, which is one of the main features of current African Pentecostalism.[58] Granted, not all Pentecostals preach the "health and wealth" message.[59] But they share much in their perception and interpretation of the Bible.

5.2 The Use of the Bible in African Pentecostalism

5.2.1 The Bible as a Devotional Book

In the scope of this research, my concern is not to analyze Pentecostal theology, which is essentially oral,[60] in order to present a systematic treatise on the Scriptures. Suffice it to note that Pentecostal and charismatic Christians are generally not much interested in formulating written doctrines and engaging in theological discussions. What matters the most is the indwelling of the Holy Spirit and the ability to preach and apply the gospel to the daily life of people. Pentecostal and charismatic Christians believe strongly that the baptism of the Holy Spirit causes the believer to feel "a new desire for God's Word."[61] This desire is dominated by a devotional approach to the Scriptures. For me, I share with many scholars the view that the Bible

---

56. Anderson, *Introduction to Pentecostalism*, 282.

57. Kalu, "'Globecalisation' and Religion," 223: "The media and modern technology are exploited to convey the new experience and millenarian theme and weave together the rural, urban and global context. Large quantities of printed materials, newsletters, pamphlets and books, audio and video cassettes, posters and stickers, television and radio programmes, drama and preaching are all pressed into the good cause." Gifford, "View," 90–91; Kalu, *African Pentecostalism*, 105–122; Anderson, *Introduction to Pentecostalism*, 132.

58. Young, "Prosperity Teaching," 4; Asamoah-Gyadu, *Contemporary Pentecostal Christianity*, xv.

59. This will be discussed in detail in the next chapter.

60. Omenyo, *Pentecost outside Pentecostalism*, 221; he refers to Hollenweger, *Pentecostalism*, 196.

61. Omenyo, *Pentecost outside Pentecostalism*, 221.

is Holy Scripture, Word of God inspired to humans, and canon entrusted to the church.[62]

The interpretation of the Bible by Pentecostals in Africa needs to be placed in the vast socio-political and religious context of the Majority World today. Philip Jenkins notes that the southward shift of the center of gravity of Christianity means that the Bible is in the hands of a different readership. He points out that currently the average Christian "is a poor person, very poor indeed" with regard to the standards set by the West.[63] Unlike many Westerners who see the societies in the Bible as far removed from them not only in time and place but also in ways of life, the Majority World readers find there the same realities they experience in their everyday life. Most of them relate their lives to biblical stories about "pressing social problems as famine and plague, poverty and exile, clientelism and corruption" as well as domination "by powerful landlords and imperial forces, by networks of debt and credit."[64] The congeniality of the Bible to African Christians is also reflected in their repackaging of the local traditional language about traditional "sustaining divinities, ancestors, and the Supreme being" to refer to God, Christ and the Holy Spirit. In this hermeneutic, they affirm that the latter "are superior to all the powers available in the people's map of their universe."[65] Ultimately, African Christians realize that "the biblical message is in its origin anything but a Western import," and find in it enough resources to cope

---

62. In Christianity, the Bible is traditionally understood as the human and divine written word that testifies to God's revelation. It is regarded as holy and thus must be handled with much care and respect. This written word, holy Scripture, "is not only God's witness to himself but also humankind's witness to God," since it was articulated by human minds inspired by God himself (Asamoah-Gyadu, *Contemporary Pentecostal Christianity*, 163). As notes Benno van den Toren, the inspiration of the Bible does not mean that it was dictated by God or that God used human authors mechanically (Van Den Toren, *La doctrine chrétienne*, 178–180). Rather, the idea is that God in his providence used human agents with their capabilities and enabled them to make use of various sources at their disposal to write his word (Van Den Toren, *La doctrine chrétienne*, 180–181). He notes that the Bible is reliable in that sense that it is God's word, testimony, revelation, canon and humans' reflection upon their experience with God. As such, the Bible is normative for Christian instruction and spirituality (Van Den Toren, *La doctrine chrétienne*, 185, 167–222).

63. Jenkins, *New Faces of Christianity*, 68.

64. Ibid.

65. Kalu, *African Pentecostalism*, 184, 266–267.

with the challenges of life.[66] It is worth noting that the perception of the Bible as a place of encounter with God and a source of salvation was strongly held by church fathers. They understood Scripture not only in terms of knowledge but also in terms of power of transformation and salvation for the reader.[67] Their conviction that through the Scriptures God speaks to the reader is shared by most African Christians, especially the ordinary readers.[68]

This approach to the Bible is most at home among Pentecostal and charismatic Christians. One can measure the impact of this on biblical interpretation inasmuch as Pentecostalism represents a significant force within Christianity in the Majority World. Anderson argues that apart from Catholic charismatics who will add the authority of the church tradition, all Pentecostal and charismatic Christians believe that the Bible contains answers to every human question and must be obeyed. For this reason, he notes, their reading of the Bible pursues one goal; that is, "to find there something that can be experienced as relevant to their felt needs."[69] In other words, they are not interested in the meaning of the text itself, but in the meaning it has for them.[70] This is rooted in the belief that the Holy Spirit illuminates the believing readers and vivifies the Bible for them.[71] Borrowing from Cheryl B. Johns, Kalu writes that "Pentecostal hermeneutics is praxis-oriented with experience and Scriptures being maintained in a dialectical relationship. The truth must be lived in life experiences."[72] At the same time personal and communal experiences are interwoven in biblical interpretation among Pentecostals. Asamoah-Gyadu observes that when charismatic churches emerged in Africa in the 1970s there was a general discontentment towards historic mission churches and their approach to the Bible, which was perceived

---

66. Jenkins, *New Faces of Christianity*, 69.
67. Decock, "On the Value," 61–62, 67–69.
68. Ibid., 61: "Furthermore, in the pre-modern Christian approach, the meaning of the Scriptures was seen primarily in the context of God's living relationship to the readers, an approach which is close to that of most ordinary readers in Africa."
69. Anderson, *Introduction to Pentecostalism*, 222.
70. Ibid., 222–223.
71. Ibid., 223.
72. Kalu, *African Pentecostalism*, 184.

as "either neglecting biblical teachings or diluting the biblical message to suit the liberal lifestyles of their members and their indifference to such truths as the experiences of the Holy Spirit."[73] Omenyo argues that the reverential attitude to the Bible is shared by most ordinary African Christians and can be interpreted "as a reaction to their perception of the attitude of some ministers/priests of their respective mainline churches, who in their view treat the Bible as a document of the past and approach it with a critical mind."[74]

In contemporary African Pentecostalism the Bible is thus used to address "existential situations" of people.[75] Biblical promises are invoked even in prayers as spiritual resources and applied literally to believers' various experiences either to acquire "spiritual and material welfare" or to defeat all types of evil powers and misfortune in life.[76] The common use of biblical verses or themes in the form of "bumper-stickers" on cars, houses and other properties is a way of appropriating their message by both individuals and corporations.[77] This led Paul Gifford to say that for Pentecostals the Bible has ceased to be a historical document written to readers in the past to become "a record of covenants, promises, pledges, and commitments between God and his chosen."[78] In Kenneth J. Archer's words, the Bible is read "as a presently inspired story."[79] Pentecostals share the strong belief that as the Word of God, the Bible contains a special message to every generation; "God speaks regularly and directly to his people today, individually and corporately" as he did in former times.[80] It is with this conviction that biblical narratives that illustrate God's supernatural interventions especially through Old Testament heroes are exploited most to address the present situation of people. The believer appropriates biblical texts, with a firm conviction that what happened

---

73. Asamoah-Gyadu, *Contemporary Pentecostal Christianity*, 161.
74. Omenyo, *Pentecost outside Pentecostalism*, 222.
75. Asamoah-Gyadu, *Contemporary Pentecostal Christianity*, 162.
76. Omenyo, *Pentecost outside Pentecostalism*, 222.
77. Kalu, *African Pentecostalism*, 266.
78. Gifford, "Ritual Use of the Bible," 179.
79. Archer, *Pentecostal Hermeneutic*, 94.
80. Omenyo, *Pentecost outside Pentecostalism*, 222.

to these heroes will repeat itself in the present situation.[81] It has to be noted that Pentecostals believe that thanks to the baptism of the Holy Spirit, believers are enabled "to hear the Lord speak to them through the Bible" in a particular situation and that the Holy Spirit helps "the reader to take a particular passage of Scripture and address it to his present life situation."[82] This belief is rooted in the high value accorded to the spiritual gifts such as "the utterance of wisdom," "utterance of knowledge" and "prophecy" (1 Cor 12:8, 10). Moreover, Pentecostals believe strongly in God's revealing action to believers through visions and dreams as attested in the Old Testament and in the experience of early Christians. It is especially believed that an anointed "man" or "woman of God"[83] is entitled to proclaim biblical declarations and to actualize them with a performative effect in the lives of the hearers.[84]

Since current Pentecostalism in the Majority World is strongly characterized by the theologies of power and prosperity, biblical texts related to these themes are exploited selectively and in most cases not much attention is paid to their original contexts. Such a selective reading of the Bible is not proper to Africa.[85] The practice occurs wherever ordinary people seek to appropriate the Scriptures as a source of comfort and guidance for their lives. But when it becomes an established and systematic practice which affects larger audiences, it is worthwhile to pay a great deal of attention to it. Paul Gifford notes that "much use of scripture is fairly loose; the text is a launching pad for ideas that may have a rather tenuous link back to the text."[86] This practice, which is common to famous televangelists even outside Africa, enables a preacher to produce a series of sermons out of a single verse. Asamoah-Gyadu gives the example of the Jacob narrative to show how biblical texts are often distorted due to the hermeneutics of power and

---

81. Kalu, *African Pentecostalism*, 267; Gifford, "View," 86.

82. Omenyo, *Pentecost outside Pentecostalism*, 222.

83. As notes J. B. Bangura, the titles "man of God" and "servant of God" are unofficially used to refer respectively to male and female founders of charismatic ministries in Sierra Leone (Bangura, *Charismatic Movement*, 61, n. 120). These titles are generally extended to all charismatic preachers in many African countries.

84. Gifford, "Ritual Use of the Bible," 180, 183.

85. The same phenomenon can even be found in other religions based on sacred books.

86. Gifford, "Ritual Use of the Bible," 179.

prosperity underlying neo-Pentecostalism.[87] Jacob, whom a critical reader will perceive as a cheater, is presented as the model of a skillful man who knows how to bring God's blessings to fruition. It is worth noting that this positive view on Jacob's tricks can be dated back to the patristic era. John Chrysostom argues that Esau proved his ingratitude to God when he failed to value his birthright. He concludes that Esau's dignity as a firstborn was transferred to Jacob, whom he depicts as a virtuous man, to fulfill God's plan. But later, John Chrysostom explains that this happened because of Esau's lack of self-control. He admonishes his hearers not to think that there was any deceitful element in Jacob's actions since everything had been arranged by God beforehand.[88] For his part, Augustine explains that Jacob's apparent trick in Genesis 27 must be interpreted spiritually and that it is not a real trick.[89]

In African Pentecostal hermeneutics, historical and critical questions are not raised.[90] Gordon Fee points out that Pentecostals have regularly displayed a general neglect of "scientific exegesis and carefully thought-out hermeneutics."[91] Kalu notes that since the 1980s, Pentecostals have begun to pay attention to scholarly hermeneutics, but that there is still "a rejection of the scholarly gymnastics in philosophical and liberal biblical interpretation."[92] He observes that for most Pentecostals, the search for a non-literal reading of the Bible is absent. They think that "the pain of the human condition is too excruciating to allow them to indulge in involuted exegesis. Philosophical niceties seem like a luxury."[93] For Gifford, the Pentecostal reading of the Bible cannot be termed fundamentalist. He explains that even if Pentecostals claim that the Bible is inerrant, it is so only "in what it promises for me" and not "in what it claims about

---

87. Asamoah-Gyadu, *Contemporary Pentecostal Christianity*, 164.
88. Chrysostom, *Homilies on Genesis*, 46–67; from between 385 and 388 CE.
89. Augustine, *Sermones*, 190–201.
90. Bangura, *Charismatic Movement*, 25, 62.
91. Asamoah-Gyadu, *Contemporary Pentecostal Christianity*, 164, quotes Fee, "Hermeneutics and Historical Precedent," 121.
92. Kalu, *African Pentecostalism*, 266.
93. Ibid.

history or science."[94] Its trueness is discovered in one's personal life and experientially.[95]

Pentecostals seek correspondences between the Bible and people's real-life situations.[96] As noted earlier, narrative texts are the most cherished and apt to offer such similarities. This link between the understanding of biblical text and human experience as the main feature of Pentecostal hermeneutics is demonstrated by the prominent role that personal testimonies play in preaching and teaching. Personal stories are told as a confirmation of the supernatural interventions of God in human life recounted in the Bible.[97] The often-repeated expression "full gospel," which is essentially Christ-centered, refers to this view that God intervenes in all areas of human life thanks to the spiritual gifts granted to the believers to perform miracles in the name of Jesus.[98] Gatwa characterizes this teaching as a "popular theology of possibilities" since it insists on the miraculous happening in daily human experience.[99] However, Gifford observes that in African Pentecostalism, testimonies do not center on deliverance from sin and vice; increasingly they are about the powerful anointing of the preacher through which the blessing has eventuated.[100]

Correspondence between biblical texts and existential experiences are also sought and exploited with regard to different circumstances of nations.

---

94. Gifford, "Ritual Use of the Bible," 187. Kalu rightly observes that "Enlightenment and liberalism, fundamentalism and evangelical neo-orthodoxy – each has left imprints" on the art of biblical interpretation. In the same manner, the hermeneutical exercise has changed over the time among Pentecostals: "In early Pentecostalism, the Bible was the Word of God and understood at its face value. The operative principle of interpretation was the conviction that exegesis was best when it was as rigidly literal as it could credibly stand. The horizons of the past and present were fused with the pragmatic hermeneutical leap. Allegorization eased the appropriation of the text, and preaching was spontaneous but not relegated to professional clergy" (Kalu, *African Pentecostalism*, 266). However, Kalu's characterization of early Pentecostalism is puzzling. It is difficult to reconcile rigid literalism and allegorization. Moreover, it is not clear what Kalu calls "allegorization." Perhaps, it is better to argue that early Pentecostals unconsciously admitted different meanings of biblical texts as was the case in patristic interpretation for instance.

95. Archer, *Pentecostal Hermeneutic*, 97.
96. Anderson, *Introduction to Pentecostalism*, 223.
97. Ibid., 224–225, 227.
98. Ibid., 225, 229.
99. Gatwa, "God in the Public Domain," 329.
100. Gifford, "Ritual Use of the Bible," 188.

For instance, the collapse of African economies is explained as the consequence of the bloodshed through internecine wars and other atrocities.[101] To support this interpretation, the Cain and Abel narrative is brought in since it states that the land did not give its produce because it was polluted with blood. Kalu observes that the question to be raised about this use of the Bible should not be whether socio-political situations may be spiritualized. In his view, one rather has to ask whether such a spiritualized diagnosis of the realities takes seriously into account the data provided by social scientific analysis and does not reject social activism as one of the strategies for social transformation.[102]

The eschatological aspect of Pentecostal hermeneutics also deserves attention here. Most Pentecostals read the Scriptures passionately, especially prophetic and apocalyptic books, and strive to find their fulfillment in the present history with much stress on the end of time. This approach to the Bible is reminiscent of the *pesher* method attested in the Dead Sea Scrolls from the Qumran community.[103] As observes Werner G. Jeanrond, the members of this community "claimed a special knowledge of divine mysteries" which would confer on them the prerogative "to apply biblical prophecies to current and even contemporary events."[104] The use of this technique by Jewish and Pentecostal readers shows their "belief in the eternal message" of the Scriptures "and a need to find guidance for today in the divine message of yesterday."[105] With regard to current Pentecostalism in Africa, the eschatological reading of the Scriptures is sometimes the

---

101. Kalu, *African Pentecostalism*, 183.

102. Ibid., 183, 216.

103. The word *pesher* is the transcription of the Hebrew term פשר which means interpretation (Charlesworth, *Dead Sea Scrolls*, Vol. 6B, 1). It can designate either a commentary or a technique. The *pesher* method considers that the Scriptures contain divine mysteries about history in general, and the history of the Qumran community in particular (1QpHab 2.9-10). These mysteries are revealed by God to the Righteous Teacher, the leader of this community (1QpHab 7.4). In *pesher* readings scriptural passages have a direct contemporary application to the readers' situation. A word or text allusion is related to a present person or place and the context of the source is ignored. For instance, in the *Habakkuk pesher*, references to the Chaldeans are straightforwardly applied to the Romans without any attempt to justify the application (http://www.insula.com.au/sciandrel/CreationLecture/hermeneutics.html, accessed on 14 April 2015; Charlesworth, *Dead Sea Scrolls*, Vol. 6B, 2.

104. Jeanrond, *Theological Hermeneutics*, 17.

105. Reif, "Aspects," 148.

expression of a protest against and a critique of the present world alienated from God and full of injustices. It is a quest for an alternative order in which life as a gift from God is dignified. In this perspective, Kalu rightly notes that such a reading "helps the audience recognize the signs of the times and discerns what God is doing in today's world. This becomes empowerment for a 'counterworld imagination.'"[106] Hence the accentuation of the "realized eschatology" by many Pentecostal churches nowadays. Out of the conviction that the new era has come about through Pentecost, these churches proclaim the benefits of the biblical imagery of the New Jerusalem and Zion. They insist that "healing, deliverance and prosperity" are now accessible to "the poor, the oppressed and the dispossessed."[107] However, this biblical interpretation has also often distracted people from this world's preoccupations to focus on the hereafter.[108]

The pragmatic hermeneutics held by Pentecostals often uses the Bible eclectically with no attention to the historical and literary context. It leads to some misinterpretation and thus misappropriation of the Bible. This may include the omission or oversight of important elements of the Christian faith, such as God's ability to turn the worst of the sinners into useful agents as revealed in the Jacob story.[109] This pragmatism sometimes turns into a literalism which confuses biblical times and the present. It gives rise

---

106. Kalu, *African Pentecostalism*, 267.

107. Anderson, *Introduction to Pentecostalism*, 234.

108. The relationship between this world and the next to come, and the attitude expected of Christians is serious matter in Christian theology. D. Fergusson wonders whether there is a way of "affirming the apocalyptic notion that the kingdom of God will be established only by the divine recreative act at the end of history, without thereby diminishing our commitment to this world." He indicates that the biblical promise about the kingdom of God acts in two ways: "First, it empowers those who are called to serve God in the present. The context of New Testament teaching about the apocalypse is one in which the consolation of the future is never allowed to distract from the present. The eschatological chapters towards the conclusion of Matthew's gospel are fraught with warnings about neglecting the service of God in the present. The Son of Man already confronts us in the poor, the sick, the hungry. The discourse about the end of the world should not be (though it often is) allowed "to abstract the reader from the challenge of facing the cost of the shadow of suffering and martyrdom." Second, it instills into the present, despite its miseries and trials, a sense of joy and celebration. This is a quality of Christian existence made possible between the resurrection of Jesus and the end of the world. It is the result of the eschatological tension between the now and the not yet of God's promise to us" (Fergusson, "Eschatology," 239–240).

109. Asamoah-Gyadu, *Contemporary Pentecostal Christianity*, 164.

to some legalistic practices like the covering of the head for women. Also, some expressions of Christianity have emerged out of such a literal reading of biblical texts. It will suffice to cite here the example of some American groups within the Holiness movement which defend adamantly the literal interpretation of Mark 16:17–18 about the signs which will accompany the believers to accredit the trueness of their message.[110] Known as "Snake Handlers," "Poison Drinkers" or "Sign Followers," these Christians argue that handling serpents and drinking poisonous substances safely demonstrate the working of the Holy Spirit as do the healing of the sick, casting out demons and speaking in tongues.[111] They insist that all these scriptural truths need to be valued and experienced as a whole in the end-time Christian community. It is believed that these signs, like the *charismata* mentioned in 1 Corinthians 12 and 14, function as an empirical demonstration of God's presence in the community's worship services.[112] Another drawback to this kind of hermeneutics is that it legitimizes a biased systematization of Pentecostal doctrines.[113] For instance, Paul's teachings about the resurrection of the dead and the coming of the Lord Jesus recorded in 1 Thessalonians 4:13–17 are naturally supplemented with apocalyptic texts from Isaiah, Daniel, Zechariah, the canonical gospels, other Pauline epistles and the book of Revelation to construct a detailed chronological presentation of the end of time scenario.[114]

5.2.2 The Talismanic and Symbolic Use of the Bible

The holiness of the Bible plays an important role in African Christianity, especially in Pentecostal churches. The sacredness of the Bible implies also

---

110. Anderson, *Introduction to Pentecostalism*, 223. That biblical text reads: "And these signs will accompany those who believe: by using my name they will cast out demons; they will speak in new tongues; they will pick up snakes in their hands, and if they drink any deadly thing, it will not hurt them; they will lay their hands on the sick, and they will recover." In biblical traditions, the ability to tread unharmed upon dangerous animals like lions, serpents and dragons (Ps 91:13) or to pick up venomous snakes with one's hands and drinking poison and yet remain safe was seen as an indication of divine protection (Uehlinger, "Snake/Serpent," 68).

111. http://holiness-snake-handlers.webs.com/. These American Christians constitute non-denominational churches within the Holiness movement.

112. Archer, *Pentecostal Hermeneutic*, 94.

113. Kalu, *African Pentecostalism*, 267-268.

114. Nsanzurwimo, *Histoire de l'Église*, 192–202.

its supernatural character.¹¹⁵ This is reflected for instance in the spirituality and practices of early African prophets who emerged in various parts of the continent between 1910 and 1950.¹¹⁶ Besides a cross, staff, or a bowl with holy water, these charismatic figures wandered with a Bible and used it in therapeutic activities. They took seriously the African traditional belief in spiritual forces but preached that the power of Christ was able to overcome them. The Bible was regarded as the source of the new power offered to Christians. For instance, prophet Wadé Harris from Liberia would place a Bible on a suffering person's head to effect healing.

It is with this perception of the Bible that it can be placed under the pillow of a person who sleeps to provide protection from any sort of harm. In this case the Bible is used as a "substitute for the charms and amulets that unbelievers bury on their properties" to spare them from evil powers.¹¹⁷ The belief in witchcraft, which is a pervasive feature for many African people, makes this practice very important for the survival of those who think to be under attacks of witchcraft from their ill-intentioned neighbors or enemies. Asamoah-Gyadu explains that this talismanic use of the Bible is not surprising if we also consider that the Qur'an which preceded it on the sub-Saharan African soil was read and used to the same end.¹¹⁸ But the roots of the talismanic use of Scripture go back to ancient Christianity, since the belief in the existence of invisible forces was an important component of the third century cosmology.¹¹⁹ Different ways to overcome them were also worked out. Roukema writes that several sources indicate that Christians

---

115. Asamoah-Gyadu, *Contemporary Pentecostal Christianity*, 160, 168, 170.
116. Kalu, *African Pentecostalism*, 35, 36; Asamoah-Gyadu, *Contemporary Pentecostal Christianity*, 171, 177; Omenyo, *Pentecost outside Pentecostalism*, 67–72.
117. Asamoah-Gyadu, *Contemporary Pentecostal Christianity*, 169, 177.
118. Ibid., 176.
119. Roldanus, *Church*, 23: good invisible beings were called "angels," messengers of God; whereas the bad ones were known as "demons." Besides the threats from demons, other limitations which put pressure on the soul and which human beings were eager to overcome by attaining communion with a higher and everlasting being were illness, mortality, economic insecurity, poverty and slavery. The cultivated people tried to achieve this in "a rational and intellectual manner," whereas the ordinary people resorted to "magic practices, incantations, exorcism or visiting a 'holy man,' who obviously disposed of better forces to lighten the burdens of life." In the face of the Eastern cults of mysteries and their promise to provide this victory through initiations, the Christians presented "Jesus as the nations' teacher whose teachings unmasked the tricks of the demons." This teaching which emerged with the second-century Christian apologists was developed by third century

carried amulets with biblical texts on them and that some church fathers passed a very positive judgement on this practice.[120] Besides the first lines from the four New Testament gospels, other prominent passages inscribed on these amulets were those in which Jesus teaches about the kingdom of God, his healing and exorcisms (Matt 4:23–25) as well as the Lord's Prayer. There were also amulets with selected verses from Psalm 91 which are about protection from malicious forces. Other amulets consisted in extracts from other psalms or Hebrew names and angels. At the end of the fourth century John Chrysostom approved the use of such amulets by Christians. But he hastened to admonish his hearers to write the commands of the gospel in their minds.[121] His approval of wearing amulets is also demonstrated in his sermon on almsgiving in 1 Corinthians 16. After telling his audience that almsgiving is "the chief of good things" of practical morality, John Chrysostom compared it with another practice – evidently popular among his flock – to convince them about the high value of charitable giving.[122] The father indicated that a Gospel hanging by one's bed for a peaceful sleep would have no effect if one neglected almsgiving.[123]

Amulets were expected to offer protection from "illness, demons, and misfortune."[124] Moreover, for John Chrysostom, the presence of holy books in a house not only drives out demons from it, but also will enable those who live in it to keep away from sin.[125] The same belief in the prophylactic

---

Christian thinkers. The general claim was that Christ "is the unique and universal mediator of salvation."

120. Roukema, "Early Christianity and Magic," 371–372.

121. Chrysostom, *Homiliae ad populum Antiochenum* 19.4 (PG 49:196; NPNF I, 9:470). He writes: "Dost thou not see how women and little children suspend Gospels from their necks as a powerful amulet, and carry them about in all places wherever they go. Thus do thou write the commands of the Gospel and its laws upon thy mind." He adds that "the Gospel will be thy surer guardian, carrying it as thou wilt then do, not outside, but treasured up within; yea in the soul's secret chambers."

122. Chrysostom, *Hom. 1 Cor.* 43.4 (PG 61:373; NPNF I, 12:258).

123. Chrysostom, *Hom. 1 Cor.* 43.4 (PG 61, 373; NPNF I, 12:262). The father writes that "since not even the Gospel hanging by our bed is more important than that alms should be laid up for you; for if you hang up the Gospel and do nothing, it will do you no such great good." In this context the word "Gospel" refers to texts or extracts from canonical gospels.

124. Roukema, "Early Christianity and Magic," 372.

125. Chrysostom, *Ad homilias de Lazaro* 3.2 (PG 48:994); translation retrieved from the internet at http://www.tertullian.org/fathers/chrysostom_four_discourses_03_

effect of biblical books and texts is also reflected in Augustine.[126] The latter cheered the Christian who would lay a Gospel on his head as a cure against a headache instead of running to pagan amulets and sorcery. At the same time, Augustine admitted that using pagan amulets and sorcery happened quite frequently in his congregation. As in ancient Christianity, the use of the Scriptures for apotropaic and prophylactic effect in current African Pentecostalism points to the value attached to the content of the Bible as the sacred Word of God.

In other contexts, the Bible is used symbolically within African Pentecostalism.[127] It is common to find a copy of the Bible perpetually placed on the pulpit not only in some charismatic churches, but also in Reformed congregations. In all cases, this Bible that is never read symbolizes God's presence among the believing assembly when gathered together or the fact that God's people must have access to God's Word. When it is buried under the foundation of the church building, the practice expresses the belief that Jesus Christ is the cornerstone of his people. The gift of a Bible to candidates for ordination in many Protestant churches points to the view that it is a source of authority.

Monjang Lee writes that the critical attitude of most Western theologians towards the Bible "reflects the collapse of Christendom and the failure of Christianity" in the West.[128] Asamoah-Gyadu observes that the Bible lost its authority for many in the West after it was deprived of "its status as more than a sacred book, through a process of biblical relativism and gradual demystification."[129] However, he recognizes that critical hermeneu-

---

discourse3.htm; accessed on 18 May 2015.

126. Augustine, *In Joannis Evangelium Tractatus CXXIV* 7, 7; 7, 12 (CCSL 36, 71; 73), 165–166.

127. Asamoah-Gyadu, *Contemporary Pentecostal Christianity*, 171, 177.

128. Lee, "Reading the Bible," 149. On page 151, Lee indicates that from an Asian perspective the act of reading the Bible does not aim at enabling the Christian to become more familiar with its teachings or to be a good minister or teacher of the Scriptures. Rather, he emphasizes, the ultimate objective in reading the Scriptures is "to upgrade ourselves and become like our Master, Jesus Christ"; in other words, we desire to get "spiritual insights through awakening and enlightenment" and then work for "the embodiment of those insights through meditation, personal application and practice to achieve personal transformation – to become like Jesus Christ in our thought, word, and deed."

129. Asamoah-Gyadu, *Contemporary Pentecostal Christianity*, 169. Mutombo-Mukendi ("Le nouveau culte," 99) surmises that the scralization of scientist rationalism

tics is needed in theology but warns against "the unreflective adoption" of academic approaches to biblical texts.[130] Following Fee, he recommends the integration of spiritual experience in biblical exegesis so that the Bible remains the book of the Christian community.[131] Fee's perceptive remarks deserve mention here.

> Taking Scripture away from the believing community, the exegete made it an object of historical investigation. Armed with the so-called historical-critical method, he thus engaged in an exercise in history, pure and simple, an exercise that appeared all too often to begin from a stance of doubt – indeed, sometimes of historical skepticism with an anti-supernatural bias. Using professional jargon about form, redaction, and rhetorical criticism, the exegete, full of arrogance and assuming a stance of mastery over the text, often seemed to turn the text on its head so that it no longer spoke to the believing community as the powerful word of the living God.[132]

I agree with Fee and Asamoah-Gyadu that biblical interpretation will be meaningful only if its starting point remains the sacredness of Scripture so that its content might be taken seriously as well. In African Pentecostalism, biblical interpretation takes the presence of the "supernatural" as a guiding hermeneutical principle.[133] Therefore, failure to give heed to the existence of "a supernatural and experiential element in Christianity" can only lead to the ruin of faith and take knowledge of the Bible and theology itself as any other academic field.[134]

---

as the only way to explain reality and access knowledge has had negative effects on our societies. He feels that it must be challenged to admit other perspectives.
    130. Asamoah-Gyadu, *Contemporary Pentecostal Christianity*, 169.
    131. Ibid., 170.
    132. Fee, *Listening to the Spirit*, 8.
    133. Asamoah-Gyadu, *Contemporary Pentecostal Christianity*, 172.
    134. Ibid., 178.

Conclusion

In the present chapter I described Pentecostalism as a global movement which has reshaped the face of Christianity worldwide in the twenty-first century. There are many Pentecostal denominations whose differences are reflected in doctrines, liturgies, structures, rituals and so on. But all of them emphasize and promote the experience of the working of the Holy Spirit and the practice of spiritual gifts in the Christian life and church liturgy. Pentecostalism as a charismatic movement is also significantly attested among the mainline Protestants and the Roman Catholic Church.

The rapid growth of Pentecostalism in the Majority World has shifted the center of gravity of Christianity southwards in terms of the number of adherents. It was noted that although the Azusa Street movement played a leading role in the spread of Pentecostalism worldwide, renewal movements with charismatic orientation developed in Africa, Asia and Latin America without any direct influence from the West. Today, most Pentecostal churches have developed independently from those founded in the West at the beginning of the twentieth century. The number of Pentecostal and new charismatic churches continues to increase in Africa and attract younger, educated and urban audiences.

The conviction that the Bible is God's Word encourages Pentecostals to seek in it resources to address human felt needs. I pointed out that the selective use of the Scriptures to articulate Pentecostal teachings often ushers in unwarranted interpretations and appropriations. The talismanic and symbolic use of the Bible, bold pronouncements of biblical texts and names, and anointment with oil for various purposes remind us of the ancient use of Christian amulets and other beliefs rooted in the Roman Catholic tradition.[135] As in the ancient church, these Pentecostal rituals can be seen as an alternative to pagan magic prohibited in Christianity, although its dynamics are still alive and operative in people's minds even after their conversion to Pentecostalism.[136] Also, Pentecostalism emphasizes power, victory and success. This is applied not only to spiritual matters, but

---

135. I noted elsewhere that these rituals can rightly function as sacraments in the believer's life: Asamoah-Gyadu, *Contemporary Pentecostal Christianity*, 136–140.

136. Roukema, "Early Christianity and Magic," 374, 378.

also to physical needs of wealth and health. The African continent with its worldview where the quest for life in fullness is conducted in a real combat against evil powers has becomes a fertile ground for Pentecostalism.

It is important to note that the challenges and opportunities related to Pentecostalism as sketched above are not restricted to the Majority World. The type of Pentecostalism I discussed has also found its way to the North through migrant churches as Claudia Währisch-Oblau's study attests. Whereas she admits that European Protestant churches do not have to adopt uncritically everything from migrant Pentecostal and charismatic churches, she encourages the former to recognize the latter as part of the movement of God's Spirit at work throughout history.[137] She thus pleads for the emergence of "an attitude of respect and humility" as the only attitude which can bring about a successful dialogue between both groups of churches for the sake of the common call to participate in God's mission.[138]

As I noted before, a considerable part of the Pentecostal and charismatic churches accept the prosperity gospel as one of their defining characteristics. The next chapter will discuss in depth the teachings of the prosperity gospel movement in Africa.

---

137. Währisch-Oblau, *Missionary Self-Perception*, 335.
138. Ibid.

CHAPTER 6

The Prosperity Gospel in Sub-Saharan Africa

As Pentecostalism continues to grow in sub-Saharan Africa, the message on health and wealth commonly called the prosperity gospel predominates most of its discourses. As we will see below, this message links Christian giving and material prosperity. Since 2 Corinthians 9:6–11 seems to support this view, I will seek to understand how these teachings on prosperity are articulated in some forms of Pentecostalism in Africa. My focus will be on the aspect of wealth rather than on health. Before I analyze the strengths and weaknesses of the prosperity gospel movement in Africa, it is important to say a word on its historical background.

6.1 Background

The names "prosperity gospel" and "health and wealth" came from the opponents of the movement which designated itself as the "Word of Faith," "Positive Confession" or the "faith message."[1] The origin of this movement is generally traced back to early American Pentecostalism in the first half of the twentieth century. This teaching "was an indirect development from Pentecostal 'realized eschatology,' the ministries of independent healing evangelists, and in particular, the writings of independent Baptist pastor E. W. Kenyon."[2] Kenyon (1867–1948) "taught the 'positive confession of the Word of God' and a 'law of faith' working by predetermined divine

---

1. Anderson, *Introduction to Pentecostalism*, 65, 217; Idahosa, *I Choose to Change,* 107.
2. Anderson, *Introduction to Pentecostalism*, 217.

principles."³ The phrase "What I confess, I possess" was a cornerstone of his belief and teaching.⁴

Concerning health, he argued that "healing is a completed work of Christ for everyone, to be received by faith whatever the evidence or circumstances. The use of medicine was inconsistent with faith."⁵ Antoine Nouis indicates that the movement developed in the 1960s in the USA and spread in North America before it flourished in Africa.⁶ In various parts of the world different Pentecostal preachers "have propounded a modified form of this teaching to suit their own contexts,"⁷ and it has become "a prominent teaching of many Pentecostal and Charismatic churches worldwide."⁸ Kenneth Hagin, generally seen as the founding father of the Faith Movement, expanded Kenyon's views and taught that "every Christian should be physically healthy and materially prosperous and successful," a teaching that he drew from some biblical verses.⁹ He argued that "it was not enough to believe in what the Bible said; the Bible must also be confessed, and what a person speaks (confesses) is what will happen."¹⁰ For his part, Kenneth Copeland took Hagin's thoughts further with much insistence on material prosperity. He therefore "formulated 'laws of prosperity' to be observed by those seeking health and wealth" and explained poverty as a curse to be countered by faith.¹¹

Anderson rejects the view of some critics who try to link the Word of Faith with the teachings of Norman Vincent Peale's "Positive Thinking," with a dualistic materialism, with the nineteenth century "New Thought" of Ralph Waldo Emerson or even with Christian Science.¹² He suggests

---

3. Ibid., 65, 217.
4. Chilenje, "Challenges," 12.
5. Anderson, *Introduction to Pentecostalism*, 217.
6. Nouis, "Une hérésie séductrice," 7.
7. Anderson, *Introduction to Pentecostalism*, 66.
8. Ibid., 217.
9. Ibid., 217.
10. Ibid., 218.
11. Ibid., 66.
12. Ibid., 219. For instance, Mutombo-Mukendi ("Le nouveau culte," 103–104) argues that the origins of the prosperity gospel must be associated with the American pragmatism of the nineteenth century according to which the value of a theory or something else is measured on the basis of its concrete results. He explains that this was accompanied

that it might be better to find its roots in the teachings of early Pentecostal preachers like Smith Wigglesworth who emphasized faith and wrote in 1924 words which are often quoted by the Word of Faith preachers: "I am not moved by what I see. I am moved only by what I believe."[13] But it remains true that today's prosperity teachers get inspiration from Norman Vincent Peale's book about the theme "Success through a Positive Mental Attitude," widely available in pirated editions.[14]

6.2 The Major Teachings of the Prosperity Gospel

The prosperity gospel emphasizes material wealth and health as noted previously. However, it is not a homogeneous movement. One might rightly speak of prosperity gospel theologies. This is due to the fact that the prosperity teachings are more of an oral theology than a written one. The prosperity gospel presents itself mostly as "a rhetorical and experiential teaching in which the appeal is as much tied to the language used and the personality of the proponent as to the theological content."[15] In addition, there are considerable differences between the preachers of this teaching in some of its details. Therefore, it is not possible to attempt a systematic presentation of its theology. But there are some common principles that one will find in prosperity discourses with varying degrees of emphasis depending on individuals and contexts. Victor Chilenje points out five main principles of the teachings of prosperity preachers in Zambia.[16] These are "sowing

---

by developments in psycho-social theories emphasizing individualism, self-dependency and practicability which insisted that truth had to produce tangible results in order to be believed. Similarly, faith was expected to yield tangible effects to be genuine. Mutombo adds that the prosperity gospel sermons are undergirded by the psychological presupposition of Positive Mental Attitude which implies that one's positive or negative thoughts will produce positive or negative results respectively. This is the philosophical framework of the laws of prosperity formulated by preachers. Kalu (*African Pentecostalism*, 256) observes that some scholars find the roots of this movement in the second-century Gnosticism which emerged in the church at different times of its history.

13. Anderson, *Introduction to Pentecostalism*, 219.
14. Gifford, "View," 87.
15. Young, "Prosperity Teaching," 4.
16. Chilenje, "Challenges," 14–16.

a seed" through tithes and offerings;[17] the principle of sowing and reaping;[18] proclaiming and having; the power of blessing through the Abrahamic covenant; and the atoning work of Christ. Willem-Henri den Hartog and Basilius Mbanze Kasera mention three principles for the case of Namibia: seed sowing, faith as a way to success and positive thinking.[19] Jean Bosco Bangura identifies three main theological motifs of faith, seed sowing and anointing which underlie the prosperity message in Sierra Leone.[20] Within the limits of this research and as announced in the introduction of the current chapter, reflections on the prosperity gospel will mainly focus on the motif of giving as a source of financial growth.

6.2.1 Atoning Death of Christ, Abrahamic Covenant and Prosperity

The foundational element of the prosperity gospel is that God wants all his children to be prosperous in all areas of life.[21] This view is deduced from the reading of 3 John 2 in the King James Version: "Beloved, I wish above all things that thou mayest prosper and be in health, even as thy soul prospereth."[22] The prosperity gospel affirms that through the suffering and death of Christ, God has provided for all the needs of human life. As a consequence, every Christian believer has been entitled to "the victory over sin, sickness, and poverty."[23] It is said that Christians have not only the right but also the responsibility to claim this prosperity.[24] This share in economic prosperity and good health through Christ can be attained "merely by a positive confession of faith."[25] Thanks to the media, especially

---

17. Ibid., 14. Giving to God is to "plough back." It is also said that one's giving "gives an identity to God," a way of saying that the act of giving will make God recognize the giver as "His faithful child."

18. The difference between this law and the former is not clear. It seems to me that both amount to the same thought of reciprocal giving.

19. Den Hartog and Mbanze Kasera, "Het welvaartsevangelie in Namibië," 17–19. I am indebted to Gerard Lof for the English translation of this article.

20. Bangura, "Charismatic Movement," 172.

21. Young, "Prosperity Teaching," 4–5.

22. The NRSV reads: "Beloved, I pray that all may go well with you and that you may be in good health, just as it is well with your soul."

23. Mbe, "From Asceticism," 47–48.

24. Young, "Prosperity Teaching," 4.

25. Mbe, "From Asceticism," 47–48.

television, the prosperity gospel preachers have "promoted the concept of the big man and the big God whose will is to prosper His people materially, physically, and spiritually because the blood of Christ's atonement and many promises in the Scriptures assure this."[26] Closely related to the redemptive death of Christ is the Abrahamic covenant as another principle of prosperity. It is strongly affirmed that as this "covenant was a legal contract, so is the promise part of a spiritual contract."[27] Therefore, in their quality of Abraham's spiritual descendants by virtue of Romans 4:16–17; 9:8 and Galatians 3:29,[28] every Christian must claim and access God's promise of generosity to their spiritual father.[29]

6.2.2 Faith and Prayer as Ways to Material Prosperity

The prosperity gospel teaches that faith is the key to prosperity. Jesus' saying about the need for the disciples to have faith "the size of a mustard seed" to perform miracles is frequently invoked to teach this principle (Matt 17:20; Luke 17:6). And faith here is not just belief, trust, hope or a correct attitude before God.[30] Neither does it amount to fully relying on and obeying the triune God as suggests Lameck Banda.[31] Rather, it is "acting on the word, speaking into reality what does not exist, and dreaming and envisioning the desired goals."[32] It is this understanding of faith that informs prayer perceived as a tool to access the blessings promised to Abraham.[33]

The conceptualization and practice of prayer is important in every religion. In Christianity and especially in Protestantism, prayer expresses the believer's total dependence on God for one's everyday life and destiny. But

---

26. Kalu, *African Pentecostalism*, 115.
27. Ibid., 255.
28. Chilenje, "Challenges," 16–16.
29. Behind this affirmation lies the story of the fall of the first Adam for whom God had destined success and material prosperity, but whose disobedience occasioned a relational and financial crisis. Fortunately, the obedience of Christ, the second Adam, has reinstated the believers into their divine rights (Mutombo-Mukendi, "Le nouveau culte," 103).
30. Banda, "Dialoguing at 'Mphala'," 63.
31. Ibid., 64. Here Banda draws on L. L. Morris' understanding of this concept: "Faith means laying hold of the promises of God in Christ, relying entirely on the finished work of Christ for salvation, and on the power of the indwelling Holy Spirit of God for daily strength" (Morris, "Faith," 360).
32. Kalu, *African Pentecostalism*, 255.
33. Ibid., 255–256; Bangura, "Charismatic Movement," 122.

Pentecostalism takes the concept of prayer further and links it to the notions of power, spiritual fight and victory. As said earlier, in Pentecostalism, spoken words are believed to have a performative power. Therefore, prayer must "be positive, bold, and decisive to be effective."[34] This understanding of the power of speech, found in the Old Testament, is strongly rooted in African traditions. Parents can curse or bless their descendants. Moreover, in African traditional religions, it is believed that people can domesticate spirits and use them to harm others. This can be done "through words, thoughts, attitudes, and behavior in sorcery or witchcraft practices."[35] As I noted previously on the use of amulets in the ancient church, the question of magic was taken seriously, as is reflected in the discussions devoted to it by some ancient Christian writers.[36] Origen, for instance, could acknowledge the intrinsic forces of human utterances both in the pagan world and the Christian context.[37] Obviously, the practice of prayer in different religious traditions functions with the same belief.

In Pentecostalism in general and in the prosperity teachings in particular, the main function of prayer is to shake the realm of evil powers thanks to its empowerment by the Holy Spirit.[38] It is believed that praying in tongues is more powerful than any other form of prayer in addressing

---

34. Asamoah-Gyadu, *Contemporary Pentecostal Christianity*, 35.

35. Kalu, *African Pentecostalism*, 177. Witchcraft is defined by Kalu as "the use of human psychic powers to do evil" whereas sorcery "employs magical incantations, implements, objects, medicine, and other paraphernalia." But in either case, "curses could be put on individuals and families by the envious or wicked people."

36. Roukema, "Early Christianity and Magic," 367–378.

37. Origen was of the view that pagan charms and invocation of some names of demonic powers had some supernatural effect in their context: Origen, *Homilies on Joshua* 20, 1 (SC 71), 406–409. But he strongly affirmed that for Christians "the words and names of Holy Scripture are even more powerful" (Roukema, "Early Christianity and Magic," 374). He explained that the effect of the Christian use of these holy words and names is due to the fact that God's angels hear them as they are pronounced by Christians. In his apology against Celsus who had accused Jesus of using magic/charlatanism to accomplish his powerful deeds, Origen denied that Christians get power from any incantations. Rather, added Origen, they invoke Jesus's name and the stories about him to cast out demons (Origen, *Contra Celsum* I, 6 (SC 132); cf. also I, 46; II, 49 (SC 132); VII, 4; VIII, 58 (SC 150). Though Origen said that this use of Jesus' name and stories about him is especially effective when it is done with sincerity and authentic belief, he indicated that the name of Jesus can sometimes effectuate wonders even when it is recited by evil men.

38. Asamoah-Gyadu, *Contemporary Pentecostal Christianity*, 35.

critical situations.³⁹ As remarks Asamoah-Gyadu, Pentecostals refer to Romans 8:26–28 to affirm that Paul "endorses praying in tongues because through such prayer the Spirit helps believers to overcome the weaknesses evident in the limitations of their language as they seek to communicate with God."⁴⁰ A similar belief can also be found in Origen who argues that magic names invoked by pagans as well as the biblical names of God hold an intrinsic power and that their effect materializes mostly when they are used in original languages.⁴¹ In the specific case of prayer, Clement of Alexandria (towards the end of the second century CE), held that prayers were more powerful when pronounced in a foreign language rather than in Greek.⁴² An unconscious dependence on this magical conception of foreign words is reflected in the use of foreign languages perhaps as a surrogate of the gift of tongues among Pentecostal and charismatic Christians. In prayers, especially in the case of deliverance, exorcism or any other pressing need, people will spontaneously resort to some formulae in a foreign language to give more impetus to one's prayer. To give an example in the Rwandan language (Kinyarwanda), the commonly used expression in such critical circumstances is "*Mu izina rya Yesu*" to rebuke evil powers.⁴³ Those who know some Swahili will find it more powerful to say "*Kwa jina la Yesu.*" Those who favor French or English will use respectively "*Au nom de Jésus*" or "*In the name of Jesus.*" This is relevant to our discussion here since such a practice is normally found among people who are even more fluent in Kinyarwanda than they are in those foreign languages.⁴⁴ Another

---

39. Ibid., 36.
40. Ibid., 43.
41. Origen, *Contra Celsum* I, 24–25 (SC 132); V, 45 (SC 147); VI, 32 (SC 147).
42. Clement, *Stromateis* I, 143, 6 (SC 30; The Fathers of the Church 85).
43. The point here is not to ask whether or not praying in the name of Jesus does make any effects. In other words, the issue at stake is not to know if the statement itself carries some powers. Rather, the example illustrates the belief that making that statement in a different language is stronger than pronouncing it in one's own language.
44. It is true that in the case of our denomination, the Pentecostal church in Rwanda, the use of Swahili can result from the fact that the first missionaries who introduced Pentecostalism in Rwanda spoke this language. In some cases, those who are more fluent in foreign languages will reasonably find it easy to utter such formulae in the language they are better able to express themselves in rather than in Kinyarwanda. For historical reasons, there are many Rwandans who do not have a full command of their mother tongue, the only national language we have.

illustration of the magical conception of foreign words can be found in the understanding and use of the Hebrew word "Halleluiah" which is popular among Pentecostals. Several times I have personally heard Pentecostal preachers explaining that the word expresses praise to God; the only thing that believers will be busy with in eternity. They infer from this that this word is the language from heaven since it refers to the worship which the celestial beings render to God continually. In their view, the heavenly nature of this expression is supported by the fact that in all Bible translations it is only transliterated and not translated. Many a charismatic preacher will say that a single pronouncement of "Halleluiah" drives demons many miles away from the place where it is shouted in faith. Thus, doing so as much as believers can will be salutary.

It is remarkable that the above understanding of prayer is informed not only by the biblical notion of demons, but also by the African traditional belief according to which "things do not happen by chance" and that evil powers oppress people and deprive them of "health, wealth, and wellbeing."[45] In this context of African Pentecostalism, the notion of African traditional deities has merged with the biblical belief in the existence and the workings of demons and evil powers hostile to human wellbeing. Affliction can be the result of breaking the moral code.[46] In Rwanda, the function of the traditional religion was to preserve relational harmony between the living, the ancestors and the physical universe. Failure to comply with the moral codes would inevitably bring hazards upon individuals and communities.[47] This belief is shared by the Old Testament where it is repeatedly said that "obedience and active maintenance of the covenant with God" offers welfare.[48] Bearing in mind this transcendental dimension of

---

45. Asamoah-Gyadu, *Contemporary Pentecostal Christianity*, 44. Gifford, "View," 88–89, 91; Kalu (*African Pentecostalism*, 178, 189) argues that the challenge to the Christian missionary in Africa remains "how one should witness the gospel in a highly spiritualized environment where recognizing the powers has not been banished in a Cartesian flight to objectivity and enlightenment." He concludes that Pentecostalism "derived its coloring from the texture of the African soil and from the interior of its idiom, nurture, and growth; its fruits serve more adequately the challenges and problems of the African ecosystem than the earlier missionary fruits did."

46. Kalu, *African Pentecostalism*, 177.

47. Karamaga, *Evangile en Afrique*, 149.

48. Kalu, *African Pentecostalism*, 179.

human life, it is no surprise that poverty and failure in life can on occasion be traced back to demonic actions that call for exorcism. Furthermore, many believe that one's business can collapse not only because of deficiency in managerial skills, but also as a result of demonic activities orchestrated by a witchdoctor.[49] In an article on the burning question regarding the attitude "modern Ghanaians" could adopt towards their culture, Meyer wrote that there was a pervasive belief among Pentecostals that one's present problems could originate from "ancestral curses" as a punishment for the sins committed by previous generations.[50] In the same vein, the existence prior to conversion of any ties with some rituals of African traditional religions generally considered as a medium through which Africans had been serving the devil unconsciously, are thought to cause existential hazards to believers.[51] So prayer for deliverance is recommended in such a spiritual climate to liberate individuals from their harmful past.

It is not possible here to elaborate on the paradoxical relationship between Pentecostalism and African cultural heritage. It will suffice to simply note that African Pentecostals are "generally very hostile to African traditional religions."[52] As noted earlier, these religions are even demonized since traditional worship is considered a place where Satan operates "in the guise of traditional spirits."[53] In this, Pentecostals take further the attitude of the colonialists in general and of many Protestant missionaries in particular towards African cultures and traditions.[54] However, I have shown that in many respects African Pentecostalism resonates with a variety of sub-Saharan African traditions and that this accounts for its growth on this continent. Kwame Bediako demonstrates that for instance, prophet William Wadé Harris and Cardinal Emmanuel Milingo from Zambia articulate their theological thoughts on healing, exorcism and pastoral care "consciously in relation to the thought-patterns, perceptions of reality and concepts of identity and community which prevail within the worldview of

---

49. Ibid., 177.
50. Meyer, "Make a Complete Break," 323.
51. Ibid., 322.
52. Asamoah-Gyadu, "Make a Complete Break," 23.
53. Meyer, "Make a Complete Break," 322.
54. Ibid., 318, 326.

African societies."⁵⁵ Bediako emphasizes that they do so "not as a matter of convenience," but because they consider "that the spiritual universe of the African primal world does offer valid perspectives for articulating Christian theological commitments."⁵⁶ Their strategy meets Cox's view according to which one of the two main conditions for a new religion to grow consists in demonstrating the ability "to include and transform at least certain elements of pre-existing religions which still retain a strong grip on the cultural subconscious."⁵⁷ Meyer is thus right to write that the often-repeated call by Pentecostals to a complete break with African traditions is more problematic than it appears; and is in fact impossible to achieve.⁵⁸ The truth is that the dynamics of those traditions referred to as past realities continue to exist in Pentecostalism.⁵⁹ The same view is worded by Asamoah-Gyadu when he says that even where "traditional religions as overt religious forms may be receding under pressure from the Christian advance," "their values, beliefs, and realities" have found new expressions in Christianity in general and in Pentecostalism in particular.⁶⁰ Anderson's depiction of the relationship between Korean Pentecostalism and shamanism is well suited to

---

55. Bediako, *Jesus and the Gospel*, 86.

56. Ibid.

57. Cox, *Fire From Heaven*, 218–219. The second condition is that this new religion must be able "to equip people to live in rapidly changing societies where personal responsibility and inventiveness, skill associated with a democratic polity and entrepreneurial economy, are indispensable." In this chapter I argue that some Pentecostals show commendable initiatives to empower their church members and that there is a pressing need to insist on this area of discipleship and Christian formation.

58. This invitation to shun one's old traditions echoes the complex situation which the apostolic church had to face in Greco-Roman society. Some examples are worth mentioning here. Participation of Christians in the meals and other celebrations in which food was offered to the pagan deities was such an important issue at Corinth that Paul had to address it in his letters (1 Cor 8 and 10). And it seems that he finally prohibited "any participation in idol offerings, with the exception of food sold in the market" (Roukema, "Paul's Admonitions," 257. Later, in a different context, we learn that the non-participation in such ceremonies by Christians was shocking and occasioned some hostility against them from their social environment (1 Pet 4:1–5; 3:17). The imperial cult is also another area where Christians were called to confess their intransigent loyalty to their faith as the book of Revelation reveals. In situations like these Christians understood that indulging in such practices would ultimately compromise their allegiance to Jesus Christ whom they confessed as Lord and Savior.

59. Meyer, "Make a Complete Break," 318.

60. Asamoah-Gyadu, *Contemporary Pentecostal Christianity*, 23; Mbiti, *Bible and Theology*, 128.

characterize the African context. Korean Pentecostal leaders state that there is no room for shamanism in their practices since they oppose it as they also reject divination. In this particular context, Anderson prefers "to consider Pentecostalism as a culturally contextual form of Korean Christianity interacting with and confronting shamanism; both continuity and discontinuity with the old religion are kept in creative tension."[61]

In my view, this dialectic of interaction and confrontation between Pentecostalism and African traditions is an ongoing process and is characteristic of any cultural context. In Rwanda, for instance, an interesting development has taken place as to the revalorization of ancestral traditions. Unlike the Roman Catholic Church, Pentecostal churches did not have any practices or liturgy for commemorating the dead as the Rwandan tradition would recommend. In the aftermath of the 1994 genocide against Tutsi, efforts to put in place such liturgical tools have become a necessity since each year the country observes a period of genocide commemorations.[62] This presupposes, as Meyer perceptively suggests, that Pentecostals should not perceive African traditional heritage as a satanic reality that a believer must get rid of at all costs.[63] At the same time, it is germane for Christians to realize that the gospel as the message about Jesus' life, deeds, death and resurrection is "essentially constant and unchanging" whereas

---

61. Anderson, *Introduction to Pentecostalism*, 241.

62. The history of the Christian church is full of such examples of interaction and confrontation between Christianity and older religions. We observe the same relationship between the nascent Christianity and Judaism from which it sprang. And when the Christian faith moved into non-Jewish land, the same dynamics were ignited. The controversies over the place of the Mosaic law in the economy of salvation was one of the crucial issues that the early church was confronted with as some New Testament writings like Romans and Galatians reveal. Later, in the ancient church, as I noted, the attitude of Christians in a pagan world continued to be an important concern for church leaders. I remarked that, for instance, although the mainstream church did condemn pagan magic, pagan beliefs found new life in the Christian faith and practices. In the Roman Catholic Church, the Second Vatican Council (1962–1965), whose aim was to update "its pastoral attitudes, habits, and institutions to make them more effective in the changed conditions of the modern world," made important resolutions as to the revalorization of local and national traditions. In the area of liturgy, decisions were made among other things on the "use of Latin and modern languages; incorporation of local and national customs or traditions; making liturgy an effective influence in society" (Trisco and Komonchak, "Vatican Council II," 407–418; here on pp. 407, 415).

63. Meyer, "Make a Complete Break," 328–329.

people's traditions and cultures "are constantly changing and transitory."[64] The Christian gospel asserts that the cross and the resurrection of Jesus are core factual events rather than fiction, without which our faith becomes useless (1 Cor 15:14).[65] It is thanks to this uniqueness and novelty of the gospel that it questions and purifies our respective traditions to fulfill their religious intuitions about God, his workings and his will as Creator and Savior.[66] But people employ their cultures and their beliefs to understand, interpret and celebrate the Christian message; the result being the emergence of a Christianity "which bears both the local imprint and also a universal imprint."[67] With regard to African Pentecostals, Kalu writes perceptively that they "take the African map of the universe seriously, acknowledging that culture is both a redemptive gift as well as one capable of being highjacked."[68]

Coming back to the perception and practice of prayer in African Pentecostalism, the prosperity gospel teaches that God will meet all the requests that the believer presents to him. This is expressed through many texts about prayer such as Mark 11:24: "So I tell you, whatever you ask for in prayer, believe that you have received it, and it will be yours." Nouis indicates that the literal reading of this verse highlights four stages to apply in a prayer of faith: to proclaim these promises; to act and behave in accordance with this confession; to receive or acquire what was prayed for

---

64. Mbiti, *Bible and Theology*, 7, 19; L. Newbigin, quoted by Anderson (*Introduction to Pentecostalism*, 234), concedes that every communication of the gospel is culturally conditioned. But he cautions that the gospel itself "is not an empty form into which everyone is free to pour his or her own content." Rather, Newbigin writes, its content remains "Jesus Christ in the fullness of his ministry, death, and resurrection."

65. Van Den Toren, *La doctrine chrétienne*, 18 ("L'Évangile présuppose que la croix et la résurrection sont des événements objectifs de l'histoire, et sans lesquelles notre foi serait vaine").

66. This is also how I understand Jesus's saying that he has not come "to abolish the law or the prophets . . . but to fulfill" them (Matt 5:17). Even to the delicate question of the ancestral function in Africa the Christian gospel offers an answer. Kwame Bediako (*Jesus and the Gospel*, 29–31) explains that although ancestors are sacralized, they are always recognized as humans limited by death. He adds that Jesus, without losing his divine nature through incarnation, "has achieved a far more profound identification with us in our humanity than the mere ethnic solidarity of lineage ancestors can ever do." Moreover, he continues, the Christian affirmation of Jesus's eternal nature and his resurrection from the dead places him much beyond ancestors.

67. Mbiti, *Introduction to Pentecostalism*, 20.

68. Kalu, *African Pentecostalism*, 179.

and to give testimony.[69] Asamoah-Gyadu explains that in Pentecostalism, prayer needs to follow certain strategies to be efficient. The main "requirement is faith, but additionally, prayers are considered more effective if they are based on Scripture, said in tongues, proclaimed with authority, militant, use words that resist the devil, and ask for the fulfillment of specific promises."[70] Three reasons are given to motivate this characterization of prayer. Jesus himself confronted demons with a commanding voice; the believer has been granted the same authority by the Holy Spirit; and the words of believers are expected to reflect this "performative power."[71] The text of Acts 4:23–31 gives confidence to Pentecostals concerning their belief in the close relationship between prayer and the manifestations of the power of God.[72]

6.2.3 Christian Giving and Financial Prosperity

Another principle taught by the prosperity gospel preachers consists in the farming imagery of sowing and reaping which says that the harvest is proportionate to the amount sowed. A series of texts are used to support the teachings (Prov 11:24; Mark 10:30; Luke 6:38; Acts 20:35; 2 Cor 9:6 and Gal 6:7). The seed is understood in terms of tithes and offerings.[73] The prosperity gospel affirms that God blesses free givers in proportion to the amount of offering one gives, which is literally called "banking in faith."[74] Some preachers speak of the so-called "seed-faith" concept according to which the "Old Testament tithing to God out of obligation was replaced by a New Testament version – giving in order to expect a blessing."[75] Since this is a spiritual law, some argue that even a non-believer who follows it will get financial breakthroughs since faith itself generates financial prosperity.[76] In

---

69. Nouis, "Une hérésie séductrice," 7: "Dites-le (proclamation que l'on possède déjà), faites-le (action en phase avec cette proclamation), recevez-le (exaucement), racontez-le (témoignage)."
70. Asamoah-Gyadu, *Contemporary Pentecostal Christianity*, 51.
71. Ibid., 56.
72. Ibid., 57.
73. Kalu, *African Pentecostalism*, 256.
74. Mbe, "From Asceticism," 57.
75. Coleman, *Globalization*, 42.
76. Chilenje. "Challenges," 15.

this context, planting a "seed" amounts to giving funds to the church or to the preacher regarded as God's agent.[77]

As noted earlier, in contemporary African Pentecostalism giving is closely linked to prosperity, both material and spiritual, and this concerns individuals as well as nations.[78] Among the models which explain the emergence of the teaching of prosperity in African Pentecostalism, Nimi Wariboko, quoted by Asamoah-Gyadu, mentions the covenant paradigm, which says that God grants prosperity to individuals and nations "according to either the covenant of giving or the covenant of good efforts."[79] He indicates that individuals get prosperity as a result of tireless "sacrificial giving" not only of money but also of "time and effort to the church," which will lead to national economic blossoming.[80] However, Asamoah-Gyadu is right to write that "the covenant of sowing and reaping'" in Pentecostal teaching is not based on sacrifice, but on what he calls "transactional giving."[81] The amount of the seed determines the extent of the harvest.[82] This way of thinking is for instance voiced by Matthew Ashimolowo.[83] It is interesting to note that he quotes 2 Corinthians 9:6 where the apostle says that "the one who sows sparingly will also reap sparingly, and the one who sows bountifully will reap bountifully." I will come back to this when I deal with the use of 2 Corinthians 8–9 by the prosperity preachers in Africa. They insist that Abraham's and Jacob's resources were the result of their faithful tithing.

In this philosophy of giving, non-tithing Christians are seen by some as worse than armed robbers since they steal from God whereas the latter do so from their fellow human beings. Pastors, their spouses and their children "have become real-life examples of the faithfulness of God to those who

---

77. Gifford, "View," 88.
78. Asamoah-Gyadu, *Contemporary Pentecostal Christianity*, 79.
79. Ibid.; Wariboko, "Pentecostals Paradigms," 37.
80. Asamoah-Gyadu, *Contemporary Pentecostal Christianity*, 79.
81. Ibid.
82. Ibid., 90.
83. Ashimolowo, *Coming Wealth Transfer*, 192. He is the Senior Pastor of Kingsway International Christian Centre in the UK. Besides his pastoral and evangelistic activities on an international level, he is a businessman.

give towards his work in tithes and offerings."[84] Some pastors and their families live a luxurious life thanks to this to such an extent that some purchase their own private jets.[85] As for Dag Heward-Mills[86], he writes that tithing Christians prosper whereas non-tithers become poor since they have nothing to reap.[87] Giving tithes not only is a way to secure further financial prosperity, but it is also a way to protect one's wealth. I personally remember one peripatetic evangelist who traveled throughout the congregations of our denomination in my area in 2012 with a message of prosperity. He used the same terms as those of insurance companies. He reminded the audience that people pay a premium to an insurance company to have their properties protected. In the same way, he added, believers need to give a special offering to God to protect their belongings. To reinforce this exhortation, he referred to Abraham sacrificing his son Isaac. Everyone was thus encouraged to offer one's "Isaac" to secure God's blessings and protect the rest of their possessions.

The importance of the "seed-harvest" principle among African Pentecostals is explained by the fact that it brings important sums of money needed to run and expand their activities.[88] My experience as a pastor in a Pentecostal congregation has brought me into closer contact with this phenomenon. I remember the day when we were in the executive council of our parish and the financial report revealed that the church finances had decreased significantly. As many Pentecostal pastors would interpret that report, it was concluded that this was a sign of a decline in spiritual life of the members of the congregation as a whole.[89] It was said that there was an urgent need to insist on teachings about tithes and offerings. To this end, the name of the above-mentioned prosperity preacher who had previously sojourned in the congregation was suggested.

---

84. Asamoah-Gyadu, *Contemporary Pentecostal Christianity*, 89.

85. Anderson, *Introduction to Pentecostalism*, 134; Asamoah-Gyadu, *Contemporary Pentecostal Christianity*, 88; Mutombo-Mukendi, "Le nouveau culte," 95.

86. He is the Bishop of the Lighthouse Chapel International headquartered in Ghana.

87. Heward-Mills, *Why Non-tithing Christians*, 1–6.

88. Gifford, "View," 88; Asamoah-Gyadu, *Contemporary Pentecostal Christianity*, 87.

89. Heward-Mills, *Why Non-tithing Christians*, 29.

While non-tithing Christians are treated harshly, unbelievers are also not spared as far as their resources are concerned. Some Pentecostal preachers teach that God will dispossess unbelievers of their resources and give them to those who will use them to spread Christian mission.[90] This is for instance the case for Eastwood Anaba of the Fountain Gate Chapel in Ghana.[91] It is clear for him that this wealth will be transferred to faithful tithing believers. As notes Asamoah-Gyadu, the logical conclusion of this train of thought is that "God exists to serve monetary needs of believers in order that his kingdom might expand."[92]

In contemporary African Pentecostalism, giving to God is also done through an offering to the man or woman of God. After a man or woman of God has ministered to people, it happens that Christians are asked to anoint him or her, which is done in the form of a special offering to this particular person. It is believed that this offering will open new opportunities in the life of the giver.[93] This "transactional giving" borrows from the Scriptures but also resonates with African traditional religions. In the latter, "ancestors and deities are fed periodically as a way of sustaining cultic relationships that enable the benefits of health, abundance, longevity, and various forms of prosperity to flow from the transcendent realm towards the human realm."[94] Consequently, the misfortune of individuals and communities will be interpreted as the logical result of "non-fulfillment of religious obligations, such as not performing appropriate sacrificial rituals or neglecting ancestors and deities."[95] This belief ties in with Malachi 3:7–9 which declares that non-compliance with tithing obligations brings divine punishment.

However, there is a need to clarify some points about the African practice of offerings in traditional religions. It would be a mistake to think that the African rituals referred to in the previous paragraph implies that people expect that all their needs will always be fulfilled by deities and spirits.

---

90. Asamoah-Gyadu, *Contemporary Pentecostal Christianity*, 93.
91. Anaba, *Breaking Illegal Possession*, 46.
92. Asamoah-Gyadu, *Contemporary Pentecostal Christianity*, 94.
93. Ibid., 81.
94. Ibid.
95. Ibid., 81, 89.

The belief in divine providence coexists with the conviction that God is ultimately sovereign and that his blessings cannot be purchased. In the Rwandan context for instance, there is a saying which goes "*Imana iraguha ntimugura*" (God gives to you, you do not buy from him). As Pentecostals exploit the African traditions, there is a need to dialogue with it in a more comprehensive way which integrates its sometimes paradoxical views.

6.2.4 Anointing as a Route to Prosperity

Another theological motif of the prosperity gospel teaching is the anointing with olive oil.[96] There are various purposes for anointment: "anointing for change" or "anointing for breakthrough" and so forth.[97] Prosperity preachers claim to receive special divine revelations and empowerment to mediate healing and success in people's lives and undertakings. Biblical texts like Exodus 29:7; Mark 6:13 and James 5:14 are invoked to anoint not only the sick for healing but also those who are to undertake a journey, to sit for an exam or start a new business. The anointing is meant to remove all obstacles to the success and wellbeing of the seeker. Anointing with oil is performed in Pentecostal circles not only by the clergy but also by gifted lay people as a means of divine grace. In this case, it would rightly operate as a sacrament in the believers' spirituality.[98] In some contexts, anointing practices may sound magical to an outsider. Granted, the adjective "magical" is used here in its neutral sense and does not refer to practices that the Christian tradition associates with demonic influence. Rather, it designates the view that a rite in itself is believed to produce a supernatural effect.[99] These rites include the anointing of the tools that one uses in one's trade or daily activity, "and washing the feet of believers so that they could step into wealth, victory, and promotions."[100] This religious act is not an invention by Pentecostals. There exist similar practices in the Roman Catholic Church

---

96. Bangura, "Charismatic Movement," 172–173.
97. Asamoah-Gyadu, *Contemporary Pentecostal Christianity*, 125.
98. Ibid., 136–140.
99. Roukema, "Early Christianity and Magic," 370.
100. Kalu, *African Pentecostalism*, 143, 258; Gifford, "View," 59; Asamoah-Gyadu, *Contemporary Pentecostal Christianity*, 123, 142. The fact that Mark 6:13 says that the disciples expelled demons and anointed the sick with oil to heal them, and that James (5:14–15) exhorts his readers to pray for the sick and anoint them with oil gives ground to this practice performed by the prosperity preachers.

tradition. In the ancient church anointment with blessed oil was believed to grant strength, healing and deliverance from demonic powers.[101] We learn that the blessing of a new house, a new ship would guarantee secure usage.[102] The blessing of fields was meant to protect them against locusts and other animals. Railways were blessed for safe traffic; even weapons were anointed to seek victory over enemies.[103] Similarly, today some Pentecostal preachers speak of "anointing for vengeance" against enemies.[104] Moreover, on occasion, the one who seeks anointing pays for the olive oil to be used and the payment depends on the individual's financial status. This practice of selling spiritual benefits cannot pass unnoticed and criticisms have been formulated not only by observers but also by some insiders.[105]

6.3 A Positive Import of the Prosperity Gospel?

6.3.1 A Genuine Quest for the Fullness of Life Promised by the Scriptures

Critics of the prosperity gospel often fail to appreciate some insights it can offer to global Christianity.[106] Anderson agrees that horrific practices of "exploitation by power- and wealth-hungry preachers" are reported but alerts to the danger of generalization. In his view, this generalizing stance prevents people from appreciating "the selective reconstructions and creative innovations made by some of these new Pentecostals in adapting to radically different contexts from those of the 'prosperity preachers' of the USA."[107] I agree with those who think that there are some benefits we can get from the prosperity gospel teachers. From this vantage point, the

---

101. Hippolytus, *Trad. ap.* 5.2; *Apostolic Constitutions* 8.29 (SC 336, 232–233).
102. *Rituale Romanum Pauli V. Pontificis Maximi jussu editum*, 220–227.
103. *Pontificale Romanum Clementis VIII ac Urbani VIII jussu editum ac a Benedicto XV recognitum et castigatum*, 365–367, 591–592.
104. Asamoah-Gyadu, *Contemporary Pentecostal Christianity*, 133.
105. Ibid., 132–133, 140–143.
106. G. Fee depicts it as "an insidious disease" which is rapidly infecting American Christianity and which "has very little of the character of Gospel in it." However, his remarks as to the failures of this trend of Pentecostalism are relevant to our discussion too (Fee, *Disease*, 7).
107. Anderson, *Introduction to Pentecostalism*, 131.

prosperity gospel should be seen as "a genuine protest against certain tendencies in the mainline churches" as rightly observes Hermen T. Kroesbergen.[108] In fact, it appears to us as a quest for dignity and ways of experiencing the fullness of salvation available through Christ in the face of the pressures and precariousness of life. Our task should therefore be to make every effort to "distinguish a genuine prosperity gospel from theologically unacceptable forms of it."[109]

In fact, the prosperity teaching is based on a certain way of reading the Bible that one needs to consider in order to appraise it. The prosperity gospel resonates with the Old Testament understanding of poverty.[110] Kalu explains that the Hebrew tradition points out six causes of poverty: "the oppression of the rich, religious apostasy, social alienation, ecological causes, human factors, and self-alienation or lifestyle."[111] Religious apostasy comprises "rebellion against God's will, Sabbath-breaking, the neglect of cultic responsibilities, and failure to tithe."[112] Social alienation here refers to war and other shortcomings in terms of bad governance. Ecological causes include natural disasters and public health issues. Human factors comprise emigration and other activities which do not promote sustainable management of natural resources. Self-alienation is about personal conduct including "laziness, sloth, drunkenness, a wasteful life style, extravagance, the love of wine and women, disobedience to parents, immorality, sexual orientation, and fraudulence."[113] Kalu adds that in this context, prosperity is equated with "God's *shalom*" which is a relational harmony between God, humans and nature.[114] The Old Testament insists that prosperity is given

---

108. Kroesbergen, "Prosperity Gospel," 78.
109. Ibid., 78, 86. Drawing on Kierkegaard's interpretation of Abraham's sacrificing Isaac, Kroesbergen sets four criteria for this task: to understand faith as an expression of gratitude to God rather than a means to manipulate him; to consider the value of tradition and resignation; to think the prosperity gospel as a personal undertaking realized in full submission to God, and to focus on God and not on us. In this context, resignation means renouncing all one's claims to something as Abraham did to Isaac by agreeing to sacrifice him. He insists that Abraham "did not make the movement of resignation and faith because he knew that they were the right tricks to get what he wanted."
110. Kalu, *African Pentecostalism*, 257.
111. Ibid.
112. Ibid.
113. Ibid.
114. Ibid., 258.

by God (Deut 18:8; Prov 10:22; Eccl 5:19) and is linked with the covenant (Deut 28:29; 29:9).[115] But it also shows that hard work leads to economic prosperity.[116] Kalu underscores that in a covenantal relationship, tithing is more than offering money, but rather an expression of "obedience to and reliance on God."[117] As for the New Testament, Kalu notes that Jesus added some elements which cause poverty, especially demonic agency. In Kalu's view, when Jesus expelled demons from their victims, he thereby showed "an example of poverty-alleviation and a method of accessing prosperity."[118] At the same time, Jesus set repentance, remaining in the Word and decisive relationship with other believers as conditions for accessing the promises of prosperity. However, Kalu does not provide any precise text in which this teaching occurs. He goes on to say that the apostolic teaching on faith, the workings of the Holy Spirit and the power of the word need to be considered as we reflect on the prosperity gospel faith. Although he does not provide the biblical reference he has in mind, and it is arguably evident that he is referring to 2 Corinthians 9:6–14, Kalu states that the apostles "encouraged believers to give generously because giving would bring earthly and heavenly returns and promote evangelization."[119] He rightly concludes that "the moral explanation of poverty cannot be avoided and the appeal to supernatural causality is palpable."[120] He maintains that the prosperity gospel in general remains "within the stream of orthodoxy" and concedes that individual preachers have added some questionable practices that they claim to have received through a divine revelation to illustrate the law of sowing and reaping used by Paul in 2 Corinthians 9.[121] For Kalu, some other preachers have gone far in seeing material prosperity as God's will and the sign of his blessing, whereas poverty and suffering are seen as divine

---

115. Zulu, "Fipelwa na baYaweh," 29.
116. Ibid., 30.
117. Kalu, *African Pentecostalism*, 258.
118. Ibid.
119. Ibid.
120. Ibid. Young ("Prosperity Teaching," 14) admits that "ignorance, sin and evil often can be the causes of pain and suffering" and that this can occur both at personal and communal levels. However, he observes that the Christian response to pain and poverty needs to "be rooted in the pain and poverty of Christ – the cross" rather than in the reciprocal giving proposed by the prosperity gospel.
121. Kalu, *African Pentecostalism*, 259.

curse. He insists that the problem with the prosperity gospel is not about the availability of biblical texts to support it, but the way these are interpreted. Dustin W. Ellington invites the believers to go beyond the prooftexting of the prosperity teachings and look at "the main aims, themes, and lines of thought of biblical books and the canon of Scripture as a whole."[122] He insists that "The wider literary context of biblical verses clarifies their meaning and places responsible limitations on their use."[123] In the same vein, Bangura observes that there is a need for the global church to reassess the pervasive themes of blessing and curse which are often associated with Israel's obedience and disobedience to covenantal terms in the Old Testament.[124] This is to the point as long as the prosperity preachers insist that believers need to appropriate covenantal promises as Abraham's spiritual descendants through Jesus's redemptive work (Rom 4:16–17; 9:8; Gal 3:29).

6.3.2 Audacity to Address Real-Life Problems

The second benefit we can get from the prosperity gospel remains its ability to address existential needs of people by drawing upon their traditions and biblical resources. For Kalu, the popularity of the prosperity gospel on the African continent lies in the fact that it resonates with "indigenous concepts of salvation, abundant life, and goals of worship."[125] These issues matter a great deal, especially because most of the African population is confronted with the problems of collapsed economies and globalization, as well as political instability. Moreover, those who have been taught that poverty, suffering and humility are the indication of true Christian faith and that they will enjoy abundance in the hereafter are inclined to embrace the prosperity teachings.[126] In other words, the overemphasis on spirituality and the demonization of wealth in most mission-founded churches has created a fertile soil for the prosperity gospel.[127] The latter sustains the poor's

---

122. Ellington, "Is the Prosperity Gospel Biblical?" 37.
123. Ibid., 37.
124. Bangura, "'Abraham's blessings are mine!'," 43.
125. Kalu, *African Pentecostalism*, 259; Bangura, "'Abraham's blessings are mine!'," 41.
126. Chilenje, "Challenges," 17; Young, "Prosperity Teaching," 16.
127. Zulu, "Fipelwa na baYaweh," 31.

hope for a radiant future.[128] But the prosperity gospel attracts adherents not only among the poor but also among the rich.[129] I recall that in the African context, the movement appeals to all social classes. Those who have acquired some possibilities of betterment will expect further uplifts whereas the disadvantaged and underprivileged will easily expect miraculous intervention as a way out of misery. As for the rich who can afford to "sow substantial seeds," they will have another motif to flock to the prosperity gospel. They "appreciate being held in high esteem by the prosperity gospel pastor, and are happy to claim their wealth as a blessing from God."[130]

The bourgeoning of new Pentecostal churches which focus on the prosperity gospel signals "that there are unresolved questions; such as the role of 'success' and 'prosperity' in God's economy, enjoying God *and* God's gifts, including physical healing and material provision, and the holistic dimension of 'salvation'."[131] Anderson explains that the Christian gospel includes the promise of a share in the practical fruits of divine grace.[132] The prosperity gospel reflects Pentecostal soteriology in which salvation means "conversion and empowerment."[133] By conversion Pentecostals understand liberation from sin and a constant fight against it and other powers of alienation while one serves God and humanity. It is significant that charismatic Christianity gives expression to one aspect of God's nature as "the source of wealth, potentialities, and abilities, and the believer must acknowledge that unless God approves of an endeavour it will fail (Ps 75:7, 10)."[134] At this level, it is right to say that the prosperity theology embraces the Old Testament "covenant theology, the concept of salvation and the atoning death of Christ."[135]

The prosperity gospel resonates with African traditional culture in that sense that African anthropology understands the goal of everyday life in

---

128. Anderson, *Introduction to Pentecostalism*, 302.
129. Nouis, "L'hérésie de la prospérité," 10.
130. Chilenje, "Challenges," 18.
131. Anderson, *Introduction to Pentecostalism*, 134.
132. Asamoah-Gyadu, *Contemporary Pentecostal Christianity*, 44–45.
133. Kalu, *African Pentecostalism*, 260, 261.
134. Asamoah-Gyadu, *Contemporary Pentecostal Christianity*, 44.
135. Kalu, *African Pentecostalism*, 261.

terms of pursuit of "vitality and abundant life."[136] Although Africans believe in personal efforts, they are strongly aware that "supernatural realities" play a key role in their success or failure.[137] As I indicated earlier, the prosperity gospel tends to explain all human misery with reference to the activity of evil powers. Both the African traditions and the prosperity gospel emphasize a transcendent dimension of human life. Paul himself or his disciple later says that human life is a real battlefield and that believers need to be equipped to that end (Eph 6:10–20).[138] Specifically, verse 18 recommends the Christians to "Pray in the Spirit at all times in every prayer and supplication." This spiritual combat, commonly known as "spiritual warfare," is supported by the belief that spiritual powers "take control of individuals, communities and nations."[139] In the above-quoted text, as in African traditional religions, human existence is precarious since evil forces strive to prevent "individuals, families, and communities from living a prosperous life."[140] The visible world in which human life evolves is in perpetual interaction with the invisible world.[141] Andrew Walls asserts that Western theology emerged from the Enlightenment universe and is thus its substantial product. He notes that it ignores "some of the most crucial situations, because it has no questions related to those situations" like those connected with the spiritual universe of African peoples.[142] He adds that "The Bible is not an Enlightenment book" and that many peoples in the world live in a larger universe, with constant activity across an open frontier

---

136. Ibid.

137. Asamoah-Gyadu, *Contemporary Pentecostal Christianity*, 45.

138. It is remarkable that after Matthew and James, Ephesians is the third book most frequently employed for preaching, for instance in the Church of the Lord (Aladura) in Nigeria for preaching. More specifically, Eph 6:10–20 is the most used passage of this epistle for sermon texts (Mbiti, *Bible and Theology*, 117). Mbiti indicates that the awareness of the workings of "these powers and principalities" is strongly rooted in African Christians' minds.

139. Anderson, *Introduction to Pentecostalism*, 231. Some scholars go beyond the recognition of Paul's reference to the existence of spiritual forces which confront and degrade human societies. M. Maggay argues that "powers" and "principalities" might also mean some "life systems and structures that entrench the demonic" in the sense that they perpetuate oppression, injustice and ruin all efforts for social and economic development of nations (Maggay, "To Respond," 50-51).

140. Kalu, *African Pentecostalism*, 177.

141. Ibid., 178.

142. Walls, "Afterword," 203; Jenkins, *New Faces of Christianity*, 90–127.

between the empirical and the spirit worlds, and face "issues for which Western theology has no resources."[143] For this reason, he rightly argues that there is a need to widen our theological agenda in Africa to respond to these needs. In his view, this means to elaborate a broader "theology of the principalities and powers" which deepens "our theology of evil, illuminating the nexus between personal sin and guilt on the one hand, and systemic, structural evil on the other that has stalled much Western theological discussion."[144] Walls recalls that the encounter between Hellenistic culture and Christianity in the early centuries of its existence pushed the latter to produce creeds and the beginnings of classical theology. He then wonders whether the encounter between Western theology and the Majority World will not yield fruitful experiences. While this encounter is vital to any quest of mutual understanding and enrichment, it is important to be aware that the many overlaps and layers of difference between what is generally termed the "West" and "the South" regarding living conditions of people are also attested in theological discourses. For instance, many USA and Canadian preachers teach the same prosperity gospel as articulated in contemporary Africa, Asia and Latin America. Indeed, I have demonstrated that the movement originated from the USA before it was spread in the Majority World.

6.3.3 A Reverential Attitude to the Bible as God's Word

The seriousness with which most of the proponents of the prosperity gospel take biblical promises is a third positive element we can learn. Their valorization of the supernatural in the Christian faith especially with regard to wealth and health calls into question the rationalistic attitude which discounts, relativizes or rejects the miraculous in the Bible.[145] After all, it is a biblical belief that God is powerful, faithful, the source of what we have and are and that he is willing to bless his children. This understanding of God is also felt in mainline mission churches where people regularly offer

---

143. Walls, "Afterword," 203.

144. Ibid. Mutombo-Mukendi ("Le nouveau culte," 90–91) shows that prosperity gospel preachers have developed a teaching on the various beings referred to in Col 1:16; 2:10, 15; Eph 1:21; 3:10; 6:12, indicating the harmful mandate assigned by the devil to each category.

145. Anderson, *Introduction to Pentecostalism*, 190–192.

different donations as an expression of gratitude to God for any happy event or success in life.¹⁴⁶ It is only with this belief that believers can confront the pressures and peculiarities of life in the hope that their efforts will yield fruits. The same message was given to Israel in the testing of the Babylonian exile and needs to be taken seriously: "For surely I know the plans I have for you, says the LORD, plans for your welfare and not for harm, to give you a future with hope" (Jer 29:11). It is in this respect that biblical narratives such as David fighting against Goliath can be used to foster confidence and not let overwhelming difficulties daunt us.¹⁴⁷ Anderson recognizes that "with its positive message of not accepting the status quo but striving for improvement in life, these forms of Pentecostalism have struck at the psychological heart of poor societies."¹⁴⁸ More importantly, there are some prosperity gospel preachers who also engage in social promotion. The case of Yonggi Cho in South Korea is a well-known example. This pastor has initiated extensive programs in social promotion, some of which have benefitted North Korea.¹⁴⁹ Bangura recognizes that in Sierra Leone charismatic churches have realized the limitations of their preaching on prosperity and started some initiatives in community development.¹⁵⁰ These churches raise funds to run their projects, which is laudable and remains one of the strengths of Pentecostalism as Anderson points out.¹⁵¹ In Namibia, the emergence of the first church of Pentecostal orientation in 1958, the Apostolic Faith Church, is another example on African soil. This church brought in the district of Nsanje "a novel religious formula" since "it provided small entrepreneurs, such as the founders themselves had become, with an ethic and a set of behavioral rules geared to safeguard their newly won position vis-à-vis their kinsmen and neighbours."¹⁵² The

---

146. Asamoah-Gyadu, *Contemporary Pentecostal Christianity*, 45.
147. Gifford, "View," 87.
148. Anderson, *Introduction to Pentecostalism*, 291–292.
149. Ibid., 296.
150. Bangura, "'Abraham's blessings are mine!'," 41.
151. Anderson, *Introduction to Pentecostalism*, 231; Bangura, "Charismatic Movement," 194–195.
152. Schoffeleers, *Pentecostalism and Neo-Traditionalism*, 32, 33, 34. However, Schoffeleers indicates that one of the negative sides of the success of these churches was that the masses living on subsistence farming in general and among them the elderly in

formula proved so effective that it was taken up by other later Pentecostal churches in the 1970s and its influence was felt beyond the district with some variations. From my personal experience in the Pentecostal Church of Rwanda, the oldest and largest of this kind in the country, I see that the adoption of a new spiritual orientation gives rise to some improvements in people's living conditions. This view is corroborated by the fact that until very recently, a popular explanation of the betterment among Pentecostals held by their neighbors was that the new converts were given money by the church. This indicates that a certain visible change had taken place in a positive way and had been witnessed by outsiders. Lovemore Togarasei holds the opinion that the prosperity gospel can contribute to entrepreneurship to alleviate poverty in Africa. He says that some prosperity preachers also teach "entrepreneurship skills" to prove to their followers that the prosperity gospel is true.[153] He gives the example of a sermon by Enock Sitima of Bible Life Ministries in Gaborone which he himself listened to.

> In the sermon, Sitima attributed poverty in Africa to four causes, which he identified as nomadic mentality, consumer mentality, civil servant and salary mentality. He defined nomadic mentality as the inability to focus on one thing, resulting in one losing direction in life. Consumer mentality was defined as the spirit of always spending what one has instead of thinking about investment. In line with the general Pentecostal discouragement of employment, civil servant and salary mentality was defined as the spirit of seeking employment instead of creating employment.[154]

One may not agree with this preacher on the view that "God never intended his followers to be employed but to be employers,"[155] but it is remarkable that his thoughts promote an entrepreneurial spirit. It is true that there are not many sermons of this kind among the prosperity preachers. Togarasei affirms that similar teachings have pushed many Pentecostals

---

particular were gradually isolated from their sphere of influence. And this, he contends, had inevitable consequences on spiritual, social and economic levels.

153. Togarasei, "African Gospreneurship," 123, 124.
154. Ibid.
155. Ibid.

to initiate their own businesses which have contributed to the alleviation of poverty through job creation. He concludes that by emphasizing that "God wants his children to live successful lives, Pentecostalism gives many Africans a positive mindset that they can make it in business through God, rather than by waiting for a Western donor to extend a helping hand."[156]

All the positive elements of the prosperity gospel presented in this chapter may not be shared by all. But at least they invite us to be critical of our own conceptualization of prosperity from a biblical and theological point of view. However, these should not obscure the serious concerns that this movement raises not only among outsiders but also among those that it attracts.

6.4 Concerns about the Prosperity Gospel

6.4.1 Moral and Social Weaknesses: Greed, Inequalities and Unaccountability

The prosperity gospel is seen by some as a result of the non-engagement with socio-political injustices of some sections of Pentecostalism that spiritualize these issues and make material prosperity a spiritual virtue.[157] Others go further and regard this movement as the reproduction of "the worst forms of capitalism in Christian guise."[158] In my view, they are partially right inasmuch as the prosperity gospel promotes blatant inequalities between the elite of preachers who benefit from it and those who are constantly exhorted to sow their seeds in the hope of experiencing breakthroughs in life.[159] Moreover, Bangura points out that in Sierra Leone, for instance, this teaching has activated the "desire for material wealth which was lying latent" in the country's traditional worldview.[160] It is therefore possible to say that the belief that one will receive a hundredfold what one has given nurtures

---

156. Ibid., 125.
157. Anderson, *Introduction to Pentecostalism*, 278, 283.
158. Ibid., 131.
159. Den Hartog and Mbanze Kasera, "Het welvaartsevangelie in Namibië," 19.
160. Bangura, "Abraham's blessings are mine!" 40.

the spirit of consumerism and greed among the rich.[161] For Kroesbergen, the prosperity gospel is biblically, theologically and historically at variance with the Christian faith.[162] He explains that it is factually erroneous since its promises of wealth and health are openly contradicted by the experience of poverty, illness and even death that befall believers.

The methods used by the prosperity gospel preachers to raise funds are often questionable and even immoral. Bangura observes that many preachers have taken advantage of the credulity of poor people to exploit them and aggravate their misery.[163] In some cases, the preachers of prosperity persuade people, and sometimes those with a low level of education and financial resources to give all that they would live on in the hope to receive multiplied returns. Once this is done these preachers never show up again in the area. In most cases the promises do not materialize and the givers are left hopeless.[164] Nouis does not hesitate to call this teaching a form of swindle (*escroquerie*).[165] In such a case, this designation is justified inasmuch as the application of the so-called laws of prosperity by these hopeless givers benefit the preacher only.[166] In fact, the strategies used to apply the seed sowing principle in fund raising by prosperity preachers are open to corruption and do not promote accountability. This is partially due to the fact that the churches that propagate the prosperity gospel are "non-denominational and independent, and the pastor is the highest organizational authority."[167] It is therefore no surprise that the prosperity gospel can promote greed and selfishness on the side of those who preach it and hope to live on the financial income it generates for the church or individual preachers.[168] Worse, the gospel is commercialized as a commodity.[169] It is

---

161. Nouis, "L'hérésie de la prospérité," 10: "Dans les pays riches, elle est une réponse aux aspirations matérialistes de personnes en quête d'une justification de leurs désirs"; Anderson, *Introduction to Pentecostalism*, 291.

162. Kroesbergen, "Prosperity Gospel," 79.

163. Bangura, "Abraham's blessings are mine!" 40.

164. Chilenje "Challenges," 19.

165. Nouis, "L'hérésie de la prospérité," 10.

166. Mutombo-Mukendi, "Le nouveau culte," 105.

167. Chilenje, "Challenges," 21.

168. Ibid., 20.

169. Kalu, *African Pentecostalism*, 145.

worthy of note that the prosperity preachers are mostly attracted by urban areas. They generally refuse to go to rural areas because people do not have enough resources to sow a seed. In mainline churches, harangues on giving beyond what one can afford make people believe that the God preached is for the rich only.[170] As far as African Christianity is concerned, I recall that the prosperity teachings are found at varying levels not only in Pentecostal and charismatic churches, but also in mainline Protestant denominations.[171] Kalu is amazed at the fact that "mission-founded churches are borrowing the Pentecostal strategies to raise funds"; some Presbyterians have started to pay tithes, for instance.[172]

In this climate where success, victory and wealth are held up as indicators of authentic life, the prosperity preachers exercise psychological pressure on believers.[173] In the face of financial and health problems, refuge in prayer, seed sowing and neglect of other ways to address these problems can have enormous consequences. Those who are attracted to these teachings might develop a spirit of laziness and parasitism since they are brought to believe that everything will happen by miracles.[174] Also, to see financial success as a synonym of prosperity and a sign of God's approval can lead to moral depravity. In fact, one can acquire wealth through immoral ways such as corruption and even witchcraft practices in a context where economic advancement is seen as a spiritual virtue.[175] Indeed, there are stories about some Christians who resort to such immoral ways and witchcraft to acquire material wealth in the African context. Another challenge from the prosperity gospel lies in the rejection of the use of medicine by some of its adherents. This attitude may inevitably endanger people's lives.

The vulnerability of the prosperity gospel has also been assessed from a socio-political perspective. The presupposition that power and success

---

170. Chilenje, "Challenges," 11–12.

171. Bangura, "Charismatic Movement," 169. In Zambia, it is reported that this teaching is influencing both Pentecostal and Reformed churches. In a positive sense, the emergence of the prosperity gospel in the country has challenged mainline churches to engage with the matter of health seriously: Kroesbergen, "Introduction," 6.

172. Kalu, *African Pentecostalism*, 145.

173. Den Hartog and Mbanze Kasera, "Het welvaartsevangelie in Namibië," 20.

174. Gifford, "View," 92.

175. Zulu, "Fipelwa na baYaweh," 31.

in all areas of life attest that one serves the most powerful God makes the prosperity gospel preachers vulnerable to manipulation. Besides the fact that they can manipulate devastated poor people as noted above, they themselves can be manipulated by corrupt politicians, military and business rulers not wanting them to tackle the real causes of poverty. These spiritual leaders exploit the African belief in the role of human intermediaries such as traditional sorcerers or diviners who are believed to have special powers to negotiate with the invisible world and to restore harmony when life is threatened.[176] These preachers feel proud to be invited by political, military and business leaders to help to solve socio-political crises in a given context. They are often caught in the trap of corrupt rulers as they play the role of spiritual counselors, intercessors and exorcists of the powerful. In this context, those attracted by the teachings of prosperity are victimized in two ways: they are robbed of their wealth by dishonest preachers while their autocrat rulers continue to exploit them being confirmed in their practices by the moral authority of the same prosperity gospel preachers. In other words, the spirit of clientelism deprives the latter of the ability to challenge those who oppress the people and maintain them in poverty. These preachers seek protection and accreditation from political leaders who willingly respond to this need because they are aware of the socio-political impact that the spiritualizing teachings of the latter have on the population whose poverty is often the result of bad governance.[177] In their quest for social and financial interests, both groups of leaders oppress and exploit those under their responsibility. This led Mutombo to wonder whether the prosperity gospel is not a form of socico-economic and political globalization which is affecting the masses of the poor globally.[178] It is true that this critique needs

---

176. Mutombo-Mukendi, "Le nouveau culte," 81, 101, 103, 123–128, 131–132.

177. Corrupt political leaders encourage religious leaders who hypnotize the masses by spiritualizing their social misery, a way of preventing and silencing socio-political demands from the people if they manage to understand the real cause of their poverty (Zognong, *Le christianisme outragé*, 26–28, 56–60).

178. Zognong (*Le christianisme outragé*, 7–26) gives a positive answer to this question. He notes that Christianity is abused by the liberalization of religion in Africa characterized by the emergence of self-proclaimed prophets of Pentecostal persuasion who manipulate the Bible and exploit the credulity of illiterate and devastated poor on the continent. For him, political leaders' indifference to this phenomenon demonstrates a deliberate complicity with those preachers of prosperity who benefit from it to the detriment of the masses of poor people in their audiences.

to be formulated for all religious leaders in sub-Saharan Africa because this temptation to gain glory is constantly present before them.

On a different level, the way in which the prosperity gospel preachers exploit African traditional beliefs raise some concerns. Their insistence on witchcraft as the main cause of human misery is "socially disruptive."[179] It often gives rise to suspicions and quarrels among people. The tendency to see evil powers behind every event prevents people from seeing the causes of their misery in social and political structures. In other words, human responsibility is obscured or overshadowed. Therefore, the ethics of hard work and tenacity in life are often discounted, and other alternatives for addressing social problems and diseases like HIV/AIDS come to nought.

6.4.2 Theological Shortcomings

Criticism has been aimed at theological shortcomings of the prosperity gospel resulting from its overemphasis on success in the present life to the detriment of other fundamental aspects of Christian salvation. The first drawback to be mentioned here is its neglect or non-recognition that suffering is also a part of human life. Carried to its logical conclusion, the view that God wants his children to prosper in all the areas of life implies that "to be in poverty or to be chronically ill is to be outside of God's will for his or her life, whether that be because of sin, ignorance or lack of sufficient faith."[180] The prosperity gospel teachings on tithes and offerings disappoint and harm faithful tithing Christians who yet experience tough existential hardships.[181] Since this movement understands authentic Christian life in terms of success, when one's prayer does not receive a positive answer, the common explanation given will be that there must be something wrong in the believer's life, a hidden sin not confessed.[182] Today, so many factors

---

179. Gifford, "View," 92.

180. Young, "Prosperity Teaching," 5; Meyer ("Make a Complete Break," 323–326) indicates that S. Y. Kwami, a Ghanaian charismatic pastor, teaches that believers need to be delivered not only from generational curses, individual past sinful life, occultist ties, demonic possession and denominationalism, but also from "acute poverty." She concludes that for some Pentecostals "poverty is not so much regarded as a socio-economic condition, but rather as a (result of) sin, while 'blessings of the Lord' are supposed to materialize in prosperity." (Meyer, "Make a Complete Break," 323); Fee, *Disease*, 8–9.

181. Asamoah-Gyadu, *Contemporary Pentecostal Christianity*, 101.

182. It is also believed that, according to the passage of Dan 10:12–13, territorial spirits can hinder divine answers to believers' prayers (Gifford, "View," 85; Bangura,

explain the financial misfortune that many African Christians are going through. And this affects everybody regardless of their religious allegiance. One may argue that even in times of failure the Christian is still loved and maintained by God's grace as Asamoah-Gyadu observes.[183] Furthermore, one should avoid giving the impression that hardships befall non-tithers whereas faithful tithing Christians are spared. One should imagine the disastrous consequences of incriminating discourses by the prosperity preachers on the spiritual, psychological and social life of a Christian confronted with tough situations. Nouis can therefore conclude that the prosperity gospel vehicles a theology of curse and suspicion.[184] And since one's level of faith is gauged by the material wealth it attains, the prosperity preachers can grade believers according to their wealth.[185] In the face of unfulfilled promises despite the seed sown, believers might end up falling into a division between the rich and the poor, the righteous and the unfaithful, and rise in a revolt against God and the church.[186] Ultimately, this will introduce "the concept of a superior class of believers who can and do effect" prosperity in their everyday life.[187] In this climate, Den Hartog and Mbanze Kasera are right to write that the prosperity gospel can lead to secularism.[188] People may gradually become skeptical about any relevance of religion in human existence. Correlatively, Gifford thinks that the

---

"Charismatic Movement," 122). To respond to this situation of disillusionment, members are sometimes called to thank God because they are at least still breathing; which is much more precious than all other unfulfilled desires one might have presented to God. Also, it happens that the pastor explains that the non-fulfillment of expected achievements was God's intention to preserve the believer from some serious hazards. Gifford reports the case of a pastor who told the congregation "the story of a woman he knew who missed her plane, only to find that that plane was the one crashed into the Pentagon on 9/11" just to tell people that "what we might see as a setback need not be" (Gifford, "Ritual Use of the Bible," 194).

183. Asamoah-Gyadu, *Contemporary Pentecostal Christianity*, 102.
184. Nouis, "Une hérésie séductrice," 7.
185. Young, "Prosperity Teaching," 7.
186. Bangura, "Abraham's blessings are mine!" 40. Chilenje ("Challenges," 21) notes that in Zambia the prosperity gospel has created divisions and hatred among the congregations, based on their financial income. He deplores that pastors in financially viable congregations refuse to release their surplus to support their colleagues in poorer congregations. Instead, the former continue to encourage the latter to engage in seed sowing in order to receive divine blessings.
187. Young, "Prosperity Teaching," 7.
188. Den Hartog and Mbanze Kasera, "Het welvaartsevangelie in Namibië," 20.

tension between the belief in a positive confession of success and the non-fulfillment of promises made by the anointed spiritual leader is one reason that leads members to keep switching churches.[189] The real danger of the prosperity teaching is evident here and must be tackled.[190] Its overemphasis on success and power excludes any provision for suffering and persecution and makes it impossible to side and "identify with the poor and oppressed in their afflictions."[191]

In other words, an important element of Christian theology is lacking or is partially handled in the prosperity gospel discourses, that is, the centrality of the cross. Pentecostalism overemphasizes the theology of experience, glory, and power and fails to grasp the full meaning of the cross in Christianity.[192] A one-sided approach to the cross presents it as a sym-

---

189. Gifford, "Ritual Use of the Bible," 194.

190. The Evangelical Alliance in the United Kingdom has produced an elaborated evaluation of the beliefs and practices of the prosperity gospel movement. The document indicates that Western Evangelicals have adopted a middle path as to the issues of wealth and health: "Between the mortification of the flesh and the narcissistic cult of the body, between self-indulgence and self-denial, between the covetous pursuit and the monastic repudiation of wealth, the evangelical church in the West has aspired to walk an ideal middle path of right living, responsible stewardship, and moderation in all things . . . We acknowledge with thanksgiving that God is the source of all good things and that he satisfies the material needs of his children. We safeguard the priority of spiritual commitments. We remain an integral part of the modern economy without having to feel that we have become totally indifferent to the plight of the world's poor. We give proper recognition to the fact that the planet cannot sustain a culture of rampant consumerism, and that we must learn to be good managers of God's creation." Evangelicals are equally aware of two major risks this ethos of moderation runs: the restriction of "the diversity and scope of Christian life and witness" by becoming uncomfortable with the more extreme ways of living; and the loss of "the radical nature of discipleship" by easily merging with the modern life of Westerners (Perriman, *Faith, Health and Prosperity*, xvi, xvii). In fact, missiological enterprise entails a constant reflection on the marks of authentic Christian *kerygma*. This mission as a mandate entrusted to the church must be understood in a holistic way. Five main features of mission have been proposed by theologians and preachers from different corners of the world as a good working basis to this end: to proclaim the Good News of the Kingdom (the life and work of Jesus being at the center); to teach, baptize, and nurture new believers; to respond to human needs by a loving service; to seek and transform unjust structures of society; and to strive to safeguard the integrity of creation and sustain and renew the life of the earth (Ross, "Introduction: Taonga," xiv).

191. Anderson, *Introduction to Pentecostalism*, 299.

192. Ibid., 190: "When the Spirit or faith in God's power or healer is seen as a quick-fix solution to human distress and want, there is a tendency to disparage the role of suffering in the lives of those Christian believers whose needs seem to remain unanswered. There are not always instant solutions to life's problems, and spirituality should not be measured in terms of success. People are not only convinced by the triumphs of Christianity but also

bol of power, victory and glory but fails to accommodate sufferings and persecution. The idea that God chose to reveal himself through a humiliated and crucified Messiah continues to be foolishness as Paul would say (1 Cor 1:18). To use Luther's words, the prosperity gospel overemphasizes the *theologia gloriae*, "theology of glory," and discounts the *theologia crucis*, "theology of the cross."[193] For his part, Ellington observes that the theme of the believer's union with Christ as the result of Jesus's death is missing in the prosperity gospel teachings.[194]

The centrality of the cross in the Christian faith tells us that not only God's grace grants victory and power through the resurrected Christ, but also that we receive the same grace to bear hard experiences and yet continue to experience God's goodness (2 Cor 12:9). Tom Smail is right to say that we should not succumb to the impression that our positive confession of biblical promises and our bold prayer can always remove every struggle from our way.[195] The Christian life is all about sharing in Jesus's resurrection and his life and death as well, as notes James Dunn.[196] Young indicates that the type of Christology involved in the prosperity gospel is wanting. The movement misses the incarnation of Jesus by taking his miracles as "a limitless wealth-generating mechanism" rather than as the signs of the irruption of God's kingdom in human history.[197] By doing so the prosperity gospel, perhaps unconsciously, denies the fact that Jesus really shared our humanity and its limitations.

---

by its perseverance in trials. The Spirit is also a gentle dove, a Spirit of humility, patience and meekness, of love, joy and peace. Overemphasizing the power of the Spirit often leads to bitter disappointment and disillusionment when that power is not evidently and immediately manifested. Pentecostal pneumatology should not only provide power where there is lack of it, but should also be able to sustain people through life's tragedies and failures, and especially when there is no visible outward success."

193. McGrath, *Luther's Theology of the Cross*, 149.

194. Ellington, "Is the Prosperity Gospel Biblical?" 37: "Christ's death brings a union between Christ and believers that leads believers to follow Christ's own pattern of life, and that pattern tends to involve suffering and self-renunciation. In its teaching on the Christian life, the prosperity gospel fails to take the cross of Christ into account."

195. Smail, "Cross and the Spirit," 65.

196. Dunn, *Christ and the Spirit*, 205.

197. Young, "Prosperity Teaching," 13.

The theological weaknesses of transactional giving and the conceptualization of faith are evident.[198] I wrote earlier in this chapter that Pentecostals in general use scriptural references selectively and neglect or fail to put them in tension with the rest of the Bible. This gives rise to misinterpretations and misappropriations of biblical passages and concepts. Asamoah-Gyadu points out three main theological drawbacks to this type of giving.[199] For most people blessings always mean material wealth and giving is considered only in quantitative terms. Moreover, this giving does not integrate other fundamental aspects of worship to God. According to Asamoah-Gyadu the most dangerous aspect of transactional giving is that giving turns into "simony, the practice in which Simon the sorcerer sought to buy the power of the Holy Spirit with money," which understanding Peter rejected harshly (Acts 8:20).[200] One can find a kind of correspondence between the prosperity gospel and the purchase of indulgences in view of the afterlife during the pre-Reformation period.[201] We meet here the presupposition that the Roman Catholic Church was entitled to administer the merits of Christ and the saints to relieve someone from temporal punishment for sins in purgatory.[202] The belief that one can pay money to be granted this relaxation of penalties is similar to present-day teaching that one's giving attracts divine blessings. In fact, today's prosperity preachers deceive their hearers "into buying themselves hoped-for release from obstacles in this life."[203] In both cases of indulgences and prosperity teachings, divine favors are mediated by an act of giving money to the church. Ultimately, this giving undermines God's sovereignty to determine humans' destiny. God is reduced to a business partner who has to grant the desires of those who have fulfilled their obligations through tithes, offerings and positive confessions. It is as if human offerings were able to influence God's decisions. Wright concludes that a "gospel" that sells blessings or anything else is in fact a prostituted message that denies the suffering grace which is intrinsic

---

198. Mutombo-Mukendi, "Le nouveau culte," 93–94.
199. Asamoah-Gyadu, *Contemporary Pentecostal Christianity*, 99–100.
200. Ibid., 100.
201. Ibid., 102.
202. Teselle, "Indulgence," 607; Bühler, "Justification," 708.
203. Wright, *Mission*, 280.

to the cross. In his view, as the apostle Paul opposed vehemently those who would carry out the preaching ministry for their profit at Corinth (2 Cor 2:17), today the church should name the prosperity gospel a heresy and reject it outrightly.[204]

In the same vein, the conceptualization of faith by the prosperity gospel is questionable. Referring to the document issued by Le Conseil National des Evangéliques de France, Nouis explains that the prosperity theology has shifted the center of faith from God to human beings who are able to make things happen at their whim by means of prayer.[205] God is therefore fully subordinated to humans' desires. Banda notes that whereas the reformed understanding of faith is theocentric, the prosperity gospel teachings hold an anthropocentric perception of this concept.[206] In the prosperity gospel, God's Spirit and faith are used in a magical way to manipulate God to meet the believer's needs.[207] This confiscation of faith by human agents often leads to pride to the detriment of God's glory.[208] While it is true that Jesus used the power of the word to overcome hindrances to wellbeing, Kalu reminds us that his exhortation to his followers "to seek, knock, and ask" implies that he envisioned "the possibility of delay and the value of perseverance and hope."[209] Paul, who taught much about prayer and faith, writes that he "appealed to the Lord" – he did not command or reclaim healing as a right – when he was tormented by a thorn in the flesh (2 Cor 12:8)[210]. Jesus also challenged the simple understanding of poverty and prosperity. His warnings against the love of money and the world, his ascetic life and insistence on self-denial and sufferings, self-giving and generosity are

---

204. Ibid., 279–280.

205. Nouis, "L'hérésie de la prospérité," 10: "Dieu n'a plus qu'à être au service des décisions de sa créature."

206. Banda, "Dialoguing at 'Mphala'," 64: "On the one hand, the Reformed tradition seems to be more theocentric in its understanding of faith. God stands out as the ultimate actor in the bestowing of faith to humanity, and humanity, in return, answers in faith to what God has done. On the other hand, the prosperity gospel movement appears to be more anthropocentric in its conceptualization of faith. Humanity is primarily the architect of faith, where a person takes the initiative and applies one's efforts in the exercise of faith."

207. Anderson, *Introduction to Pentecostalism*, 218.

208. Young, "Prosperity Teaching," 13.

209. Kalu, *African Pentecostalism*, 258.

210. Mutombo-Mukendi, "Le nouveau culte," 108.

revealing (Mark 8:34–38; 10:17–31; Luke 12:16–21). For Jesus, these experiences are determinant in the life of his disciples.

From the above, it is clear that the prosperity gospel distorts the doctrine of salvation by making success and wellbeing the measure of spirituality and the sign of God's approval. While we need to affirm that Christ's salvation includes spiritual and worldly benefits affecting the whole of human existence, the prosperity gospel preachers should realize that "this is nowhere portrayed in the Bible as an irreversible law of cause and effect."[211] Moreover, the Old Testament texts, mostly from Deuteronomy and the wisdom literature, which teach that God will bless his people as long as they are obedient to him are counter-balanced for instance by the books of Job and Habakkuk which speak of the misfortune and suffering of the righteous.[212] Gifford concedes that the declarative and performative use of the Bible generates hope and that the assurance that "all the biblical promises are yours and must provide incentives in conditions where it is all too easy to give up."[213] However, he cautions that "the improvement possible in Africa simply by believing and persevering must necessarily be limited."[214] Besides the recognition that there is no cause-effect relationship between Christian salvation and material prosperity, believers need to acknowledge and make good use of all the available resources with which they have been entrusted to secure material prosperity and welfare. This teaching is strongly affirmed in the Old Testament which affirms at the same time that prosperity is given by God, as said earlier. In my view, Jesus's parable of the talents also highlights that each believer must use their potential to fructify what is available (Matt 25:14–30). This text should not be restricted to spiritual matters. In the same vein, Paul's exhortations to work with one's hands (1 Thess 2:9) and fight idleness (1 Thess 5:14; 2 Thess 3:6–13) as ways of meeting one's needs need to be taken seriously. Perhaps, the example of Mensa Otabil who,[215] without resorting to any rituals or miracles,

---

211. Anderson, *Introduction to Pentecostalism*, 219, 220.

212. Young, "Prosperity Teaching," 12.

213. Gifford, "Ritual Use of the Bible," 194.

214. Ibid.

215. He is the Senior Pastor of the International Central Gospel Church in Accra, Ghana.

insists on success, motivation, self-reliance and self-confidence, needs to be emulated. He explains that poverty cannot be overcome nor success be realized through faith, gifts, "anointing miracles, rituals, or deliverance," but "by work, through education [...], and through national political reform."[216] So "planning" and "vision" are among the key concepts of his teachings. All this is encapsulated in the notion of empowerment which, in my view, deserves much attention in contemporary African Pentecostalism.

Conclusion

The teaching on health and wealth commonly called the prosperity gospel whose origin can be traced back to early American Pentecostalism in the first half of the twentieth century is one of the predominant features of contemporary African Pentecostalism. This chapter has focused on the aspect of material wealth. Although the prosperity gospel is not a homogeneous movement, I attempted a summary of its common teachings which might occur in prosperity discourses with varying degrees of emphasis depending on individuals and contexts. The atoning death of Christ and the Abrahamic covenant were presented as the two main bases for the belief that God wants all his children to be prosperous in all areas of life. As descendants of Abraham through the mediation of Christ, Christians have the right to claim victory over sin, sickness and poverty available thanks to the redemptive death of Christ. Faith and prayer, the two other principles of the prosperity gospel, are indicated to Christians as the means to acquire that threefold victory.

As is the case in Pentecostalism in general, prayer is expected to carry performative power and serves mainly to dismantle the realm of evil powers thanks to its empowerment by the Holy Spirit. It is most efficient when performed in tongues. This understanding of prayer is informed not only by the biblical notion of evil spirits and demons, but also by the African traditional belief according to which nothing happens by chance and evil powers oppress people and deprive them of every sort of enjoyment in their living. It reveals the paradoxical relationship that exists between Pentecostalism and African cultural heritage. Whereas African Pentecostals

---

216. Gifford, "View," 91, 92.

are generally hostile to African traditional religions, they function with the same cosmological views. I concluded that this dialectic of interaction and confrontation between Pentecostalism and African traditions is an ongoing process characteristic of any cultural context.

The fifth main teaching of the prosperity gospel explored in this chapter is Christian giving which is perceived as a reliable way to financial success. It emphasizes the farming metaphor of sowing and reaping which says that the harvest is proportionate to the amount sowed. In this context, the seed refers to tithes and other types of offerings. The importance of the "seed-harvest" principle among African Pentecostals is explained by the fact that it brings important sums of money needed to run and expand their activities. While tithing Christians expect financial breakthroughs, non-tithing Christians and unbelievers are threatened that God intends to dispossess them of their resources to benefit those who will use them to spread Christian mission. The last major teaching of the prosperity gospel explored in this chapter was the practice of anointing as a route to material wellbeing. Anointing is performed to mediate different forms of positive change in one's endeavors.

The strengths and weaknesses of the prosperity gospel have also been assessed in this chapter. Concerning the positive aspects, I registered its genuine quest for the fullness of life promised by the Scriptures, its audacity to address real-life problems, and its reverential attitude to the Bible as God's Word. On the negative side, I identified some shortcomings. These are mainly moral and social weaknesses in the form of greed, inequalities and unaccountability promoted by the practices of fundraising and the kind of luxurious life attested among most preachers of the movement. Also the insistence on witchcraft as the main cause of human misery generates suspicions and quarrels among people, and prevents them from identifying the genuine causes of their misery in social and political structures. On a theological level, it was observed that the overemphasis on success in the present life fails to integrate suffering and failure in Christian salvation. This is mainly due to a selective reading of the Bible which does not strive to put in tension various biblical texts for a broader understanding and application of their message. Against a one-sided interpretation of the cross, I pleaded for the view that God's grace grants victory and power through the resurrected Christ, but also that we receive the same grace to bear hard experiences and yet continue to experience God's goodness. The recurrent explanation of poverty and other forms of misfortune confronting Christians as a result of failure in faith and in giving to God was seriously challenged. This kind of giving, which can be regarded as a transaction between God and humans, and the view of faith presented above undermine God's sovereignty to determine humans' destiny.

All in all, the prosperity gospel teaches a realized eschatology inasmuch as it promises a full wellbeing in the present.[217] Within this trend of Pentecostalism there is a gradual and significant move from the longing for the second coming of Christ and the end of time to the enjoyment of the fullness of Christian salvation in the believer's present life.[218] While it is important for Christians to affirm that Christ's salvation includes spiritual and worldly benefits affecting the whole of human existence, this is presented nowhere in the Bible in terms of an irreversible law of cause and effect. These promises are truly biblical and believers should take stock of them as Young observes, but it is equally important to allow Scripture to interpret Scripture because "Theology cannot be based on proof texts isolated from the context."[219] In the following and last chapter of this study, I will investigate the use of 2 Corinthians 8–9 in the African context marked by the prosperity gospel.

---

217. Anderson, *Introduction to Pentecostalism*, 301.

218. Young, "Prosperity Teaching," 12. But Zognong (*Le christianisme outragé*, 26–28) writes that preachers of prosperity use apocalyptic teachings to provoke fear among their hearers and manipulate them for financial interests.

219. Young, "Prosperity Teaching," 3.

CHAPTER 7

The Reading of 2 Corinthians 8–9 in Africa Today in Dialogue with the Prosperity Gospel

I come now to the concluding reflections of this research. In the previous chapter I discussed the use of the Bible in today's African Pentecostalism dominated by the prosperity gospel. Now I would like to assess the way 2 Corinthians 8–9 is quoted and employed in the same context. I will limit myself to quotations in written, published works, and will not investigate the oral use of these chapters in sermons. This investigation attempts a learning dialogue with the prosperity gospel over the motives of Christian giving as reflected in 2 Corinthians 8–9. I will discuss the points at which there is tension between my reading of the text, some elements of its interpretation encountered in the reception history, and the perspectives put forward by the prosperity gospel teachers. The purpose of this confrontation of views will be to build up a constructive and well-informed debate.

At this juncture, it is important to ask again the questions I raised in the introduction of this research. To what extent does the concept of grace, which is central to Paul's thoughts in 2 Corinthians 8–9, feature in the prosperity gospel discourses? What are the motivations of Christian giving and the attitude towards possessions according to this trend of theology? To what extent is care for the poor perceptible in the prosperity gospel readings of our passage? These last two questions will enable me to discuss the question raised by most of the authors studied in the reception history of 2 Corinthians 8–9 who see some dangers in material wealth and point to the Lord's voluntary poverty as the guiding principle of Christian generosity. My intent here will be to see if this motive can be promoted in a poverty-ravished continent like Africa; and if possible how to articulate a theology of stewardship and giving. The presence or absence of this motive in contemporary African Pentecostalism will equally be investigated. At the same time, I will reflect on the motive of reward, whether in this life or in the hereafter, whether or not meritorious, and whether or not atoning, encountered in most of the authors studied in the reception history of 2 Corinthians 8–9.

However, I do not pretend to present an exhaustive presentation of the use of 2 Corinthians 8–9 by African preachers of the prosperity gospel. The identification of all the existing literature on this question is a daunting task. This becomes understandable if we keep in mind the fact that the prosperity gospel – and Pentecostalism in general as I observed earlier – is above all an oral tradition. I will thus consider six famous African preachers whose voices are undoubtedly representative of the prosperity gospel movement on the African continent. In addition to Matthew Ashimolowo, Mensa Otabil and Dag Heward-Mills whom I have already mentionned in the previous chapter, these include David O. Oyedepo,[1] Enoch Adejare Adeboye,[2] and Beson Andrew Idahosa.[3] The amount of space allocated to each of them in the following pages is solely decided by the extent to which they refer to 2 Corinthians 8–9 in the literature at our disposal. Morever, the fact that all of them happen to be from West Africa may be explained by the fact that it is one of the parts of the world in which Pentecostalism is flourishing most.[4] Correspondingly, it is from there that we find an important number of Pentecostals who not only preach the prosperity gospel but also write books to disseminate their ideas across the globe. As I noted in chapter five of this study, most of contemporary Pentecostal preachers operate in interdenominational networks and make use of new technologies

---

1. D. O. Oyedepo is the Presiding Bishop of the Living Faith Church Worldwide, with a network of churches all over Nigeria and in most African nations.

2. E. A. Adeboye is the General Overseer of the Redeemed Christian Church of God and President of Christ Redeemer's Ministries in Nigeria. He is a PhD holder in Mathematics and former Senior Lecturer at the University of Lagos.

3. Archbishop B. A. Idahosa was the founder of the Church of God Mission International with headquarters in Benin City, Ghana.

4. Anderson, *Introduction to Pentecostalism*, 9, 43, 131, 127.

and media to reach a larger audience. It is thus possible that there might be exchange of resources and views; hence mutual influences among the prosperity gospel preachers. All this explains the many overlaps and similarities that the reader finds in the teachings, as presented in the next pages.

7.1 Matthew Ashimolowo: 2 Corinthians 9:5–13[5]

7.1.1 The Motivations for Giving

Ashimolowo notes that human nature does not easily accommodate giving. Naturally, he says, human beings strive to get all that they can and keep it for themselves.[6] However, Ashimolowo observes that God provides his blessings to people so that they become a blessing to others. In his words, God "wants us to be a conduct, a pipeline through which He can reach people who are thirsty, broken and in need of being wet with the blessing of God."[7] To illustrate his view Ashimolowo adduces Genesis 12:2 where God told Abraham that he would bless him to make him a blessing to his generation. In Ashomolowo's view, one is ultimately empowered to empower others.

Concerning the motivations for giving, Ashimolowo indicates that Christianity itself proceeded from "the reaching out and giving" demonstrated by God's act of giving his Son according to John 3:16.[8] He explains that giving and receiving is a process that fosters the perpetuation and enjoyment of life. He takes his illustration from the farming domain to say that if one delights in the sweetness and nutritious value of grapes and fails to plant them, these very grapes will just "end with one generation and with one usage."[9] Similarly, he writes that this is true for our body. Besides the fact that it has to produce energy for life, if it "fails to give out wastage, what was enjoyed in eating becomes a painful experience."[10] Other motivations for giving enumerated by Ashimolowo are that God's instruction

---

5. Ashimolowo, *Coming Wealth Transfer*, 187–205.
6. Ibid., 187.
7. Ibid., 188.
8. Ibid., 189.
9. Ibid.
10. Ibid.

about this act pursues our benefit (Luke 6:38; Phil 4:17); it is "an expression of love" and "a mark of maturity";[11] the quality of one's giving is an indication of progress in the likeness with God (Matt 7:11).[12] Ashimolowo adds that giving frees believers from worldly wealth and connects them to God and to other people's blessing.[13] For this, Ashimolowo quotes again Genesis 12:2 about the promise of blessing given to Abraham so that he would become a blessing to others. He opines that by engaging in giving the believer is ultimately involved in God's mission because finances make possible the sending of preachers of the gospel (Rom 10:14–17).[14] He insists on the close relationship between giving to mission enterprises and material blessing:

> Believers need to give because it helps to reach the lost. Those who are committed to the spreading of the gospel must recognize that this great cause would only be possible from the giving of believers. Giving is necessary because it is what establishes financial blessing in the life of a Christian. The force of financial blessing is released as we give our money.[15]

To support this view Ashimolowo quotes 2 Corinthians 9:6: "The point is this: the one who sows sparingly will also reap sparingly, and the one who sows bountifully will also reap bountifully." He explains that "Giving is the planting of a financial seed in order to experience a financial harvest"; it is thus a deposit which increases before God because "the force of financial blessing is released as we give money."[16] It is clear that for Ashimolowo one must give and expect a financial breakthrough of some kind. He emphasizes this idea by quoting Galatians 6:7: "Do not be deceived; God is not mocked, for you reap whatever you sow." He concludes that one's harvest is in fact proportionate to one's level of giving. A little further, Ashimolowo

---

11. Ibid. On page 194 Ashimolowo argues that for this reason Jesus said that "It is more blessed to give than to receive" (Acts 20:35).

12. Ibid., 190–191.

13. Ibid., 191.

14. Ibid., 191–192. He notes that "one of the key reasons God wants us to give is for the establishment and promotion of His kingdom"; failure to do so results in one's "financial barrenness" as well as other family and social problems (ibid., 207, 208–228).

15. Ibid., 192.

16. Ibid., 190, 192.

multiplies Old Testament quotations to say that God established inviolable laws that "seed must produce after its own kind" (Gen 1:11–12) and that "seedtime and harvest time would not cease" (Gen 8:22). He adds that "Our giving is one of the highest forms of sacrificial worship" because we participate "in the process of creating a financial future" as we give.[17] To conclude his reflection on the motivations for giving, Ashimolowo indicates that it is "a principle of prosperity in contradiction to secular opinions, but which provokes the blessings of the Lord."[18] In his view, this is substantiated by Proverb 11:24–25: "Some give freely, yet grow all the richer; others withhold what is due, and only suffer want. A generous person will be enriched, and one who gives water will get water." This contrast consists in the fact that many people think that one's wealth increases by hoarding one's possessions while in fact, he insists, blessings come by releasing what one possesses.[19] The last reason for giving according to Ashimolowo is that it "honours God as the Lord of all" and at the same time establishes the covenant between the believer and God (1 Chr 29:10–14, 16).

7.1.2 The Kinds of Offerings and Ways of Giving

Ashimolowo shows that believers are expected to give freewill offerings because they participate in the determination of the amount to be given. He explains that freewill offerings flow from a heart of gratitude for the benefits received from God, and establish fellowship with him.[20] Another type of offering that Christians should give mentioned by Ashimolowo is what he calls "a vow or pledges," that is to say a commitment that one makes "to serve the Lord with a special offering, either prior to or after a breakthrough."[21] Concerning the way the duty of giving to God needs to be done, he indicates that it must be a continuous practice done with love and desire to please God and bless others (1 Cor 13:3; 2 Sam 24:24). It is in this context that Ashimolowo quotes 2 Corinthians 9:5–13 extensively in order to instruct that "It is not the level of giving alone that is important;

---

17. Ibid., 193.
18. Ibid.
19. Ibid., 193–194.
20. Ibid., 195, 196.
21. Ibid., 199.

it is the attitude of the giver that is paramount."[22] He explains that "our offerings stay on earth while our attitude is what God receives."[23] He finds that it is for this reason that Paul elaborates on the true nature of giving in this passage. Ashimolowo understands that the purpose of one's generosity "is defeated and the blessing hindered" if giving is done "outside a heart of love, generosity and cheerfulness."[24] He continues by suggesting that one should carefully reflect on and plan one's giving (1 Cor 16:2). Ashimolowo quotes Luke 6:38 to underscore again that "the quality and quantity of your seed determines the quality and quantity of your harvest. Bear in mind that once you set the percentage or level of giving, you have already fixed the level of blessing that will flow to you."[25] Whereas he intimates that the believer must give whatever the circumstances are, Ashimolowo tempers his tone and submits that one's offering should be according to one's means.

> Certainly God never wants a person to go beyond their ability in the giving of their offering. It is no use giving and jeopardizing the happiness of the giver, but make sure that you never come before the Lord empty handed.[26]

Ashimolowo roots his view in 2 Corinthians 9:7: "Each of you must give as you have made up your mind, not reluctantly or under compulsion, for God loves a cheerful giver." He warns that although fasting, praying and prophesying are commendable actions in Christian life, they cannot replace the act of giving that he depicts as an "act of covenant."[27] Similarly, he admonishes believers not to go before the Lord empty handed.

To sum up, one surmises that according to Ashimolowo the most important motivation for giving is the expectation of tangible returns from God, especially financial prosperity. This is clear from the summary that he provides at the short section in which he answers the question as to why we should give.

---

22. Ibid., 202.
23. Ibid., 203.
24. Ibid., 202.
25. Ibid., 203.
26. Ibid., 204.
27. Ibid.

It opens the windows of heaven, it rebukes every financial devourer, and it stops them dead in their tracks. Giving becomes your powerful seed for a future great harvest. It is not an act that is carried out flippantly, but must be thought through and prayerfully approached. It is the most powerful principle of God designed to be a blessing to both the giver and the recipient. The natural mind may not understand it – it cannot see how letting go will lead to receiving abundance. However, God's Word stands that it is the one who scatters that increases.[28]

It turns out that in the above-mentioned quotation Ashimolowo's reference to the opening of "the windows of heaven" and the "financial devourer" hints at the passage of Malachi 3:10–11 which speaks explicitly of material blessings as a result of faithful tithing. In the prosperity gospel terminology, the term "harvest" is the equivalent of breakthrough and may indicate money, a job, promotion, good health, children and any other form of success.[29] The traditional African traditions and Pentecostal beliefs agree that such devourers comprise "witches and wizards, envious relatives, demons, and those with evil supernatural abilities to derail others in their financial affairs and other progress in life."[30]

It is surprising that Ahimolowo never quotes 2 Corinthians 8–9 when he deals with giving for philanthropic purposes.[31] It is also questionable whether giving as it is presented by Ashimolowo can rightly be called "one of the highest forms of sacrificial worship" while one is encouraged to give as a kind of investment that will bring sure increase; in other words, a way to ensure one's financial future.[32]

---

28. Ibid., 194–195.
29. Asamoah-Gyadu, *Contemporary Pentecostal Christianity*, 83.
30. Ibid., 89. He notes that the pervasive traditional belief in witchcraft produces many stories "about money mysteriously disappearing from wallets, money safes, and closets, for which people seek supernatural intervention, some from shrine priests and others from deliverance Pentecostal pastors. When Christians are faithful in their tithing, God insulates them and their endeavours from devourers, so that they can prosper in health and wealth."
31. Ashimolowo, *Coming Wealth Transfer*, 222–228.
32. Ibid., 193.

7.2 Mensa Otabil: The Principles of Productivity and Multiplication

In his *Four Laws of Productivity: God's Foundation for Living*, Otabil illustrates his teaching by quoting 2 Corinthians 9:10: "He who supplies seed to the sower and bread for food will supply and multiply your seed for sowing and increase the harvest of your righteousness." Otabil argues that God our Creator "purposively placed within the earth everything necessary for life, health and happiness, and then provided us with the mental and intellectual ability to maximize and efficiently utilize these resources."[33] To enable humans to achieve this quality of life, Otabil notes, God put in place some "laws and principles" to regulate the relationship between "creation and the Creator," violation of which results in "lack, poverty, depression and recession."[34] These laws indicated by Otabil encompass productivity, multiplication, replenishment, and the submission of creation. Explaining the law of productivity, he writes that whoever "desires to progress in life must learn to operate" this principle.[35] Here he employs Paul's statement in 2 Corinthians 9:10 quoted above. He writes that God sees to it that he provides each and every one with a seed to be fructified. For Otabil, the problem is that one fails to discover one's seed and keeps staring at and envying other people's wealth. He indicates that the seed entrusted to each individual is worthier than wealth and that seeds are diverse. One may receive a seed of intellectual work, another that of manual work or other kinds of talent. Otabil opines that since the seed in this context means "the gift" God freely placed in each individual, it needs to be prayed for and discerned for a good use.[36] He esteems that the parable of the talents (Matt 25:14–28) is all about this principle of multiplication.[37] While he recognizes that some appear to be "multi-gifted," Otabil warns that they end up in confusion and even in poverty because they lack focus.[38]

---

33. Otabil, *Four Laws of Productivity*, 2.
34. Ibid., 2, 3.
35. Ibid., 26.
36. Ibid., 26–29.
37. Ibid., 53.
38. Ibid., 37–42.

Otabil quotes again 2 Corinthians 9:10 to illustrate his second principle, that of multiplication.[39] Here multiplication is explained as a second step which follows that of production of our initial "masterpieces" and consists in the expansion of our abilities. In Otabil's view, God's principles function in all areas of human life.[40] It is remarkable that his understanding of God-given talents entrusted to each individual is more related to skills than to material possessions. Otabil's views here can promote empowerment of believers since they insist on the ethics of responsibility.

7.3 Dag Heward-Mills: The Law of Sowing and Reaping

7.3.1 Tithing: 2 Corinthians 8:7

As he presents twenty spiritual problems which deflect people from paying their tithes, Heward-Mills uses 2 Corinthians 8:7 to explain one of them: "People do not pay tithes because they only obey sections of the Word of God."[41] In 2 Corinthians 8:7 Paul writes: "Now as you excel in everything – in faith, in speech, in knowledge, in utmost eagerness, and in our love for you – so we want you to excel also in this generous undertaking." Here Paul invokes the Corinthians' excellence in spiritual matters to exhort them to a similar performance with regard to the collection for the poor Christians in Jerusalem. For Heward-Mills, this verse serves as an exhortation to tithing, which practice he considers the major key to prosperity.[42] He understands it as the "most basic principle of sowing and reaping" which leads God

---

39. Ibid., 46.
40. Ibid., 49–52.
41. Heward-Mills, *Why Non-tithing Christians*, 31.
42. Ibid., 6–7. Further, he also explains ten reasons why God instituted the tithe: a way to express gratitude to God, a means for God's people to remember where they were saved from, a prayer of thanksgiving, an opportunity to allow believers to enjoy the remaining ninety percent of one's income, a source of payment for God's ministers, a way to help the needy and helpless, to get resources to respond to some other secular needs, a way to bless his people, a test of obedience (ibid., 71–82). Coming back to tithing as a route to prosperity, Heward-Mills writes that God ordained this practice "to create a peculiar and unusual group of prosperous and blessed people on the earth." He concludes that God's intention has been embodied in the Jewish people's history.

to rebuke one's prosperity devourer.[43] Heward-Mills quotes Malachi 3:11 to emphasize this function, and in his opinion the greatest blessing, of tithes. Without explaining in what these unchecked devourers consist, he indicates that they are behind the failure of individuals and nations who receive important amounts of money but remain poor. Although Heward-Mills recognizes the value of hard work, he explains that these efforts fail if the individual does not tithe faithfully since tithing is the major key to prosperity.[44]

It is interesting to note that Heward-Mills also refers to 1 Corinthians 16:1–2 in his teaching on tithes. Although this quotation is extraneous to the main text studied in this research, it is worth mentioning since it equally deals with Paul's collection: "Now concerning the collection for the saints: you should follow the directions I gave to the churches of Galatia. On the first day of every week, each of you is to put aside and save whatever extra you earn, so that collections need not be taken when I come." Heward-Mills argues that some people fail to tithe since "they think it is an Old Testament law and does not apply to them."[45] As if the above quotations from Paul were not convincing, Heward-Mills admits that instructions on tithing are mostly found in the Old Testament. Then he invokes additional scriptural evidence to prove that there exists continuity between both Testaments as far as spiritual and doctrinal resources are concerned. He concludes that *"Tithing was before the Law, during the Law and after the Law!"*[46]

7.3.2 How to Activate the Principle of Sowing and Reaping: 2 Corinthians 9:6–10

Heward-Mills discusses the ways Christians can activate the law of sowing and reaping. After explaining that life on earth in its various manifestations is perpetuated by "the miracle of the seed," he affirms that even money,

---

43. Ibid., 3–5. In his view, once such devourers are rebuked "it takes just a little to make you a rich person. When you are without this blessing, you will seek better jobs and earn more money but always fail to become rich. When the devourer is rebuked, you may not earn that much but your bucket will fill quickly and soon begin to overflow" (ibid., 4).

44. Ibid., 6–7.

45. Ibid., 44.

46. Ibid., 45 (Italics in original).

though inanimate, "contains the mysterious power of seed."[47] He finds support in Paul's exhortation in 2 Corinthians 9:6–10:

> The point is this: the one who sows sparingly will also reap sparingly, and the one who sows bountifully will also reap bountifully. Each of you must give as you have made up your mind, not reluctantly or under compulsion, for God loves a cheerful giver. And God is able to provide you with every blessing in abundance, so that by always having enough of everything, you may share abundantly in every good work. As it is written, "He scatters abroad, he gives to the poor; his righteousness endures forever." He who supplies seed to the sower and bread for food will supply and multiply your seed for sowing and increase the harvest of your righteousness.

Heward-Mills subsequently makes a comment for application. He indicates that whenever we pay our tithes we are sowing a seed in God's house which will activate "the laws of sowing seeds and reaping harvest" and at the same time we are inadvertently creating wealth for ourselves.[48] Among the fifteen laws of sowing and harvesting which are set in motion by tithing, there are two which deserve mention here since Heward-Mills illustrates them with a scriptural proof from 2 Corinthians 8–9. The first principle says that "You must plant LARGE AMOUNTS OF SEED."[49] Heward-Mills explains that the reason for this is that in any entrepreneurial activity there must be some losses.[50] 2 Corinthians 9:6 is quoted as a scriptural authority to support this reasoning. The Bible version that he uses here does not favor Paul's metaphorical language: "But remember this – if you give little, you will get little. A farmer who plants just a few seeds will get only a small crop, but if he plants much, he will reap much."[51] Drawing

---

47. Ibid., 116.
48. Ibid.
49. Ibid., 118 (Upper-case letters in original).
50. Ibid., 119.
51. The Living Bible (TLB). As its editors indicate, "The Living Bible is a paraphrase of the Old and New Testaments. Its purpose is to say as exactly as possible what the writers of the Scriptures meant, and to say it simply, expanding where necessary for a clear understanding by the modern reader" (https://www.biblegateway.com/versions/The-Living-Bible-TLB/).

upon the parable of the sower in Mark and Matthew, Heward-Mills explains the necessity of sowing a big amount. In his view, apart from the fact that some seeds will never develop, many others will be lost.[52] He resorts to the analogy with a man's reproductive capabilities. He explains that a man's sperms number millions for the simple reason that most of them will be lost before they reach the right ground. He goes on to show that if these sperms are fewer than forty million, it will be very difficult for one to cause a pregnancy. These biological remarks enable Heward-Mills to reinforce his teaching on faithful tithing:

> This truth means that some of the offerings you give will be lost as seed that falls by the wayside. There is no way to determine which one will be lost and which one will fall onto good ground. That is why you have to keep on sowing because some of your seeds will be lost anyway. Coming to church many times and being given many opportunities to give your tithes and offerings will definitely increase your chances of reaping a harvest.[53]

The second law that Heward-Mills justifies with a reference to 2 Corinthians 8–9 reads: "USE SOME of your harvest AS A SEED."[54] Again he prefers The Living Bible to better express his teaching on tithing. Moreover, he applies capital letters to highlight the point he is making (i.e. tithing as planting a seed): "For God, who gives seed to the farmer TO PLANT, and later on good crops to harvest and eat, will give you more and more SEED TO PLANT and will make it grow so that you can give away more and more fruit from your harvest." Heward-Mills urges his readers to remember to pay their tithes when the blessings come since that is the first thing to do as a way to render honor to God. Failure to do so, he warns, will definitely bring poverty in the future.[55] Heward-Mills continues his teaching on tithing by answering the question of the ineffectiveness of tithes for some people. Having explained that tithes will yield the expected

---

52. Heward-Mills, *Why Non-tithing Christians*, 120.
53. Ibid., 119.
54. Ibid., 124 (Capital letters in original).
55. Ibid., 125.

results only if they are combined with obedience in other areas of Christian life, he identifies ten reasons why tithes fail to work for some people.[56] For Heward-Mills, the tithe is a peculiar offering and that one of the reasons why it becomes ineffective is when it is not acceptable. He defines three reasons that cause an offering to be so: "the unrighteous life of the giver, the secret worship of idols and thirdly not having been given in proportion to what we received."[57] It is for the third cause that 2 Corinthians 8:12 is adduced as a proof-text. Heward-Mills' view is that Paul's teaching in this verse is that "God always looks at what you have before assessing what you have brought to Him."[58]

It is interesting to note that Paul's exhortations on the collection become an important scriptural authority for Heward-Mills to teach tithing. I recall here that in my exegetical analysis of 2 Corinthians 8:15, I noted that Paul does not refer either to the practice of tithing or to other fixed regulations on giving enunciated in the Old Testament to convince the Corinthians to give their contributions for his collection. I suggested that this omission probably indicates that he holds to the principle of the voluntary character of Christian giving. As one reads Heward-Mills's arguments, one gets the sense that tithing functions in a quasi-magical manner to bring about divine blessings.

7.4 David O. Oyedepo

In his *Covenant Wealth*, Oyedepo points out that our salvation is about deliverance from both sin and any other form of destruction connected to it. He asserts that we are thus "called into a life of abundance and glory, not degradation and shame."[59] After discussing the misconceptions on wealth and the distinction between worldly possessions and wealth proceeding from the kingdom of God, Oyedepo explains the purpose of the latter. In his view, "wealth in the kingdom" or "covenant wealth," as he calls it, is the

---

56. Ibid., 165–173.
57. Ibid., 168.
58. Ibid., 170.
59. Oyedepo, *Covenant Wealth*, 6.

"proof of our redemption."[60] To support this idea he quotes 2 Corinthians 8:9: "For you know the generous act of our Lord Jesus Christ, that though he was rich, yet for your sakes he became poor, so that by his poverty you might become rich." He writes that after the fall of Adam, poverty is one of the main "consequences of sin" and that the coming of Jesus into the world meant "to take us into glory, thereby making wealth a part of our redemptive package."[61] Oyedepo justifies this interpretation by the fact that through Jesus's resurrection believers were "raised up with Him and are seated together with Him in heavenly places" where there exists no "poor place."[62] Elsewhere Oyedepo expresses the same view and illustrates it by a quotation from Ephesians 2:6 which explicitly says that God has "raised us up with him [Jesus] and seated us with him in the heavenly places in Christ Jesus."[63] He contends that since "God is the Most High" it is impossible to be his son and resemble him when you live with failures. Success in everything is the birthright and destiny of born-again Christians thanks to Jesus's redemptive work. But he insists that Christians need to discover God's secrets to succeed in whatever they undertake. It is remarkable that Oyedepo dwells much on the principles of self-discipline, sense of duty and responsibility, hard work as well as positive thinking and confession rather than on giving as a miraculous route to success and material prosperity.

The interpretation of Paul's statements presented above by Oyedepo calls for some comments. In the third chapter of this study, I argued that Jesus's self-impoverishment indicates his incarnation and earthly life as a whole. I noted that the richness and poverty of Christ do not denote

---

60. Ibid., 21, 26, 35.

61. Ibid., 36.

62. Ibid., 37.

63. Oyedepo, *Exploring the Secrets of Success*, 5, 227. Among other texts he cites the parable of the talents to demonstrate that every born-again Christian has been provided with a talent, an ability to be used profitably. After quoting Luke 6:38 about reciprocal giving, he criticizes those believers who have wrongly "thought that giving is the only thing to do to become financially successful." While he reiterates that God is faithful and that he will assuredly fulfill his promises to those who give, he pleads for a balance between giving and hard work: "It is the blessing of the Lord that maketh rich, that is why by strength shall no man prevail. So, giving is the foundation for the ultimate result you get through working" (158, 159, 162). Oyedepo also teaches about care for the poor but in this respect he does not refer to 2 Cor at all. The resources used are Ps 41:1–3; Prov 21:13; 19:17; Ps 41:1–3; Mark 14:7; etc.

material wealth and destitution but the renunciation of heavenly glory to assume the human condition. As for his making the Corinthians rich, I understood that Jesus's redemptive work, which is an act of divine grace, has benefitted believers (Eph 3:8). Paul says that he chose to live as a poor person, working with his hands for subsistence (1 Cor 4:11; Phil 4:11–12; 2 Cor 11:9; 1 Thess 2:9; 2 Thess 3:7–8; Acts 18:3; 20:34) and that through his ministry the Corinthians have been enriched (1 Cor 1:5). In my view, there can be no doubt that God's salvation includes worldly things that we need in order to live. However, I am tempted to say that 2 Corinthians 8:9 is not well suited to support this truth. Above all, the view that financial prosperity is the proof of our redemption reduces Christian salvation to material things. This can hardly be supported by a careful reading of the Scriptures.

Another difficulty raised by Oyedepo's interpretation is the literal and unilateral affirmation that believers have been raised and seated in heaven with the resurrected Jesus. Such a reading seems to suggest that the believer is no longer affected by any earthly constraints and contingencies. In my understanding, Paul's view is that the believers' life is now guided by new principles different from those of this world in its alienation from God. The evangelist John, who is the champion of the realized eschatology, speaks of this ambivalent life of Jesus's followers. They are in the world but they do not belong to it. It is remarkable that the evangelist insists that Jesus said clearly that he was not asking his Father to take his disciples out of the world, but rather to protect them against the devil, and cause them to commit themselves to unity and sanctification (John 17:9–20). This implies that the disciples, like their fellow humans, will have to face the challenges of everyday life including poverty.

7.5 Enoch Adejare Adeboye

Among Adeboye's spiritual publications I will consider *The Ultimate Financial Breakthrough* in which he refers to 2 Corinthians 8–9. Against a backdrop of the general affirmation that it is God's intention to provide his children with financial success, Adeboye sets out to lead the reader to the discovery of the secrets of wealth beyond expectations.[64] He states that the story of the widow of Zarephath offers seven principles for such a quick move. He goes on to explain that this widow used her little flour and oil to make a meal for the prophet Elijah and that by doing so she experienced abundance for her future living. For the purpose of this study I will investigate one principle, the only one which is connected to 2 Corinthians 8–9: "Sow When It is Practically Difficult To Do So."[65] Adeboye clarifies that like the widow whose offering is commended by Jesus in Mark 12:41–44, the one of Zarephath (1 Kgs 17:7–16) sowed the last provision she had at a time when it looked "exceptionally inconvenient for her."[66] He infers that the level of giving is not determined by what one gives but by what is left after giving. Then he writes that this sacrificial giving is reflected in the Macedonian Christians who gave to Paul's collection in spite of their extreme poverty (2 Cor 8:2–3).[67] From the quotation of this passage Adeboye carries on with an actualizing *parenesis*:

> Even if you are poor today, God can make you richer than the richest man in your community. If you put into practice the type of giving exemplified by the widow, you can give your way to prosperity by offering the type of gifts which God delights in. If widows can give all that they have, why do people who are in a better financial state not give more? God is looking for sacrificial givers: – those who will give even when it is not convenient.[68]

He supplements this call to sacrificial giving by quoting Paul when he asks the Corinthians to give as one has decided and with joy (2 Cor 9:7). This quotation allows Adeboye to add that if one wants "to attract God's attention with giving," one should give when it seems inconvenient because God will bless such a giver.[69] Further he insists that the only reason that

---

64. Adeboye, *Ultimate Financial Breakthrough*, 11.
65. Ibid., 13 (Capital letters in original).
66. Ibid., 14.
67. Here Adeboye writes by mistake that it is the Corinthians who gave out of deep poverty.
68. Adeboye, *Ultimate Financial Breakthrough*, 15.
69. Ibid., 15, 16.

led God to choose this widow of Zarephath among many others was "the act of giving."[70]

Some remarks on Adeboye's ways of reading Paul deserve mention here. First, it is difficult to know whether the Macedonian Christians later rose out of their poverty as a result of their donation to Paul's collection. Unlike the widow of Zarephath who was assured by God through his prophet that her "jar of meal will not be emptied and the jug of oil will not fail until the day that the LORD sends rain on the earth," nothing indicates that the Macedonians participated in the collection with the expectation that they would experience financial breakthroughs in return. Second, we can also wonder how to reconcile Paul's affirmation that the Macedonian Christians were still poor though they had committed their lives to the Lord, and Adeboye's view that God's will is to pour financial prosperity upon his children. Should we speculate that God waited until the Macedonians got involved in the collection to bless them materially, if in fact this happened? All these observations demonstrate that the causal relationship between giving and material wealth is more problematic than it appears even though there might be numerous biblical references to support it. Above all, the type of giving defended by Adeboye in this book can hardly be termed sacrificial because by giving one anticipates some breakthroughs.[71] Rather, it is perhaps better to call it "transactional giving" to use Asamoah-Gyadu's expression.[72]

7.6 Benson Andrew Idahosa

In this section I consider Idahosa's book entitled *I Choose to Change*. In the foreword, Colin Urquhart contends that "No subject can be sure to cause so much contention among Christians today as that of prosperity," and that it is clearly true that God wants his children to experience prosperity. He explains that this truth is plainly taught in the Old Testament and that Jesus Christ came to manifest God's kingdom on earth.[73] Urquhart denies

---

70. Ibid., 15, 69.
71. Ibid., 53–54.
72. Asamoah-Gyadu, *Contemporary Pentecostal Christianity*, 79.
73. Urquhart, "Foreword," 7.

that Idahosa teaches "a prosperity gospel" because he does not propose to the reader a "get rich quick" formula. He maintains that Idahosa "expounds the biblical truth that prosperity is an aspect of God's purpose for His children and is to be seen alongside other aspects of His plan."[74]

Idahosa starts his book with the affirmation "GOD'S WEALTH IS YOURS"[75] and subsequently quotes 2 Corinthians 9:11: "You will be enriched in every way for your great generosity, which will produce thanksgiving to God through us."[76] After testifying that God changed his attitude to success and prosperity, Idahosa deplores that many Christians continue to live in "ignorance, unbelief and confusion" on this matter.[77] He also emphasizes that it is not God's will that Christians live in sin, guilt, dispossession, and failure.[78] Rather, Idahosa affirms, God's salvation meets spiritual, physical and material needs of humans. In his view, it only takes a born-again Christian to claim God's "promises and act upon them by faith."[79] He argues that this is possible through Christ's victory over death, poverty, fear, failure and the like. It is worth noting that Idahosa explains that God's intention to bless and make his children prosper stands as long as their motives are right. He writes that the motive is right when we desire to have *"plenty and left over"* to contribute to the advancement of God's work on earth. Idahosa supports his assertion by quoting 2 Corinthians 9:8, 10–11 from The Living Bible.

> God is able to make it up to you by giving you everything you need and more so that there will not only be enough for your own needs but plenty left over to give joyfully to others . . .[10] For God, who gives seed to the farmer to plant, and later on good crops to harvest and eat, will give you more and more seed to plant and will make it grow so that you can give away more and more fruit from your harvest.[11] Yes, God will give you much so that you can give away much, and when we take

---

74. Ibid.
75. Idahosa, *I Choose to Change* (Capitals in original).
76. Ibid., 9.
77. Ibid.
78. Ibid.
79. Ibid., 10.

your gifts to those who need them they will break out into thanksgiving and praise to God for your help.

In Idahosa's view, Paul's statement that God will "supply all your needs" implies that "He must provide money."[80] He adds that God will surely grant Christians money because they need it both to meet their own needs and expand his work on earth. He indicates that Christians have only to learn the divine secret about financial, spiritual and physical blessings.[81] Referring to John 10:10, Idahosa states that the Christian experience is all about "superabundance, beginning with salvation of the soul" because everything that God accomplishes is on a grand scale.[82]

As I contended earlier, Christian life is made of ups and downs. The view that failures, losses and sufferings have no place in God's salvation neglects a fundamental truth of biblical theology, namely the cross. I am aware that one might respond that the cross was Christ's way to victory. But Jesus's sayings that his followers will have to suffer and be persecuted like their Master or that each of them must take up their cross (Mark 8:34–35; 10:38–39) contradict this view. Similarly, Paul's testimonies about the hardships of apostleship rule out that unilateral interpretation of the cross in terms of success (2 Cor 1; 4; 6; 12).[83] In other words, the notions of power, authority and success need to be redefined. Instead of seeing them solely in a perspective of triumphal journey from victory to victory, it is germane to integrate the view of service and perseverance. This is what Jesus taught his disciples about the perception of greatness. When James and John asked to be seated on either side of Jesus's throne (Mark 10:37) – this request was

---

80. Ibid., 11, 113. On page 69 he writes that giving is directed to God, Christians, and the poor (Mal 3:10; Rom 12:13; Prov 19:17). However, it is surprising that no reference is made to Paul's collection which is specifically a donation to the poor Christians in Jerusalem.

81. Idahosa does not restrict his teaching to giving. He strongly believes that each believer is a steward and that they have been granted seeds to plant. However, Idahosa does not relate this teaching to 2 Cor 8–9. The seeds he mentions include "soil to cultivate, oceans to sail, mountains to scale, deserts to conquer, rivers to harness, minerals to mine and forests to utilize," as well as "brain and spirit with which to receive His creative ideas" (Idahosa, *I Choose to Change*, 16).

82. Ibid., 61.

83. Mutombo-Mukendi ("Le nouveau culte," 98, 122) insists that suffering is part of human condition in general and of Christianity in particular. He concludes that Christianity without suffering is not Christianity.

formulated by their mother according to Matt 20:20–21 – they were told by their Master that whoever wanted to be great among others had to be their servant (Mark 10:43–45). But this does not mean that he denied that there would be leaders in a Christian community. Rather, he challenged the disciples to have a different understanding of authority and power since he first indicated to them how these notions were abused among the Gentiles (Mark 10:42). In this new perception of greatness, leaders should recognize that they do not create authority and power, but that they receive them from God to serve others for the glory of the one who granted them to his human agents. It is only in this way that God's power can be a weapon against the evil for Christian believers.

Moreover, it is hard to accept Idahosa's tendency to give the impression that in 2 Corinthians 9:8, 10–11 God's provision is equated with money. In my view, Paul says in 2 Corinthians 9:11 that the Corinthians will be constantly enriched, and that this enrichment encompasses both economic and spiritual blessings just as God's grace in 2 Corinthians 9:8a encapsulates both dimensions of God's provision. Nevertheless, Idahosa's interpretation which grasps the close relationship between wealth and mission in Paul's instruction about the collection deserves some recognition. I argued that Paul understands God's purpose in enriching the Corinthians to be that they might demonstrate every sort of generosity; that they may abound in every good work. This is another way of saying that the believers' possessions must participate in the promotion of their missionary calling in the world.

7.7 Discussion and Evaluation

A constructive discussion with the prosperity gospel in sub-Saharan Africa requires the recapitulation of the exegetical conclusions drawn from 2 Corinthians 8–9 in the third chapter of this study. It was pointed out that the notion of χάρις is central to Paul's thought in the conceptualization of his collection. The Macedonians' enthusiastic giving is perceived by Paul as triggered by God's χάρις and as an example to be emulated by the Corinthians. In the same vein, the self-impoverishment of Jesus Christ for the enrichment of believers is also depicted as the χάρις, grace of our Lord Jesus Christ, his generous act which enriched the Corinthians.

The collection is termed χάρις, a generous undertaking, a generous gift. Contributing to it is also χάρις, a privilege. It is also said that God is able to provide joyful givers with πᾶσαν χάριν, material and spiritual resources. So, serving the saints through the collection is an expression of God's χάρις in the life of a believer; it is an aspect of righteousness on the part of the latter. Christian believers in Jerusalem are expected to return χάρις, gratitude in terms of thanksgivings to God and intercessional prayers on behalf of the Corinthians. In the same breath, Paul invites the Corinthians and other Achaean churches to join him in worship to God for his surpassing gift of salvation, as he himself expressed χάρις to him for enabling Titus to serve among the Corinthians.

Five motivations were drawn from 2 Corinthians 8–9: Divine grace triggers true giving; imitation of the Lord Jesus Christ in his self-impoverishment to benefit Christians; the sense of solidarity and interdependence among believers; the belief that God will continue to provide for the needs of joyful givers and the conviction that one's giving creates a dynamic fellowship in which the material needs of the poor are met and the latter long to interact with their benefactors and address their gratitude to God. Therefore, God and others are put at the center of the act of giving. While the notion of αὐτάρκεια, sufficiency does not aim at self-enjoyment but to constantly serving those in need, divine provisions to the giver are not a reward because even the initial resources needed to serve the needy stem from God.

Concerning the way of giving, Paul wants the Corinthians not to misinterpret his commendation of the Macedonians who gave beyond their means, as if he was expecting the former to do the same. He tells them that one must decide what one will give and this according to one's ability.

In the following pages of this research, the dialogue with the prosperity gospel in sub-Saharan Africa over the motivations of Christian generosity in light of 2 Corinthians 8–9 will be carried out in a constant interaction with the long tradition of the hermeneutics of 2 Corinthians 8–9 from late Antiquity to the Reformation time. However, this discussion cannot cover all the points highlighted in the previous paragraph simply because I have been analyzing isolated quotations and not running commentaries by the prosperity preachers. Therefore, the following points will occupy my attention:

- The concept of grace in the hermeneutics of 2 Corinthians 8–9
- The farming metaphor of sowing and reaping
- The ways of giving and care for the poor
- Christian κοινωνία
- The Lord's voluntary poverty and attitude to material possessions
- A theology of stewardship and giving.

7.7.1 The Concept of Grace in the Hermeneutics of 2 Corinthians 8–9

The concept of grace, which captured the attention of John Chrysostom, Theodoret of Cyrus, Ambrosiaster, Thomas Aquinas and Calvin, is hardly present in the preachers of prosperity I studied. The Macedonians' giving to the collection is an act of grace. Chrysostom and Theodoret emphasize this by indicating that cooperation between divine grace and human will drives humans to achieve good deeds. Adeboye refers to the Macedonian Christians sacrificial giving (2 Cor 8:2–3) as he expounds his teaching on the principle of seed sowing. But I contended that his interpretation gives to the reader the impression that the Macedonians gave their contributions in the hope that they would be rewarded financially, which is not what Paul says. I also showed that these Christians who were commended by Paul were poor. This contradicts the prosperity gospel principle according to which being poor implies being outside God's will because financial prosperity is a part of our redemption.

Coming back to the concept of grace, one can speculate that Paul's idea that the Macedonians had been given the grace to take part in the collection is implicitly alluded to by the prosperity gospel teachers through their concept of seed. They explain that the seed may mean any talent or material things entrusted to every believer and that needs to be fructified. Correspondingly, Heward-Mills mentions even the "tithing talent" that one needs to use according to God's will for the sake of the kingdom of God.[84] However, these preachers do not explicitly refer to God's grace, whereas Paul does so.

---

84. Heward-Mills, *Why Non-tithing Christians*, 48.

7.7.2 The Farming Metaphor of Sowing and Reaping

Through the analogy with sowing and reaping in 2 Corinthians 9:6–11, Paul expresses one aspect of Jewish beliefs, the retributive justice of God. God reciprocates the good deed accomplished by the faithful. Paul presents it as one of the motivations for the Corinthians to complete their contributions to the collection. This belief in recompense for one's giving is picked up with varying levels of emphasis by the church fathers we encountered in this research. Thomas Aquinas and Calvin also feel comfortable with it. However, there are also sharp discrepancies in the nature of reward. Although John Chrysostom admits that God takes care of the faithful giver – and he urges believers to seek only what is necessary for their life – he insists that one's wealth is multiplied in heaven. Theodoret refers to reward with much sobriety and clarity. He points out that God is the provider for the believers and thus he will continue to grant them what meets their daily needs. He recognizes that the giver should expect in the present life to receive spiritual benefits and possible reciprocation of the assistance given out as alms. Ambrosiaster for his part writes that those who assist the needy in accordance with God's will receive a double reward for their sowing. He means here that these givers have their resources multiplied so that they continue to practice good deeds; and ultimately they will receive the reward from God in the world to come. Thomas Aquinas explains that generous giving increases one's merits for divine recompense which covers both spiritual things and material possessions. Calvin rejects the idea that our giving to the needy should be stimulated by the hope of any kind of worldly returns as a way of compensation since God's blessing is much more precious than earthly possessions. But he strongly defends the view that believers certainly receive benefits in proportion to one's giving. Calvin points out that the giver's harvest comprises both spiritual rewards of eternal life and material blessings that God bestows upon generous people so that they may continue to assist the needy.

Interestingly enough, the principle that God reciprocates Christian giving is very much at home among the prosperity gospel circles. However, it is remarkable that the prosperity gospel preachers insist on one aspect of God's reciprocation. It is constantly said that the believer's offering, generally referred to as a seed, will be multiplied. The principle of proportionality between what is given and the returns to be expected is strongly emphasized. From the parable of the sower, for instance, Adeboye formulates an interesting principle suggesting that one has to sow on good ground. He explains that the produce of the seed in the good soil is exemplified in the believers' lives as follows: the thirtyfold return is gained by those who give to the members of their church; the sixtyfold return is secured when one gives to a servant (man or woman) of God; whereas the hundredfold return is achieved when an offering is directed to the high priest, also called the head of the sons of the prophets (the highest church leader?)[85] This restriction of God's reward to material wealth in the present life is a development of realized eschatology characteristic of some forms of Pentecostalism in Africa as notes Anderson.[86] In the previous chapter, I remarked that there is a perceptible move from the longing for the return of Christ and the end of time to the enjoyment of the fullness of the Christian salvation in the believer's present life.[87] Anderson writes that "A realized eschatology which always sees the 'not yet' as 'already' may be no worse than one that sees the 'not yet' always as 'not yet'."[88] He explains that one of the reasons for the rise of independent and Pentecostal churches in the Majority World is that many people had the sense that existing Christian missions were "exclusively concerned with the 'not yet,' the salvation of the soul in the life hereafter, and that little was done for the pressing needs of the present life, the 'here and now' problems addressed by Pentecostal and independent churches."[89] My intention here is not to opt for either aspect to the detriment of the other. The point which I am trying to make is that there is a need to formulate a balanced teaching which keeps in a constant

---

85. Adeboye, *Ultimate Financial Breakthrough*, 18, 19. As he explains the parable, the first two types of giving and their corresponding benefits are supported by scriptural quotations: Gal 6:9–10 and Matt 10:41 respectively. For the third category he invokes the widow of Zarephath as the one who "sowed into the life of Elijah." In doing so, Adeboye adds, the widow "was able to access the source of superabundant blessings as she reaped a hundredfold return." He explains that her benefit was not restricted to food for the remaining part of her life, but that even the death which was threatening her and her child was avoided.

86. Anderson, *Introduction to Pentecostalism*, 301.

87. Young, "Prosperity Teaching," 12.

88. Anderson, *Introduction to Pentecostalism*, 220.

89. Ibid.

and energizing tension the benefits of the "already" and the expectations of the "not yet" of God's salvation through Christ for believers.

7.7.3 The Ways of Giving and Care for the Poor

From the outset, it is important to note that all the ancient authors I considered treat 2 Corinthians 8–9 unanimously as Paul's teaching on almsgiving. John Chrysostom insists on the fact that one should give abundantly and voluntarily. But he lays emphasis on the fact that God judges the value of alms not on the basis of their amount, but on that of the giver's inner disposition. In his view, almsgiving must be a continual practice for a Christian. Theodoret points out that God measures the offering by the capacity of the giver. Therefore, he suggests that giving should be voluntary and done in a joyful spirit. For Ambrosiaster, since all things are God's property, one should give as much as one is able to. For Thomas Aquinas, almsgiving as a genuine expression of piety should be a permanent practice fulfilled promptly, abundantly and joyfully. For his part, Calvin emphasizes that we are allowed to give only what we are able to. He states that in the context of 2 Corinthians 8–9, almsgiving is so important inasmuch as it is an aspect of righteousness. That giving needs to be directed to the poor is so strong in Calvin's mind that he asserts that negligence of it amounts to defrauding the poor of their due. Correspondingly, he warns that miserly rich people together with their possessions are threatened by a curse.

On closer consideration, there are both similarities and discrepancies between the conceptualization of Christian giving sketched above and the teachings developed by the prosperity gospel preachers I studied in relation to 2 Corinthians 8–9. Pentecostal preachers favor the idea that one must sow as much as one can and insist on the misfortune which will befall unfaithful givers. The main difference between present charismatic preachers and the former readers that I considered in this research lies in the beneficiary of Christian generosity. I observed that in the prosperity gospel discourses I studied, the authors never relate their quotations from 2 Corinthians 8–9 to assistance to the needy. This is more puzzling if we consider that the same authors allot some sections of the books I analyzed to giving to the poor. Quotations from 2 Corinthians 8–9 are restrictively used to support the payment of tithes and other offerings to the church and ministry. Moreover, giving is presented as a route to material prosperity since it prompts divine material blessings. However, their insistence on the link between Christian giving and mission is laudable and remains in line with Paul's thought elsewhere.[90] It might foster the sense of duty in every church member if it is well reflected on and applied. Correspondingly, this teaching can be a source of economic empowerment and self-reliance for churches especially in the Majority World today. But for a faithful interpretation of 2 Corinthians 8–9 I think that one needs to bear in mind that Paul sets the aims of his collection as follows: "for the rendering of this ministry not only supplies the needs of the saints but also overflows with many thanksgivings to God" (2 Cor 9:12). Also, as I argued, Paul perhaps thought that in the future the economic conditions could change in Jerusalem and Corinth due to different factors which would place Jerusalem in better economic conditions to reciprocate the gift received (2 Cor 8:14). All things considered, Paul's collection is above all a charitable giving, an undertaking motivated by God's grace.

7.7.4 Christian κοινωνία

The question of what it means to be a church matters a lot in this dialogue with the prosperity gospel. As noted in my earlier interpretation of 2 Corinthians 8–9, Paul uses the term κοινωνία to mean the Macedonians' participation in his collection for the saints in Jerusalem (8:4). In 9:13 the same word conveys the idea of sharing one's resources with others. The exegetical analysis of 2 Corinthians 8–9 has enabled me to point out five motivations spelled out by Paul to exhort the Corinthians to complete this project as they had pledged. Two of them reflect Paul's view that Christians should live in interdependence and mutual support. First, Paul wanted the Corinthians to share his belief in the possibility that in the future the Corinthians would benefit from the generosity of the Jerusalem church in case of a reversal in economic conditions (8:13–15). Second, the apostle hoped that his collection would generate the sense of fellowship between the Corinthians and the Jerusalemite Christians. He anticipated that it would relieve the needs of the poor Christians in Jerusalem and drive the

---

90. In Phil 4:15–16 Paul received donations from the Philippians to support his mission in the province of Macedonia. According to 2 Cor 11:8–9 the Macedonians sent him financial support and he continued to minister to the Corinthians free of charge.

latter into longing and intercessional prayers for the Corinthians and worship to God (9:12–14).

Elsewhere in his letters Paul depicts the local church as a body with a variety of members working in interconnectedness (Rom 12:4–8; 1 Cor 12:12–31). In the context of the collection, Paul goes further to show that this mutual interdependence should exist between Christian congregations. As noted erlier, one will remember that in Romans 15:25–31 Paul expects that his collection will be seen as a tangible symbol of this mutual inderdependence between both Jewish and Gentile Christian communities. This view remains true regardless of whether the collection is regarded as an expression of the unity between the two wings of early Christianity (Munk, Safrai and Tomson) or as an attempt to restore the unity disrupted by several controversies and opposition which Paul had been facing from his Jewish counterparts in his mission to the Gentiles (Dunn). In any case, it is remarkable that in the conceptualization of his collection for Jerusalem, Paul seeks to convince his Gentile congregations to appropriate and express his understanding of being church as a κοινωνία of individual believers, but more importantly among Christian communities. This had to materialize through the financial gift collected by congregations in Greece for the needy among Jewish Christians in Jerusalem.

The concept of κοινωνία used by Paul with regard to his collection for Jerusalem has captured John Chrysostom's attention. In his view, the apostle termed the collection a κοινωνία to teach the Corinthians that they are both givers and receivers. Chrysostom explains that in addition to the thanks addressed to God for the collection received, the saints in Jerusalem will pray to God seeking to see the Corinthians and witness the χάρις that has been granted to the latter. In his reading of Paul in this context of the collection, John emphasizes the idea of interdependency among people which, he maintains, reflects God's will. It is true that in his sermons John focuses much on mutual interdependence among his congregants rather than among different parishes of his patriarchate.

Paul's perception of the church in the sense of the community of all believers is badly missing in most preachers of the prosperity gospel. This is probably due to the fact that this theological trend is dominated by individualistic and selfish principles as demonstrated in my treatment of the phenomenon in the sixth chapter of the present study. The state of affairs is facilitated by the non-denominational and independent character of most of the churches that propagate the prosperity gospel; they are built on one person-leadership structure in which the pastor is the ultimate managerial authority. I maintained earlier that this remains true since prosperity teachings promote blatant inequalities between the elite of preachers who, entrapped by greed, benefit from them and those who are constantly exhorted to sow their seeds in the hope of experiencing breakthroughs in life.[91] It goes without saying that in such a context, fundraisings aiming at relieving the needs of poor members in a given congregation or within other congregations, let alone the promotion of a ministry or project run by several congregations can hardly take place. The existence of networks seems to be operative not among churches but among their leaders who often invite one another to promote their own ministries.

7.7.5 The Lord's Voluntary Poverty and Attitude to Material Possessions

My exegetical analysis of 2 Corinthians 8:9, confirmed by present-day exegetes, explained the voluntary poverty of Christ in terms of an unsurpassable act of self-giving through his incarnation for the benefit for others, the expression of the Lord's grace for human salvation. The early readers of this text that I encountered earlier in this study concur with this reading. The church fathers I analyzed insist that Christ's mind is an invitation for Christians to imitate the Lord through free giving to the needy. They teach that the riches which flow to the believers are spiritual benefits and never material possessions. John Chrysostom, for instance, draws from this his praise for asceticism. For him material wealth must not be hoarded but distributed to the poor. He also emphasizes that lust for possessions and righteousness are incompatible. Like Chrysostom, Theodoret believes that perfection is contempt for material wealth and voluntary poverty. Without invoking Christ's voluntary poverty, Ambrosiaster shows a relatively negative view on material wealth. Although he does not state clearly that earthly wealth is bad, he thinks that there are some people who choose what is better and despise worldly possessions to commit themselves entirely to God's

---

91. Wright, *Mission*, 280.

things. Thomas Aquinas refers explicitly to the Lord's self-impoverishment in 2 Corinthians 8:9 to teach that Christ remained spiritually rich but made himself indigent in worldly possessions since he was deprived of everything and was in want. In Thomas' view, Christ cherished material poverty, so that believers need to imitate the Lord's example in order to become spiritually rich. It is thus understandable that with this negative view of material wealth, the idea that giving is a route to financial prosperity since it prompts divine material blessing as claims the prosperity gospel, would have been strange to the above-mentioned authors. Nor does Calvin espouse such a view though he does not show any aversion to material wealth. He only indicates that we owe possessions to God and therefore need to use them to assist the poor. For him, the Lord's self-impoverishment in 2 Corinthians 8:9 which was exemplified in the Macedonians' life is an exhortation to beneficence. The point I am making here is that there is discontinuity of thought between the former readers of our passage and the African preachers I studied in relation to the attitude to material wealth. Perhaps, Pentecostal preachers of the prosperity gospel would say that their interpretation of Paul presented above was lost during all the foregoing centuries. However, this would require a clear demonstration. In my view, a meticulous analysis of Paul's argumentation rules out the idea that he is trying to show the Corinthians a way to prosperity. Rather, Paul assures the Corinthians that God will grant them sufficiency. It would be a big mistake to equate this with prosperity, which is in most cases synonymous with superabundance in the prosperity gospel discourses.

As stated previously, the motive of the Lord's voluntary poverty is also invoked by some Pentecostal preachers in Africa today. But this is done from a different perspective which is informed by the pursuit of success in everything, both spiritually and materially. I noted that the accent is laid on the riches that stem from Christ's act. In the treatment of the literature from some figures within the prosperity gospel movement in Africa, I demonstrated that they insist that these riches encompass both spiritual and material provisions. For them, material prosperity must be claimed and enjoyed as a birthright for born-again Christians. But they indicate that this claim is justified only if one is willing to use portions of these goods as donations to the church, to the ministry or even to God's servant for evangelism. I noted that some go even further by saying that material abundance is the proof of our redemption. It is not an exaggeration to say that the prosperity gospel preachers reverse the flow by sacralizing material wealth which in their view had been demonized by most of the historical Christian traditions in Africa. The only problem strongly denounced by the prosperity preachers with regard to material possessions is the believer's unwillingness to give them out. This is why Ashimolowo, for instance, asserts that giving reflects our "detachment from earthly possessions and our attachment to the person of God."[92] However, although giving is strongly advocated by the prosperity gospel teachers as a route to economic blossoming, no atoning function is credited to it as almsgiving was perceived by John Chrysostom for instance.

The fundamental question to be raised in relation to giving is to what extent the Lord's self-impoverishment for the enrichment of believers as a motivation to assist the needy is embodied in the type of giving promoted in the form of Pentecostalism I have been discussing so far. I observed that in the prosperity writings which I studied, 2 Corinthians 8–9 is never invoked in the area of Christian giving for philanthropic purposes. However, I do not think that the Lord's self-impoverishment implies that poverty is to be seen as a virtue. On the contrary, the point made by Paul is that as Christ dispossessed himself of his riches for the sake of humans, Christians need to appropriate his mind. Marshall, who specifies that the example of Jesus remains the foundational element of the theology of 2 Corinthians 8–9, expresses this idea very aptly: "It emerges incidentally from the form of Paul's statement that poverty is not a good in itself, an ascetic ideal to be cultivated for its own sake; rather it is a condition that is voluntarily endured in order that a lot of other people who are poor may be enriched."[93] There is no doubt that, interpreted in this way, this motive remains good news which must be proclaimed even in a poverty-ravished continent like Africa. All we need is a biblically grounded theology of stewardship and giving.

---

92. Ashimolowo, *Coming Wealth Transfer*, 191.
93. Marshall, *New Testament Theology*, 287–288.

7.7.6 A Theology of Stewardship and Giving

The belief that all our resources are God's is very positive and has given rise to the spirit of generosity in Africa.[94] We learn from Kalu for instance, that in the aftermath of the Liberian civil war, many born-again Christians in Nigeria took leave of absence from their jobs and went to serve in Liberia in different domains.[95] From the same perspective, a certain number of ministries started "financial investment houses and other businesses to assist members, provide jobs, and fund projects."[96] He indicates that in every case charity was presented "as a virtue that God rewards; one's prosperity depends on how much one is willing to give back into the storehouse of the Lord to aid the brethren."[97] It is equally noticeable that Kalu clarifies that as Pentecostals urge every member to assist other fellow members, they teach that "one is saved by grace alone for service to others" and that exchanging material goods brings about "a foretaste of the reign of God to the present."[98]

Asamoah-Gyadu pleads for a holistic approach to Christian giving. This means surrendering first one's life to the Lord Jesus Christ as it is the case for the Macedonians (2 Cor 8:1–5).[99] Asamoah-Gyadu insists on the fact that Paul calls the Macedonians' spirit of giving a form of grace sourced from God. He explains that the Macedonian enthusiasm was not motivated by anything but to share in the ministering to the Christians in Jerusalem; they saw it as a privilege in Paul's view.[100] Asamoah-Gyadu aptly shows that the absence of this fundamental idea that giving flows out of the deep "sense of belonging to God and of being part of God's mission by contributing to the resources needed for it" results in the questioned transactional philosophy of giving.[101] The coming of Jesus Christ introduces a new perspective in the way we approach Old Testament instructions about

---

94. Asamoah-Gyadu, *Contemporary Pentecostal Christianity*, 94.
95. Kalu, *African Pentecostalism*, 222.
96. Ibid.
97. Ibid.
98. Ibid.
99. Asamoah-Gyadu, *Contemporary Pentecostal Christianity*, 94–95.
100. Ibid., 95.
101. Ibid.

giving. Asamoah-Gyadu writes that Jesus' example referred to by Paul in Philippians 2:5–11 and 2 Corinthians 8:9 indicates that God requires more than a certain percentage of our wealth. He explains that all that we are and all that we have needs to be surrendered to God.[102] He points out that in the perspective of the new covenant believers are expected to offer a part of their resources "as the Lord's rightful due in view of his claim on all that they are and all that he has entrusted to them."[103] As demonstrated in the Macedonians – and this in contrast with the man or woman of God who receives offerings and lives a luxurious life while most of the givers live in misery – funds are not raised for one's personal interests. Paul sets a very good example of how money should be handled to serve God's mission (2 Cor 2:17).[104] However, Asamoah-Gyadu writes that the notion of God's reciprocation of Christian giving is not ruled out but needs to be understood differently. It is not something to be calculated before one performs one's giving or applied magically. It is rooted in God's grace.

> The general tenor of the teaching of the New Testament is that we give to God faithfully and trust him for his grace in life, knowing that if we sow sparingly, we reap sparingly and if we sow bountifully, we reap bountifully. But that is not a magical formula, because God's hand cannot be twisted in our favour; to think otherwise is to challenge God's sovereignty. The promises of God come true by his grace and we can only trust him to fulfill these promises through his own indescribable gift, Jesus Christ who is our Lord and Saviour.[105]

Therefore, the understanding of God's provision in this context as a reward for one's giving is not Pauline. The apostle of the Gentiles makes it clear that the seed for sowing does not originate from human efforts but rather from God (2 Cor 9:10). This does not mean that Paul is encouraging idleness. Rather, he is affirming what he says elsewhere in a rhetorical question that all that we have comes from God (1 Cor 4:7). Equally wrong

---

102. Ibid., 96.
103. Ibid., 97.
104. Ibid., 96.
105. Ibid., 102.

and anti-Pauline is the thought that God is expecting that people give their offerings so that he may bless them materially in return.[106] Rather, the Christians are expected to give joyfully (2 Cor 9:7), which means in gratitude for the special gift they have received from God, Christ himself, and all the good things they have been granted through him (Rom 8:32).

Moreover, it is important to insist that the type of giving defended by Paul in 2 Corinthians 8–9 is purposed to relieve poor fellow Christians in Jerusalem. Therefore, the view that people give to receive more and more material wealth for self-enjoyment is not from Paul. Paul clarifies it when he speaks of αὐτάρκεια, sufficiency among the Corinthians (2 Cor 9:8). One receives divine provisions in order to serve those in need. One may understand that Pentecostals feel at liberty to take this text from this original setting and employ it to promote Christian giving through offerings and tithes. After all, it is still about Christian generosity. Academic exegesis should admit the broadening of the scope of biblical texts. However, this broadening of scope leaves us with a more urgent question as to what extent the resources collected by Pentecostal churches through different types of offerings are allocated to social promotion. As some Pentecostal preachers may claim that non-tithing Christians are "worse than armed robbers" since they steal not from humans but from God,[107] there is a pressing need to give heed to Calvin when he warns that, normally, not giving to the poor is defrauding them of their due. This question is crucial inasmuch as some Pentecostals, like Heward-Mills for instance, agree that among other things the tithe has been established to relieve the needy.[108]

In my view, Christian stewardship is about the believer's effort to develop a biblically and theologically grounded view of human society, and about the responsibility of all believers to build it under the lordship of Jesus. This presupposes that material wealth is neither sacralized nor demonized. Rather, it is part of God's creation and a gift or talent entrusted to human beings in general and to believers in particular to be shared with others.[109] However, believers are constantly reminded that material posses-

---

106. Mutombo-Mukendi, "Le nouveau culte," 112, 122.
107. Asamoah-Gyadu, *Contemporary Pentecostal Christianity*, 88.
108. Heward-Mills, *Why Non-tithing Christians*, 6–7.
109. Mutombo-Mukendi, "Le nouveau culte," 122.

sions can constitute a real danger if one places one's hope in them rather than in God who provided them (1 Tim 6:6–10, 17–19). Correlatively, poverty cannot be seen as a Christian value since Paul himself had to deal with it in his career and exhorted his converts to do so through manual work (1 Thess 2:9; 5:14; 2 Thess 3:6–13).

Many sub-Saharan African Pentecostals should humbly agree to learn from some prosperity gospel preachers like Mensa Otabil who insists on hard work and self-discipline, rather than on giving as a way to financial success. Moreover, the prosperity gospel preachers, who are often richer that those to whom they teach the laws of prosperity, are encouraged to learn to seriously apply them themselves by sharing their resources with the needy instead of taking the little they had to live on.[110] They should even go further and adopt Calvin's view of labor in which Calvin took up Luther's doctrine of profession as a calling from God (*Beruf* in German) to teach that through work one values oneself and makes oneself useful to the community.[111] In this way, God's work will no longer be restricted to worship-related activities such as the building of church premises and funding evangelism rallies and the like, as many still think in African Pentecostal circles. Correspondingly, the encompassing perception of God's work and the participation he expects of believers to whom he has entrusted various seeds will affect Christian giving. In Rwanda, for instance, fundraising for the above-mentioned activities, seen as properly spiritual, is almost spontaneous. This is not the case when it comes to a different kind of social promotion like building a school or a health center.

Ultimately, what Paul says about the theology of stewardship needs to be taken seriously. Since the apostle understands the Corinthians' giving to the collection as the administration of χάρις for God's glory (2 Cor 8:19), he implies that they are fulfilling their *raison d'être*.[112] Bearing this in mind, I may conclude that according to Paul in 2 Corinthians 8–9 Christian giving by nature is more about a believer's responsibility than the expectation of any form of returns either in the here and now or in the life hereafter.

---

110. Ibid., 112–113, 8. It is shocking that some preachers even encourage people to take a loan from others or a financial institution in order to get a seed to sow in the kingdom.

111. Weber, *L'éthique protestante*, 197.

112. Becker, *Paul's Usage of* χάρις, 334.

Conclusion

The discussion of the use of 2 Corinthians 8–9 by the prosperity gospel teachers in Africa has revealed to me that this text is essentially adduced to motivate Christians to give one's possessions in expectation of financial prosperity. In this context, material goods are seen as a right to be claimed and enjoyed by believers providing that they remain willing to give them out for the advancement of God's work on earth.

The principle of seed sowing and reaping is largely involved in the above hermeneutics. Laws are formulated and backed up by quotations from 2 Corinthians 8–9 to teach the believer how to activate this general principle of reaping and harvesting drawn from Paul's farming imagery in 2 Corinthians 9:6–11. In most cases, the concept of seed refers to money. But there are also instances where it is broadened to designate abilities and skills which have been given to every believer. In any case, it is emphasized that one must sow one's seed in order to have a harvest, which means financial prosperity and other opportunities of success and promotion in one's life. Hence some insist more on hard work and self-discipline rather than on giving as a way to financial prosperity. The prosperity gospel preachers have the merit of relating giving to mission. One must give to the church or to a ministry. This can take the form of normal offerings and tithes. However, in their writings 2 Corinthians 8–9 does not appear as a scriptural authority for teaching about giving for philanthropic purposes. I noted that the type of giving developed by African prosperity teachers can hardly be called sacrificial, but rather transactional.

My dialogue with the prosperity gospel teachers over the use of 2 Corinthians 8–9, in conversation with John Chrysostom, Theodoret of Cyrus, Ambrosiaster, Thomas Aquinas and John Calvin has pointed out both convergences and divergences. The centrality of the concept of grace unanimously emphasized throughout the history of the church is badly missing in the prosperity gospel discourses. The reception history of Paul's message to the Corinthians as sketched in this research demonstrates that 2 Corinthians 8–9 is solely employed for charitable purposes. The belief in reward or God's reciprocation of the believer's giving comes up in all the ancient readers of Paul referred to above. However, the nature of this reward and its time of fulfillment divide them. Whereas most of the prosperity gospel teachers insist almost exclusively on the enjoyment of material returns in the present life, ancient readers of Paul admit belief in spiritual and material recompense in the present life and in the world to come. Furthermore, except for Calvin, others show aversion to any pursuit of material wealth, considered as incompatible with righteousness.

Having considered this, I made the point that the centrality of the concept of grace in 2 Corinthians 8–9 directs that we conceptualize Christian giving in terms of responsibility, gratefulness and trust that God is faithful to his promise to take care of his children however the circumstances might be. While the Lord's self-impoverishment does not imply that poverty is to be regarded as a virtue, the Christian is constantly challenged to appropriate Christ's mind in his propensity to self-giving in order to serve and save humans.

Conclusion

The purpose of this research was to investigate the exegesis, the reception of 2 Corinthians 8–9 from late Antiquity to the Reformation, and its use in sub-Saharan African Pentecostalism today as far as the motivations of Christian giving are concerned. My contention was that Paul addressed Christian giving here primarily for a charitable purpose from which he inferred theological significance. He rooted charity in his theological framework of God's grace as a benefaction made to human beings which requires gratitude in the form of every good deed, especially care for the needy. At the same time, Paul held the Jewish view that God reciprocates generous giving performed by believers. Heuristic questions that I formulated as a guide for this research have allowed me to remain focused on its subject matter.

The question as to whether Paul imagined his collection from scratch or whether he drew on existing religious and social practices in the Jewish and Greco-Roman contexts was dealt with in the first chapter of this study. While Paul's collection has no obvious antecedent in Jewish history, I noted that in Judaism a great deal of attention is paid to care for the poor in general, and through almsgiving especially. Reward is promised to the righteous person, the one who provides for the needy; whereas God's judgement awaits whoever mistreats the poor. The idea that ethical uprightness not only meets the needs of the poor but can also protect the almsgiver, emerged with the Writings and found extensive expression in the Apocrypha. I noted that Greco-Roman society practiced different forms of benefaction prompted not primarily by love for the needy, but by the search for social praise by benefactors. Nonetheless, some low-level forms of care for the poor existed in this culture. I concluded that Paul's inspiration for the collection in favor of the poor Christians in Jerusalem must be sought not in the Greco-Roman patronage/benefaction practices, but in the Jewish conviction that the same God of Israel, who has revealed the fullness of his grace in Jesus Christ commands his people to care for the poor.

In the second chapter I discussed the question of the literary integrity of the second letter to the Corinthians. In the face of the large number and diversity of partition hypotheses advanced to account for discrepancies in 2 Corinthians, I aligned with scholars who argue that it is preferable to maintain its unity. The main reason for this position was the lack of any attestations of the alleged originally individual letters, and the unsatisfactory explanation for the motivation of their compilation. As for 2 Corinthians 8–9, I registered a stronger claim. Thanks to Stowers' insightful investigation into the use of the phrase περὶ μὲν γὰρ in classical Greek, the view that chapters 8 and 9 belonged to two originally separate letters is no longer tenable. As far as the text of 2 Corinthians 8–9 is concerned, the manuscript tradition is more or less stable. Only a few variants occupied my attention.

The questions regarding the meaning of the recurrent term χάρις in 2 Corinthians 8–9 and the tension between Paul's commendation of the Macedonians' contribution above their means (8:1–3) and his strong and repeated recommendation to the Corinthians to contribute according to one's possessions (8:11–12) were addressed in the third chapter of this work. The exegetical analysis of 2 Corinthians 8–9 reveals that Paul multiplies exhortations to stimulate the Corinthians to resume their collection. The term χάρις shows up ten times in the passage with various meanings. The Macedonians requested the χάρις, privilege (8:4), to participate in the collection termed χάρις as well (8:6, 19). Their enthusiasm in this project is seen by Paul as the effect of God's χάρις (8:1), and as an example to be emulated by the Corinthians (8:7). Paul hopes that the Corinthians' contribution will signal to the Christians in Jerusalem that God's χάρις is at work in the former (9:14). In other words, Paul sees his collection for the saints in Jerusalem as an expression of God's χάρις in the Corinthians' life; it is an aspect of their righteousness (9:10). The self-impoverishment of Jesus Christ too is depicted as the manifestation of his χάρις (8:9). Paul expresses χάρις to God both for Titus's work among the Macedonians and for the divine indescribable gift (8:16, 9:15). He depicts God as the one who is able to make χάρις abound in the form of material and spiritual resources to cheerful givers so that they continue to provide for the needy (9:8). From the insistent use of χάρις by Paul in the context of the collection, I concluded that his parenesis entails that he sees his project not as a purely humanitarian undertaking. Apart from its obvious and primary purpose to relieve the needs of the Jerusalem church, the apostle expects the collection to trigger a dynamic of fellowship not only among humans involved in it, but also between them and God (9:12–14). The apostle must have realized that his eulogy about the Macedonians for contributing above their means (8:1–3) could be easily misunderstood. Apparently, his insistence on the fact that the Corinthians should give according to one's possessions (8:11–12) aims at clarifying his statement. Paul does not expect the Corinthians to give beyond their means like the Macedonians, but to imitate the way the action of the latter matched their initial request to contribute. In doing so, the apostle remains consistent with his earlier practical advice in 1 Corinthians 16:2 in which he indicated that the Corinthians' donations had to be set aside on a weekly basis and in proportion to one's earnings. In Thomas Aquinas' view, Paul tells the Corinthians that he does not have any intention to force them to contribute beyond their means, but that he is convinced that their prompt willingness to give will ultimately lead them to do so.

Paul gives a series of motives for giving to the needy. First, he explains that God's grace produces generosity within the believer's life as exemplified by the Macedonian Christians. Second, the imitation of the Lord Jesus Christ whose generosity led him to impoverish himself for the enrichment of believers should motivate Christian generosity. Third, the belief in the possibility that in the future the Corinthians would benefit from the generosity of the Jerusalem church in case of a reversal in economic conditions is an incentive to giving to the collection. Fourth, the conviction that God will continue to provide for the needs of joyful givers paves the way for generous giving. However, God's beneficence is not understood as a reward for the believer's generosity since the initial resources needed to give to the needy are provided by God. Finally, a double purpose of Christian giving is formulated by Paul as a motive for generosity. The collection is expected to relieve the needs of the poor Christians in Jerusalem. Moreover, Paul hopes that his collection will engender a dynamic of fellowship both among humans involved in it and between them and God. By putting God and others at the center of the believer's life, Paul redefines the notion of αὐτάρκεια, sufficiency and highlights the communal essence of the Christian faith.

The exploration of some sermons and commentaries on 2 Corinthians 8–9 from late Antiquity to the Reformation period was guided by the question of how this text has been interpreted over the centuries especially with regard to the function of the concept of grace and the motives and purpose of Christian giving. All the authors considered register to varying degrees the significance of the term χαρίς in their reading of Paul. Except for Ambrosiaster, they emphasize either Paul's attributing the Macedonians' participation in the collection to the effect of God's χάρις, grace, or the fact that the project itself is termed χάρις. For John Chrysostom, Paul relates the Macedonians' zeal for the collection to God's χάρις to teach humility and emulation to the Corinthians. However, he notes that God's χάρις does not exclude human will. The full cooperation between Titus's eagerness to engage in the collection and God's grace is an example. Theodoret of Cyrus points in the same direction and insists that it is fitting that sharing in the collection is presented by Paul as a χάρις, a privilege since the Corinthians are to expect spiritual benefits which are also the various riches of divine χάρις. Thomas Aquinas argues that the *gratia* that the Macedonians have been granted is a divine free gift which comprehends endurance in afflictions and generosity through almsgiving. In his view, Paul calls this generosity *gratia* because all good that we accomplish stems from God's *gratia*. Calvin insists that Paul terms his collection God's *gratia* because all that we are and possess stems from God. Besides, helping the needy is not merely a commendable virtue; it is a special privilege, a *gratia*.

Concerning the motivations for giving, the text is strictly placed in the context of almsgiving and is never applied to Christian giving for other purposes. One motivation is strikingly common to all the earlier authors considered, the belief in reward. It is mostly drawn from Paul's reference to the metaphor of sowing and reaping in 2 Corinthians 9:6–11. For some, this reward consists in the multiplication of material resources during one's lifetime and spiritual blessings now and in the hereafter. For others, the emphasis is very much on the second aspect of recompense (i.e. spiritual benefits in the present life and in eternity). Aversion to material possessions is integral to this viewpoint. But other motivations are formulated and emphasis is placed differently. John Chrysostom notes in the first place that God himself requests alms to feed his people. The other strong reasons for Christian generosity are the hope for reward, gratitude to God for all the benefits granted to believers through Jesus' incarnation, interdependency among people as a status ordained by God, and the atoning function of alms. Theodoret notes that love for God motivated the Macedonians for the collection. He also indicates that the apostle teaches the Corinthians that just as God cares for the seed sown until it gives food to people, so he expects the Christians to give the needy the necessities of life. Another reason for the Corinthians to give generously is that they are to expect spiritual things from divine χάρις, and assistance from the saints' abundance when they themselves are in need. But the best reward the Corinthians are to hope for consists in joining the saints in endurance. For Ambrosiaster, the conviction that all things are God's property justifies almsgiving. He says that those who provide for the needy with sincerity make their gifts to God, and that these gifts are ultimately also God's because it is he who commands people to offer them. The hope for reward is another motivation for Christian generosity. This reward consists in returns in the present time and recompense in the hereafter as well. God rewards only those who act wholeheartedly as if they were depositing for themselves their treasure in God's presence. Their resources are multiplied to enable them to continue their practice of good deeds; and ultimately they will receive the reward from God in the world to come. Although Thomas Aquinas does not address explicitly the question why Christians ought to give alms, he does relate it to God's grace as I noted previously. It is thus possible that he sees the belief in divine reward as an incentive to Christian generosity. This *gratia* through almsgiving merits reward from God. Divine recompense covers both spiritual things and material possessions. Like Thomas, Calvin explains that since all that we are and possess stems from God, almsgiving is the imitation of God, our Father in heaven, who liberally provides us with all good things. While beneficence should not be motivated by the expectation of recompense, Calvin says that a double reward is promised to those who engage in true almsgiving: provisions for their own living, and enough resources to assist the destitute. This reward is also double inasmuch as it concerns eternal life and enrichment in terms of possessions in the present life.

The question of the way of giving has occupied the attention of earlier readers of 2 Corinthians 8–9. John Chrysostom writes that one should give abundantly and voluntarily. He lays emphasis on the fact that God judges the value of alms not on the basis of their amount, but on that of the giver's inner disposition. He esteems that considering the Corinthians' weakness, Paul makes a concession and allows them to give according to one's possessions. Almsgiving must be a continual practice for a Christian. For Theodoret, God measures the offering by the capacity of the giver. Therefore, giving has to be voluntary and performed in a joyful spirit. In Ambrosiaster, giving correctly means giving as much as one is able to. Thomas contends that since God multiplies alms, one must give correctly (i.e. promptly, abundantly and joyfully). Almsgiving should be a permanent practice because it is a genuine expression of piety and must be directed to the indigent. Surrender to God must precede our almsgiving. However, alms from a sinner should only be accepted if the individual does not have the intention to remain in sin. For Calvin, all believers are expected to show liberality even when confronted with extreme poverty. In other words, almsgiving should be an unceasing exercise in a Christian's life. Calvin emphasizes that the freedom given to believers to give only what they are able to must be taken seriously because a curse will fall upon miserly rich people together with their riches. For Calvin true liberality means to rely on divine providence and to give joyfully one's resources as God directs. With such a positive disposition of heart, almsgiving becomes a sacrifice pleasing to God. While no atoning function is attached to almsgiving in Calvin's thought, in the context of 2 Corinthians 8–9 it is important inasmuch as it is an aspect of righteousness whose negligence amounts to defrauding the poor of their due.

My investigation into the reception history of 2 Corinthians 8–9 has enabled me to answer the question about attitudes to wealth. John Chrysostom says that material possessions must be distributed to the poor. Correspondingly, he glorifies asceticism. He understands that lust for possessions and righteousness are incompatible. Like Chrysostom, Theodoret is aware of the danger of possessions. He perceives perfection as contempt for material wealth and as voluntary poverty. He views that Paul exhorts the Corinthians to contempt for money, which produces everlasting righteousness. Ambrosiaster shows a relatively negative view on material wealth. Although he does not state clearly that earthly wealth is bad, he thinks that there are some people who choose what is better and despise worldly possessions to commit themselves entirely to God's things. For these people God appoints rich people to provide for their food and clothing. Like John Chrysostom and Theodoret, Thomas praises material poverty. Complete devotion to God results in contempt for possessions. For this reason, it is better to give everything to the needy and, as a consequence, live in afflictions for Christ's sake. However, considering human weakness, says Thomas, one should give according to one's possessions. We find in Calvin a neutral approach to material wealth. He explains that God alone is said to know the right amount needed for everyone to meet their own needs and do good to others.

The question regarding the way 2 Corinthians 8–9 is interpreted in African Christianity marked by poverty and the prosperity gospel was addressed in the final chapter of this study. An adequate response to it required an introduction to African Pentecostalism in general and to the prosperity gospel in particular as one of its predominant features. This was the task assigned to chapters five and six respectively. Pentecostalism was depicted as a global and non-monolithical movement which has reconfigured the map of world Christianity. It was observed that all Pentecostal denominations insist on and promote the experience of the working of the Holy Spirit and the practice of spiritual gifts in the Christian life and church liturgy. Pentecostalism as a charismatic movement is also significantly attested among mainline Protestantism and the Roman Catholic Church. Today, most Pentecostal churches have developed independently from those founded in the West at the beginning of the twentieth century. The number of Pentecostal and new charismatic churches continues to increase in Africa and they are attracting younger, educated and urban audiences.

One of the characteristics of Pentecostal churches is their strong conviction that the Bible is God's Word from which resources are found to respond to human felt needs. The Bible is read selectively, which often results in unwarranted interpretations and appropriations. The talismanic and symbolic use of the Bible, bold pronouncements of biblical texts and names, and anointment with oil for different purposes is reminiscent of the ancient use of Christian amulets and other beliefs rooted in the Roman Catholic tradition. As in the ancient church, these Pentecostal rituals can be seen as an alternative to pagan magic prohibited in Christianity, albeit its dynamics are still alive and operative in people's minds even after their conversion to Pentecostalism. Another feature of Pentecostalism in sub-Saharan Africa is the rhetoric of power, victory and success which embraces all realms of human existence. The sub-Saharan Africa in which the quest for life in fullness is conducted in a real combat against evil powers has become a fertile ground for Pentecostalism in general and the prosperity gospel in particular.

The sixth chapter discussed the prosperity gospel perceived as an expression of "realized eschatology" in the sense that it promises instant healing and material wealth in the present life. It was observed that in this trend of Pentecostalism there is a perceptible move from the enthusiasm for the return of Christ and the end of time to the enjoyment of the fullness of Christian salvation in the believer's present life. This is mediated by the theme of Christ's atoning death which means victory over sin, poverty and sickness. It is said that these benefits can be claimed through faith and prayer on the basis of the Abrahamic covenant which includes all believers in Christ. Also, Christian giving and various anointing practices are taught as doctrinal truths which reveal the secrets of and open the way to financial prosperity. The supernatural is conceived of as the defining feature of true Christian life.

I observed that the prosperity gospel presents some positive aspects. It is a genuine quest for the fullness of life promised by the Scriptures. It is remarkable that while it is biblically and theologically right to affirm that Christ's salvation includes spiritual and worldly benefits to believers, the Bible never portrays this reality as an irreversible law of cause and effect. The second positive point about the prosperity gospel lies in its audacity to address real-life problems. I finally argued that its reverential attitude to the Bible as God's Word needs to be emulated by other expressions of the Christian faith. Nevertheless, I identified some shortcomings of the movement. On the moral and social side, it was noted that fundraising practices often promote greed, inequalities and unaccountability. Furthermore, the insistence on witchcraft as the main cause of human misery generates suspicions and quarrels among people and prevents them from detecting the real causes of their misery in social and political structures. Consequently, the prosperity gospel as it stands on the continent cannot be seen as a solution to material poverty and hunger confronting sub-Saharan Africa today. Rather, it aggravates the misery of those it attracts while it enriches its preachers. The theological weaknesses were also discussed. The movement's failure to integrate human sufferings and failures in the hermeneutics of the cross misses the full meaning of the incarnation of Jesus. Correlatively, it harms those believers who commit their life and deeds to God and who yet experience harsh circumstances. In the same vein, the teachings on giving and faith promoted by the prosperity gospel were found wanting for various reasons. First, they neglect or fail to put different scriptural passages in tension with the rest of the Bible; the result being that they give rise to misinterpretations and misappropriations of biblical passages and concepts. Moreover, they usurp God's sovereignty to determine humans' destiny. God is reduced to a business partner who must grant the desires of those who have fulfilled their obligations through tithes, offerings and positive confessions.

Investigation into the interpretation of 2 Corinthians 8–9 by the prosperity gospel teachers in sub-Saharan Africa has revealed that this text is almost uniquely used to support the belief that giving is a route to financial prosperity. The principle of seed sowing and reaping is largely involved in the above hermeneutics. Laws are formulated and backed up by quotations from 2 Corinthians 8–9 in order to teach the believer how to activate this general principle of reaping and harvesting drawn from Paul's farming imagery in 2 Corinthians 9:6–11. In most cases, the concept of seed refers to money. But there are also examples in which it is expanded to abilities and skills which have been given to every believer. Thus, some insist much on hard work and self-discipline rather than on giving as a way to financial prosperity. My suggestion was that such teachings should be emphasized within Pentecostalism. They are able to promote the empowerment of believers since they insist on the ethics of responsibility.

Without endorsing the transactional philosophy which underlines the type of giving taught by the prosperity gospel preachers, I appreciated the fact that they establish a strong relation between Christian giving and mission. However, I lamented that the idea of being church in the sense of a community of all believers is seriously missing. The preachers concentrate almost exclusively on sponsoring their invidivual ministries and projects or those run by their own churches. The view that congregations should work in mutual interdependence, as exemplified in 2 Corinthians 8–9, is totally absent from their discourses. Moreover, in their writings, 2 Corinthians 8–9 does not appear as a scriptural authority for teaching on giving for philanthropic purposes although this is the context in which Paul wrote these chapters. My dialogue with the prosperity gospel teachers over the use of 2 Corinthians 8–9, in conversation with John Chrysostom, Theodoret of Cyrus, Ambrosiaster, Thomas Aquinas and John Calvin has pointed out both convergences and divergences. The centrality of the concept of grace unanimously emphasized throughout the history of the church is badly missing in the prosperity gospel discourses. The reception history of Paul's message to the Corinthians as sketched in this research demonstrated that it is solely employed for charitable purposes. The belief in reward or God's reciprocation of the believer's giving comes up in all the ancient readers of Paul discussed in this study. However, the nature of this reward and its time of fulfillment divide them. They admit a belief in spiritual and material recompense in the present life and in the world to come. Except for Calvin, they all show aversion to any pursuit of material wealth which is considered incompatible with righteousness. As for the prosperity gospel teachers, they insist on the enjoyment of material returns in the present life.

It is my conviction that Pentecostals need to learn from those who preceded us in the interpretation of the Bible. I do not pretend that their readings are always normative. Concerning 2 Corinthians 8–9, there is much to be taken seriously in the role of the concept of grace and care for the needy in the conceptualization and practice of Christian giving. Also, it is useful to note that the absence of any explicit reference to previous traditions among Pentecostals does not necessarily mean that they do not make use of them at all. On closer consideration, one realizes that on a given subject matter, Pentecostals expound perhaps unconsciously the views of earlier readers. The sacralization of the practice of giving offerings and paying tithes in Pentecostalism is reminiscent for instance of John Chrysostom's view that almsgiving atones for sins. Therefore, it is useful for Pentecostals to be at least aware of this continuity and discontinuity in the ongoing task of biblical interpretation. Perhaps, it is also germane to learn that inspiration comes about not only through spontaneous illumination but also through engagement with earlier and current readers of the same biblical texts.

Again, concerning the interpretation of biblical texts, I made the point that academic exegesis should admit the broadening of the scope of biblical texts. In the case of 2 Corinthians 8–9 Paul's motives for the collection can be applied to Christian giving in general. However, I contended that the apostle's concern to use the collected funds to meet the needs of disadvantaged Christians in Jerusalem warns Pentecostal churches about the risk of neglecting the poor when they spend tremendous amounts of money on their different activities. Moreover, considering the central function of the concept of grace in 2 Corinthians 8–9, my claim was that Paul understands Christian giving much more as a matter of responsibility and expression of gratefulness than as a way of securing rewards. At the same time, it has to be noted that Paul shares the Jewish belief in God's blessing the faithful in general and the joyful giver in particular, both in the present life and in the world to come. In this case divine recompense is either a matter of God's free grace or his retributive justice.[1] God blesses the giver but he is not put into counter-obligation by the latter in the way pagan gods are.[2] Paul may have been aware that the views of merit and reciprocity could gradually undermine the fundamental element of the covenantal grace through Christ on which the Christian faith is built. Such a process seems to have taken place in theological discourses of Greek-speaking Judaism through the benefaction system, to which Philo and Josephus reacted.[3]

---

1. Harrison, *Paul's Language of Grace*, 322.

2. Ibid., 299, 350: "Whereas the honorific inscriptions, like Paul, register the disposal and return of χάριτες by benefactors and their beneficiaries, the transaction is an entirely civic affair and is very seldom related to the divine realm. Furthermore, on these rare occasions, the gods are invariably placed under counter-obligation by the cultic piety of the benefactor or community."

3. Ibid., 346.

Perhaps the order in which Paul presents to the Corinthians the motivations for them to contribute to the collection for Jerusalem reveals an order of priority. Everything starts with God's grace enabling the Macedonians to give in spite of their abject poverty (2 Cor 8:1–5) and enriching the Corinthians in Christ through spiritual gifts (2 Cor 8:7; cf. 1 Cor 1:4–5). Paul continues by showing that such a selfless giving demonstrated by the Macedonians is ultimately exemplified by the Lord Jesus Christ. Finally, he assures the Corinthians that God will provide for them. It needs to be remembered that elsewhere Paul insists on the primacy of God's benevolence to humans when they were still unable to do anything good to him (Rom 5). There he concludes that God will *a fortiori* continue his beneficence to them now that they have been reconciled to him. This is the backdrop against which one should faithfully read Paul's imagery of the sowing and reaping in 2 Corinthians 9:6–11 as the promise that God will take care of the joyful giver. This is how Paul tells the Corinthians that their giving to the collection must not be seen as a loss but as a normal way to enter God's economy of stewardship. It seems that Paul challenges the human propensity to self-serving giving expressed in different forms of benefit exchange present in all cultures to various degrees. Paul's rooting Christian generosity from the outset in the effect of God's χάρις in the life of the believer attests to the fact that in 2 Corinthians 8–9 Paul views Christian giving as essentially more concerned with the believer's responsibility than the expectation of any form of return. Therefore, the promise that God is faithful to his promise to take care of his children however the circumstances might be, needs to be taken seriously as the Word of God. This is an element of our salvation through Christ which we can never merit but receive and live out with thanksgiving. However, a sound interpretation of biblical texts in general and of Paul in particular needs to take into consideration not only the reader's context for their application, but primarily their original setting. In this way, together with other interpreters of the Scriptures, the prosperity gospel preachers will strive to allow the Bible to interpret the Bible instead of compiling proof texts isolated from their respective contexts as a way of doing theology.

For the time being it is not possible to extrapolate what will happen if the process of the sacralization of giving continues its trajectory among

Pentecostals. There is a real risk that this overemphasis on giving will gradually lead to the doctrine and practice of selling indulgences contested by the Reformers in their time. While in the late Middle Ages one would purchase indulgences for oneself or for one's relatives to obtain the removal of punishment for sins in the purgatory, today the prosperity gospel teaches that one must give offerings in order to secure God's favors. In both cases, Christian giving becomes a sacramental duty in that sense that there is a shared presupposition that offering money to the church enables the individual to access divine benefits. To put it differently, the views of merit and reciprocity characteristic of the benefaction system may gradually undermine the fundamental element of the covenantal grace through Christ on which the Christian faith is built. Consequently, the legitimate claim made by the prosperity gospel preachers that teachings on material prosperity and healing need to be acknowledged and taught by churches as integral to God's salvation through Christ's redemptive work is distorted. It risks turning into a religious philosophy which is biblically, theologically and historically at variance with the Christian faith.

Bibliography

Primary Sources

Ambrosiaster. *Commentarius in epistulas Paulinas 2, Ad Corinthios secunda.* Corpus scriptorum ecclesiasticorum Latinorum, v. 81. Vindobonae, Vienna, Austria: Hoelder-Pichler-Tempsky, 1966-1969. Translated and edited by G. L. Bray as *Commentaries on Romans and 1-2 Corinthians.* Ancient Christian Texts (Downers Grove, IL: InterVarsity Press, 2009).

Aristotle. *Posterior Analytics. Topica.* Translated by Hugh Tredennick, E. S. Forster. LCL 391. Cambridge, MA: Harvard University Press, 1960.

Augustine. *In Joannis Evangelium Tractatus CXXIV.* CCSL 36. Translated and edited by J. W. Rettig as *Tractates on the Gospel of John 1-10. Fathers of the Church 78.* Washington, DC: Catholic University of America Press, 1988.

Augustine. *Sermones.* Translated and edited by E. Hill as *The Works of Saint Augustine: A Translation for the 21st Century: Sermons III/1 (1-19) on the Old Testament.* New York: New City Press, 1990.

Beentjes, P. C., ed. *The Book of Ben Sira in Hebrew: A Text Edition of all Extant Hebrew Manuscripts and a Synopsis of all Parallel Hebrew Ben Sira Texts.* Leiden: Brill, 1997.

Bible Works 7. Philo's Works, Nestle-Aland 27th edition of *Novum Testamentum Graece*, 4th edition of *Biblia Hebraica Stuttgartensia*, Rahlf's edition of the *Septuagint*, English and French Bible versions, etc.

Calvin, John. *Commentarii in Pauli Epistolam ad Romanos.* Translated and edited by J. Owen as *Commentaries on the Epistle of Paul the Apostle to the Romans.* Grand Rapids, MI: Eerdmans, 1947.

———. *Commentarii in Secundam Pauli Epistolam ad Corinthios.* Opera Exegetica Veteris et Novi Testamenti II, 15. Translated and edited by H. Feld. Genève: Librairie Droz, 1994.

———. *Commentarius in librum Psalmorum.* Translated from the original Latin and collated with the author's French version by J. Anderson as *Commentary on the Book of Psalms*, Vol. 4. Grand Rapids, MI: Eerdmans, 1949.

———. *The Second Epistle of Paul the Apostle to the Corinthians and the Epistles to Timothy, Titus and Philemon.* Edited by D. W. Torrance and T. F. Torrance; translated by T. A. Smail. Grand Rapids, MI: Eerdmans, 1964.

Charlesworth, J. H., ed. *The Dead Sea Scrolls: Hebrew, Aramaic, and Greek Texts with English Translations*, vol. 1, *Rule of the Community and Related Documents*. Tübingen/Louisville: J. C. B. Mohr/Westminster John Knox, 1995.

———, ed. *The Dead Sea Scrolls: Hebrew, Aramaic, and Greek Texts with English Translations*, vol. 2, *Damascus Document, War Scroll and Related Documents*. Tübingen/Louisville, KY: J. C. B. Mohr/Westminster John Knox, 1995.

———, ed. *The Dead Sea Scrolls: Hebrew, Aramaic, and Greek Texts with English Translations*, vol. 6B, *Pesharim, Other Commentaries, and Related Documents*. Tübingen/Louisville, KY: J. C. B. Mohr/Westminster John Knox, 2002.

Chrysostom, John. *Ad homilias de Lazaro.* PG 48. Translation retrieved from http://www.tertullian.org/fathers/chrysostom_four_discourses_03_discourse3.htm; accessed on 18 May 2015.

———. *Homiliae ad populum Antiochenum.* PG 49. Translated by P. Schaff. (NPNF I, IX). Edinburgh/Grand Rapids: T & T Clark/Eerdmans, 1989.

———. *Homiliae in binas ad Corinthios Epistulas et commentarius in Epistolam ad Galatas.* PG 61. Translated by T. Chambers as *Homilies on the Epistles of Paul to the Corinthians* (NPNF I, XII). Grand Rapids, MI: Eerdmans, 1989. First published 1956.

———. *Homilies on Genesis* 46-67. Translated by R. C. Hill. The Fathers of the Church, 87. Washington, DC: Catholic University of America Press, 1992.

Cicero. *De Officiis.* Translated by Walter Miller. LCL 30. Cambridge, MA: Harvard University Press, 1913.

———. *De Oratore: Books 1-2.* Translated by E. W. Sutton, H. Rackham. LCL 348. Cambridge, MA: Harvard University Press, 1942.

Clement. *Stromateis 1-3.* Translated by J. Ferguson. The Fathers of the Church 85. Washington, DC: Catholic University of America Press, 1991.

De Jonge, M., ed. *The Testaments of the Twelve Patriarchs: A Critical Edition of the Greek Text.* Leiden: Brill, 1978.

Demosthenes. *Orations, Volume V: Orations 41-49: Private Cases.* Translated by A. T. Murray. LCL 346. Cambridge, MA: Harvard University Press, 1939.

1 Enoch: The Hermeneia Translation. Translated by G. W. E. Nickelsburg and J. C. VanderKam. Minneapolis, MN: Fortress Press, 2012.

Epictetus. *Discourses, Books 1-2.* Translated by W. A. Oldfather. LCL 131. Cambridge, MA: Harvard University Press, 1925.

———. *Discourses* I. Translation and Notes by R. F. Dobbin. Oxford: Oxford University Press, 1998.

Euripides. *Hippolytus*. Translation, Introduction and Commentary by M. R. Helleran. Warminster, UK: Aris & Phillips, 1995.

———. *Medea*. Edited with an introduction, a translation and a commentary by J. Mossman. Classical Texts. Oxford: Aris & Phillips, 2011.

Hippolytus. *Traditio Apostolica*. Translated by G. Dix as *The Treatise on the Apostolic Tradition of St Hippolytus of Rome*. Revised edition by H. Chadwick. London: SPCK, 1968.

Josephus, Flavius. *Antiquitates Judaicae*. Volume IV, Books 1-4. LCL 242. Translated by H. St J. Thackeray. Cambridge, MA: Harvard University Press, 1930.

———. *Antiquitates Judaicae* 1-4. Translated by S. Mason. Translation and commentary by L. H. Feldman. Leiden: Brill, 2000.

———. *The Jewish War, Volume I: Books 1-2*. Translated by H. St J. Thackeray. LCL 203. Cambridge, MA: Harvard University Press, 1927.

———. *The Jewish War, Volume II: Books 3-4*. Translated by H. St. J. Thackeray. LCL 487. Cambridge, MA: Harvard University Press, 1927.

———. *The Jewish War, Volume III: Books 5-7*. Translated by H. St J. Thackeray. LCL 210. Cambridge, MA: Harvard University Press, 1928.

La Bible Vie nouvelle: Avec notes d'études. Genève: Société Biblique de Genève, 2010.

La Bible, Traduction Œcuménique de la Bible (Nouveau Testament). Paris: Librairie Générale Française, 2000.

La Nouvelle Bible Segond: Édition d'étude. Paris: Alliance Biblique Universelle, 2002.

Leo the Great. *Sermons*. Translated by J. P. Freeland and A. J. Conway. CCSL 138. The Fathers of the Church 93. Washington, DC: Catholic University of America Press, 1996.

Martial. *De Spectaculis Liber* 1-5. Edited and translated by D. R. Shackleton Bailey. LCL 94. *On the Spectacles*, Vol. 1. Cambridge, MA: Harvard University Press, 1993.

Metzger, M., trans., ed. *Les constitutions apostoliques: Introduction, texte critique, traduction et notes*, vol. 3, livres 7 et 8. Paris: Éditions du cerf, 1987.

Novum Testamentum Graece. 28th Revised Edition by B. Aland et al. Stuttgart: Deutsche Bibelgesellschaft, 2013.

Origen. *Contra Celsum* (SC 132; 136; 147; 150). Translated by H. Chadwick. Cambridge: Cambridge University Press, 1953.

———. *Homilies on Joshua* (SC 71). Translated by A. Jaubert. Paris: Cerf, 1960.

Philo. *De Iosepho*. Translated by F. H. Colson. LCL 289. Cambridge, MA: Harvard University Press, 1935.

———. *De Posteritate Caini*. Translated by F. H. Colson, G. H. Whitaker. LCL 227. Cambridge, MA: Harvard University Press, 1929.

———. *De Sacrificiis Abelis et Caini*. Translated by F. H. Colson, G. H. Whitaker. LCL 227. Cambridge, MA: Harvard University Press, 1929.
———. *De Somniis*. Translated by F. H. Colson, G. H. Whitaker. LCL 275. Cambridge, MA: Harvard University Press, 1934.
———. *De Specialibus Legibus IV.* Translated by F. H. Colson. LCL 341. Cambridge, MA: Harvard University Press, 1939.
———. *De Vita Mosis*. Translated by F. H. Colson. LCL 289. Cambridge, MA: Harvard University Press, 1935.
———. *Legum Allegoriae*. Translated by F. H. Colson, G. H. Whitaker. LCL 226. Cambridge, MA: Harvard University Press, 1929.
———. *Quod Omnis Probus Liber sit*. Translated by F. H. Colson. LCL 363. Cambridge, MA: Harvard University Press, 1941.
Pietersma, A., and B. G. Wright. *A New English Translation of the Septuagint and Other Greek Translations Traditionally Included under That Title*. New York: Oxford University Press, 2007.
Pontificale Romanum Clementis VIII ac Urbani VIII jussu editum ac a Benedicto XV recognitum et castigatum. Paris: Jouby, 1859.
Rituale Romanum Pauli V. Pontificis Maximi jussu editum. Lyon, 1704.
Seneca. *Moral Essays, Volume III: De Beneficiis*. Translated by John W. Basore. LCL 310. Cambridge, MA: Harvard University Press, 1935.
Seneca. *Epistulae morales, Volume II: Epistles 66-92*. Translated by Richard M. Gummere. LCL 76. Cambridge, MA: Harvard University Press, 1920.
Seneca the Elder. *Declamations, Volume II: Controversiae*, Books 7-10. Suasoriae. Fragments. Translated by Michael Winterbottom. LCL 464. Cambridge, MA: Harvard University Press, 1974.
Tertullian. *La pudicité (De Pudicitia)*. Translated and edited by C. Munier, with an introduction by C. Micaelli. SC 394. Paris: Éditions du Cerf, 1993.
Theodoret of Cyrus. *Commentarius in omnes sancti Pauli Epistolas*. PG 82. Translated with an introduction by R. C. Hill as *Commentary on the Letters of St. Paul* I. Brookline, MA: Holy Cross Orthodox Press, 2001.
Thomas Aquinas. *Super II Epistolam ad Corinthios lectura*. Translated and edited by J.-E. Stroobant de Saint-Eloy as *Commentaire de la deuxième épître aux Corinthiens*. Paris: Cerf, 2005.
———. *Summa Theologiae* 34. Translated and edited by R. J. Batten as *Charity: Latin text and English Translation, Introductions, Notes, Appendices and Glossaries*. London: Eyre and Spottiswoode, 1975.
———. *Summa Theologiae* 35. Translated by T. R. Heath as *Consequences of Charity: Latin Text and English Translation, Introductions, Notes, Appendices and Glossaries*. London: Eyre and Spottiswoode, 1972.

Secondary Sources

Adeboye, E. A. *The Ultimate Financial Breakthrough*. Weybridge, UK: RoperPenberthy Publishing Ltd, 2010.

Anaba, E. *Breaking Illegal Possession: Dislodge the Enemy and Possess the Land!* Accra: Design Solutions, 1996.

Anderson, A. H. *An Introduction to Pentecostalism*. Cambridge: Cambridge University Press, 2014.

———. "Varieties, Taxonomies, and Definitions." In *Studying Global Pentecostalism*, edited by A. Anderson, 13–29. Berkeley, CA: University of California Press, 2010.

Anderson, G. A. *Sin: A History*. New Haven, CT: Yale University Press, 2009.

Antony, B. "'He Who Supplies Seed to the Sower and Bread for Food': The Pauline Characterization of God in 2 Corinthians 8-9." In *Theologizing in the Corinthian Conflict: Studies in the Exegesis and Theology of 2 Corinthians*, Biblical Tools and Studies 16, edited by R. Bieringer, et al., 305–317. Leuven: Peeters, 2013.

Anueau, J. "Sainteté-Théologie biblique." In *Dictionnaire critique de théologie*, edited by J.Y. Lacoste. Paris: Presses Universitaires de France, 1998.

Archer, K. J. *A Pentecostal Hermeneutic: Spirit, Scripture and Community*. Cleveland, TN: CPT Press, 2009.

Asamoah-Gyadu, J. Kwabena. *Contemporary Pentecostal Christianity: Interpretations from an African Context*. Eugene, OR: Wipf & Stock Publishers, 2013.

Ashimolowo, M. *The Coming Wealth Transfer*. London: Mattyson Media, 2006.

Banda, L. "Dialoguing at 'Mphala': A Conversation on Faith between John Calvin and Proponents of the Prosperity Gospel." In *In Search of Health and Wealth: The Prosperity Gospel in African, Reformed Perspective*, edited by H. Kroesbergen, 63–77. Wellington, South Africa: Christian Literature Fund, 2013.

Bangura. "'Abraham's Blessings Are Mine!' Charismatics and the Prosperity Gospel in Sierra Leone." *Geestkracht. Bulletin voor Charismatische Theologie* 70 (2012): 32–48.

Bangura, J. B. "The Charismatic Movement in Sierra Leone (1980-2010): A Mission-historical Analysis in View of African Culture, Prosperity Gospel and Power Theology." PhD Dissertation, VU University Amsterdam, 2013.

Barclay, J. M. G. "'Because He Was Rich He Became Poor': Translation, Exegesis and Hermeneutics in the Reading of 2 Corinthians 8.9." In *Theologizing in the Corinthian Conflict: Studies in the Exegesis and Theology of 2 Corinthians*, Biblical Tools and Studies 16, edited by R. Bieringer, et al., 331–344. Leuven: Peeters, 2013.

Barnett, P. *The Second Epistle to the Corinthians*. New International Commentary on the New Testament. Grand Rapids, MI: Eerdmans, 1997.

Barrett, D. B., ed. *World Christian Encyclopedia: A Comparative Study of Churches and Religions in the Modern World AD 1900-2000*. Nairobi/New York: Oxford University Press, 1982.

Barrett, D. B. *Schism and Renewal in Africa: An Analysis of Six Thousand Contemporary Religious Movements*. Nairobi: Oxford University Press, 1968.

Barrett, D. B., G. T. Kurian, and T. M. Johnson, eds. *World Christian Encyclopedia: A Comparative Study of Churches and Religions in the Modern World*, vol. 1. Oxford/New York: Oxford University Press, 2001.

Barrett, P. *The Second Epistle to the Corinthians*. New International Commentary on the New Testament. Grand Rapids, MI: Eerdmans, 1997.

Baumgärtel, F., and J. Behm. "καρδία." In *Theological Dictionary of the New Testament*, vol. 3, translated by G. Bromiley and edited by G. Kittel, 606–614. Grand Rapids, MI: Eerdmans, 1965.

Becker, E. M. *Letter Hermeneutics in 2 Corinthians: Studies in Literarkritik and Communication Theory*. Translated by H. S. Heron. London/New York: T. & T. Clark, 2004.

Becker, J. P. *Paul's Usage of χάρις in 2 Corinthians 8-9: An Ontology of Grace*. Lewiston, NY: Edwin Mellen Press, 2011.

Bediako, Kwame. *Jesus and the Gospel in Africa: History and Experience*. Theology in Africa Series. Maryknoll, NY: Orbis Books, 2004.

Bennett, T. A. "Paul Ricoeur and the Hypothesis of the Text in Theological Interpretation." *The Journal of Theological Interpretation* 5 (2011): 211–230.

Betz, H. D. *Galatians*. Hermeneia, a critical and historical commentary on the Bible. Philadelphia, PA: Fortress Press, 1979.

———. *2 Corinthians 8 and 9: A Commentary on Two Administrative Letters of the Apostle Paul*. Hermeneia, a critical and historical commentary on the Bible. Philadelphia, PA: Fortress Press, 1985.

Betz, H. D., et al., eds. *Religion Past and Present: Encyclopedia of Theology and Religion*. Leiden/Boston, MA: Brill, 2012.

Beyer, H. W. "εὐλογέω, εὐλογητός, εὐλογία, ἐνευλογέω." In *Theological Dictionary of the New Testament*, vol. 2, translated by G. Bromiley and edited by G. Kittel, 754–765. Grand Rapids, MI: Eerdmans, 1964.

Biéler, A. *La pensée économique et sociale de Calvin*. Genève: Librairie de l'université, 1959.

Bieringer, R. "Love as that which Binds Everything Together? The Unity of 2 Corinthians Revisited in Light of Αγαπ- Terminology." In *Second Corinthians in the Perspective of Late Second Temple Judaism*, Compendia Rerum Iudaicarum ad Novum Testamentum 14, edited by R. Bieringer et al., 11–24. Leiden/Boston, MA: Brill, 2014.

Bieringer, R., et al. *Theologizing in the Corinthian Conflict: Studies in the Exegesis and Theology of 2 Corinthians.* Biblical Tools and Studies 16. Leuven: Peeters, 2013.

Bleek, F. "Erörterungen in Beziehung auf die Briefe Pauli an die Korinther." *Theologische Studien und Kritiken* 3 (1830): 614–632.

Bolton, D. "Paul's Collection: Debt Theology Transformed into an Act of Love among Kins?" In *Theologizing in the Corinthian Conflict: Studies in the Exegesis and Theology of 2 Corinthians*, Biblical Tools and Studies 16, edited by R. Bieringer et al., 345–359. Leuven: Peeters, 2013.

Bornkamm, G. *Geschichte und Glaube* 2. München: C. Kaiser, 1971.

Bovon, F. "Beyond the Canonical and the Apocryphal Books, the Presence of a Third Category: The Books Useful for the Soul." *Harvard Theological Review* 105 (2012): 125–137.

Brown, C., ed. *The New International Dictionary of New Testament Theology*. Revised edition. Exeter: Paternoster Press, 1976.

Brown, R. E. *An Introduction to the New Testament.* The Anchor Bible Dictionary. New York: Doubleday, 1997.

Brown, R. E., J. A. Fitzmyer, and R. E. Murphy, eds. *The New Jerome Biblical Commentary*, London: Bloomsbury Academic, 1994.

Bruehler, B. B. "Proverbs, Persuasion and People: A Three-dimensional Investigation of 2 Corinthians 9.6-15." *New Testament Studies* 48 (2002): 209–224.

Bühler, P. "Justification." In *Encyclopédie du protestantisme*, edited by P. Gisel, 708–709. Genève: Labor et Fides, 2006.

Bultmann, R. *Der zweite Brief an die Korinther.* Kritisch-exegetischer Kommentar über das Neue Testament 6. Edited by E. Dinkler. Göttingen: Vandenhoeck & Ruprecht, 1976.

Chamberlain, W. D. "Introduction." In *Commentary on the Epistles of Paul the Apostle to the Corinthians by John Calvin*, Vol. 2, translated by J. Pringle. Grand Rapids, MI : Eerdmans, 1948.

Canivet, P. "Theodoret of Cyr." In *New Catholic Encyclopedia*, vol. 13, edited by B. L. Marthaler et al., 878–879. Detroit: Gale, 2003.

Carrez, M. *La deuxième épître de saint Paul aux Corinthiens.* Commentaire du Nouveau Testament II, 8. Genève: Labor et Fides, 1986.

Chilenje, V. "The Challenges of the Prosperity Gospel for Reformed/Presbyterian Churches in the 21st Century." In *In Search of Health and Wealth: The Prosperity Gospel in African, Reformed Perspective*, edited by H. Kroesbergen, 10–26. Wellington, South Africa: Christian Literature Fund, 2013.

Coleman, S. *The Globalization of Charismatic Christianity: Spreading the Gospel of Prosperity*. Cambridge: Cambridge University Press, 2000.

Conzelmann, H. "χαίρω, χαράν, συγχαίρω, χάρις, χαρίζομαι, χαριτόω, ἀχάριστος, χάρισμα, εὐχαριστέω, εὐχαριστία, εὐχάριστος." In *Theological Dictionary of the New Testament*, vol. 9, translated by G. Bromiley and edited by G. Friedrich, 359–376. Grand Rapids, MI: Eerdmans, 1974.

Conradie, E. M. *Angling for Interpretation: A First Introduction to Biblical, Theological and Contextual Hermeneutics.* Study Guides in Religion and Theology 13. Stellenbosch: Sun Press, 2008.

Cox, H. *Fire From Heaven: The Rise of Pentecostal Spirituality and the Reshaping of Religion in the Twenty-first Century.* London: Cassell, 1996.

Crehan, J. H. "Ambrosiaster." In *New Catholic Encyclopedia*, vol. 1, edited by B. L. Marthaler et al., 346–347. Detroit: Gale, 2003.

Dahan, G. "Introduction." In *Super II Epistolam ad Corinthios lectura*, edited by Thomas Aquinas, translated by J. E. Stroobant de Saint-Eloy, *Commentaire de la deuxième épître aux Corinthiens*, I-XLVII. Paris: Cerf, 2005.

Dahl, N. A. *Studies in Paul.* Minneapolis, MN: Augsburg Publishing House, 1977.

Danker, F. W., W. Bauer, and W. F. Arndt, eds. *A Greek-English Lexicon of the New Testament and Other Early Christian Literature.* Chicago, IL: University of Chicago Press, 2000.

Decock, P. B. "On the Value of Pre-modern Interpretation of Scripture for Contemporary Biblical Studies." *Neotestamentica: Journal of New Testament Society of South Africa* 39 (2005): 57–74.

Delling, G. "πλεονέκτης, πλεονεκτέω, πλεονεξία." In *Theological Dictionary of the New Testament*, vol. 6, translated by G. Bromiley and edited by G. Friedrich, 266–274. Grand Rapids, MI: Eerdmans, 1971.

Den Hartog, W. H., and B. Mbanze Kasera. "Het welvaartsevangelie in Namibië." *Soteria* 31 (2014): 16–23.

Dibelius, M., and H. Conzelmann. *The Pastoral Epistles.* Philadelphia: Fortress Press, 1972.

Dittenberger, W. *Orientis Graecae Inscriptiones.* 2 vols. Leipzig: Georg Olms Verlag, 1903–1905.

———. *Sylloge Inscriptionum Graecarum.* Vol 2. Lipsiae: S. Hirzel, 1898-1901.

Downey, G., ed. "Antioch." In *New Catholic Encyclopedia*, vol. 1, edited by B. L. Marthaler et al., 521–524. Detroit: Gale, 2003.

Downs, D. J. *The Offering of the Gentiles: Paul's Collection for Jerusalem in its Chronological, Cultural, and Cultic Contexts.* Wissenschaftliche Untersuchungen zum Neuen Testament II/ 248. Tübingen: Mohr Siebeck, 2008.

Dubois, M. "Mystical and Realistic Elements in the Exegesis and Hermeneutics of Thomas Aquinas." In *Creative Biblical Exegesis: Christian and Jewish Hermeneutics through the Centuries.* Journal for the Study of the Old

Testament, Supplement Series 59, edited by B. Uffenheimer and H. G. Reventlow, 39–62. Sheffield: JSOT Press, 1988.

Duff, J. *The Elements of New Testament Greek.* Cambridge: Cambridge University Press, 2010.

Dunn, J. D. G. *Beginning from Jerusalem: Christianity in the Making,* vol. 2. Grand Rapids, MI: Eerdmans, 2009.

———. *Christology in the Making: A New Testament Inquiry into the Origins of the Doctrine of the Incarnation.* Philadelphia, PA: Westminster Press, 1980.

———. *The Christ and the Spirit: Christology.* Grand Rapids, MI: Eerdmans, 1998.

Elliot, E. E. "Paul and His Coworkers." In *Dictionary of Paul and His Letters,* edited by G. F. Hawthorne, R. P. Martin and D. G. Reid, 183–189. Downers Grove, IL: InterVarsity Press, 1998.

Ellington, D. W. "Is the Prosperity Gospel Biblical? A Critique in Light of Literary Context and Union with Christ." In *In Search of Health and Wealth: The Prosperity Gospel in African, Reformed Perspective,* edited by H. Kroesbergen, 37–51. Wellington, South Africa: Christian Literature Fund, 2013.

Evans, O. E. *Saints in Christ Jesus: A Study of Christian Life in the New Testament.* Swansea: John Penry Pr, 1975.

Fee, G. D. *The Disease of the Health and Wealth Gospels.* Vancouver: Regent College, 2006.

———. "Hermeneutics and Historical Precedent – a Major Problem in Pentecostal Hermeneutics." In *Perspectives on the New Pentecostalism,* edited by R. P. Splitter. Grand Rapids, MI: Baker, 1976.

———. *Listening to the Spirit in the Text.* Grand Rapids, MI: Eerdmans, 2000.

Ferguson, E. *Backgrounds of Early Christianity.* Grand Rapids, MI: Eerdmans, 2003.

Fergusson, D. "Eschatology." In *The Cambridge Companion to Christian Doctrine,* edited by C. E. Gunton, 226–244. Cambridge: Cambridge University Press, 1997.

Finn, R. *Almsgiving in the Later Roman Empire: Christian Promotion and Practice (313-450).* Oxford Classical Monographs. Oxford: Oxford University Press, 2006.

Friesen, S. J. "Paul and Economics: The Jerusalem Collection as an Alternative to Patronage." In *Paul Unbound: Other Perspectives on the Apostle,* edited by M. D. Given, 27–54. Peabody, MA: Hendrickson Publishers, 2010.

Fritzsche, C. F. A. *De nonnullis posterioris Pauli ad Corinthios epistolae locis dissertationes duae.* Vol. 2. Lipsiae: C. H. Reclam, 1824.

Furnish, V. P. *II Corinthians: Translated with Introduction, Notes, and Commentary.* The Anchor Bible, 32A. Garden City, NY: Doubleday, 1984.

Gaertner, D. "Corban." In *Eerdmans Dictionary of the Bible*, edited by D. N. Freedman. Grand Rapids, MI: Eerdmans, 2000.

Gale, H. M. *The Use of Analogy in the Letters of Paul*. Philadelphia, PA: Westminster Press, 1965.

Gapapa, D. C. "Les nouveaux mouvements religieux." In *Histoire du christianisme au Rwanda: Des origines à nos jours*, edited by T. Gatwa and L. Rutinduka, 46–49. Yaoundé: Éditions CLÉ, 2014.

Garrison, R. *Redemptive Almsgiving in Early Christianity*. Sheffield: JSOT Press, 1993.

Gatwa, T. "God in the Public Domain: Life Giver, Protector or Indifferent Sleeper During the Rwandan Tragedies?" *Exchange* 43 (2014): 313–338.

Georgi, D. *Remembering the Poor: The History of Paul's Collection for Jerusalem*. Nashville, TN: Abingdon Press, 1992.

———. *Die Gegner des Paulus im 2. Korintherbrief: Studien zur religiösen Propaganda in der Spätantike*. Wissenschaftliche Monographien zum Alten und Neuen Testament 11. Neukirchen-Vluyn: Neukirchener Verlag, 1964.

———. *Die Geschichte der Kollekte des Paulus für Jerusalem*. Theologische Forschungen 38. Hamburg-Bergstedt: Reich, 1965.

Gifford, P. "Ritual Use of the Bible in African Pentecostalism." In *Practicing the Faith: The Ritual Life of Pentecostal-Charismatic Movements*, edited by M. Lindhardt, 179–197. New York: Berghahn Books, 2011.

———. "A View of Ghana's New Christianity." In *The Changing Face of Christianity: Africa, the West, and the World*, edited by L. Sanneh and J. A. Carpenter, 81–96. New York: Oxford University Press, 2005.

Gorman, M. J. "'You Shall Be Cruciform for I Am Cruciform': Paul's Trinitarian Reconstruction of Holiness." In *Holiness and Ecclesiology in the New Testament*, edited by K. E. Brower and A. Johnson, 148–165. Grand Rapids, MI: Eerdmans, 2007.

Gregory, B. C. *Like an Everlasting Signet Ring: Generosity in the Book of Sirach*. Berlin: De Gruyter, 2010.

Habarurema, V. "Histoire de l'Église de Pentecôte au Rwanda: Des origines à l'an 2000." In *Histoire du christianisme au Rwanda: Des origines à nos jours*, edited by T. Gatwa and L. Rutinduka, 177–230. Yaoundé, Editions CLÉ, 2014.

Halmel, A. *Der zweite Korintherbrief des Apostels Paulus: Geschichtliche und literarkritische Untersuchungen*. Halle: Max Niemeyer, 1904.

Hamilton, J. M. *Social Justice and Deuteronomy: The Case of Deuteronomy 15*. Atlanta, GA: Scholars Press, 1992.

Harkins, P. W. "John Chrysostom, St." In *New Catholic Encyclopedia*, vol. 7, edited by B. L. Marthaler et al., 945–949. Detroit, MI: Gale, 2003.

Harris, M. J. *The Second Epistle to the Corinthians: A Commentary on the Greek Text.* The New International Greek Testament Commentary. Grand Rapids, MI: Eerdmans, 2005.

Harrison, J. R. *Paul's Language of Grace in its Graeco-Roman Context.* Wissenschaftliche Untersuchungen zum Neuen Testament II/172. Tübingen: Mohr Siebeck, 2003.

Hausrath, A. *Der Vier-Capitel-Brief des Paulus an die Korinther.* Heidelberg: Fr. Bassermann, 1870.

Hartley, H. A. "Financing Paul: Money and Mission in the Corinthian Correspondence." *Scripture Bulletin* 38 (2000): 69–79.

Hendrix, H. "Benefaction/Patron Networks in Urban Environment: Evidence from Thessalonica." In *Social Networks in the Early Christian Environment: Issues and Methods for Social History,* Semeia 56, edited by L. M. White, 39–58. Atlanta, GA: Scholars Press, 1992.

Heward-Mills, D. *Why Non-tithing Christians Become Poor and How Tithing Christians Become Rich.* Wellington, South Africa: Lux Verbi. BM, 2009.

Hollenweger, W. J. *Pentecostalism: Origins and Developments Worldwide.* Peabody, MA: Hendrickson Publishers, 1997.

Hood, J. "Theology in Action: The Gospel and Social Care." In *Transforming the World: The Gospel and Social Responsibility,* edited by J. A. Grant and D. A. Hughes. Nottingham: Apollos, 2009.

Houwelingen, P. H. R. van. "Jerusalem, the Mother Church: The Development of the Apostolic Church from the Perspective of Jerusalem." *Sárospataki Füzetek* 16, no. 3–4 (2012): 11–22.

Hyldahl, N. "Die Frage nach der literarischen Einheit des Zweiten Korintherbriefes." *Zeitschrift für die neutestamentliche Wissenschaft und die Kunde der älteren Kirche* 64 (1973): 289–306.

Idahosa, B. *I Choose to Change.* East Sussex: Highland, 1987.

Jasper, D. *A Short Introduction in Hermeneutics.* Louisville, KY: Westminster John Knox Press, 2004.

Jenkins, P. *The New Christendom: The Coming of Global Christianity.* Oxford: Oxford University Press, 2012.

———. *The New Faces of Christianity: Believing the Bible in the Global South.* Oxford: Oxford University Press, 2006.

Jeanrond, W. G. *Theological Hermeneutics: Development and Significance.* New York: Crossroad, 1991.

Jeremias, J. *Jerusalem in the Time of Jesus.* Philadelphia: Fortress Press, 1969.

Johnston, R. K. "Evangelicalism." In *The Oxford Companion to Christian Thought: Intellectual, Spiritual, and Moral Horizons of Christianity,* edited by A. Hastings, A. Mason, and H. Pyper, 217–220. Oxford: Oxford University Press, 2000.

Joubert, S. *Paul as Benefactor: Reciprocity, Strategy and Theological Reflection in Paul's Collection*. Wissenschaftliche Untersuchungen zum Neuen Testament II/124. Tübingen: Mohr Siebeck, 2000.

Judge, E. A. "The Social Identity of the First Christians." *Journal of Religious History* 11 (1980): 201–217.

Kalu, Ogbu U. *African Pentecostalism: An Introduction*. Oxford: Oxford University Press, 2008.

———. "'Globecalisation' and Religion: The Pentecostal Model in Contemporary Africa." In *Uniquely African? African Christian Identity from Cultural and Historical Perspectives*, Religion in Contemporary Africa Series, edited by J. L. Cox and G. Ter Haar, 215–240.Trenton, NJ: Africa World Press, 2003.

Kamalakar Jayakumar, D. "A System of Equality and Non-acquisitiveness as a Subversion of the Greed-Based Capitalism and the Patronage System." *Asia Journal of Theology* 22 (2008): 237–254.

Kennedy, J. H. *The Second and Third Epistles of St. Paul to the Corinthians*. Methuen: London, 1900.

Karamaga, A. *L'Evangile en Afrique: Ruptures et Continuité*. Yens: Editions Cabédita, 1990.

Kim, Kyoung-Jin. *Stewardship and Almsgiving in Luke's Theology.* Journal for the Study of the New Testament Supplement Series, 155. Sheffield: Sheffield Academic Press, 1998.

Kohlenberger III, J. R., Edward W. Goodrick, and James A. Swanson. *The Exhaustive Concordance to the Greek New Testament*. Grand Rapids, MI: Zondervan, 1995.

Kroesbergen, H. "Introduction." In *In Search of Health and Wealth: The Prosperity Gospel in African, Reformed Perspective*, edited by H. Kroesbergen, 6–8. Wellington, South Africa: Christian Literature Fund, 2013.

———. "The Prosperity Gospel: A Way to Reclaim Dignity?" In *In Search of Health and Wealth: The Prosperity Gospel in African, Reformed Perspective*, edited by H. Kroesbergen, 78–88. Wellington, South Africa: Christian Literature Fund, 2013.

Lambrecht, J. *Second Corinthians*. Sacra Pagina 8. Collegeville, MN: Liturgical Press, 1999.

Lee, Moonjang. "Reading the Bible in the Non-Western Church: An Asian Dimension." In *Mission in the 21st Century: Exploring the Five Marks of Global Mission*, edited by A. F. Walls and C. Ross, 148–156. Maryknoll, NY: Orbis Books, 2008.

Liddell, H. G., and R. Scott. *A Greek-English Lexicon: A New Edition Revised and Augmented Throughout*, vol. 1, Oxford: Clarendon Press, 1925.

Lietzmann, V. *An die Korinther I/II.* Tübingen: J. C. B. Mohr, 1969.

Lohse, E. "χείρ, χειραγωγέω, χειραγωγός, χειρόγραφον, χειροποίητος, ἀχειροποίητος, χειροτονέω." In *Theological Dictionary of the New Testament*, vol. 9; translated by G. Bromiley and edited by G. Friedrich, 424–437. Grand Rapids, MI: Eerdmans, 1974.

Longenecker, B. W. *Remember the Poor: Paul, Poverty, and the Greco-Roman World*. Grand Rapids, MI: Eerdmans, 2010.

Lust, J., E. Eynikel, and K. Hauspie. *A Greek-English Lexicon of the Septuagint*. Revised Edition, Stuttgart: Deutsche Bibelgesellschaft, 2003.

Maggay, M. "To Respond to Human Need by Loving Service." In *Mission in the 21st Century: Exploring the Five Marks of Global Mission*, edited by A. F. Walls and C. Ross, 46–52. Maryknoll, NY: Orbis Books, 2008.

Marguerat, D. *Les Actes des apôtres: 1-12*. Commentaire du Nouveau Testament II.5a. Genève: Labor et Fides, 2007.

———. *Les Actes des apôtres: 13-28*. Commentaire du Nouveau Testament II.5b. Genève: Labor et Fides, 2015.

Marshall, I. H., ed. *New Testament Interpretation: Essays on Principles and Methods*. Milton Keynes: Paternoster, 2005.

———. *New Testament Theology: Many Witnesses, One Gospel*. Downers Grove, IL: InterVarsity Press, 2004

Marshall, J. *Jesus, Patrons, and Benefactors: Roman Palestine and the Gospel of Luke*. Wissenschaftliche Untersuchungen zum Neuen Testament, II/259. Tübingen: Mohr Siebeck, 2009.

Martin, R. P., ed. *2 Corinthians*. Word Biblical Commentary, 40. Waco, TX: Word Books, 1986.

Mayeur, J.-M., et al., eds. *Histoire du Christianisme* II. Paris : Desclée, 1995.

Mbe, A. R. "From Asceticism to a Gospel of Prosperity: The Case of Full Gospel Mission Cameroon." *Journal for the Study of Religion* 17 (2004): 47–66.

Mbiti, J. S. *Bible and Theology in African Christianity*. Nairobi: Oxford University Press, 1986.

McGrath, A. E. *Luther's Theology of the Cross: Martin Luther's Theological Breakthrough*. Oxford: Blackwell, 1990.

McKee, E. A. *John Calvin on the Diaconate and Liturgical Almsgiving*. Travaux d'Humanisme et Renaissance, 197. Genève: Librairie Droz, 1984.

McKenna, S. J. "Pelagius and Pelagianism." In *New Catholic Encyclopedia*, vol. 11, edited by B. L. Marthaler et al., 60–63. Detroit, MI: Gale, 2003.

Meggit, J. J. *Paul, Poverty and Survival*. Edinburgh: T. & T. Clark, 1998.

Metzger, B. M. *A Textual Commentary on the Greek New Testament. 2nd edition*. Stuttgart: Deutsche Bibelgesellschaft, 1994.

Meyer, B. "'Make a Complete Break with the Past.' Memory and Post-Colonial Modernity in Ghanaian Pentecostal Discourse." *Journal of Religion in Africa* 28 (1998): 316–349.

———. *Translating the Devil: Religion and Modernity Among the Ewe in Ghana.* Edinburgh: Edinburgh University Press for the International African Institute, 1999.

Morris, L. L. "Faith." In *New Bible Dictionary*, edited by J. D. Douglas, 357–360. Downers Grove, IL: InterVarsity Press, 1996.

Murphy, F. X. "Jerome, St." In *New Catholic Encyclopedia*, vol. 7, edited by B. L. Marthaler et al., 757–760. Detroit, MI: Gale, 2003.

———. "Leo I, Pope, St." In *New Catholic Encyclopedia*, vol. 8, edited by B. L. Marthaler et al., 474–478. Detroit, MI: Gale, 2003.

Musemakweli, E. *La dynamique de la prédication en Afrique.* Yaoundé: Editions CLE, 2003.

Mutombo-Mukendi, F. "Le nouveau culte de la prospérité en Afrique, ses fondements, et ses implications sociologiques." *Analecta Bruxellensia* 8 (2003): 78–132.

Neirynck, Frans, and Frans van Segbroek. *New Testament Vocabulary: A Companion Volume to the Concordance.* Leuven: University Press, 1984.

Nickelsburg, G. W. *Ancient Judaism and Christian Origins: Diversity, Continuity, and Transformation.* Minneapolis, MN: Fortress Press, 2003.

Nickle, K. F. *The Collection: A Study in Paul's Strategy.* Studies in Biblical Theology, 48. London: SCM Press, 1966.

Nieuwenhove, R. van, and J. Wawrykow, eds. *The Theology of Thomas Aquinas.* Notre Dame, IN: University of Notre Dame Press, 2005.

Noll, M. A. "The Future of Protestantism: Evangelicalism." In *The Blackwell Companion to Protestantism*, edited by A. E. McGrath and D. C. Marks, 421–438. Malden, MA: Blackwell, 2004.

Nouis, A. "L'hérésie de la prospérité." *Réforme* 3515 (2013): 10.

———. "Une hérésie séductrice." *Réforme* 3472 (2012): 7.

Nsanzurwimo, J. *Histoire de l'Église de Pentecôte au Rwanda.* Vällingby: Svenska Tryckcentralen, 2009.

Nyberg Oskarsson, G. *Le mouvement pentecôtiste: Une communauté alternative sud du Burundi, 1935-1960.* Uppsala: Swedish Institute of Missionary Research, 2004.

O'Mahony, K. J. *Pauline Persuasion: A Sounding in 2 Corinthians 8-9.* Journal for the Study of the New Testament Supplement Series 199. Sheffield: Sheffield Academic Press, 2000.

Oeming, M. *Contemporary Biblical Hermeneutics: An Introduction.* Translation by J. Vette. Burlington, VT: Ashgate, 2006.

Ogereau, J. M. "The Jerusalem Collection as Κοινωνία: Paul's Global Politics of Socio-Economic Equality and Solidarity." *New Testament Studies* 58 (2012): 360–378.

Olin, J. C. "Calvin, John." In *New Catholic Encyclopedia*, vol. 2, edited by B. L. Marthaler et al., 887–890. Detroit, MI: Gale, 2003.

Olson, J. E. *Calvin and Social Welfare: Deacons and the Bourse Française*. Selinsgrove, PA: Susquehanna University Press, 1989.

Omenyo, C. N. *Pentecost outside Pentecostalism: A Study on the Development of Charismatic Renewal in the Mainline Churches in Ghana*. Missiological Research in the Netherlands, 32. Zoetermeer: Boekencentrum, 2002.

Otabil, Mensa. *Four Laws of Productivity: God's Foundation for Living*. Tulsa, OK: Vincom, 1991.

Oyedepo, D. O. *Covenant Wealth*. Lagos, Nigeria: Dominion House, 1992.

———. *Exploring the Secrets of Success*. Lagos, Nigeria: Dominion, 1998.

Panikulam, G. *Koinonia in the New Testament: A Dynamic Expression of Christian Life*. Analecta biblica, 85. Rome: Biblical Institute Press, 1979.

Pásztori-Kupán, I. *Theodoret of Cyrus*. Early Church Fathers. London/New York: Routledge, 2006.

Perkins, P. "Taxes in the New Testament." *Journal of Religious Ethics* 12 (1984): 182–200.

Perriman, A., ed. *Faith, Health and Prosperity: A Report on 'Word of Faith' and 'Positive Confession' Theologies by ACUTE (The Evangelical Alliance Commission on Unity and Truth among Evangelicals)*. Carlisle: Paternoster Press, 2003.

Peterman, G. W. "Romans 15.26: Make a Contribution or Establish Fellowship?" *NTS* 40 (1994): 457–463.

Punt, J. "Some Perspectives on Paul's Economic Vision Amidst Globalisation." *Religion and Theology* 7 (2000): 325–354.

Punt, J. "He is Heavy . . . He's my Brother: Unraveling Fraternity in Paul (Galatians)." *Neotestamentica: Journal of New Testament Society of South Africa* 46 (2012): 153–171.

Quasten, J. *Patrology 3: The Golden Age of Greek Patristic Literature From the Council of Nicaea to the Council of Chalcedon*. Westminster, MD/Utrecht Antwerp: Newman Press/Spectrum Publishers, 1960.

Redditt, P. L. *Daniel*. The New Century Bible Commentary. Sheffield: T&T Clark, 1999.

Reif, S. C. "Aspects of the Jewish Contribution to Biblical Interpretation." In *The Cambridge Companion to Biblical Interpretation*, edited by J. Barton, 143–159. Cambridge/New York: Cambridge University Press, 1998.

Roldanus, J. "Le chrétien - étranger au monde dans les homélies bibliques de Jean Chrysostome." *Sacris Erudiri* 30 (1987–1988): 231–251.

———. *The Church in the Age of Constantine: The Theological Challenges*. London/New York: Routledge, 2006.

Ross, C. "Introduction: Taonga." In *Mission in the 21st Century: Exploring the Five Marks of Global Mission*, edited by A. F. Walls and C. Ross, xiii-xvi. Maryknoll, NY: Orbis Books, 2008.

Roukema, R. "Early Christianity and Magic." *Annali di storia dell'esegesi* 24 (2007): 367–378.

———. "Herman Ridderbos's Redemptive-Historical Exegesis of the New Testament." *Westminster Theological Journal* 66 (2004): 259–273.

———. *Jesus, Gnosis and Dogma*. Translated by S. Deventer-Metz. London: T. & T. Clark, 2010.

———. "Les Églises de Réveil dans la perspective du Nouveau Testament." *Perspectives Missionnaires* 61 (2011): 58–71.

———. "Paul's Admonitions on Idol Offerings (1 Cor. 8 and 10) in Patristic Interpretation" (Papers presented at the Fifteenth International Conference on Patristic Studies held in Oxford 2007). *Studia Patristica* 44 (2010): 249–258.

———. "The Value of Patristic Interpretation of the New Testament." Lecture given at the meeting of the *Studiorum Novi Testamenti Societas*, 2–6 August 2005 in Halle, Germany. Adjusted for the Master class on 24 May 2011. Protestant Theological University Kampen, 5.

Safrai, Z., and P. J. Tomson. "Paul's 'Collection for the Saints' (2 Cor 8-9) and Financial Support of Leaders in Early Christianity and Judaism." In *Second Corinthians in the Perspective of Late Second Temple Judaism*, edited by R. Bieringer et al., Compendia Rerum Iudaicarum ad Novum Testamentum 14, 132–220. Leiden/Boston: Brill, 2014.

Sanneh, L. "The Changing Face of Christianity: The Cultural Impetus of a World Religion." In *The Changing Face of Christianity: Africa, the West, and the World*, edited by L. Sanneh and J. A. Carpenter, 3–18. Oxford: Oxford University Press, 2004.

———. *Disciples of all Nations: Pillars of World Christianity*. New York: Oxford University Press, 2008.

Schmidt, A. J. *How Christianity Changed the World*. Grand Rapids, MI: Zondervan, 2004.

Schmithals, W. *Die Gnosis in Korinth: Eine Untersuchung zu den Korintherbrifen*. Forschungen zur Religion und Literatur des Alten und Neuen Testaments 66. Göttingen: Vandenhoeck & Ruprecht, 1956.

Schoffeleers, M. *Pentecostalism and Neo-Traditionalism: The Religious Polarization of a Rural District in Southern Malawi*. Anthropological Papers, 1. Amsterdam: Free University Press, 1985.

Senft, C. *La première épitre de saint Paul aux Corinthiens*. Commentaire du Nouveau Testament, 7. Genève: Labor et Fides, 1990.

Smail, T. "The Cross and the Spirit: Towards a Theology of Renewal." In *Charismatic Renewal*, edited by T. Smail, A. Walker, and N. Wright. London: SPCK, 1995.
Soden, H. F. von. "ἀδελφός, ἀδελφή, ἀδελφότης, φιλάδελφος, φιλαδελφία, ψευδάδελφος." In *Theological Dictionary of the New Testament*, vol. 1, translated by G. Bromiley, edited by G. Kittel, 144–146. Grand Rapids, MI: Eerdmans, 1964.
Spijker, G. van't. "Les nouvelles Communautés chrétiennes au Rwanda et leur défi à la formation au ministère pastoral." *Revue Congolaise de Théologie Protestante* 23 (2012): 47–66.
———. *Les usages funéraires et la mission de l'Église: Une étude anthropologique et théologique des rites funéraires au Rwanda*. Kampen: Uitgeversmaatschappij J. H. Kok, 1990.
Stählin, G. "ἴσος, ἰσότης, ἰσότιμος." In *Theological Dictionary of the New Testament*, vol. 3, translated by G. Bromiley, edited by G. Kittel, 343–355. Grand Rapids, MI: Eerdmans, 1965.
Stowers, S. K. "*Peri men gar* and the integrity of 2 Corinthians 8 and 9." *Novum Testamentum* 32 (1990): 340–348.
Strack, H. L., and P. Billerbeck. *Kommentar zum Neuen Testament aus Talmud und Midrash III*. München: Beck, 1926.
Strathmann, H. "λειτουργέω, λειτουργία, λειτουργός, λειτουργικός." In *Theological Dictionary of the New Testament*, vol. 4, translated by G. Bromiley, edited by G. Kittel, 215–222. Grand Rapids, MI: Eerdmans, 1965.
Sullivan, C. S. "Merit." In *New Catholic Encyclopedia*, vol. 9, edited by B. L. Marthaler et al., 510–514. Detroit, MI: Gale, 2003.
Synan, V. *The Holiness Pentecostal Tradition: Charismatic Movements in the Twentieth Century*. Grand Rapids, MI: Eerdmans, 1997.
Talbert, C. H. "Money Management in Early Mediterranean Christianity: 2 Corinthians 8-9." *Review and Expositor* 86 (1989): 359–370.
Teselle, E. "Indulgence." In *The Cambridge Dictionary of Christianity*, edited by D. Patte, 607–608. Cambridge: Cambridge University Press, 2010.
Thrall, M. E. *A Critical and Exegetical Commentary on the Second Epistle to the Corinthians*. Vol. 1 (I-VII). International Critical Commentary on the Holy Scriptures of the Old and the New Testaments, 34. Edinburgh: T. & T. Clark, 1994.
———. *A Critical and Exegetical Commentary on the Second Epistle to the Corinthians*. Vol. 2 (VIII-XIII). International Critical Commentary on the Holy Scriptures of the Old and the New Testaments, 34. Edinburgh: T. & T. Clark, 2000.

Togarasei, L. "African Gospreneurship: Assessing the Possible Contribution of the Gospel of Prosperity to Entrepreneurship in Light of Jesus' Teaching on Earthly Possessions." In *In Search of Health and Wealth: The Prosperity Gospel in African, Reformed Perspective*, edited by H. Kroesbergen, 113–128. Wellington, South Africa: Christian Literature Fund, 2013.

Toren, B. van den. *La doctrine chrétienne dans un monde multiculturel: Introduction à la tâche théologique.* Carlisle: Langham Global Library, 2014.

Towner, P. H. *The Letters to Timothy and Titus.* NICNT. Grand Rapids, MI: Eerdmans, 2006.

Trisco, R. F., and J. A. Komonchak. "Vatican Council II." In *New Catholic Encyclopedia*, vol. 14, edited by B. L. Marthaler et al., 407–418. Detroit, MI: Gale, 2003.

Uehlinger, C. "Snake/Serpent." In *Religion Past and Present: Encyclopedia of Theology and Religion*, edited by H. D. Betz. Leiden/Boston: Brill, 2012.

Urquhart, C. "Foreword." In *I Choose to Change*, edited by B. Idahosa, 7–8. East Sussex: Highland, 1987.

Uzukwu, G. N. "The Poverty and Wealth of the Macedonians: A Grammatical and Rhetorical Analysis of 2 Cor 8:1-5." In *Second Corinthians in the Perspective of Late Second Temple Judaism*, Compendia Rerum Iudaicarum ad Novum Testamentum 14, edited by R. Bieringer, 319–330. Leiden/Boston: Brill, 2014.

Verbrugge, V. D. *Paul's Style of Church Leadership Illustrated by His Instructions to the Corinthians: To Command or not to Command.* San Francisco, CA: Mellen Research University Press, 1992.

Währisch-Oblau, C. *The Missionary Self-Perception of Pentecostal/Charismatic Church Leaders from the Global South in Europe: Bringing Back the Gospel.* Leiden/Boston: Brill, 2009.

Wallace, W. A., J. A. Weisheipl, and M. F. Johnson. "Thomas Aquinas, St." In *New Catholic Encyclopedia*, vol. 14, edited by B. L. Marthaler et al., 11–29. Detroit, MI: Gale, 2003.

Walls, A. F. "Afterword: Christian Mission in a Five-hundred-year Context." In *Mission in the 21st Century: Exploring the Five Marks of Global Mission*, edited by A. F. Walls and C. Ross, 193–204. Maryknoll, NY: Orbis Books, 2008.

Wariboko, N. "Pentecostals Paradigms of National Economic Prosperity in Africa." In *Pentecostalism and Prosperity: The Socio-Economics of the Global Charismatic Movement*, edited by K. Attanasi and A. Yong. New York: Palgrave Macmillan, 2012.

Watson, D. F. "Rhetorical Criticism, New Testament." In *Dictionary of Biblical Interpretation*, edited by J. H. Hayes, 399–402. Nashville, TN: Abingdon Press, 1999.

Weber, M. *L'éthique protestante et l'esprit du capitalisme*. Paris: Gallimard, 2003.
Weinfeld, M. *Social Justice in Ancient Israel and in the Ancient Near East*. Jerusalem/Minneapolis, MN: Magnes/Fortress Press, 1995.
Weisheipl, J. A. *Friar Thomas d'Aquino: His Life, Thought, and Work*. Garden City, NY: Doubleday, 1974.
Weiss, J. *Der erste Korintherbrief. Kritisch-exegetischer Kommentar über das Neue Testament 5*. Göttingen: Vandenhoeck & Ruprecht, 1910.
Windisch, H. *Der zweite Korintherbrief. Kritisch-exegetischer Kommentar über das Neue Testament 6*. Göttingen: Vandenhoeck & Ruprecht, 1924.
Witherington III, B. *Conflict and Community in Corinth: A Socio-Rhetorical Commentary on 1 and 2 Corinthians*. Grand Rapids, MI: Eerdmans, 1994.
Wright, C. J. H. *The Mission of God's People: A Biblical Theology of the Church's Mission*. Grand Rapids, MI: Zondervan, 2010.
Wright, N. T. "Introduction, Commentary, and Reflections on the Letter to the Romans." In *The New Interpreter's Bible*, vol. 9, edited by L. E. Keck et al. Nashville, TN: Abingdon Press, 2002.
Young, P. R. "Prosperity Teaching in an African Context." *Africa Journal of Evangelical Theology* 15 (1996): 3–16.
Zimmerli, W. "χαίρω, χαράν, συγχαίρω, χάρις, χαρίζομαι, χαριτόω, ἀχάριστος, χάρισμα, εὐχαριστέω, εὐχαριστία, εὐχάριστος." In *Theological Dictionary of the New Testament*, vol. 9, translated by G. Bromiley, edited by G. Friedrich, 377–387. Grand Rapids, MI: Eerdmans, 1974.
Zognong, D. *Le christianisme outragé: La misère religieuse en procès*. Paris: Harmattan, 2014.
Zulu, E. "Fipelwa na baYaweh: A Critical Examination of Prosperity Theology in the Old Testament from a Zambian Perspective." In *In Search of Health and Wealth: The Prosperity Gospel in African, Reformed Perspective*, edited by H. Kroesbergen, 28–35. Wellington, South Africa: Christian Literature Fund, 2013.

Electronic sources

Abbink, J. "A Bibliography on Christianity in Ethiopia." ASC Working Paper 52, Leiden, African Studies Centre, 2003. http://www.ascleiden.nl/pdf/workingpaper52.pdf. Accessed on 1 September 2015.
"The Apostolic Tradition of Hippolytus of Rome." http://www.bombaxo.com/hippolytus.html. Accessed on 3 May 2015.
De Bruyn, T., Stephen Cooper, and David G. Hunter. "A Translation, with Introduction and Notes of Ambrosiaster's *Commentary on the Pauline*

Epistles." https://arts.uottawa.ca/cla-srs/sites/arts.uottawa.ca.cla-srs/files/debruyn.translation.ambrosiaster_0.pdf. Accessed on 29 September 2013.

Chrysostom, John. "Four Discourses, chiefly on the parable of the Rich man and Lazarus: Discourse 3: Concerning Lazarus - Concerning Reading the Scriptures - The Reason why it is not said, 'Thou hadst,' but 'thou receivedst' - Why is it that the just often fall into troubles, while the wicked escape them?" Translated by F. Allen. 1869. http://www.tertullian.org/fathers/chrysostom_four_discourses_03_discourse3.htm. Accessed on 18 May 2015.

http://holiness-snake-handlers.webs.com/. Accessed on 5 August 2014.

The Living Bible (TLB). https://www.biblegateway.com/versions/The-Living-Bible-TLB/. Accessed on 12 August 2014.

Michael, H. "St. Thomas Aquinas: Economics of the Just Society." Paper presented at the Austrian Student Scholars Conference, December 2012. http://www2.gcc.edu/dept/econ/ASSC/Papers2013/ASSC2013-HaganMichael.pdf. Accessed on 19 September 2014.

New Advent. "Apostolic Constitutions (Book VIII)." http://www.newadvent.org/fathers/07158.htm. Accessed on 3 May 2015.

Nordquist, R. "Hendiadys." http://grammar.about.com/od/fh/g/hendiadysterm.htm. Accessed on 21 May 2011.

"Pesher." http://www.insula.com.au/sciandrel/CreationLecture/hermeneutics.html. Accessed on 14 April 2015.

Saint Thomas Aquinas. "Super II Epistolam ad Corinthios lectura." Html-edited by J. Kenny and translated by F. Larcher as *Commentary on the Second Epistle to the Corinthians*. http://dhspriory.org/thomas/SS2Cor.htm. Accessed on 11 May 2015.

Langham Literature and its imprints are a ministry of Langham Partnership.

Langham Partnership is a global fellowship working in pursuit of the vision God entrusted to its founder John Stott –

> *to facilitate the growth of the church in maturity and Christ-likeness through raising the standards of biblical preaching and teaching.*

Our vision is to see churches in the majority world equipped for mission and growing to maturity in Christ through the ministry of pastors and leaders who believe, teach and live by the Word of God.

Our mission is to strengthen the ministry of the Word of God through:
- nurturing national movements for biblical preaching
- fostering the creation and distribution of evangelical literature
- enhancing evangelical theological education

especially in countries where churches are under-resourced.

Our ministry

Langham Preaching partners with national leaders to nurture indigenous biblical preaching movements for pastors and lay preachers all around the world. With the support of a team of trainers from many countries, a multi-level programme of seminars provides practical training, and is followed by a programme for training local facilitators. Local preachers' groups and national and regional networks ensure continuity and ongoing development, seeking to build vigorous movements committed to Bible exposition.

Langham Literature provides majority world preachers, scholars and seminary libraries with evangelical books and electronic resources through publishing and distribution, grants and discounts. The programme also fosters the creation of indigenous evangelical books in many languages, through writer's grants, strengthening local evangelical publishing houses, and investment in major regional literature projects, such as one volume Bible commentaries like *The Africa Bible Commentary* and *The South Asia Bible Commentary*.

Langham Scholars provides financial support for evangelical doctoral students from the majority world so that, when they return home, they may train pastors and other Christian leaders with sound, biblical and theological teaching. This programme equips those who equip others. Langham Scholars also works in partnership with majority world seminaries in strengthening evangelical theological education. A growing number of Langham Scholars study in high quality doctoral programmes in the majority world itself. As well as teaching the next generation of pastors, graduated Langham Scholars exercise significant influence through their writing and leadership.

To learn more about Langham Partnership and the work we do visit **langham.org**

www.ingramcontent.com/pod-product-compliance
Lightning Source LLC
Chambersburg PA
CBHW052011290426
44112CB00014B/2197